ALSO BY DAVID DARY

The Buffalo Book

True Tales of the Old-Time Plains

Cowboy Culture: A Saga of Five Centuries

True Tales of Old-Time Kansas

Entrepreneurs of the Old West

*Kanzana, 1854–1900: A Selected Bibliography of Books,
Pamphlets and Ephemera of Kansas*

More True Tales of Old-Time Kansas

Seeking Pleasure in the Old West

RED BLOOD & BLACK INK

RED BLOOD
&
BLACK INK

Journalism in the Old West

DAVID DARY

ALFRED A. KNOPF NEW YORK 1998

THIS IS A BORZOI BOOK
PUBLISHED BY ALFRED A. KNOPF, INC.

Grateful acknowledgment is made to the following for permission to
reprint previously published or unpublished material:
Frances Collin Literary Agent: Excerpt from *Country Editor's Boy* by Hal Borland
(J. B. Lippincott Company, 1970), copyright © 1970 by Hal Borland.
Reprinted by permission of Frances Collin Literary Agent.
University of Nevada Press: Excerpts from *An Editor on the Comstock Lode*
by Wells Drury, copyright 1936 by Farrar & Rinehart.
Reprinted by permission of the University of Nevada Press.
Barbara White Walker: Letter of March 29, 1918, from William Allen White
to Rolla Clymer. Reprinted by permission of Barbara White Walker.

Library of Congress Cataloging-in-Publication Data
Dary, David.
Red blood & black ink: journalism in the Old West /
by David Dary. — 1st ed.
p.   cm.
Includes bibliographical references and index.
ISBN 0-679-44655-9
1. Journalism—West (U.S.)—History.
2. American newspapers—West (U.S.)—History.
I. Title.
PN4894.D37   1998
071'.8—dc21   97-34373
CIP

Manufactured in the United States of America
First Edition

To the memory of those nineteenth-century western newspaper editors who used no weasel words in speaking their minds

The newspaper is the historian's surest and most nearly eternal source of information. The living event is forever gone, but the newspaper is evidence that life was here.

—Anonymous

CONTENTS

ACKNOWLEDGMENTS

I AM INDEBTED to the late Otis H. Chidester of Tucson, Arizona, who more than a decade ago renewed my interest in letterpress or relief printing, a craft I first learned in Manhattan, Kansas, from Herbert R. Miller, Nicholas Talarico, and Glen Graham nearly forty years earlier. They were gentlemen of the old school who had mastered the craft. I also am indebted to my first high school journalism teacher, Mildred Sykes, who instilled in me the need for clear and precise writing.

My debt of appreciation extends to the many printers, editors, reporters, and others involved in newspaper journalism in the Old West whose names appear throughout this work. Without their contributions this book would not have been possible.

I also want to thank those who came to my aid as I sought to locate the historic photographs and illustrations scattered throughout this book's pages. They include Deborah Brown at the Missouri Historical Society, St. Louis; and Nancy Sherbert at the Kansas State Historical Society, Topeka. John Hanks of the American Heritage Center, University of Wyoming at Laramie, went beyond the call of duty to locate specific material, as did Katherine Wyatt of the Nebraska State Historical Society, Lincoln. Mary Bogan of Special Collections at the William Allen White Library, Emporia State University at Emporia, Kansas, was most helpful, as was William Allen White's granddaughter, Barbara Walker, at the *Emporia Gazette*. Special thanks also go to Gary Kurutz and Dawn L. Rodrigues of the California State Library, Sacramento, and to Don De Witt and John Lowitt of the Western History Collections, University of Oklahoma, Norman; Ed Kelley and Mike Shannon of the *Daily Oklahoman*, Oklahoma City; Catherine Bark, librarian in the School of Journalism and Mass Communication at the University of Oklahoma; and Mark Thomas, executive director of the Oklahoma Press Association.

D. D.

PREFACE

———◆———

FOR NEARLY HALF a century journalism and printing have fascinated me. At an early age I discovered that my maternal great-grandfather had learned the printing trade as an apprentice and then worked on several newspapers. My maternal grandfather started a weekly paper to help support his political ambitions. In high school I chose to take printing courses and learned to set type, pull proofs, and run presses. I also worked on my high school newspaper. This interest led me to pursue a career in journalism, first in broadcasting and then in print.

As a working journalist I often ran into colleagues who dreamed of owning their own weekly newspaper. In nearly all cases it was just a dream. When some of them took a close look at the amount of work involved in running a weekly, their dream of escaping from the rat race made their city jobs seem like vacations. Still they dreamed and were captivated by the simpler days when there was no television or radio or other forms of mass communication created by galloping technology. In the minds of many, those days were exciting yet romantic, especially in the Old West.

This book seeks to tell the story of newspaper journalism in the Old West and to capture the social memory of newspaper journalism in the West during the nineteenth and early twentieth centuries. It also seeks to capture and affirm the flavor, emotion, and color of newspaper journalism in the vast region stretching from the Canadian border southward to the Rio Grande, and westward from the Mississippi River to the Pacific Ocean. This book, however, is not a definitive history of newspaper journalism in the Old West. Such a work, which would require dozens of volumes and a lifetime to produce, has never been published. This is the story of journalism and of many of the men and women who established and published newspapers in the West, of what they wrote and printed, and of how they worked and lived and died. It is the story of their role in settling and shaping the American West. It is the story of their legacy.

David Dary

Along Imhoff Creek
Norman, Oklahoma, 1998

RED BLOOD & BLACK INK

CHAPTER ONE

SETTING THE STAGE

*Our liberty depends on the freedom of
the press, and that cannot be limited
without being lost.*
—Thomas Jefferson

WHEN JOSEPH CHARLESS, an Irish refugee, established the *Missouri Gazette* at St. Louis in 1808, it was the first newspaper to be published west of the Mississippi River. The city then had a population of about a thousand, one-fifth of them Americans, the rest French. There were hardly enough people to support a newspaper, but Meriwether Lewis, governor of the Missouri Territory, encouraged Charless to start one since St. Louis did not have a printer of any sort, and Lewis needed someone to print the laws of the territory. He sent Charless, who was then in Kentucky, an advance of $225 in banknotes and a bill of exchange on the Bank of the United States to buy printing equipment, but the postrider carrying the funds to Charless drowned in an accident and the money was lost. Lewis considered the matter important enough that he then sent William Clark, who had accompanied him on the exploration of the Louisiana Territory after Thomas Jefferson bought the vast region from France in 1803, to Kentucky to complete the negotiations with Charless.

When Charless arrived in St. Louis early in 1808, he distributed a printed prospectus telling residents of his plans to start a paper. He rented the north room of the house of Joseph Robidoux, the founder of St. Louis, ordered a Ramage printing press from Pennsylvania and type from Louisville, and made other preparations to begin operations. But Charless became ill, and publication of the paper was delayed until July 12, 1808, four days before his thirty-sixth birthday, when he and an assistant, a printer from Kentucky named Jacob Hinkle, published the first issue of the *Missouri Gazette*. It comprised four pages and was printed on foolscap (folded paper) sheets eight by twelve inches in size. Part of it was printed in French, the rest in English. The first issue had 174 subscribers who had

In 1808 Joseph Charless, an Irish refugee, established at St. Louis the *Missouri Gazette,* the first newspaper published west of the Mississippi River. *(Courtesy Missouri Historical Society, St. Louis)*

paid, or promised to pay, the annual subscription price of three dollars in cash, or had pledged four dollars in such produce as flour, corn, beef, or pork. Six months after launching his paper, Charless was still using his columns to remind subscribers that some had failed to meet their pledges. He also urged new subscribers to pay in advance because it cost him "upwards of twenty dollars" to produce each issue, and "neither paper, types and ink could be had without cash."

Because revenues from subscriptions and advertising were skimpy, Charless made ends meet by doing job printing. Only three weeks after beginning publication, Charless was given an advance of five hundred dollars to publish 350 copies of the territorial laws. Rumors began to fly that the territorial government controlled the *Missouri Gazette.* In his columns on January 4, 1809, Charless stated that such reports were false, informing his readers that he was an independent guardian of the rights and liberties of the people.

WHEN CHARLESS ARRIVED in New York City in 1796 from Ireland, he spelled his name Charles, pronounced "Char-les," with two syllables. But when he found people using only one syllable, "Charles," in addressing him, he added the final *s* to make sure they pronounced his surname to his liking. He worked for the *Mifflin Gazette* at Lewistown, Pennsylvania, but soon left and moved to Philadelphia, where he joined another Irish refugee, Matthew Carey, who owned a printshop. While employed in Carey's shop, Charless helped to produce there one of the first quarto editions of the Bible printed in America, something that remained a point of pride with him for the rest of his life. Charless's name appears on the title page of that Bible.[1] In 1800, Charless moved west to Lexington, Kentucky, and with a partner, Francis Peniston, established the *Independent Gazetteer,* a paper first issued on March 29, 1803. Charless soon became sole owner of the paper, but in March 1804 he sold out to Thomas Anderson and moved to Louisville, Kentucky. There, in 1807, Charless established another paper, the *Gazette and Western Advertiser,* which he sold two years later when he moved to St. Louis and established the *Missouri Gazette.*

IT HAD TAKEN 150 years for a vigorous and independent press to develop along the eastern seaboard. At that rate, to a casual observer of the time, it would take another 200 years for the press to develop in the vast region between the original colonies and the Mississippi River. But a new spirit had captured the nation after the close of the American Revolution: In all walks of life people enjoyed a liberating sense of freedom, and a restless stream of humanity began moving westward. Most people followed the major waterways instead of trying the more difficult overland travel through trackless forests. Hands down, the most important route west was the Ohio River, which flows nearly a thousand miles from its origin in Pennsylvania through the rolling country of Ohio, across Indiana, and along the southern edge of Illinois, to where it runs into the Mississippi at Cairo. Numerous smaller rivers flow into the Ohio, including the Muskingum, Hocking, Scioto, Miami, and Wabash. Settlement along the Ohio between the Appalachian Mountains and the Mississippi River developed rapidly.

Following the settlers, and in some instances traveling with them, were printers like Joseph Charless, who pushed toward the setting sun, stopping, often by instinct, to unload their handpresses, cases of type, type sticks,* supplies of paper, and other equipment and start a newspaper.

---

* A type stick, often called a composing stick, is used to hold letters, numerals, and other symbols as type is set and arranged in lines. Made of metal, and varying in length from four to twelve inches, type sticks can be adjusted for desired column width. Their depth of about two inches enables the typesetter to set several lines of type. See Appendix A.

The first newspaper established west of the Appalachian Mountains was the Pittsburgh *Gazette,* founded in 1786 by John Scull and Joseph Hall. They had their small press brought by wagon across the Alleghenies while their paper stock was transported by packhorse train to Pittsburgh, then a village of three hundred people. When they ran out of paper, they had to borrow the cartridge paper used in ammunition shells from the commandant at Fort Pitt to keep publishing. The situation improved eleven years later, when a small paper mill was established not far from Pittsburgh.[2]

John Bradford, a surveyor who came west after the American Revolution, became the first person to set up a press within the boundaries of United States territory west of the Appalachian mountains and immediately south of the Ohio River. When Bradford, a Virginian, arrived at Lexington, Kentucky, in 1786, he was granted the free use of a lot on the condition he set up a printshop. He liked the arrangement and sent to Philadelphia for a press and printing equipment. In due time everything came by packhorse and wagon over the mountains to Pittsburgh and down the Ohio River some four hundred miles by flatboat to Limestone, Kentucky (then called Maysville), and again by horse and wagon to Lexington. Bradford then learned the basics of printing and published the first issue of the *Kentucke Gazette* on August 11, 1787, only thirteen years after the first English settlement at Harrodsburg, south of Lexington. The *Kentucke Gazette* was founded primarily to promote statehood for the territory. William Henry Perrin, a Kentucky historian of journalism, wrote in 1888 that during the paper's early years, copies "were taken to the different settlements by the postriders, and when it arrived the best reader among the inhabitants would mount a stump and never stop until he had read the paper through, advertisements and all."[3]

Unlike John Bradford, however, most of the men who started early newspapers west of the Appalachians were experienced printers. George Roulstone, a native of Boston, had published newspapers in Massachusetts and North Carolina before starting the first paper (1791) in what is now Tennessee at Hawkins Court House, later renamed Rogersville. Roulstone named the paper the *Knoxville Gazette* because he intended to move it to Knoxville, which was to become the territorial capital in 1792. Roulstone published the first issue in Knoxville in May 1793.

Another printer from Kentucky, William Maxwell, holds the distinction of establishing the first newspaper north of the Ohio River and west of the Allegheny and Blue Ridge Mountains. In 1787, six years before Maxwell's arrival, Congress created what it called the North-West Territory. A settlement called Losantiville was soon established where the Licking River joins the Ohio. When General Arthur St. Clair arrived to become governor, the name Losantiville did not please him, and he changed it to Cincinnati, the name of the Pennsylvania society of Revolutionary War officers of which he was president. Maxwell, a native of New Jersey and a veteran of the Revolution, arrived in Cincinnati with his small press and a few fonts of type and set up his equipment in a log cabin that stood on the corner of what are now Front and Sycamore Streets. There, on November 9, 1793, he published the first issue of the *Centinel of the North-Western Territory*, adopting the Boston spelling of "Centinel." His four-page paper was eight and a quarter by ten inches in size. On the third page, Maxwell told his readers he had mislaid the list of advance subscribers and asked them to call at the newspaper office for their copies. The *Centinel's* motto, borrowed by Maxwell from eastern newspapers, was "Open to all parties but influenced by none."[4]

To the south in the Mississippi Territory, Benjamin M. Stokes, another printer, acquired a small press purchased in London in 1790 and brought to the region by an army officer to print the territorial laws. With the help of one R. T. Sackett, Stokes started the *Mississippi Gazette* at Natchez in September 1800. Still another printer, Elihu Stout, who had learned the printing trade from John Bradford in Kentucky, decided to start his own newspaper at Vincennes, located on the Wabash River in the Indiana Territory. On July 31, 1804, the first issue of Stout's *Indiana Gazette* appeared. Stout, a native of Virginia and boyhood friend of Patrick Henry, continued to publish the paper until 1806, when his office and printing equipment were destroyed by fire. He ordered a new press, type, and other equipment and resumed publication on July 4, 1807, renaming his paper the *Western Sun*.

Stout and other printers who established newspapers between the Appalachians and the Mississippi River were for the most part imitators, not originators. They were conformists who used eastern newspapers as their models and made do with what little mechanical printing equipment they had. Almost all their work was done by hand.

Their presses were made of wood and differed little from those used by Johann Gutenberg and his rivals nearly four hundred years earlier. Such individually made wooden presses were expensive, heavy, and cumbersome. The printer would push a bar that twisted a wooden screw attached to a plate to make the impression of inked type on paper. Whether printed sheets were uniform in appearance depended on the pressure exerted on the bar by the printer. The process was improved in 1796, when Adam Ramage, a Scottish immigrant working in Philadelphia, replaced the old-fashioned slow-moving wooden screw with a faster triple-threaded, rapid-motion screw and an iron bed and plate. This "toggle-and-lever" combination supplied more pressure on the impression, thereby providing printed sheets of uniform appearance. The Ramage press was stronger and faster to operate, and cost less, than the wooden presses. A printer could procure a new Ramage press and enough type to start a small paper for seven or eight hundred dollars, or a used Ramage and type for two or three hundred.

When Joseph Charless obtained a Ramage press to print the first issue of his *Missouri Gazette* in 1808, it was the only printing press west of the Mississippi, a distinction that lasted until 1815 when another press, probably a Ramage, was brought to St. Louis through the efforts of Charless's enemies. Although he made many friends in St. Louis, Charless remained an independent and outspoken editor. He criticized the military for its clumsy handling of campaigns on the frontier, during the War of 1812. He attacked the army for excessive drinking, gambling, and card-playing. He also rounded on the local courts for their treatment of Indians. And when, in February 1814, five or six armed men visited his office in an attempt to intimidate him, Charless defended himself with his shillelagh. The men left. But they were so angry that they raised a thousand dollars to start a competing paper, advertising for a printer in newspapers to the east of St. Louis. One of their advertisements, which appeared in the Lexington (Kentucky) *Reporter*, read:

> TO PRINTERS: The people of St. Louis are desirable [*sic*] of procuring a printer at that place. A man of correct Republican principles with even moderate abilities would satisfy them, though it is unquestionable that the profits of a well-directed press would richly reward the labors of a man of genius and acquirements.[5]

Charless's opponents succeeded in attracting Joshua Norvell, a printer and lawyer, who in May 1815 established the weekly *Western Journal* in St. Louis. But Norvell apparently was not the "genius" Charless's opponents had sought, because the paper failed sixteen months later, in September 1816, by which time Norvell had left for Arkansas. During the spring of 1817 a printer from Cincinnati, Sergeant Hall, established a new paper named the *Emigrant and General Advertiser*, but it also did poorly. In 1818 it was taken over by Isaac N. Henry, Evarist Maury, and Thomas Hart Benton and renamed the *St. Louis Enquirer*. Benton later became a U.S. senator from Missouri. Henry, Maury, and Benton apparently used the printing equipment and press Norvell had left behind.

BEYOND ST. LOUIS to the west there were no printing presses. The pattern of settlement continued to follow the major waterways, but large and deep streams were fewer in number west of the Mississippi. The chief tributary flowing eastward into the Mississippi is the Missouri River, starting in Montana and eventually joining the Mississippi just north of St. Louis. The close proximity of the mouth of the Missouri to St. Louis no doubt contributed to the increased settlement along the river. The population of the Missouri Territory doubled between 1804 and 1810, and by 1817 perhaps sixty thousand people called it home, most of them living close to the Missouri or in St. Louis and along the Mississippi. The settlement of Franklin was established in 1817 about 150 miles west of the Mississippi, on the north bank of the Missouri. Two years later the town of Boonville was founded on the south bank, opposite Franklin. On April 23, 1819, the first newspaper published west of St. Louis was established at Franklin by Nathaniel Patten, Jr., a native of Massachusetts, in partnership with Benjamin Holliday, Jr., a Virginian. Patten had learned the printing trade on a Boston newspaper. The four-page paper, printed on a Ramage press, was called the *Missouri Intelligencer and Boon's Lick Advertiser*. Its price was three dollars a year if paid in advance or four dollars if paid at the end of the year. The pages were eight by eighteen inches, with five columns to a page.

The first issue had about a hundred subscribers. The paper contained several advertisements, ranging from a notice of unclaimed letters at the post office to a woman's petition for separation from her husband because of desertion. Gradually Patten, who was the *Intelligencer*'s editor as well as publisher, began including local news, such as the following item from the June 3, 1823 issue: "Within a few days past our river has risen to a height unprecedented in the memory of the oldest citizen of this country. It is now, however, slowly ebbing, and there is every reason to believe that the present rise will produce no unhappy effects." From the beginning Patten included much of the same fare printed by the St. Louis papers, which had in turn been clipped from eastern newspapers. From the October 7, 1825, issue: "A young lady of 18 was lately killed by lightning in Lebanon, Connecticut, and her breast shattered in a shocking manner—supposed to be in consequence of her wearing a steel corset. Have a care, ladies." Patten often used poetry to fill empty space in his paper, including the following verse:

"A Young Swain's Lament"

I wish I was the corset bone,
    That's to thy lovely breast;
That I might be, both night and day,
    To thy fair bosom prest.
I wish I was the china cup,
    From which you drink your tea;
For then I know at every sip,
    You'd give a kiss to me.[6]

The first steamboat to ply the Missouri River was the *Independence.* Constructed at Pittsburgh especially for use on the shallow Missouri River, it took thirteen days to make the journey upstream from St. Louis to Franklin, arriving on June 5, 1819. The return trip downstream required only three days.[7] Such steamboats soon brought more settlers up the Missouri River, and with them came more printers. By 1820 there were five weekly newspapers in Missouri, including two in St. Louis, and one each at Franklin, Jackson, and St. Charles.

While the Missouri Territory could claim five papers by 1820, the Arkansas Territory to the south, established in 1819, could claim only one. Soon after the latter was formed, William Edward Woodruff, a young printer then working in Tennessee, sensed opportunity there. He took a

With two canoes lashed together to hold printing equipment, William Edward Woodruff and another young man poled up the White River to Arkansas Post and established the *Arkansas Gazette* on November 20, 1819. *(Courtesy Arkansas Gazette Foundation)*

just-purchased printing press, type, and other equipment and set out by
boat down the Cumberland, Ohio, and Mississippi rivers to the mouth of
the White River. When Woodruff learned that the White River was not
open for navigation, he lashed two canoes together, loaded his printing
equipment on them, and poled the rest of the way to Arkansas Post, the
territorial capital, located on the north bank of the Arkansas River. There,
on November 20, 1819, Woodruff published the first issue of the *Arkansas
Gazette.* When the capital was permanently moved to Little Rock, the
paper moved too, publishing its first issue there on December 29, 1831.[8]

The settlement of the region between the Appalachians and the Mississippi River was so rapid that ten new states were added to the Union between 1790 and 1821. Missouri was admitted in 1821 and Arkansas in 1836,
as the twenty-fourth and twenty-fifth states, respectively. But beyond the
western borders of Missouri and Arkansas, there was little settlement for
nearly twenty years. The region, labeled by explorers the Great American
Desert, lacked major waterways deep enough to allow reliable steamboat
travel. Most early explorers who crisscrossed the region had left the false
impression in the minds of easterners that the land was not arable and that
no civilized human could—or would—want to live where only Indians
resided.

But far to the southwest of Missouri and Arkansas, in Spanish Texas,
such misconceptions did not exist. Bernardo Gutiérrez de Larta, an adventurer, brought a small army from Louisiana into what is now eastern
Texas in August 1812, and declared the establishment of the Republic of
Texas. With Gutiérrez came his fellow adventurer José Alvarez de Toledo,
who brought a printing press and several fonts of type. When Gutiérrez
was driven from Texas, the press was moved to Louisiana, although Alvarez soon returned to Nacogdoches, where in May 1813 he published *El
Mejicano,* the first newspaper printed in Texas. It supported Mexican independence from Spain.[9]

Six years later, in 1819, two Americans, Horatio Bigelow and Eli Harris—who had worked on newspapers in Georgia, Kentucky, and Tennessee—joined an expedition organized by Dr. James Long, an American
angry that Texas had been given to Spain, to "Americanize" eastern Texas.
Long declared Texas an independent republic and established his embry-
onic government in Nacogdoches. On August 14, 1819, Bigelow and Harris
brought out the *Texas Republican.* The paper lasted two months, until the
town was recaptured by Mexicans and the printing office destroyed.

After Mexico gained independence from Spain in 1821, it was eight
years until another newspaper appeared in Mexican Texas. Milton

Slocum, a twenty-six-year-old printer from Massachusetts, established the *Mexican Advocate* in Nacogdoches in September 1829. He took the oath, required by the Mexican government, that he would not disturb the peace by publishing seditious material. Although no copy of the paper has survived, it is known to have been printed in both Spanish and English and to have promoted land purchase. That same year Godwin B. Cotten, a veteran newspaperman from New Orleans, started another weekly newspaper, the *Texas Gazette,* in San Felipe, a town founded in 1823 by Stephen F. Austin with the approval of the Mexican governor. The first issue of Cotten's paper contained four nine-and-one-half-by-twelve-inch pages, each of which had three columns. An annual subscription cost six dollars in cash or produce. The first insertion of an advertisement cost one dollar for ten lines and fifty cents for each subsequent insertion. Although Cotten claimed to be in his thirties, a contemporary later described him as "a genial old bachelor of fifty or thereabouts."[10]

By 1827 Mexican authorities were trying to halt American immigration to Texas, but they had little success, and by the early 1830s about twenty thousand Americans had settled in Texas. After General Antonio López de Santa Anna became dictator of Mexico in 1823, American settlers in Texas set up a provisional republican government. Texians, as these settlers called themselves, then captured the Mexican stronghold at San Antonio. Meanwhile, Joseph Baker and Thomas H. and Gail Borden, Jr. decided to start a paper that would be "tool to no party, but would fearlessly expose crime and critical error wherever met with."[11] Their paper, the *Telegraph and Texas Register,* was started at San Felipe de Austin on October 10, 1835, nine days after the first shot had been fired in the Texas Revolution. Early the following year Santa Anna gathered a large Mexican army and marched to recapture San Antonio, where Texians had fortified the Alamo. When word reached San Felipe that the Alamo had fallen, the *Telegraph and Texas Register,* on March 17, 1836, carried the first reports of the battle under a banner headline with the now famous slogan "Remember the Alamo." The reports were then picked up and reprinted by other newspapers throughout the United States. Later, when the Mexican army advanced toward San Felipe, the *Telegraph and Texas Register* was moved to Harrisburg. But Santa Anna and his army soon captured and burned that town as well, including the newspaper office, throwing the press and type into the bayou. (The press was later raised from the waters and used to print other Texas papers.) The Bordens and Baker escaped capture and quickly ordered a new press and more type from Cincinnati. On August 2,

1836, they reestablished their paper at Columbia, the first capital of the Republic of Texas.[12]

To the north of Texas and west of Missouri and the Territory of Arkansas, Congress in 1830 had set aside a vast but indefinite area of the Louisiana Territory, some six hundred miles from north to south and two hundred miles in width, as a permanent home for Indians. Beginning in 1831, numerous tribes were moved from the states and territories east of the Mississippi into this unknown region, one of the most shameful acts in U.S. history. Nonetheless, along with the Indians came newspapers established by missionaries and teachers who ministered to the involuntary emigrants.

Among these missionaries was Jotham Meeker, who had been born in Hamilton County, Ohio, in 1804, and had learned the printing trade in Cincinnati when the town was less than two decades old. In 1825 Meeker's life was suddenly changed when he heard Robert Simerwell, a Baptist missionary to Indians, preach in Michigan. At the age of twenty-one Meeker himself became a missionary among the Potawatomie Indians in what is now southern Michigan. There he met Isaac McCoy, a Baptist minister and champion of the Indians, who headed the mission. In 1830, however, Meeker retired from his post, returned to Cincinnati, married a young woman who had also been a missionary in Michigan, and found work as a printer. Isaac McCoy left Michigan for the Arkansas Territory to work with the Cherokees along the Arkansas River. In 1831 McCoy persuaded Meeker to return to missionary work in Michigan, where the latter began to experiment with devising "for the Indian languages an orthography which might be written or printed with the ordinary characters" of the English language.

In the spring of 1833, Meeker was ordered to abandon his Michigan mission and to go to Indian Territory with a printing press and equipment, which he obtained in Cincinnati at a cost of $468.13. Meeker and his wife then traveled by steamboat to Independence, Missouri, near the big bend in the Missouri. From there they went overland to the new Shawanoe mission, located a few miles southwest of what is now Kansas City, Missouri. There, in January 1834, Meeker set up his printing press. To create written forms of Indian languages which had till then only been spoken, Meeker adapted the Roman alphabet to his purpose, assigning to various letters new sounds that existed in the given Indian tongue in the place of their usual English sounds. He spent much of his first year printing books for Indians and teaching them to read.

In 1835, having taught the Indians at the mission to read, Meeker published the *Siwinowe Kesibwi,* which in English means *Shawnee Sun,* the first newspaper to be printed wholly in an Indian language. Meeker, who kept a daily journal for about twenty years, made the following entries concerning the first issue of his monthly:

FEBRUARY

18 Commence setting types on the 1st No. of Shawanoe Sun. . . .
19 Composition on the Sun. . . .
20 Composition. . . .
21 Finish composition on the Sun—make up, and take proof.
23 Read proof & correct the Sun. . . .
24 Print the first No. of the Shawanoe Sun. . . .
25 Distribute types and clear up the office. . . .
26 . . . Fold up all of the Sun. Very cold.[13]

Meeker printed some hundred copies of the first issue of the *Shawnee Sun.* Johnston Lykins, another missionary, was listed as editor. The paper continued publication until about 1844. Meeker may have been the first printer in the world who had to teach his readers how to read before he could issue his newspaper.[14]

Nine years after Meeker started the *Shawnee Sun* in eastern Kansas, two other Indian-language newspapers appeared more than a hundred miles to the south in what is now Oklahoma. The *Cherokee Messenger* began publication in August 1844 at the Cherokee Baptist Mission located near modern Westville. The paper was printed in Cherokee, listing Rev. Evan Jones as editor and H. Upham as printer, but it lasted for only thirteen issues. The following month another paper was issued at Tahlequah, printed in both English and Cherokee. It was called the *Cherokee Advocate* and was edited by William Potter Ross, a graduate of Princeton University and nephew of a Cherokee chief. Ross advised his readers in the first issue that the paper's subscription price was "three dollars per annum except to those persons who read only the Cherokee language, and they shall pay two dollars." Later all Cherokees who could not read English received the paper free.[15]

BY THE 1840s the spirit that captured the nation following the American Revolution had resulted in the annexation of Texas and the addition of Oregon and California to the United States. These events reflected the sweeping nationalism often labeled "Manifest Destiny." For some Americans the spirit meant that the United States had a natural right to occupy all of the land between the Atlantic and Pacific. Many people believed it was their nation's foreordained destiny, and simply an extension of the freedoms enjoyed in a country only seventy years old. Others accepted their government's actions as testimony that God had granted the United States title to the vast region west and southwest of the Louisiana Territory.

When representatives of Mexico and the United States signed the Treaty of Guadalupe-Hidalgo on February 2, 1848, the signers were unaware that gold had been discovered nine days earlier near Coloma, on the south fork of the American River in California. Had gold not been discovered, several decades might have passed before California attained the minimum population of sixty thousand needed for statehood. Of course the mass migrations to California created an almost immediate demand for news. Although Don Augustin Vicente Zamorano, secretary to the Mexican governor, had brought the first printing press to California during the summer of 1834, the first newspaper was not published until a dozen years later: on August 15, 1846, five weeks after the U.S. flag had been raised over Monterey and California was proclaimed a part of the United States. Walter Colton, chaplain of the U.S. frigate *Congress* and a onetime editor of the Philadelphia *North American,* decided to start a newspaper called the *Californian* at Monterey with the help of Robert Semple, a Kentuckian who stood at six foot eight in his stockings and dressed in buckskin with a foxskin cap. They were also assisted by Joseph Dockrill, a crew member from the *Congress.* It is possible Colton had acquired the old wooden-frame Ramage press purchased in Boston by Zamorano and shipped to California twelve years earlier. In his diary on Saturday, August 15, 1846, Colton wrote:

To-day the first newspaper ever published in California made its appearance. The honor, if such it be, of writing its Prospectus, fell to me. . . . The press was old enough to be preserved as a curiosity; the mice had burrowed in the balls; there were no rules, no leads, and the types were rusty and all in pi [mixed together]. It was only by scouring that the letters could be made to show their faces. A sheet or two of tin were procured, and these, with a jackknife, were cut into rules and leads. Luckily we found, with the press, the greater part of a keg of ink; and now came the main scratch for paper. None could be found, except that used to envelop the tobacco of the cigars smoked here by the natives. A coaster had a small supply of this on board, which we procured. It is in sheets a little larger than the common-sized foolscap, and this is the size of our first paper, which we have christened the Californian.

Though small in dimensions, our first number is as full of news as a black-walnut is of meat. We have received by couriers, during the week, intelligence from all the important military posts through the territory. Very little of this has transpired; it reaches the public for the first time through our sheet. We have also, the declaration of war between the United States and Mexico with an abstract of the debate in the senate. A crowd was waiting when the first sheet was thrown from the press. It produced quite a little sensation.[16]

The *Californian* was published each Saturday, one-half printed in English, the other half in Spanish. An annual subscription was five dollars, while a single issue cost twelve and a half cents. For many years the legend persisted among early California journalists that Colton printed his paper with Spanish type, which has no *w*s and therefore had to use two *v*s to form the letter *w*. But anyone who closely examines the early editions can see there is no truth to the legend. Colton simply did not have a sufficient supply of *w*s and resorted to using *v*s only after running out of *w*s.

On January 9, 1847, up the coast from Monterey at Yerba Buena, California's second paper, the *California Star,* was established by Samuel Brannan, a Mormon and native of Maine. He and a colleague, Edward Cleveland Kemble, had arrived at Yerba Buena in July 1846 by ship from New York, where Brannan had published two Mormon journals, *The Prophet* and the *New-York Messenger.* Kemble had been his assistant. Brannan brought with him his printing press and type, and a large supply of newsprint. The press and equipment were first located on the second floor of a mule-powered gristmill on what became Clay Street, between Montgomery and Kearny, in San Francisco, although before the first issue of the *California Star* was published, its printing office was moved to a newly constructed adobe building close to the Customs House.

Brannan had planned on starting a paper in California before leaving New York City. He had even had the masthead engraved. Shortly after they arrived, however, Kemble joined John Charles Frémont's battalion of volunteers and set off to conquer and annex California to the United States. Brannan then hired Elbert P. Jones, a lawyer from Tennessee, as temporary editor, who wrote in the first issue of the *California Star,* January 9, 1847, that while he was on "the editorial tripod, all private pique, personal feeling and jealousy will be laid aside."[17]

Walter Colton, onetime
editor of the Philadelphia
North American, started the
first newspaper in California,
the *Californian,* in 1846
at Monterey. *(Courtesy
California State Library)*

Maine native Samuel Brannan, a
Mormon, started California's second
newspaper, the *California Star,* in
1847 at Yerba Buena (San Francisco).
(Courtesy California State Library)

When copies of the *California Star* reached Walter Colton, editor of the *Californian* at Monterey, he noted in his columns: "We have received the first two numbers of a new paper just commenced at Yerba Buena. It is issued upon a small but very neat sheet, at six dollars per annum. It is published and owned by S. Brannan, the leader of the Mormons, who was brought up by Joe Smith himself, and is consequently well qualified to unfold and impress the tenets of his sect."[18] When Jones read the *Californian*'s comments, he forgot his high resolve and wrote the following in the January 23, 1847, issue of the *California Star*:

We have received two late numbers of the "Californian" a dim, dirty, little, paper printed in Monterey on the worn out materials of one of the old California WAR PRESSES.

It is puplished [*sic*] and edited by Walter Calton [*sic*] and Robert Semple, the one a WHINING sycophant, and the other an OVER-GROWN LICK-SPITTLE. At the top of one of the papers we find the words "please exchange." This would be considered in almost any other country a bare-faced attempt to swindle us. We would consider it so now were it not for the peculiar situation of our country which induces us to do a great deal for others in order to enable them to do a little good. We did think of charging the men of the Californian five dollars and seventy five cents "to-boot" between papers, but as it seems to be their determination to "hump" themselves in future, while on the editorial tripod, we have concluded to give our paper to them this year, so as to afford them some insight into the manner in which a Republican newspaper should be conducted. They appear now to be awfully verdant.

Edward C. Kemble helped Samuel Brannan establish California's second newspaper, the *California Star,* in 1847. *(Courtesy California State Library)*

A review of the early issues of the paper as edited by Jones shows other such intemperate outpourings, but things changed after Edward Kemble was discharged from Frémont's army and returned in early April 1847 to work with Brannan on the newspaper. After Brannan went east, leaving Kemble in charge, Jones submitted a fierce editorial which was rejected by Kemble. As Kemble later recalled, "Then there was quickly arranged without music a lively and engaging waltz around the printing office to the utter consternation and discomfiture of types, 'forms,' stools and everything that stood in the way." Kemble ejected Jones from the office. The April 17, 1847, issue of the *California Star* announced that Jones was no longer associated with the paper.[19]

That same month at Monterey, Robert Semple became sole proprietor of the *Californian* and two weeks later moved the paper to San Francisco, which had just changed its name from Yerba Buena. Interestingly, the discovery of gold at Sutter's Mill in January 1848 was ignored by both the *Californian* and the *California Star,* perhaps because it was local news and readers already knew about it. The *Californian* did not print any mention of the discovery for nearly two months until on March 5, under a small one-line heading, "Gold Mine Found," the following short item appeared:

In the newly made raceway of the Saw Mill recently erected by Captain Sutter, on the American Fork, gold has been found in considerable quantities. One person brought thirty dollars worth to New Helvetia, gathered there in a short time. California, no doubt, is rich in mineral wealth; great chances here for scientific capitalists. Gold has been found in almost every part of the country.

The value of a gold rush to the economy perhaps spurred the *California Star* to publish an extra edition on April 1 telling of the discovery. Two thousand copies were sent to Missouri for distribution. Within a month gold fever had not only hit nearly all Californians but the nation as well. Both papers suspended publication because their printers and most of their San Francisco readers had left for the goldfields. Within months, however, San Francisco was a boomtown. Before 1848 ended, the two papers combined and, on January 4, 1849, became the *Alta California.* A little more than a year later, on January 23, 1850, the newspaper became a daily.

Journalism had arrived in the Far West. But in that vast and mostly unsettled region between Missouri and California, the prairie and plains and the Rocky Mountains had only been crisscrossed by explorers, mountain

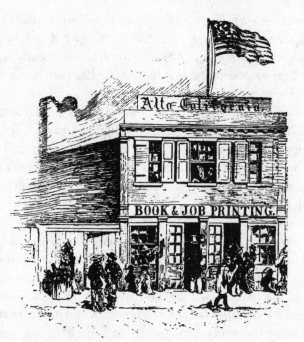

An artist's drawing of the office of the *Alta California* about 1850, when the paper became a daily. *(Courtesy Bancroft Library, University of California)*

men, missionaries, traders, immigrants bound for Oregon or California, and a few journalists. The stage had been set. During the next half century, the spirit of the westward movement would see the settlement of the vast region from Texas northward to Canada, and from Missouri westward to the Pacific, and with the settlers would come printers to establish more newspapers in the traditions of those they followed.

CHAPTER TWO

NO WEASEL WORDS

Editors were great characters in those days, intensely interesting to study, gifted with imagination, always partisan, never neutral, and thoroughly imbued with the vision that the function of an editor was to enlighten, educate, interest and entertain, and gosh, how they did it!

—Cecil Howes

THERE IS A HAZARD in trying to generalize about the writing style of early newspaper editors in the American West. Each editor's style was very personal and was the product of upbringing, experience, and education. Though no two editors had the same style, those who had mastered the English language did have one thing in common—there was a precision in what they wrote. Their writing was terse and pointed. Most were proud to take sides on any question, and none was ever averse to replying, "Yes, I wrote that."

From colonial days well into the nineteenth century, newspaper writing in America followed a literary style. Stories were organized and written in chronological order as they were in Europe and England. The writing tended to be formal, and the writer did not hesitate to inject subtle opinion. The stories were loosely presented in the narrative, often rambling form of an English theme, with the writer using more words than necessary, embellishing the central point. But this style gradually changed because of the influence of penny papers produced for the masses in New York City, especially James Gordon Bennett's New York *Herald*. Most editors in the West were not originators and sought to imitate the successful editors and papers in the East. Bennett put some needed ingredients into American journalism—spice, enterprise, aggressive news coverage, and a writing style that was fresh, original, and clear. Journalism historian Frederic Hudson, writing in 1873, described the *Herald*'s writing as in the "French style, with an infusion of the dash and vigor of the young Republic." American journalists, he wrote, "had previously aped that of modern England—solid, argumentative, heavy. They were the solemn communications of Honestus, Scaevola, Americus, Publius, Scipio, written by veteran politicians and retired statesmen; the antiquated philosophy of one age turned into editorial articles for the next. . . . But Mr. Bennett changed all this in the *Herald*. He made each article and each paragraph tell its own story."[1]

Like Bennett, the best editors in the West were masters of vigorous English. They knew or concocted virile expressions. They applied the barbed epithet when they thought it would do the most good. They understood the value of editorial abuse in attracting readers, to show pride in their papers, or to show their indignation about rival editors or people they did not like. While the masters of such style would eventually be found in nearly every western territory and state, Kansas probably had more of them than any other place in the West during the late 1850s and early 1860s because of the struggle to make Kansas a free state. From the beginning, Kansas editors were compelled to take sides on the question of slavery. They were outspoken and had the drive and force of crusaders. Their abusive manner probably was the result of enthusiasm, but they often generated animosities. These editors were rarely neutral or nonpartisan even when writing about nonpolitical matters.

This was especially evident after armed Missourians crossed the border into the Kansas Territory in 1855 to vote illegally on whether Kansas should go slave or free. Papers on both sides of the question held their ground, but at Lawrence, Josiah Miller and R. G. Elliott, owners of the *Kansas Free State*, attacked George W. Brown, editor of the *Herald of Freedom*, also published in Lawrence, although both were free-state papers. On April 7, 1855, the *Kansas Free State* observed:

> It was exceedingly amusing to see how very much some men were alarmed in this place on the day of election. The editor of the *Herald* was concealed most of the day, until near night, then, loaded down with revolvers and bowies, sneaked over to the polls and voted after the Missourians dispersed. A number of others did not go to the polls at all. There was no danger. . . .
>
> Nothing is so ridiculous and contemptible as the manner in which he [Brown] has managed the *Herald*. At first he, through fear and a desire to get more subscribers, got up a very tame, dough-faced paper, or at least those distributed in the Territory were such, we heard it intimated that a different edition was sent East. We noticed him several times, and finally he began to work right in the Free State ranks, until last week he issued two or three editions, one for the Missourians, containing no

anti-slavery at all, the other for the East, rabid in its denunciation of pro-slavery men, and the third for a medium class of thinkers. – Such a coward might do in Conneautville, Pennsylvania, but we have but little use for him in the ranks of freedom, in Kansas. – We have suspected these various editions of the same paper for some time, but now we are convinced of their existence, as we have them on our table, procured enveloped, under the pretense of wishing to send some to Missouri and Massachusetts.

Proslavery papers emphasized their views on the subject but also took aim at one another when it came to the economic survival of their towns. The *Kansas Weekly Herald* at Leavenworth and the *Squatter Sovereign* in Atchison frequently took potshots at each other because their towns were bitter rivals for trade and commerce. On May 11, 1855, Leavenworth's *Kansas Weekly Herald* opined:

> It is with great reluctance we condescend to notice anything from the vituperative pen of the insignificant, puerile, silly, black-guard who at present presides over the Editorial conduct of the *Sovereign*. Atchison may be, but Leavenworth is not the place where Peter Pindar's remark, "every black-guard scoundrel is a king," is recognized by the community. . . . The egotistical dupe of the *Sovereign* thinks we are a representation of the verdancy of Virginia. . . . Be that as it may, we can retort by saying that the mendacity of Missouri is represented in the person of one R. S. Kelley, of Atchison.

R. S. Kelley, editor of the Atchison *Squatter Sovereign,* counterattacked by calling the editor of the *Herald* the scum of the earth, a blackguard, and a muckraker, among other terms of scorn—which prompted a fresh barrage from the latter in the *Herald* of June 1, 1855:

> The low, silly, garrulous numbskull of the *Squatter Sovereign,* yclept Kelley—the contemptible, whining, *blind puppy* of Atchison, that answers to the name of "Bob," continues to pour forth his tirade of abuse upon us with unrelenting fury. . . .
> The *Sovereign,* in speaking of our "*low flung* language," says:
> "He can assail no one but in the language of the doggery."
> It is to be presumed that when we assail a *dog,* it will be in language intelligible to him. We look upon Kelley as a *dog,* and consequently thought the "language of the doggery" suitable to the occasion. . . .

In the peroration of the *Sovereign's* article, Kelley becomes exceedingly bellicose, and gives us to understand he "*will fight.*" This does not frighten us: if Kelley *wishes* to fight, and will designate some time and place for that purpose, we will meet him. . . .

Certainly the words were often hotter when a free-state editor and a proslavery editor exchanged barbs. Such a clash occurred between Solomon "Sol" Miller, editor of the *Kansas Chief,* published at White Cloud, and Thomas J. Key, editor of the *Kansas Constitutionalist,* a strong proslavery paper established at Doniphan in 1856. Their towns were located on opposite sides of Doniphan County in northeast Kansas. This exchange began on August 20, 1857, when Miller printed the following in his *Kansas Chief:*

It is well known that Gov. Walker has declared that the Constitution shortly to be formed for Kansas, shall be submitted to a vote of the people; and it is also known that the President has promised that Walker shall be sustained in this policy. This has called out Thomas J. Key, editor of the Doniphan *Constitutionalist,* who is one of the Delegates elect from this County. (It is said, but we hardly believe it, that he every morning sticks his head into an empty flour barrel, and yells, at the top of his voice, "*Honorable Thomas J. Key!*" just to hear how it sounds; and that he has all the little boys hired, with candy, to exclaim, when he walks the streets, "There goes *Honorable* Thomas J. Key!"

Key then responded to Miller in his *Kansas Constitutionalist:*

There is a small sheet published at White Cloud, called the *Chief,* said to be edited by one Sol Miller, which we seldom see. In the last number the editor devotes nearly a column to the "Honorable Thomas J. Key," as he calls us, and he succeeds admirably in misrepresenting us, telling lies upon us. His article has about as much sense as Black Republican articles generally, such for instance, as "three groans for McNulty."

The editor of the *Chief* wishes us to bring him into notice, but we do not wish to pollute our columns with such trash, unless forced to do so. We would gently hint to the cross-eyed, crank-sided, peaked and long razor-nosed, blue-mouthed, nigger-lipped, white-eyed, soft-headed, long-eared, crane-necked, blobber-lipped, squeaky-voiced, empty-headed, snaggle-toothed, filthy-mouthed, box-ankled, pigeon-toed, reel-footed, goggle-eyed, hammer-hearted, cat-hammed, hump-shouldered, blander-shanked, splaw-footed, ignoble, Black Republican, abolition editor, to attend to his own affairs or we will pitch into him in earnest.

To this Sol Miller retorted in the September 10, 1857, issue of the *Kansas Chief*:

"Honorable" Thomas J. Key Gets Savage! – In a late number of the Doniphan *Constitutionalist,* (which the *gentlemanly* publisher neglected to send us,) the editor takes satisfaction upon us, by calling us all the hard names he ever heard of – hard names being the only argument he understands. Among other things, he calls us a Black Republican, and a liar! – says we want him to bring us into notice – threatens to kick us – and seeming to exhaust his vocabulary of hard words, concludes with a tirade of slop-shop expressions, purporting to come from some hireling lick-spittle in his employ, who is taught and commanded to proclaim, "What a mighty man is Thomas J. Key, my master!" This latter was unnecessary, as his editorials are always a mess of botch-work, which could not be made worse if he were to try. Now, that dig hurt our feelings *awfully!* We must acknowledge, we did not exactly tell the truth about him. We said his name was Thomas Jefferson Key. We beg Thomas Jefferson's pardon – it should have been Thomas Jack-ass Key! (No insult intended to jack-asses generally.) But the idea that we want him to bring us into notice – goody [*sic*] gracious! Do we want a skunk to fling his filth upon us, that people may notice us? It would be far preferable to being brought into notice by such a burlesque upon humanity as Thomas J. Key! But to think that such wretches are sent to form a Constitution for the government of decent people – the thought is humiliating![2]

Sol Miller did not limit his verbal attacks to editors of proslavery papers. On one occasion, in his December 29, 1859 issue, Miller lobbed a volley at the editor of a newspaper in the neighboring town of Iowa Point:

In the name of the editorial fraternity, we contend that the editor of the *Chief* should not so underrate the intelligence of the reading community as to outrage common sense, and "write himself down an ass" in one single paper – Iowa Pint [*sic*] Paper.

Nature has not favored us as some others we know of. We know of editors not "far about," who will readily be recognized as asses, without the scratch of a pen!

We have heard of hybrids of various descriptions, but only once of a cross between the quadruped and insect. That isolated case is the editor of the Iowa Point *Dispatch*—he is half "fyste" and half tumble-bug! His quadruped nature is indicated by his bark, and his insect nature, by the substance he delights to revel in!

"Venerable," of the *Dispatch,* acknowledges his indebtedness to us, to the amount of a hundred barrels of corn.—Keep your corn, neighbor, for home consumption; if we should have a hard Winter, provender for asses will be scarce in the Spring!

When an editor at Marysville, Kansas Territory, took a potshot at the town of White Cloud, Miller let go another blast in the February 16, 1860, issue of the *Kansas Chief*:

The Marysville *Democratic Platform,* a paper about half the size of the *Chief,* containing about a dozen sticks of reading matter, and requiring three persons to edit it, is getting wolfish, and makes the following threat: "When we are not crowded with sensible news, and no longer have room in our columes [*sic*] for interesting and respectable [*sic*] items, we will attend to your case - "Sol Miller." Don't—we adjure you to don't! Do not let our case interfere with the "respectable" items in your paper. If we are to fare half as badly in your interesting "columes" as the English language does, our case is hopeless indeed!

One observer of early Kansas editors described the language used as being "without equivocation, innuendo, double talk or double meaning. It is generally incisive and sometimes mordacious. It doesn't wiggle, wobble or waver, beat about the bush, put out a smoke screen, play hide and seek or dodge the issue and does not stoop to demagoguery. It contains no weasel words."[3]

Such writing did not stop when Kansas was admitted as a free state in 1861. In fact it continued through most of the rest of the nineteenth century, although as the old editors died or retired, it declined. By 1880 Dan Anthony, owner and editor of the *Leavenworth Times,* was leading the pack. A good example of his writing style is his attack on A. F. Collamore, the Leavenworth correspondent for the *Kansas City Times,* and two other men who Anthony charged have "for years been associates and participants . . . in whiskey drinking, gambling and debauchery. The trio embraces three of the lowest, dirtiest, filthiest scoundrels that ever infested any place on earth."[4] Two days later, Collamore responded in the columns of the *Kansas City Times*:

> The fiendish, bloodthirsty proprietor of the Leavenworth *Times,* is so fearfully low down and utterly despicable, here, where he is thoroughly *known,* that the very dogs, the sorriest mongrels or the mangiest Spitz, would, in a certain contingency, pass him by, and cross a county writhing with agony, in search of a *cleaner* post. For twenty-two years, it has been his habit to call decent men, who opposed his lunacies, "*dirty dogs*," "*gamblers*," "*skunks*," "*drunkards*," "*scoundrels*," etc. His beast-iality of disposition, and brutishness of heart, have banished him from the walk of life of every *gentleman,* and he stalks through our streets, despised, shunned, and hideous to the sight of those who, with gentle instincts or cultivated habits, loathe disagreeable disgusting surround-ings. Ignoring decency, to answer an argument, or refute a charge, he even resorts to his vocabulary of billingsgate which springs spontaneous from a putrid heart, and scatters his blackguardism in very poor Eng-lish. Gentlemen, congregated on the sidewalk, scatter at his approach, as though a cyclone of epidemic pestilence was imminent, and ladies shudder, as they drop their veils and shrink with horror, when they real-ize his vicinage.[5]

If such a diatribe were published today about a prominent local figure, legal action undoubtedly would follow. Dan Anthony had twice been mayor of Leavenworth, had served several terms as postmaster, and in most quarters was viewed as one of the city's most honored and respected citizens. But until about 1890 editors and publishers in the West were not that concerned about libel or defamatory statements. Until the 1860s few libel suits had been filed against newspapers anywhere in the nation. Libel laws were passed by states and not the federal government, and Americans knew the First Amendment of the Constitution called for freedom of the press. In the late 1860s, however, with the growth of cities and newspapers came an increase in the number of libel suits filed in the nation, especially in the East. In 1869, for instance, there were at least 756 libel suits pending against editors. One observer in 1873 wrote that they had been filed "by personages who claim a plaster of greenbacks for their wounded reputations."[6]

Most editors and publishers in the West did not worry much about libel suits since state defamation laws were a morass of contradictory doctrines, and the cases involved often conflicted widely. The courts were slow in hearing such cases, and judges too lax in trying them. During the 1870s few people were prosecuted for libel anywhere in the nation. By the 1880s, however, the rise of yellow journalism as practiced by Joseph Pulitzer and the Scripps brothers in the East stimulated efforts to shore up libel laws. Tougher standards were applied by appellate courts, and editors and publishers in the East began to take notice and became more cautious about avoiding defamation. Aware of what was going on in the East, western newspaper editors also started to pay more attention to threats of libel.[7]

By the mid-nineteenth century, printers in the West were being called editors of their papers. Many wrote their local items in pencil or pen and ink. After they edited and revised their copy, it was set into type and printed. The editor did it all. To save time some editors actually composed stories as they stood at the typecase setting each word. This habit may itself account for the terse and pointed style of many editors: They learned to make every word count.

While many weekly papers became known for the writing of their editors, some dailies gained national reputations because of the writings of their reporters. One such paper was the *Territorial Enterprise*, started at Genoa in what became Nevada in 1858. It moved to Carson City in 1859, and then in 1860 to the booming mining town of Virginia City. There the *Territorial Enterprise* became a magnet for some of the best writers in the West, including Mark Twain, Dan De Quille, Joe Goodman, Alf Doten, and Wells Drury.

Drury, who started on the competing Gold Hill *Daily News* but soon moved to the *Enterprise*, recalled years later that the paper's reporters "scattered gems of thought and shafts of wit through their columns, lending life and color to the current history of their sagebrush plains and ore-bearing crags and canyons. . . . Every reporter wrote what he pleased and hung the copy on the 'hook.' The printer set it as written, and it went through that way."[8]

In 1862 a tall, thin young man named William Wright, who used the pen name Dan De Quille, went to work as a reporter on the *Enterprise*. Born in Ohio, he moved to Iowa at age eighteen and began writing for local newspapers and sending articles to *Graham's Monthly Magazine*, published in Philadelphia. In 1857 he went to California as a prospector, and then to Nevada in 1861. By that time he had become a regular contributor to the *Golden Era*, California's leading literary journal. On the basis of his work for the *Golden Era*, De Quille was offered the job as editor of local news on the *Enterprise*. He accepted and stayed with the paper for more than thirty years, reporting the news and writing a regular column called "Quille-Drops." He knew the mining business well but wrote stories on any subject. He had a truly remarkable vocabulary. De Quille also found time to write articles for papers in Salt Lake City, San Francisco, and Iowa. His writing displayed humor, a wonderful use of anecdotes, and a flair for vivid description.

The following charming example of De Quille's work is taken from the *Territorial Enterprise*, March 17, 1877:

The foreman of a certain mine counted among the Comstocks, having reason to think that the men working in a particular drift were doing a good deal of soldiering, took occasion the other day to satisfy himself in regard to their underground operations. Quietly advancing along the drift, without a warning light of any kind, he found the men all comfortably seated with their backs braced against the side walls.

One of them was just saying: "I presume I can tell you the greatest story about stealing honey that any of you ever heard."

"Will you be kind enough to hold on with that story?" said the foreman, coming to the front.

Instantly all the men were on their feet. As they were fairly caught, however, it was useless to make a sudden show of industry. They therefore awaited somewhat anxiously what further their foreman might have to say.

He then proceeded: "You see, if you tell your wonderful honey story, here, but few of the men in the mine will be able to hear it. Now, as it is undoubtedly a very amusing thing, I wish all the men to have the pleasure of listening to it. Go on with your work, and this evening you shall tell the story at the boardinghouse, when all may hear it."

With this the foreman turned and marched away, while the men fell to work heartily, feeling much ashamed of having been caught soldiering.

That evening after supper, much to the surprise of the workmen of the mine, all were requested to remain, as a matter of great importance was about to be brought to their notice. All remained, wondering what was coming. Not a few feared there was to be a heavy drafts or a general discharge. All were next asked to range themselves around the room on chairs, properly placed for a comfortable lean against the walls. The cooks, waiters, and dishwashers were next called in and seated. A large armchair was then placed at the upper end of the room, to a seat in which the hero of the great honey story was invited.

The foreman then stated to the meeting that he had in store for them a great treat—nothing less, indeed, than the most remarkable story about stealing honey ever heard since the invention of that industrious insect, the honeybee. The story would be told them by the gentleman occupying the armchair at the head of the hall. Said gentleman had intended relating the story to a few men that day in one of the drifts of the mine, but he had been prevailed upon to await the present opportunity, when all would be able to hear the best thing of the age.

All eyes were turned toward the blushing occupant of the armchair, who was so bewildered and stunned that for a time he was unable to utter a word. "Well, the story," cried the foreman. "Begin the story!"

Something must now be done by the man in the armchair. He arose and said: "I can't tell the story here. I shall not try. You may give me my time—discharge me!"

"We are very sorry to lose the great honey-stealing story," said the foreman, "as we are all ready to hear it from first to last, but if you can't tell it we must do without it, I suppose." Turning to the men, he then said: "Here is the only place where I will have any telling of stories. When a man has a good story to tell, I shall so arrange it that he may have the use of this room and I shall discharge the next man who has a good thing to tell and refuses to relate it when called upon."

The man who is in possession of the great honey story has not yet told it, and not a man in the mine can now be induced to admit that he knows or ever knew a story of any kind. Storytelling is at a discount there.

The man who hired De Quille was Joseph T. Goodman, editor of the *Enterprise,* and the best-known editor on the Comstock. He helped to push the paper into national prominence by stressing human interest stories and giving writers free rein. It was Goodman who also hired Samuel Langhorne Clemens, who first used the pen name Mark Twain while writing for the *Enterprise.* Clemens grew up on the banks of the Mississippi River at Hannibal, Missouri, where, at the age of fourteen, he went to work for Joseph P. Ament, founder in 1848 of the weekly *Missouri Courier.* Two years later Clemens's brother Orion established the Hannibal *Journal.* Young Clemens secured his release from the apprenticeship with Ament and went to work for his brother. When Orion was absent, Samuel edited the paper. About two years later, young Clemens decided to strike out for himself and went to St. Louis, where he got a typesetting job on the *Evening News.* A later journey took him to New York, where he worked for a printing firm at low wages; then to Philadelphia, where he worked on the

In 1863 Samuel Clemens began signing his dispatches to the *Territorial Enterprise* at Virginia City with the pseudonym Mark Twain. *(Courtesy California State Library)*

Inquirer and *Public Ledger;* and on to Cincinnati, where he was employed for several months by a printing company.

When Sam Clemens's brother received an appointment as territorial secretary for Nevada in 1861, Sam went with him to Carson City. He tried his luck with a timber claim and then at mining but found no success in either. While engaged in mining in the Esmeralda district, he wrote several humorous letters to the *Territorial Enterprise,* signing them "Josh." Those letters brought him a twenty-five-dollar-a-week job offer from editor Goodman. Clemens walked nearly seventy miles to accept the newspaper job in Virginia City. He eventually went to Carson City to make daily reports on the doings of the legislature. It was there, on February 2, 1863, that for the first time he signed his daily dispatch with the pseudonym Mark Twain. Under that name, by which he was known for the remainder of his life, he established his literary reputation.

When Samuel Clemens went to work for the *Enterprise,* the paper's senior editor was Dan De Quille, six years older than Clemens. It was De Quille who edited Clemens's first copy and who supposedly taught him the technique of humorous writing that eventually brought him fame. Although Clemens worked for only twenty months on the *Enterprise,* he gained quite a name for himself in that short time. In 1863 he was attacked by a rival paper, the Virginia *Evening Bulletin,* which—among other disparaging remarks—reported: "At the solicitation of about 1500 of our subscribers we will refrain from again entering into a controversy with that beef-eating, blear-eyed, hollow-headed, slab-sided ignoramus, that pilfering reporter, Mark Twain." The *Bulletin* had apparently come off second best on some point of reporting against the man whose remarkable imagination was even then working at full speed.

The *Enterprise* was a very personal paper in that readers knew the writers by name, and their prominence made them well known during the 1860s and 1870s, its most successful years. Such an approach to journalism was similar to that used by Horace Greeley in his New York *Tribune,* but opposite to that of Henry J. Raymond, who started the *New York Times* in September 1851. Raymond was impersonal and gained a reputation as a reasonable and objective editor willing to compromise. Both approaches had their adherents in the West.

When William Rockhill Nelson founded the *Kansas City* (Missouri) *Evening Star* in 1880, he did not give his reporters bylines. They worked in anonymity. It was the paper and not the individual that received credit for the well-written local stories. Nelson hired men of brains and ambition and inspired them, despite small salaries, to create a distinctive and powerfully influential newspaper. Although not a writer himself, Nelson demanded terse, sharply etched descriptive writing without unnecessary verbiage.

For example, when Thomas Nast, whose cartoons had helped to break the Tammany Hall political machine in New York City, passed through Kansas City on September 18, 1886, an unidentified *Star* reporter wrote:

Mr. Thomas H. Nast of New York city, the celebrated cartoonist, arrived in the city last night via the Wabash and left on the Santa Fe this morning on a visit to his son at Silverton, Colorado. Mr. Nast was seen at the depot this morning by a reporter for *The Star* in section number three of the sleeping car Granada, just before his departure. Contrary to the stories that have been from time to time circulated in the west about his failing health, the broken physical condition and the story that his eyes were giving out, the celebrated artist was found to be looking the very picture of health. His keen eyes seem just as clear and bright as they were when he was preparing daily surprises for the American public by

William Rockhill Nelson founded the *Kansas City* (Missouri) *Evening Star* in 1880. He was not a writer but hired the best possible reporters and writers and inspired them to create a distinctive and powerfully influential newspaper that gained a national reputation for quality journalism. *(Author's collection)*

his strong, clear cut, vigorous and highly satirical caricatures of Tweed, B. Gratz Brown and Horace Greeley fifteen or sixteen years ago.

In appearance Mr. Nast is below the medium size of a full but not obese figure. He has a slightly foreign air betraying his French, or rather Belgian origin. He wears at present a somewhat "wiry" moustache and a full beard slightly cropped on the cheeks but growing in a full goatee at the chin.

Although the first practical typewriters appeared on the market in 1874, and some eastern newspapers soon began employing them, many editors in the West and elsewhere viewed the invention as either a toy or an instrument of business and were slow in adopting it except for business correspondence. Nelson refused to allow typewriters in his news- and editorial rooms for several years because he felt that they encouraged wordiness in his writers. One may well wonder how he would react to the use of computers in countless newsrooms today.

TERSE AND POINTED writing was a hallmark of many papers in the West, and not just those that became well known. For instance, the following news item appeared in the *Grant County Herald,* published at Silver City, New Mexico, on March 21, 1875:

> We learn that on Friday, Jose Garcia, who lives at the Chino copper mines, caught his wife in flagarante delicto – we leave the reader to guess the crime – Jose, then and there, gave her the quietus with an axe. She's dead – deadest sort of dead, and it is said that Jose did not run away and intends to face the music.

Terseness and pointedness, of course, could be and often were carried to extremes—as, for example, in the columns of the *Frontier Index,* a newspaper edited by Legh Freeman, which moved with the Union Pacific railroad as it built across Nebraska and Wyoming. During Ulysses S. Grant's first campaign for the presidency in 1868, Freeman, in the *Frontier Index* of May 19, labeled Grant a "whisky bloated, squaw ravishing adulterer . . . monkey ridden, nigger worshipping mogul . . . hell-born satrap . . . tanbark, stinking aristocrat . . . double-dealing hypocrite . . . libertine seducer, and polygamic squaw keeper . . . leather-headed howling, debaucher . . . ," and a "California barroom-bummer."

This kind of foul-mouthed (and what today we recognize as deplorably racist) abuse, while not necessarily raising a paper's public esteem, got the readers' attention and provided entertainment for them in a period before radio and other forms of canned entertainment. Rival editors in the same town also often kept the pot boiling as they exchanged invective or provoked one another to editorial combat. Soon after Thompson B. Ferguson started the *Watonga* (Oklahoma) *Republican* in October 1892, he began goading the editor of the *Rustler,* the town's other paper. In one of his sharpest attacks, on November 29, 1893, Ferguson—who later became governor of Oklahoma—wrote: "The ignorant, egotistical, scrawny, miserable, contemptible, disgusting, measley, mangey, depraved, lying, hypocritical, blear-eyed, dough-faced, idiotic, dwarfed, pinched-up, squaking old numskul [*sic*] of the ex-Rustler ghost still continues to impose himself upon a people who are even more completely disgusted with him than were the Nebraska people who compelled him to make a premature and hasty exit."

Editors' writing skills were tested when exchanges developed, especially between two or more communities in the same county, each vying to become the county seat. In Kansas alone there were nearly thirty such battles—they were often called wars—during the late nineteenth century, and editors in the warring towns went out of their way to attack one another and the residents of the rival community. When the towns of Woodsdale and Hugoton were competing to become the county seat of Stevens County in far southwest Kansas, the editor of the *Hugoton Herald* observed in print:

Now if we had Sam Wood and the deadheads, who came over from Springfield to attend to our business, tarred and feathered, we would have our dirty work done for the spring. The adherents of Wood are an itinerant class of gamblers, toughs and disreputable roustabouts, the most despicable followers the heart of such a contemptible old villain could wish.[9]

In the struggle between the towns of Ingalls and Cimarron in Gray County, Kansas, M. Schiffgen, editor of the Cimarron *Jacksonian,* gave vent to the following on August 2, 1889:

We are onto the lopeared, lantern-jawed, half-bred and half-born whisky-soaked, pox-eaten pup who pretends to edit that worthless wad of subdued paper known as the Ingalls Messenger. He is just starting out to climb the journalistic banister and wants us to knock the hayseed out of his hair, pull the splinters out of his stern and push him on and up. We'll fool him. No free advertising from us. Murphy, k.m.a. [kiss my ass].

The Ingalls *Messenger* ceased publication about a year later.

The editor of the *Advisor* at Voltaire, Kansas, wrote in the April 22, 1886 issue:

The snooping propensities of the Colby *Cat* are fully equal to those of the old "yaller" variety, and like the "yaller" cat, is continually in trouble by reason of it. For the past winter the Colby feline has been too much engaged in Sheridan county to smell much in any other direction, but the vigorous kicking it has received from that quarter has driven it out and now the nose of the beast is in this county. We are loaded for bear and don't want to monkey with cats, but if some things continue, there will be an excellent opportunity for some one to start a manufactory of fiddle strings in Thomas county.

The dugout (*center*) housed the printing plant of the *Thomas County Cat,* established in 1885 at Colby in northwest Kansas. The sod house (*right*) provided living quarters for the proprietors, D. M. Dunn and E. P. Worcester, who sold the paper in 1890. *(Courtesy Kansas State Historical Society)*

Most of the early editors who engaged in such attacks usually avoided legal action, but the later ones sometimes got into legal trouble. Thus, when T. W. Eckert, editor of the Arkansas City (Kansas) *Traveler,* attacked the departing editor of the *Enquirer,* another paper in town—"It is reported that Charlie McIntire may soon take charge of Greer's supplement in this city. Charlie is all right. In fact, anybody would be an improvement on the eunuch who is snorting around in the basement, but unable to do anything."—these remarks cost Eckert seven hundred dollars in a libel judgment.[10]

Consider also the following example from the *Arizona Sentinel,* March 20, 1875:

It remained for San Francisco, the great metropolis of the Pacific Coast, to send to the United States Senate the biggest fool of them all. Senator Hager, in his speech in the Senate, on the Indian Appropriation Bill, asserted that Arizona was a "nearly worthless country." What does he know about Arizona? Nothing. He is totally ignorant of the Territory and its resources and to make such a barefaced, gratuitous lying assertion, is disgraceful to the country and to his constituency.

In Kansas, where law and order and what passed for civilization had arrived in nearly every community by the late nineteenth century, almost all the hard-hitting editors had either mellowed or died. Just after the turn of the century, William Allen White, the well-known editor of the *Emporia Gazette,* complained in the columns of his paper that for some years there had not been a really good row between editors:

There is in progress in a small Kansas town, at the present time, a newspaper row that reminds one of the halcyon days when the rag across the street was edited by a lop-eared leper. Unfortunately for the picturesque in journalism, the lop-eared lepers are nearly all dead, or in the poorhouse. We seldom hear of them any more, and we sigh for the touch of a vanished hand, and the sound of a voice that is still. . . .

In this Kansas row, one of the editors is described as a hyena that prowls the night. The hyena that prowls by night replies that his antagonist is, to all intents and purposes, a polecat. The polecat appears slightly dazed by this rebuke, but rallies bravely, and intimates that the hyena would consider it no crime to steal the coppers from the dead man's eyes, although such charges involve nature faking, for what would a hyena do with coppers—or, for that matter, why should a dead man wear them on his eyes?

The hyena ignores this accusation and expresses his profound conviction that the polecat would rob a widow's hen roost. And so the cheerful controversy proceeds. It is really refreshing, as viewed from a distance, and it is too bad that the prominent business men . . . are always butting in to stop it. They ought to be sending marked copies of the local papers all over the country to cheer up a doleful world.[11]

Over time the editors and their writing changed, and by the 1920s the personal opinions of most editors were usually couched in polite language because the West had changed. It was not as wild. Westerners had acquired a sense of permanence and transplanted the institutions and government found in the East. Editors and publishers paid more attention to the business of newspapers and sought to make their papers more respectable. But in the process a staid dullness replaced the vigor and colorful language that had once graced their columns.

CHAPTER THREE

POLITICS

*I shall preserve the liberty of the Press
as long as I am able to control one.*
—Joseph Charless

LONG BEFORE NEWSPAPERS appeared in the American West, the marriage of journalism and politics had been consummated in the East during the American Revolution. The courtship began when newspapers published the writings of patriots who cited social and economic conditions as reasons why the colonies should be independent. Many colonial newspapers became significant players in what was really a political struggle aimed at obtaining freedom.

After the colonies gained their independence, the debate over what form of organized government the new nation should have took center stage. There were those who wanted George Washington crowned king. Most did not, although almost everyone wanted him to head whatever government was established. The Articles of Confederation, adopted on March 2, 1781, proved unsatisfactory because, fearing a central government with too much power, their authors left the states too much power to permit a central government to function efficiently.

As the debate unfolded, newspapers published the views of John Adams, Thomas Jefferson, Alexander Hamilton, and others and then reported what occurred when delegates gathered in Philadelphia on May 25, 1787, for the Constitutional Convention. After more than three months of debate, the delegates submitted a Constitution on September 17 that addressed the natural rights of man and granted certain powers to a central government while reserving other powers for the states. The delegates had considered adding a citizens' Bill of Rights to the Constitution, but at the time there was general agreement that such material would be superfluous since the states had already guaranteed such rights in their own constitutions. By the late 1780s, however, there were growing fears that a powerful central government was incompatible with liberty. When the nation's first

Congress met in 1789, James Madison put forth a series of constitutional amendments affirming the individual's right to life, liberty, and property. Quickly ratified by the states, the ten amendments became law only a year after the last of the states, Rhode Island, had ratified the basic Constitution.

Almost as a passing reference, the press was included in the First Amendment, which reads:

> Congress shall make no law respecting an establishment of religion, or prohibiting the free exercise thereof; or abridging the freedom of speech, or of the press; or the right of the people peaceably to assemble, and to petition the Government for a redress of grievances.

While there is little evidence that the Founding Fathers spent much time debating press freedom, they knew well the role played by newspapers during the Revolution. Papers had instructed and directed readers on political matters, including issues and candidates, and had also provided criticism of local and national administrators. The importance of this service may have convinced the Founding Fathers of the need for a free press, which, under the First Amendment, cannot be restricted legally without a constitutional amendment, meaning that neither the president nor Congress can abridge the freedom of the press without running into resistance from the courts.

By the late 1780s many newspapers were speaking with authority on countless subjects, and readers no longer regarded most newspaper editors as merely printers issuing publications to which others contributed ideas: The editors of such papers became opinion leaders.

When Joseph Charless printed and distributed the prospectus for his *Missouri Gazette* in 1808, he recognized the role of newspapers in the new nation, and the responsibilities of an editor. His prospectus read in part:

> It is self evident that in every country where the rays of the Press is [*sic*] not clouded by despotic power, that the people have arrived at the highest grade of civilization, there science holds her head erect, and bids her sons to call into action those talents which lie in a good soil, inviting civilization. The inviolation of the press is coexistent with the liberties of the people, they live or die together, it is the vestal fire upon the preservation of which, the fate of the nation depends; and the most pure hands officiating for the whole community, should be incessantly employed in keeping it alive.[1]

Charless's prospectus served as his declaration of faith in the freedom of the press as part of the fundamental rights of all citizens.

Like so many other printers who established newspapers during and after the American Revolution, Charless was a man of clear and firmly held opinions who spoke his mind in person and in print. He was a strong supporter of Thomas Jefferson and the Louisiana Purchase. Early in 1809 Charless printed the following editorial, stating his political support for both and at the same time lambasting the eastern press:

> Big Swamp Louisiana! What citizen is there, who is in the smallest degree alive to the prosperity of our happy country, who does not feel indignant at the gross falsehoods and ignorant philippics published against the Jefferson administration, concerning the purchase of Louisiana? We would recommend these incendiary editors to the study of geography, and they will discover that Louisiana possesses a soil equal to any other State or Territory in the Union. Rich in minerals, numerous navigable rivers and many other advantages place this desirable country far above the calumny of the miserable scribblers. Give us industrious planters, and in a short period Louisiana will become the bright star in the Federal constellation.[2]

As other newspapers were established in Missouri, their editors not only expressed their views in their columns but gradually began to report political news. Initially papers published the journals of the Missouri legislature while lawmakers were in session. Soon papers had reporters covering the legislative sessions. In some instances the editors themselves covered the sessions, sending reports back home to be published by their papers. The papers also printed letters from readers expressing their views on political affairs. These letters were often published with short commentaries by the editors referring readers to longer stories on the subject elsewhere in the paper. Most early editors believed that their newspapers should be advocates of principles and not people. In the eyes of many, it was immoral to support individuals without any thought of the fundamental truths for which they stood. Thus the publication of the doctrines of political parties was emphasized by editors who sought balance and consistency in their columns. In turn, the leaders of political parties hoped that their doctrines would influence readers.

Missouri newspapers paid considerable attention to national politics, especially the Missouri Compromise of 1820, which decreed that slaveholding should not be permitted north of the Thirty-eighth Parallel except in Missouri, which was admitted as a slave state while Maine was admitted as a free state. The nation's sectional balance was thus maintained, along with political stability, even after Texas was admitted as a slave state in 1845 and California as a free state in 1850. Proslavery people were seemingly pacified because under the Missouri Compromise the future territories of New Mexico and Arizona would be brought into the Union as slave states.

But everything changed with the passage of the Kansas-Nebraska Act in 1854. Under the Missouri Compromise, Nebraska would have been free and Kansas slave, but the Kansas-Nebraska Act repealed that portion of the Missouri Compromise barring slavery north of 36° 30′ west of the state of Missouri. It left the question of slavery in the new territories up to the people who would draft the constitutions of those states. Overnight, slavery became a national issue. Free-state and proslavery supporters hurried to the new territory to try to determine which way Kansas would go. Unlike anywhere else in the West, national politics would be responsible for creating and dominating the early Kansas press, much as the American Revolution governed the developing press along the Atlantic seaboard late in the eighteenth century. Henry King, whose newspaper career in Kansas and Missouri spanned the nineteenth and early twentieth centuries, later observed: "Kansas is perhaps the only place on the face of the earth of which it has been said that a newspaper was started before there was any [local] news to print."[3] National politics dominated the columns.

When the Kansas Territory was opened to settlement in the spring of 1854, George W. Gist, a proslavery businessman at Weston, Missouri, quickly organized a town company, crossed the Missouri River, and laid out a town site near Fort Leavenworth, just across the river from Weston. Gist urged his son-in-law, William H. Adams, who published a weekly newspaper at Weston, to start a paper there. Adams took his printing press and equipment across the river on a ferry, set it up under an old elm tree on the site of what would become Leavenworth, Kansas, and prepared to publish the *Kansas Weekly Herald,* the first newspaper in the Kansas Territory.

A day or two after Adams' press was set up, a traveler happened upon the editor as he was setting type for the first issue of the *Herald.* The traveler later wrote that Leavenworth consisted of only "four tents, all on one street, a barrel of water or whiskey under a tree, and a pot, on a pole over a fire. Under a tree, a type-sticker had his case before him and was at work on the first number of the new paper, and within a frame, without a board on side or roof, was the editor's desk and sanctum."[4]

Soon after the first issue was printed, a one-story frame structure was completed to house the newspaper. Adams moved his press, printing equipment, and belongings into the new building. Within days of the move, a proslavery man from Louisiana visited the office and later wrote:

A visit to the printing office afforded a rich treat. On entering the first room on the right hand, three law 'shingles' were on the door; on one side was a rich bed, French blankets, sheets, table cloths, shirts, cloaks and rugs, all together; on the wall hung hams, maps, venison and rich engravings, onions, portraits and books; on the floor were a side of bacon carved to the bone, corn and potatoes, stationery and books; on a nice dressing case stood a wooden tray half full of dough, while crockery occupied the professional desk. In a room on the left, the sanctum, the housewife, cook and editor lived in glorious unity, one person. He was seated on a stool, with paper before him on a piece of plank, writing a vigorous knockdown to an article in the Kickapoo *Pioneer,* a paper of a rival city. The cook-stove was at his left, and tin kettles all around; the corn cake was 'a-doing,' and instead of scratching his head for an idea, he turned the cake and went ahead.[5]

From the beginning the purpose of Adams's *Kansas Weekly Herald* was to build political support to make Kansas a slave state, but the paper was rather bland. Adams was primarily a printer and not skilled in writing or in editorial matters. Perhaps because of this and the need for more financial backing, after only six issues of his paper, Adams took a new partner, Gen. Lucien J. Eastin, former editor of the St. Joseph (Missouri) *Gazette.* Eastin took over the paper's editorial chores and began to emit fiery pronunciamentos in support of slavery in Kansas.

The full name of the Kickapoo *Pioneer,* referred to by the *Herald*'s Louisiana visitor, was the *Kansas Pioneer,* a weekly paper that had been started in the new town seven miles north of Leavenworth. The publisher and editor was A. B. Hazzard, who installed the new press and printing equipment in one room on the second floor of an old log building that had been used by missionaries at the Kickapoo Indian Mission. Hazzard's paper was bitterly proslavery and anti-Leavenworth, but after Leavenworth won out as the principal city in the county, Hazzard's paper died, and he sought greener pastures, moving to Savannah, Georgia, to publish a paper.

The first newspaper in the Kansas Territory opposed to slavery was started by John Speer, a printer from Ohio. He had gone to the territory in the spring of 1854, soon after it was opened to settlement. He selected what is now Lawrence as the place to publish his paper. The town, which had been laid out by the Emigrant Aid Company from New England, was located on the Kansas River about thirty-five miles south of Leavenworth. While Speer did not bring a press or printing equipment with him, he wrote editorials for his new paper hoping to have the first issue printed by the *Kansas City* (Missouri) *Enterprise.* But when the proprietor of the *Enterprise* learned that Speer opposed slavery, he refused to do the printing. Speer then tried to have his paper printed by the proslavery *Kansas Weekly Herald* at Leavenworth, but was again told no. Frustrated, Speer returned to Ohio, had the paper, called the *Kansas Pioneer,* printed there, and returned to Kansas Territory to distribute it. The first issue was dated October 18, 1854. But, once back in Kansas Territory, Speer learned that A. B. Hazzard had started his proslavery *Kansas Pioneer* at Kickapoo. To avoid confusion Speer changed the name of his free-state paper to the *Kansas Tribune.* After his press and equipment arrived, Speer published the second issue of his renamed paper on January 5, 1855.

The second free-state paper, the *Herald of Freedom,* was also located at Lawrence, and its first issue, like that of Speer's paper, was printed in the East. George Brown was selected by the Emigrant Aid Company, headquartered in New England, to start a free-state paper in Kansas Territory at a new town, to be called Wakarusa, being settled by immigrants sponsored by the company. Brown had the first issue of his paper printed at Conneautville, Pennsylvania, and dated it October 21, 1854. When he arrived in the Kansas Territory, he learned that the new town had been named Lawrence, not Wakarusa. In the second issue, he duly changed the place of publication.

The third free-state paper in Kansas Territory, also established in Lawrence, was the *Kansas Free State,* started in January 1855 by Josiah Miller and R. G. Elliott, although the newspaper's office was destroyed about four months later by a group of Missourians who came to Lawrence. By then Lawrence had become the principal free-state town in the territory, while Leavenworth, Kickapoo, and Atchison—all three located on the Missouri River—were strong proslavery towns. The free-state and proslavery editors exchanged hundreds of bitter volleys, but they also found time to report local news, including less incendiary politics. The editor of the *Leavenworth Weekly Herald* included a little humor in the following piece published on December 10, 1859:

Dr. H—— tells a good story at the expense of our worthy ex-city marshal. While the latter was endeavoring to rescue the team [of horses] which broke through the ice on election day, he broke through himself, and came very near drowning. As the ice was giving way, and he about going down, he exclaimed at the top of his voice, "I have not voted—I have not voted!" Of course he was rescued, as candidates could be found within the hearing of every man's voice.

As students of American history know, the free-state cause won, and Kansas was admitted to the Union as a free state on January 29, 1861. But for Kansas editors, the years 1854 to 1861 were filled with intense feelings and desperate determination. The political lines were drawn with unmistakable precision, leaving no refuge or middle ground where an editor could hide. Conditions created a partiality for aggressive campaigning, and for disregarding any impulses toward brotherly kindness and patience. Not only were editors on the firing line, but they helped to bring about the news they published. They and their constituents made no distinction between politics and other questions of the day.

One observer wrote:

If an editor were 'agin' something he was also 'fernist' the personality that was sponsoring whatever project the editor happened to be 'agin' at the moment. There was no distinction between editorial freedom and personal freedom in those days. If an editor objected to any program or the views of any person it was taken to be personal as well as political opposition to the proposal under discussion. So it is no wonder that editorial viewpoints bred personal animosities. The times and conditions were such that no other course was open, they believed, as did their constituents and those whom the editors opposed. There is an old dogma, "If you believe you are right, let there be no deviation from the charted course." That was firmly imbedded in the minds and personalities of the men and women who constituted the citizenship of Kansas in those early days. And it applied to the editorial brethren as well as to the ordinary sovereign squat – meaning Mr. Average Citizen.[6]

The political turmoil in Kansas attracted not only national attention but eastern newspapermen. Horace Greeley, who supported the new Republican Party, was on his way overland to California during the late spring of 1859 when he stopped over in Kansas to attend a territorial Republican convention at Osawatomie. When Democrats learned he was coming, the *Leavenworth Weekly Herald* reported: "We find the so-called Republicans of Kansas sending all the way to New York for the great Agamemnon of Black Republicanism—Horace Greeley—to aid in the organization of their party in this Territory. He comes with a platform in his breeches pocket."[7]

After Greeley learned what Kansas Democrats were charging, he wrote articles for the territory's Republican papers saying that there was not a shadow of truth to the charges, that no one, either in or out of Kansas, had asked him to attend the Osawatomie convention. Greeley did attend the convention, but if he had hoped to play an active role in it, his hopes were in vain. The Kansas Republicans treated him with the courtesy due the great editor, but conducted their deliberations without his participation. After the convention adjourned, Greeley was asked to speak. Nearly a thousand people heard him talk for an hour and a half as he reviewed old political parties; the steady growth of slave power; and the origin, history, principles, and objects of the Republican Party. Some Kansas editors printed Greeley's speech in full as he continued his westward journey to the goldfields of the far western Kansas Territory, in what is now Colorado.

In 1868 Henry W. Talcott, from Indiana, and Nelson F. Acers, from Illinois, both attorneys, bought the weekly *Allen County Courant* in Iola, Kansas, and changed its name to *Neosho Valley Register*. A year later Acers sold his interest to Talcott, who published the paper until he sold it in 1871. This photo was taken about 1870, when Iola had a population of less than a thousand residents. *(Courtesy Kansas State Historical Society)*

Because of the role the Kansas struggle played in the creation of the Republican Party, Abraham Lincoln decided to visit the territory in November 1859, only a few months after Greeley. By then the fight to make Kansas a free state was almost over. The free-staters had won and Kansas was knocking for admission into the Union. Lincoln had become an important figure in the newly formed Republican Party. On the afternoon of November 30, 1859, Lincoln arrived by train at St. Joseph, Missouri, and was met by two Kansas newspapermen, Mark Delahay and Daniel W. "Web" Wilder. Delahay was a former Illinois newspaperman and attorney whose wife was Lincoln's cousin. Delahay had started a free-state newspaper at Leavenworth, but a proslavery mob sacked his office and threw his printing press into the Missouri River. Wilder, a Kansas leader of the new Republican Party, was editor of the *Elwood Free Press,* a free-state paper. Delahay and Wilder escorted Lincoln on a ferry across the Missouri River to Kansas, where the future president spent seven days speaking in several towns and talking to citizens. Free-state newspapers reported the visit, as did eastern newspapermen in the Kansas Territory, including Henry Villard and Albert D. Richardson, who were in the settlement of Troy when Lincoln spoke. Richardson later wrote:

In the imaginative language of the frontier, Troy was a town—possibly a city—but, save a shabby frame courthouse, a tavern and a few shanties, its urban glories were visible only to the eye of faith. It was intensely cold. The sweeping prairie wind rocked the crazy buildings, and cut the faces of the travelers like a knife. . . . There was none of the magnetism of a multitude to inspire the long, angular, ungainly orator, who rose up behind a rough table. With little gesticulation—and that little ungraceful—he began, not to declaim, but to talk in a conversational tone, he argued the question of slavery in the territories in the language of an average Ohio or New York farmer. I thought, "If the Illinoisans consider this a great man their ideas must be very peculiar." But in ten or fifteen minutes I was unconsciously and irresistibly drawn by the clearness and closeness of his argument. Link after link it was forged and welded, like a blacksmith's chain.[8]

It was not until after the future president left the Kansas Territory and made his now famous speech at Cooper Union in New York City on February 27, 1860, that editors in Kansas and national correspondents like Richardson realized that Lincoln had first tried out those remarks on people in Kansas. Three months after the Cooper Union speech, Lincoln was nominated for the presidency in Chicago, and on November 6, 1860, he was elected the sixteenth president of the United States. By then newspaper editors in the Kansas Territory who had supported Lincoln felt much pride in the role they and their papers had played in doing so.

Even before the passage of the Kansas-Nebraska Act, the character of national politics had begun to change. The Whigs and Democrats had been the chief political parties. The Democrats championed westward expansion, but the Whigs consistently opposed it, along with most measures of concern in the West. The fate of the Whig Party was soon sealed, and it disappeared as a formal organization by 1857. By then plans for the future development of the West were playing a crucial role in the formation of the Republican Party, which came to dominate the political culture of Kansas. Elsewhere in the West the influence of politics and of journalism's coverage were more subdued.

In the Rocky Mountains from the Montana Territory south to the New Mexico Territory, the discovery of gold and silver created mining towns before anyone gave much thought to politics. It is not surprising that most editors in the new hurriedly built towns proclaimed their papers independent to gain widespread approval. One Colorado miner, H. G. Hawley, wrote in his diary on August 6, 1860: "I hear nothing about politics out here as every body is for money and not for office."[9]

In most instances, however, it did not take editors long before they became involved in partisan debates, supporting one candidate over another or declaring allegiance to a political party. By then journalism was changing because of politics. Many editors were assuming partisan roles in politics, which elevated them to leadership roles in civic and political matters. But at the same time most editors had little time nor did they seek time to analyze how the partisanship reflected in their papers' columns was helping to build new governments by transplanting eastern laws and customs into the West.

But not all eastern ways applied in the West. The long-functioning power structures common in the East, along with apathy and the tendency to trust those in control, tended to concentrate governmental functions in the hands of certain classes, groups, or families. In the new towns of the West, no such structure existed. If a person could convince neighbors that he had energy and ability, was willing to identify with the interests of the people and follow their advice, he could achieve political power regardless of his background.

Some editors sought to obtain political power by taking a partisan position in their newspapers. Not all were successful. The editor of the *Colorado*

Miner, published at Georgetown, thought that there were enough Republican voters in town to support his paper. He was wrong and returned to an independent policy. But in Montana, a few weeks after the *Herald* was founded at Helena by Robert Fisk during the middle 1860s, the paper supported the Republican cause after Fisk was given about $15,000. When William Clagett was elected a delegate to Congress from Montana, Fisk was rewarded again—his brother was appointed collector of customs.[10]

BY THE LATE nineteenth century, it was not uncommon in larger cities for political factions to operate their own papers. In Montana rival copper kings owned the *Daily Miner* at Butte and the Anaconda *Standard,* located in the same county. On November 9, 1898, the morning after an election, both papers reported the electoral results. First the *Daily Miner:*

> By coercion, intimidation and bribery the returns show that the Dalycratic ticket has managed to force itself upon Silver Bow County. A more disgraceful election was never witnessed in Montana. The freedom of the ballot and honesty in elections has become a farce in the light of the methods used by the Dalycratic heelers.
>
> That the Dalycrats bought all the purchasable element no one in the city doubts. Election day, every irresponsible loafer and bum in the city was shouting for Marcus Daly and jingling in their pockets the price of their votes. The better element, the representative element of Butte, does not appear to be in the majority in Silver Bow County. The returns show that good government by and for the people was beaten.

The Anaconda *Standard:*

> In spite of a wholesale buying of votes, repeating and fraudulent balloting as indulged in by an unscrupulous opposition, the forces of honesty and decency in Silver Bow County were rewarded yesterday when the entire Democratic ticket won by a handsome majority. That the lying and thieving tactics of the Clark forces availed them little is proven by the results of yesterday's balloting.

The prospects of political spoils motivated many editors in Montana and elsewhere in the West, but not those in the young New Mexico Territory, which—when opened in 1850—included what is now Arizona and part of modern Colorado. Santa Fe was the region's commercial and political center; Albuquerque was only a sleepy farming settlement of about twelve hundred souls and not large enough to support a paper. The region's economy was poor, and there was great poverty and illiteracy. Between 1847 and 1879 only sixty-three weekly newspapers were published in what is now New Mexico, and many were short-lived. The editors of nearly all these papers took a live-and-let-live position, while two groups of citizens, each with its own newspaper, sought to control politics. One group was composed of federal officers who allied themselves with prominent members of the Spanish-American community. Their paper was the Santa Fe *Weekly Gazette,* founded in June 1851 by James L. Collins. The other group was led by Jose M. Gallegos, a former priest who tended to oppose American rule. His political colleague was Spruce M. Baird, a lawyer from Texas, who published the Santa Fe *Amigo del País* and *El Democrata,* partisan papers published during political campaigns. At about the time the Civil War began, Baird returned to Texas and Gallegos soon joined what had been his opposition. A new group was then formed, led by J. F. Chaves, who quickly aligned himself with some of the federal officers and W. H. Manderfield and Thomas Tucker, two printers who had become publishers of the Santa Fe *Weekly New Mexican.* Between 1851 and 1869, it was impossible to label the groups along party lines because both claimed to represent whatever party was in power nationally. But beginning in 1869, the Chaves group took a leading role in the New Mexico Republican Party. T. B. Catron and S. B. Elkins soon dominated the group, which consisted of federal officials, prominent Spanish Americans, and the publishers of the Santa Fe *New Mexican.* This group became known as the Santa Fe Ring.

Little was written about this group until after more newspapers were established in the New Mexico Territory during the 1870s. Perhaps the first paper to attack the Santa Fe Ring was the Las Cruces *Borderer,* established in 1871 by N. V. Bennett, a Democrat and native of New York. About a year after he started his paper, Bennett accused the Santa Fe *New Mexican* of being nothing more than the mouthpiece of a corrupt group of political demagogues. The *Borderer,* however, suspended publication just before Bennett died in 1876. On April 1, 1876, the *Grant County Herald,* located in the mining boomtown of Silver City, reprinted an editorial from the New York *Sun* naming Catron and Elkins as leaders of the Santa Fe group and adding that Elkins expected to be a U.S. senator once New Mexico became a state. Six months later, and probably responding to stories in both the *Herald* and the *Sun,* the Santa Fe *Weekly New Mexican,* October 17, 1876, reported that no such ring existed and added:

The word "ring" has of late years grown into very common use, and it is applied very generally and liberally. It is used generally to designate any combination or association of men for any and whatever purpose. It is a favorite word with disappointed aspirants for political favor, sore heads, unsuccessful place seekers, chronic mischief makers and fault finders and noisy demagogues. It is especially a pet word with ambitious outs who are impatient to get in, and above all with fellows who, having lately held office, have been found incompetent or unworthy and been kicked out. It has been the fashion for the classes above named, and even of a more reputable class of Democratic politicians, to talk a great deal of what they term a "Santa Fe Ring" . . . which has no existence except in the distempered brain of fussy demagogues and place hunters.

Democrats quietly continued to blame the Santa Fe Ring for all of the evils that beset the territory, especially after S. M. Ashenfelter, who had married into the Bennett family, became editor of the *Grant County Herald.* He reprinted a piece from the St. Louis *Republican,* charging that the Santa Fe Ring bribed members of the New Mexico territorial legislature to do its bidding. Ashenfelter told his readers the Santa Fe Ring did exist and did manipulate the territorial legislature to reward northern Spanish-American counties at the expense of southern Anglo-American Democratic counties.

About a year later, on September 14, 1878, the Santa Fe *New Mexican* reported that William Breeden, territorial Republican chairman, had asked Democrats for more specific charges upon which territorial officials could take legal action. Several days later, on September 21, S. M. Ashenfelter responded in the *Herald:*

During the last eight or ten years many and grievous complaints have been made throughout the territory of the acts of oppression by which that combination of individuals known as the Santa Fe Ring has maintained its ascendancy. It is generally understood that this ring is made up of government officials whose interests are not identified with those of the Territory, but who have come out from the east, because in the division of political spoils, an office in New Mexico fell [to] their lot. Does anyone doubt that in case the Democratic party won in the next national contest, a new set of cormorants would be foisted upon our people, and that a new ring would be organized in Santa Fe? Does anyone believe that such a ring would hold the welfare of the people in higher esteem than the gratification of their own selfish ends?

Whether the Santa Fe Ring was guilty of everything Ashenfelter and other Democrats charged is not known, but a later Democratic administration in New Mexico secured criminal indictments against many ring members, although only a few were convicted.

While many editors in the New Mexico Territory began rejecting political domination in the 1880s, some did not. At Las Vegas, New Mexico, forty newspapers, including eight dailies, were published between 1879 and 1912, during which time the town's population increased from about 1,500 to 7,000. Nine of the forty papers, including three dailies, were directly sponsored or encouraged by politicians. Many of the other papers sold their editorial opinions to the highest bidder. During this period three of the town's editors were appointed postmasters, while still other appointed positions were used to reward or to motivate other publishers.[11]

The rise of the Republican Party created tough times for Democrats and editors who supported them not only in New Mexico but in neighboring Colorado Territory, which was established in 1861. Perhaps it was only natural that Colorado Republicans and a Denver newspaper made the most out of a sensational story involving a not-very-remarkable man named Alferd Packer. It all started in the fall of 1873, when a group of Utah prospectors organized a trip to Colorado's rich San Juan goldfields. While looking for a guide, they learned of a man sitting in a Salt Lake City jail who knew the territory. They offered to bail him out if he would lead them to the gold. The man was Alferd Packer, a native of Pennsylvania who had served in the Union Army during the Civil War, and he agreed. It was winter when the party reached the San Juans. They were warned to stay put until spring, but a small splinter group, led by Packer, foolishly set off into the rugged mountains early in 1874. The following spring only Packer emerged, appearing sleek and well fed for a man trapped in the mountains for sixty days, and he had quite a bit of money. Suspicious local officials questioned Packer, who broke down and made two confessions. He told how the party became trapped and that his five companions died or killed each other, or he had killed them, and how he had lived off portions of their bodies. Packer, dubbed a man-eater, was jailed in Saguache, but escaped with the aid of an accomplice on August 8, 1874. About eight years later Packer was arrested again near Fort Fetterman, Wyoming; he was returned to Colorado. Before the trial, the *Rocky Mountain News* in Denver, on March 13, 1883, reported, perhaps tongue in cheek, that Packer was known as a renegade Republican who had eaten five of the seven Democrats in Hinsdale County. When Packer was tried in early April 1883, found guilty, and sentenced to death, one account claims Judge Melville G.

Gerry, a native of Georgia and a Southern gentleman of the old school, meted out the death sentence as follows:

> "Stan' up, yah voracious man eating son of a bitch, stand up!
>
> "They was sivin Dimmicrats in Hinsdale County, and ye eat five of them, God damn ye!
>
> "I sintins ye t' be hanged by the neck until ye're dead, dead, dead, as a warnin' ag'in reducin' the Dimmycratic population of th' state."

Another version has Judge Gerry saying: "Alferd Packer, you voracious Republican cannibal, I would sentence you to hell but the statutes forbid it."

In truth district court records, as reported by the *Rocky Mountain News,* April 14, 1883, indicate that the political affiliations were a myth, and that Judge Gerry actually lectured Packer with a great deal of compassion in sentencing him:

> It becomes my duty as the Judge of this Court to enforce the verdict of the jury rendered in your case, and impose on you the judgment which the law fixes as the punishment of the crime you have committed. It is a solemn, painful duty to perform. I would to God the cup might pass from me. You have had a fair and impartial trial. You have been faithfully and earnestly defended by able Counsel. . . .
>
> A jury of twelve honest citizens of the County have sat in judgment on your case and upon their oaths they find you guilty of wilful and premeditated murder – a murder revolting in all its details. . . .
>
> For nine long years you have been a wanderer upon the face of the earth, bowed and broken in spirit; no home; no loves; no ties to bind you to earth. You have been, indeed, a poor, pitiful waif of humanity. I hope and pray that in the spirit land to which you are so fast and surely drifting, you will find peace and rest for your weary spirit which this world cannot give. Alferd Packer, the judgment of this Court is that you be removed from thence to the jail of Hinsdale County and there confined until the 19th day of May, A.D. 1883, and that on said 19th day of May, 1883, you be taken from thence by the sheriff of Hinsdale County, to a place of execution prepared for this purpose at some point within the corporate limits of the town of Lake City, in the said County of Hinsdale, and between the hours of 10:00 A.M. and 3:00 P.M. of said day, you, then and there, by said sheriff be hung by the neck until you are dead, dead, dead, and may God have mercy upon your soul!

That night a lynch mob gathered, apparently determined to relieve the Hinsdale County sheriff of his obligation to carry out the judge's sentence. Packer was quickly moved from Lake City to the jail in Gunnison. His attorney appealed the decision to the Colorado Supreme Court on the technicality that Packer had been charged under territorial jurisdiction but tried under state jurisdiction. In 1883, three years later, a second trial was held, and the jury returned a verdict of guilty of manslaughter for each of the five victims. Packer was sentenced to eight years on each count—a total of forty years. Packer was about forty-four years old when he was taken to the Colorado state penitentiary at Canon City to serve his sentence.

Colorado newspapers were not through with Packer, however, although his last spectacular appearance there had little to do with politics. He remained in prison occupying his time making horse-hair rope and bridles until 1901, when Polly Pry, a columnist for the *Denver Post*, visited the state penitentiary at Carson City while researching a story on prison reform. There she met and interviewed Packer. She returned to Denver and told Frederick G. Bonfils and Harry H. Tammen, owners of the *Denver Post*, about Packer.

Bonfils, who had been in the real estate and lottery businesses, and Tammen, a onetime bartender, had joined forces in 1895 to buy the *Post*. Although dynamic publishers, they were ruthless and irresponsible. They used giant banner headlines printed in red ink which emphasized their highly sensational approach to news. They asked Polly Pry and lawyer William W. "Plug Hat" Anderson to get Packer paroled. Bonfils and Tammen wanted to employ him as a sideshow freak in a circus they owned. The state's governor did grant Packer a parole, but only on the condition that he go to Denver and remain there for six years and nine months. That eliminated the possibility of Packer's appearing with the circus when it toured outside of Denver. Packer paid lawyer Anderson a fee of twenty-five dollars. Although there are several versions of what happened next, when Anderson visited Bonfils, Tammen, and Polly Pry at the *Denver Post*, Bonfils supposedly demanded half of the fee Anderson had received. When Anderson refused, Bonfils struck him in the face. Anderson left but returned with a revolver and entered the office without knocking. He shot Bonfils in the neck and chest and Tammen in the shoulder and chest as both men ducked under Polly Pry's full skirt. Anderson was waiting to use the last bullet in his revolver when Bonfils raised Polly's skirt to see what was happening. When Anderson saw Bonfils shaking like a leaf and perspiring heavily, he started laughing and put the gun away. Bonfils and Tammen survived. Anderson was arrested on charges of assault with intent to murder, and was tried three times—after two hung juries, a third panel found him not guilty.[12]

THE PAGES OF newspapers published in the West between the late 1860s and about 1900 reflect the fact that there was little real difference nationally in the policies of the Democrats and Republicans. Both avoided the chief issues of American life and in their political campaigns for support relied on trite phrases such as "party loyalty." Perhaps precisely because of this, local politics and political reporting in this period are more colorful. For instance, on May 7, 1880, the weekly Logan (Kansas) *Enterprise* published the following:

> One of the members of the city Council made the statement previous to the election that in case he was elected "that he proposed to crow over it before the d——d little sons of b——s of the Enterprise," and in case we gave him any back talk "that he proposed to spit in our face and then pound it in." If the gentleman wishes to do us a serious injury we would recommend that he fill the large vacuum under his nose with pulverized guano before trying the experiment.

The above paragraph is mild when compared to another front-page story found in the Los Angeles (California) *Broad-Axe,* a weekly established "to lay low monopolies, rings, and robbing politicians" during the 1875 campaign. The paper was edited by W. C. Wiseman. After another paper, the *Los Angeles Daily Independent,* took some political potshots at Wiseman, he responded in the August 31, 1875, issue of the *Broad-Axe* under the headline:

THE BASTARD SQUIRT
CALLED THE DAILY INDEPENDENT

The hired tool of Black Republicanism, under cover of the Independent party, is still peging away at the Broad-Axe. Go on, little Bastard, squirt, flunkey. You cannot raise to the dignity of a sycophant, or a yellow, bobtailed, mangy dog. You have tried but failed. And in your efforts have sank low down into the salevated cesspools of corruption, from whence you eminated. Carrying with you large sums of money wrongfully assessed from Independent candidates, to publish the fatherless Bastard that has ruined and damned their hopes of election. A fatherless Bastard cannot inherit from its blood kindred a name or favors from the public. But could have told the names of the dark lantern Federal Brigade dads of the filthy bantling called the Daily Independent, and thereby saved us the trouble of having to publish it. . . . Was there ever before such an outrage? Pirates, thieves, and highway robbers, have more honor and would scorn to be guilty of so mean and dastardly an act. The shame of snolegosters of the said Bastard Banttling, not content with their ill-gotten gains, envies the BROAD-AXE—take us to task for charging candidates $10 for their announcements and that candidates paid it rather than get out abuse. That cannot be so, for we have not written a single abusive line against county candidates of either party; but have from time to time spoken well of all, and still say that all are honorable gentlemen on both tickets, and we could cordially support many of the Independent nominees if they were not found in such bad company—company that would tarnish the reputation of a sheep-killing dog, to wit the said snolegosters.

Most newspapers welcomed paid advertisements by politicians, but few offered credit even to candidates they might favor. Mrs. J. E. Ramey, editor of the weekly *Porter* (Oklahoma) *Enterprise* and one of many women editors in the West, published the following rates in her May 12, 1916, issue:

POLITICAL ANNOUNCEMENT FEES.

The price for political announcements, to be run from the time the announcement is given us for publication until close of the primary, will be as follows:

For Congress	$20.00
For State and Senatorial office	$15.00
For County office	$10.00
For County Commissioner	$5.00
For Justice of the Peace, Constable, Etc.	$2.50

All political announcements will be Strictly Cash in Advance. Positively no partiality will be shown in this respect.

But in hard economic times some editors openly tried to use their political affiliations to make ends meet. The editor of the *Denver Daily Gazette*, a Democrat, asked every Democrat to persuade friends and neighbors to subscribe. "Remember, by doing so . . . you just so much add to your influence . . . and strengthen the hands of your fellow Democrats." How successful this editor was is not known.[13]

In the first issue of the *Territorial Topic,* published on August 1, 1889, at Purcell, Chickasaw Nation, Indian Territory, editor H. T. Miller told his readers:

> Having no secular or sectarian creeds which we wish to force down the people, our columns are always open to those who desire to discuss issues of this kind.
>
> Being faithful adherents to that noble old party of our forefathers, which is "of the people, for the people and by the people," we reserve the right to advocate its principles whenever and wherever the opportunity offers itself.

The *Topic,* however, appears to have been in the minority, since nearly all small-town weekly papers in the West during the late nineteenth and early twentieth centuries tended to be politically partisan. Still, that did not mean they did not report news of the opposition. Some editors felt a responsibility to report opposing political views. Most papers printed verbatim the State of the Union messages of the U.S. presidents and the messages of the territorial or state governors. But there were those editors whose papers only attacked the opposition. They expected their readers to accept a partisan view of political life as provided by the editors or by regular correspondents. In one instance both newspapers in Manhattan, Kansas—the *Nationalist* and the *Republic*—supported my grandfather, Archie W. Long, a Jeffersonian Democrat, when he ran for and was elected mayor in 1909. The town's two papers continued to support him after the election in what was primarily a Republican community. But when the *Nationalist* was designated the official city paper and given the business of publishing city legal notices, C. A. Kimbell, editor of the *Republic,* began attacking Mayor Long, who soon quietly established a third paper, the *Riley County Democrat.* Long hired Albert H. Hammond to sell advertising and to edit the four-page weekly. Obviously the paper's editorials, many written by my grandfather, supported his views. For example, the April 3, 1911, issue included the following:

> "The next council will have some very important work to attend to the coming year, if it does its full duty. There are three matters of vital importance to the future of Manhattan. A complete city sewer system should be provided for at an early date. The waterworks plant should be extended to give service and fire protection to practically every section

of the city. Plans should be discussed and perfected for paving a street to the college. These matters are outside the usual work of the council, and will involve the expenditure of more than $100,000."

No, mam [*sic*], the foregoing is not an extract from the city administration's platform, although the administration has been following the good suggestions therein made. It is an extract from the *Republic* of March 24, 1908, a year or more before Editor Kimball got mad at A. W. Long and commenced trying to "get even" with him. Tut, tut, brother, throw off your spite and dyspepsia. Brace up! Let us all pull together for a better and bigger Manhattan. The students at the College and people of neighboring towns are laughing at your boyish tactics.

Although Long's name does not appear in any issue of the paper as publisher, he continued to publish the *Riley County Democrat* until he lost an election for state representative in the Kansas legislature. The paper soon ceased publication.

In May 1909, at about the same time that my grandfather established a weekly to support his own political ambitions, C. C. Hendricks, a physician from Pittsburgh, Pennsylvania, moved to Albuquerque, New Mexico, intent on starting a newspaper to establish himself as a champion of the causes of the common people. Hendricks had served in the U.S. Army Medical Corps in the Philippine Islands and claimed to have a law degree. With no previous newspaper experience, Hendricks rented office space, arranged for the Western Union Telegraph Company to run a loop to the office, subscribed to the Hearst leased-news wire service, employed a press telegraph operator and other people, made arrangements with a local printer, and on May 18, 1908, brought out the first issue of the *Albuquerque Sun,* an afternoon paper published six days a week.

From the start he wrote and published editorials attacking prominent men in town in hopes of gaining the favor of the masses. Hendricks struck out blindly at friend and foe alike, in editorials deliberately designed to provoke and infuriate those against whom they were directed. Soon Hendricks began attacking public officials as well, including the regents of the University of New Mexico and then university president William G. Tight, who was quite innocent of any wrongdoing. Tight tired of the attacks and resigned. Hendricks then went after the Albuquerque police department. His editorial published in the *Sun* on June 3, 1909, said in part: "Men and women of this community are held up on the highways of the City almost at the whim of our executives, who hold high court and try the case without jury, without complaint, without even hearsay evidence to base the charge on." And the next day his lead editorial began: "There is not a woman in this town who is safe in leaving her home, either alone or with her husband or brother. She is liable to arrest at the whim of any officer of the law."

One police officer, William Phillips, a man more than six feet tall, decided he would "beat the hell" out of Hendricks for his attacks on the police department. Phillips entered the *Sun* office and apparently went after Hendricks. Moments later Hendricks apparently landed a right cross to Phillips's jaw, knocking him to the floor. Hendricks picked Phillips up from the floor by the seat of the pants, took him to the door, and tossed him out on the sidewalk. Later that day, June 4, 1909, the *Sun* published a story with a headline that read:

COWARDLY ASSAULT ON EDITOR OF SUN BY POLICE OFFICER.

Police Officer William Phillips invaded the editorial offices of the *Sun* this morning and assaulted Editor Hendricks of the *Sun,* threatening to kill him, while Hendricks was sitting at his desk writing editorials. Phillips rushed into the room and waving an editorial of yesterday's issue of the *Sun,* assaulted the editor and an altercation ensued. District Attorney Frank W. Clancy, who has a law office next door, tried to restrain the combatants.

A few days later Phillips resigned from the police department and returned to being a carpenter. Later, however, he filed suit against the *Sun* and Hendricks asking for $25,000 for injuries suffered in the incident and for damage to his reputation. As for the *Sun,* Hendricks soon closed the paper and returned to Pennsylvania, giving up any hope of becoming a U.S. senator from New Mexico championing the cause of the common people.[14]

Trying to identify the financial backers of papers established for political reasons is often difficult. In some instances politicians were even tied to more than one newspaper in a community—as witness the story of New York–born Richard Cunningham McCormick, a small, dapper man with red hair. After being named secretary of the Territory of Arizona in 1863, he left Washington, D.C., and headed west. Passing through New Mexico, he purchased an old Ramage printing press and some type from a New Mexico editor. In the Arizona Territory, McCormick published the first issue of the *Arizona Miner* on March 9, 1864, at Fort Whipple, the temporary capital. In that first issue McCormick told his readers that local rather than national affairs would occupy the paper's chief attention. A few

months later, when the territorial capital was moved to Prescott—
McCormick named the town Prescott in honor of historian William H.
Prescott—the *Miner* also moved there. McCormick was appointed territorial governor in 1866, and he operated the *Miner* until the fall of 1867,
when he sold the paper to John H. Marion. At about the same time, the territorial legislature, meeting in Prescott, voted to move the capital to Tucson, and McCormick purchased an interest in Arizona's oldest newspaper,
the *Weekly Arizonian,* which had been established at Tubac in 1859. Soon
the paper was moved to Tucson, with McCormick purchasing a Washington handpress* for it in the fall of 1868, at about the time he stepped down
from the territorial governor's post and was elected as the Arizona Territory's third delegate to Congress.

Early in 1869 a young Canadian, Pieron W. Dooner, was hired as a
printer by the paper. Within a few months he became editor. The appearance of the paper improved, and its contents became more lively. Under
Dooner the newspaper changed its name, dropping the second *i,* making it
the *Weekly Arizonan.* Dooner figured that since the territory was Arizona
and not Arizonia, the paper's name should be based on the territory's.

Although the *Weekly Arizonan* claimed to be an independent paper,
it was obviously friendly toward McCormick. John Marion, who had
purchased McCormick's *Miner* at Prescott, began attacking him. When
McCormick announced in 1870 that he would seek reelection as territorial
delegate to Congress, Dooner and the *Arizonan* supported McCormick,
but Marion and the *Miner* supported the opposing Democratic candidate.
Then, in late summer or early fall of 1870, Marion visited Tucson and met
Dooner for the first time in person. What happened is still a matter of
conjecture but Dooner soon withdrew his paper's support of McCormick.
On Saturday, September 24, 1870, McCormick visited the office of the
Arizonan and met with Dooner. During the meeting Dooner offered to sell
the newspaper to McCormick for three thousand dollars. According
to one account, McCormick said he would think about it and come back
the next day. McCormick did return the next day, but with several men
who dismantled the Washington handpress and carried it away, piece by
piece. Dooner, who was helpless to stop them, was furious. Within an
hour Dooner started restoring the old press the paper had used before
McCormick purchased the new one. Although it was missing parts,
Dooner managed to get the old press operating and soon printed an edition of the *Arizonan* telling his readers that McCormick and his people

* See Appendix A.

were trying to destroy Arizona's only newspaper so they could carry out
their system of fraud and mendacity. McCormick's Republican friends
replied that Dooner had actually tried to blackmail McCormick by offering
to sell him the paper.

Four days later a one-page flyer was circulated throughout Tucson. It
announced the forthcoming establishment of a new newspaper, to be
called the *Arizona Citizen*. The first issue appeared on October 15, 1870,
with John Wasson as editor. Wasson wrote:

> To all those familiar with the circumstances which induced its publica-
> tion, no apology need be given for the large space occupied with politi-
> cal matters, and they will not expect a change until after the ensuing
> election. In the interim, court proceedings and other official doings in
> Tucson, matters of local interest to the public, the movement of troops,
> etc., will receive due attention in our columns.

Whether McCormick had a business interest in the paper is not known,
but it supported his reelection as Arizona's delegate to Congress, while
Dooner and the *Arizonan* supported McCormick's opponent. The editors, however, did not confine themselves to the issues or to the candidates. They soon chose to attack each other. Dooner labeled Wasson the
territorial governor's lackey, as well as

> . . . a servile, self-asserting, and stupid upstart. . . . As the gaily painted
> moth, clothed from the slime and filth of earth, which flits around the
> lighted candle and finally expires in the flame, so this worthless upstart,
> but yesterday dragged from the gutters of political and social corrup-
> tion, and clothed, for an hour, from the spoils of official prostitution,
> awaits his doom in the flame of honest, popular indignation which will
> soon accomplish the extirpation of the infamous rabble of which he is an
> acknowledged member. This salable tool is the mouthpiece selected by
> McCormick through which to fling calumny and vituperation at honest,
> industrious and honorable men – men possessing independence of
> character, and ambition of a standard too exalted to value the flattery of a
> sycophant or the acquiescent smiles of a cynic.

Wasson's attacks on Dooner were not as violent, but at one point he referred to "his imbecility in the past, his brash exhibition of ingratitude and
turpitude," and asked, "Whenever was this shameless editor honest?" He
described Dooner as "a poor worm, having shown himself utterly untrust-

worthy." As Election Day neared, Wasson issued a mock apology: "The galoot Dooner will please pardon us for omitting extended mention of him as our space is too precious to waste upon such an obscure and despised being. He is publicly gangrened." McCormick won reelection, and within a few months thereafter the *Arizonan* ceased publication.[15]

Anyone flipping through the yellowing pages of old western newspapers or turning the crank on a reader displaying microfilmed copies of the papers cannot help but smile when running across political items such as the following, which appears on the front page of the *Stockton* (California) *Journal* for January 11, 1851:

Singular Proceedings: Joe Barker, the Mayor of Pittsburg [California] who was elected while in jail, on a conviction of street preaching and street riots, is giving the goodly people of the Iron city a great deal of trouble. He is determined to show them that Joe Barker is Mayor, and that his enemies shall taste the sweets of the dungeon he so long enjoyed. He has arrested the Sheriff for misdemeanor, the Catholic Bishop as a nuisance, and the City Council for a conspiracy, and threatens to imprison any judge who on *habeas corpus* discharges any of his prisoners. After he had committed the city council to jail, he closed his speech with the following emphatic remarks: "We want (said he) one reform, and then we will be able to get along. Hang all the Judges, drive out half the lawyers, and put down the grog-shops."

CHAPTER FOUR

EXPRESSING OPINION

*Don't imagine for one moment that this paper
is published expressly to please you.*
—William C. Brann

THERE WAS NO clear separation between news and opinion in the early newspapers of the American West. Printers who edited papers thought nothing of including their personal opinions in factual news stories—but then, this had been the practice of editors in the East since colonial times. And early American newspapers had copied the literary style of those in England and Europe.

In the West one of the earliest examples of mixing news and opinion in a newspaper story appeared in the May 31, 1809, issue of Joseph Charless's *Missouri Gazette,* published at St. Louis. He wrote:

A few days ago, a barn at the north end of this town, the property of Mr. P. Chouteau, was burned by a vagabond party of Indians who infest this town and neighborhood. Last Monday appeared to be a day of jubilee among them, parading the streets with bottles of whiskey, which are openly sold to them by every retailer in defiance of the laws; during these orgeries [*sic*] an Indian by the name of Squinoai, attacked an Ottoway woman in the most populous part of town, and at mid-day, put her to death by thrusting an arrow into her neck and down her body; much mischief is apprehended if some of our whiskey merchants are not made examples of.

Charless saw nothing wrong in expressing his opinions when reporting on current events: It was his newspaper, and he could print what he wanted. In a two-column report entitled "A Glance at Europe," which appeared on the front page of his paper, Charless, a native of Ireland, expressed his grudge against England and predicted that it would soon fall to

Napoleon. Charless often printed long and cumbersome reports that read like essays under the heading "For the Missouri Gazette" over such pseudonyms as "Cato," "A Bystander," "Cicero," and "An Actual Settler." These reports, usually on political matters, sometimes covered a page or two and occasionally ran for several issues.

Charless was firmly opposed to dueling. On January 2, 1811, he wrote: "Should the following mode of treatment be practised in all cases of the Duelling mania, there is no doubt but it would entirely remove the disorder. 'A good beginning—James Henry who lately killed Malaki P. Varaian in a duel at Sackets Harbor, has been convicted of manslaughter and sentenced to ten years imprisonment.' " Five months later, in his May 30, 1811, issue, Charless again attacked the practice of dueling, but withheld the specific details of a recent duel, explaining:

> As many of our readers might expect a relation of 'an affair of honor!' which took place last week, we presume they will applaud our motive when we inform them that it is no want of respect to our patrons which induces us to withhold such information. A barbarous custom hooted at by civilized society, falling daily into merited contempt, should (we humbly conceive) never be noticed by the journalists but with the language of Cervantes, the inimitable author of Don Quixotte.

As late as 1823, however, the *Missouri Gazette* was still reporting on duels. On January 20 of that year, Charless noted: "Two more persons have been killed in duels near St. Louis. Their names are Messrs. Waddle and Crow. It must be a vicious state of society in which the pistol is the umpire of every controversy."

Whether Charless's published views had any effect on ending the practice of dueling is not known, but the practice of mixing opinion and fact had a profound impact in Texas, when the *Telegraph and Texas Register,* published at San Felipe, reported on the fall of the Alamo in March 1836. Editors Gail and Tom Borden provided on March 17 the first sketchy information on the Mexican attack that had killed 187 Texans eleven days earlier. Then, a week later, the paper carried another story containing the names of the known dead, including Jim Bowie, William Barret Travis, and James B. Bonham. In their second story the editors set facts aside, injecting comments intended to arouse and enrage the readers and thereby keep their loyalties alive. The March 24, 1836, story read in part:

MORE PARTICULARS RESPECTING
THE FALL OF THE ALAMO

That event, so lamentable, and yet so glorious to Texas, is of such deep interest and excites so much our feelings that we shall never cease to celebrate it, and regret that we are not acquainted with the names of all those who fell at that Fort, that we might publish them, and thus consecrate to future ages the memory of our heroes who perished at the Thermophlae [sic] of Texas. . . .

At day break of the 6th inst. the enemy surrounded the fort with their infantry, with the cavalry forming a circle outside to prevent escape on the part of the garrison. The number consisted of at least 4000 against 140! General Santa Ana commanded in person, assisted by four generals and a formidable train of artillery. Our men had been previously much fatigued and harassed by [aggravating] and incessant toils, having experienced for some days past a heavy bombardment and several real and feigned attacks. But, American valor and American love of liberty displayed themselves to the last; they were never more conspicuous; twice did the enemy apply to the walls their scaling ladders and twice did they receive a check; for our men were determined to verify the words of the immortal Travis, "to make the victory worse to the enemy than a defeat." A pause ensued after the second attack, which was renewed on the third time, owing to the exertions of Santa Ana and his officers; they poured in over the walls, "like sheep." The struggle, however, did not even there cease—unable from the crowd and for want of time to load their guns and rifles our men made use of the butt-ends of the latter and continued to fight and to resist, until life ebbed out through their numberless wounds and the enemy had conquered the fort but not its brave, its matchless defenders; they perished but they yielded not: only one remained to ask for quarter which was denied by the unrelenting enemy—total extermination succeeded, and the darkness of death occupied the memorable Alamo, but recently so teeming with gallant spirits and filled with deeds of never-failing remembrance. We envy not the feelings of the victors, for they must have been bitter and galling; not proud ones. Who would not be rather one of the Alamo heroes, than of the living of its merciless victors! Spirits of the mighty, though fallen! honours and rest are with ye: the spark of immortality which animated your forms, shall brighten into a flame, and Texas, the whole world, shall hail ye like demi-gods of old, as founders of new actions, and as patterns for imitation![1]

The *Telegraph and Texas Register*'s story was picked up by other papers, and a legend was born. It made those who died at the Alamo heroes, and gave the battle immortality almost overnight.

The practice of editors expressing their opinions in news stories continued west of the Mississippi, as more newspapers were established in Texas, Missouri, and California. After giving a portion of the facts, an editor for no apparent reason would insert a stock phrase such as, "This writer has constantly held the opinion that . . . ," or "Right here it may be worth noting that . . . ," at which point he would state his personal views. Early western editors, like those in the East, sold their newspapers by subscription to people who could pay in advance the six to ten dollars a year required. Readers were generally educated people with the means to pay. Readers unable to pay often were given old copies of newspapers or learned secondhand what had been published. But in September 1833, Benjamin Henry Day established the daily New York *Sun,* sold copies on the streets for a penny each, and attracted readers who could not afford to subscribe to other papers. Day became successful because of the growing population of New York and the large number of residents who could afford a penny newspaper. While Day's penny paper concept was not then adopted in the West, he found that his readers were more interested in factual news than in opinion, and he began to eliminate opinion from news stories and stress impartiality.

James Gordon Bennett adopted this policy when he founded the penny New York *Herald* in 1835, as did Horace Greeley, who established the daily New York *Tribune,* a two-cent paper, in 1841. Greeley gradually introduced cultural reporting, and by the late 1840s was also presenting stimulating ideas in essay form. These "editorials," as they became known, were kept separate from news stories and identified as opinion. This practice, like objective news reporting, would eventually spread to other newspapers, including those in the West.

Initially a professed Whig (the party opposed to popular rule), Greeley worked through his paper to benefit common people. With no formal education, he learned by experience. He allowed a few other journalists to express their opinions in editorials, but he did not endorse all of them. Greeley seemed to sense that the United States was experimenting with democracy, and that it must continue doing so if democracy was to be kept dynamic. His readers seemed to sense this, as well as Greeley's sincerity and consciousness of responsibility to them.

Initially the changing journalistic practices in the East were limited to daily papers in the growing cities, especially New York. In the West, how-

Horace Greeley was a personal journalist. His editorials in the weekly New York *Tribune,* which was circulated in the West, influenced many western editors who sought to emulate Greeley's style in the columns of their papers. *(Courtesy Kansas State Historical Society)*

ever, there were no dailies and no cities until San Francisco became a major trading center, following the California gold rush. Outside San Francisco western papers were still small weeklies published by printers who also served as editors and operated their papers in a leisurely manner and followed the old practice of mixing fact and opinion in their stories. This began to change by the middle 1850s, especially in the newly opened territories of Kansas and Nebraska and a bit later in the New Mexico and Nevada territories, because Horace Greeley began publishing a weekly *Tribune* primarily for readers outside New York, especially those in the West. A one-year subscription cost two dollars, but Greeley gave free subscriptions to weekly newspaper editors anywhere if they gave him free subscriptions to their weeklies.

Through his weekly *Tribune,* which had a circulation of 112,000 in 1854 and many times that number of readers, Greeley's influence not only on readers but on journalism in the West was enormous. Historian James Ford Rhodes observed:

These readers were of the thorough kind, reading all the news, all the printed speeches and addresses, and all the editorials and pondering as they read. The questions were discussed in their family circles and with their neighbors, and, as differences arose, the *Tribune* always at hand, was consulted and re-read. There being few popular magazines during this decade [the 1850s], the weekly newspaper, in some degree, took their place; and through this medium, Greeley and his able coadjutors spoke to the people of New York and the West, where New England ideas predominated, with a power never before . . . known in this country.[2]

Western editors saw how Greeley's editorials, presented separately from objective news stories, reflected a sense of responsibility toward his readers. Many papers began to borrow Greeley's techniques, including the *Texas State Gazette,* a weekly printed in Austin. It prepared the way for Southern secession by molding opinion through editorial discussions and the publication of timely articles and essays by prominent Southerners. When war came the *Gazette,* April 20, 1861, published the following editorial:

DECLARATION OF WAR

By the act of the Northern Black Republican President, the two governments are precipitated into a war. The peaceful and conservative course of the Confederate Government is before the world, and will command its confidence and respect. The deliberation and coolness which have marked the conduct of President Davis and his able advisers, ought to have met with a better result. The existence of a foreign military armament on our soil without our consent was itself an act of war, and but for the common desire to avoid shedding the blood of a kindred race, President Davis would have long ago opened that fire upon Fort Sumter. But he was willing to negociate [*sic*] with Lincoln's government, and to settle all matters peacefully. The commissioners sent on to Washington have, after a long and unnecessary delay on the part of Lincoln's government, been told that they cannot be officially received; and now the only course left us is to eject the foreign invader off our soil by force. The telegraph brings the news that our batteries have been opened upon Fort Sumter, and the next news will be its capture. But there will be perhaps, sad loss of life to the occupants. It was known to Lincoln that we would capture this fort at any time, and the blood which flows is upon his own hands.

At the start of the Civil War, the only Unionist newspaper in Texas was the *Alamo Express* at San Antonio, edited by James P. Newcomb, but his opinions were silenced in May 1861, when the paper was destroyed by the extremist Knights of the Golden Circle and Confederate Rangers.[3]

Because of Horace Greeley's influence, the use of editorials became commonplace in western newspapers during and after the Civil War. It was not until the early 1880s, however, that another form of expressing opinion developed. Eugene Field, managing editor of the Denver *Tribune* from 1881 to 1883 (but better known later for his sentimental children's verse), pioneered the column form of editorial writing, which depended for effect on short barbed paragraphs, as opposed to the older, longer editorial form, which attempted to approach a subject from all angles. This shorter form, adopted by many western papers, left room on the editorial page for more writers.

The growth of western towns following the Civil War enabled many weeklies to become daily newspapers, and towns often had two or more papers competing for readers. It was then that editors of dailies began emulating the practices of successful eastern papers by separating opinion from news. Perhaps a few western editors were influenced by James Parton's essay, which appeared in the spring 1866 issue of *North American Review*. Parton wrote:

> The prestige of the editorial is gone. . . . There are journalists who think the time is at hand for the abolition of editorials, and the concentration of the whole force of journalism upon presenting to the public the history and picture of the day. The time for this has not come, and may never come, but our journalists already know that editorials neither make nor mar a daily paper, that they do not much influence the public mind, nor change many votes. . . . The news is the point of rivalry; it is that for which nineteen-twentieths of the people buy newspapers; it is that which constitutes the power and value of the daily press; it is that which determines the rank of every newspaper in every free country.[4]

While many western dailies separated opinion from news in their columns and others ignored editorials altogether and concentrated on news, a majority of the weeklies in the West continued to mix news and opinion. Both weeklies and dailies, however, went on publishing the opinions of their readers in the form of letters, sometimes on page 1. One interesting letter to an editor was published by the Larned, Kansas, *Weekly Chronoscope*, on November 25, 1887:

To the Editor of the Chronoscope.

I wish to say a few words to our grocery merchants through your

paper. It is rather a delicate subject to handle. It has been the practice of
the grocers to set their vegetables outside on the walk, and all know we
have an innumerable number of dogs, and some of them pretty tall dogs,
too, and it looks as if they drink from some mineral spring. What we
housekeepers want is for the grocers to place their vegetables on boxes
and barrels above the high water mark. Your wire screens on the baskets
are not water tight. When a housekeeper goes shopping for turnips,
beets, cabbage and celery they don't want peas. . . .

Housekeeper

Some editors of dailies in the larger western cities believed that news
shaped public opinion more than editorials did, and that readers bought
their papers more for news than for the opinions expressed in editorials.
Successful editors soon realized that if their editorial opinions were to be
accepted, their papers first had to report on the issues. This "agenda setting," as it is called today, paved the way for papers to express opinions on
issues they reported in the news. Editors who sought to form public opinion only through editorials found that they were not successful unless their
topics reflected public concerns created by straight news reporting.

A review of a cross-section of the larger newspapers published in the
West during the late 1880s suggests that their editorials were more focused
and more carefully written than in the years before. It also suggests that
several forms or types of editorials were emerging.[5] Whether editors established labels for the various types is not known, but there were distinctive
differences. One type was simply *informational,* where the writer restated
the facts of a recent news story and explained its importance. Another type
could be described as *interpretive,* presenting with brevity the facts of a
particular story much like the informational form, but then explaining why
it was important, its hidden significance, and what it meant to readers. Still
another was *argumentative.* This latter type was nothing new. In fact it had
dominated the expression-of-opinion form used by many editors much
earlier. Dan Anthony, who published and edited the Leavenworth,
Kansas, *Evening Bulletin,* wrote such an editorial, "Sunday Laws," in the
May 23, 1865, issue:

This morning, C. R. Morehead & Co. were arrested and brought before
the recorder for a violation of the Sunday laws, in permitting [wagon]
trains to be loaded from their warehouse on Sunday. The goods did not
belong to them, but were left in storage by a Mexican trader. The mayor
was applied to, and gave *written* permission to the Mexicans to load the

teams, and also *"ordered the policemen not to interfere, or to arrest the parties."* The city attorney *refused* to prosecute the case, and moved that a nolle pros. [motion to discontinue] be returned, which was granted by the court.

We do not find fault with this course, only in this: it is making fish of one and flesh of another. The German is hauled up for practising an innocent game on Sunday, roundly fined, and threatened with an iron jacket, if he dare drink his glass of lager or pitch a game of quoits on Sunday.

We were hauled up before his Honor, charged with carrying concealed weapons. We proved that we had a permit from the acting mayor, and that it was custom, usage, and in accordance with the charter. A fine of ten dollars was imposed. The city attorney did not move a nolle pros. in our case.

O ye gods, and the good people of Leavenworth! look out for these men *"who strain at a gnat and swallow a camel."*

Another type of editorial saw the writer *call for action* by first explaining a situation and then calling on readers for some specific action to solve it. If immediate action was not needed, very skilled writers might use the *persuasive* editorial to convince readers by suggestion, inference, and thoughtful psychology on how to resolve a potential problem. Sometimes such editorials were direct and to the point, as the following example from the *Chase County Leader,* at Cottonwood Falls, Kansas, shows:

The damage to the contents of farmers' wagons by loose stock, the past week, is a burning shame and disgrace. It is enough to drive every bit of trade from the town. A man cannot leave his wagon to go into a store to trade without having the entire contents pulled out and trampled under foot by town horses and cattle. We saw a woman drive into town yesterday, with a quantity of hay in her wagon to feed her team during her stay, and before she got half way down Broadway there were fifteen head of horses and cows following and trying to eat the hay. Business men comprise a majority of the city council and a decent consideration of the welfare of their patrons should be sufficient inducement for them to stop the nuisance.[6]

Still another type of editorial, one that had been around from the earliest days of journalism in the West, could be labeled *entertaining*. This form gave editors the opportunity to have some fun and usually capitalized on satire, humor, and comedy in the news to entertain their readers. One such satirical editorial appeared in the *Olwyhee Avalanche,* published at Ruby City, Idaho Territory. On December 30, 1865, the paper denounced hurdy-gurdy houses, gambling, and excessive drinking of bad whiskey in these words:

In review of the past year, think whether you have fought ye "tiger" nobly; contributed freely to the support of frail femininity, done your share towards ridding this community of bad whiskey and paid your reckoning therefore; and done the fair thing by the hurdies. If you have, by all means continue to do so. It is a plain proposition that the "tiger" must be fought. He's a beast containing little of the milk of human kindness, and aside he's seldom insulted by being tackled. Those who have fought him during the past year are better schooled to worry about him. . . . It is the duty of such to fight him vigorously. Suppose you have come off second best—it was a mere scratch that it so turned out. Go after him the coming year with renewed vigor. Pit into him during the winter season when he's lean. While doing so, never think of the many short meals you've eaten or cold sleeps in consequence; nor of the wife and children who need your dust; but fight him determinedly, for if you do not he'll grow bold and perhaps thirst for blood. . . .

Benedicts and bachelors who have paid your money to bedeck and sustain puts, go in and never mind your mammas, wives or sweethearts. Your mammas and wives probably won't hear of it, physicians are mum, and your sweethearts, if they do know, will overlook these natural acts and defend you—especially if you've got plenty of money. If you've tried to exhaust the community of bad whiskey—of all men you are the best calculated to continue the operation. If saloon men *will* keep bad liquor, teach them that it shall grow no worse on their shelves. Admitting that you experience headaches, you must not forget the free beds given you and the official attentions received. . . .

The gay and festive cusses who have generously donated a fair living to fiddlers and hurdies, need not our words of cheer to spend the coming year's earnings as they did the one just gone. They need not fear of having to run these *she*-bangs alone—the coming summer will amply replace the veterans on the retired list.

While the writing of newspaper editorials by the 1860s had generally improved over those of the late 1840s, many were still wordy and stilted because not all printers were good writers or editors. By the late 1860s, however, many printers who had some success at publishing newspapers had sold their papers to people with formal educations and with good writing skills.

Not all editors wrote or even attempted to write editorials. When Anne H. Martin became editor of the *Carson News,* a Democratic afternoon paper in Nevada, she was untrained in journalism and struggled merely to edit the news. She did not write editorials. But a man named Daily, a tall, courtly gentleman who was editor of the rival *Nevada Tribune,* a Republican paper, frequently walked down the street from his office to the *Carson News,* entered the office, bowed low to Anne Martin, walked quietly to her desk, and wrote a vituperative editorial in answer to the abusive attack he had written for his own paper that morning.[7]

A similar situation was recalled by William A. Keleher, who took a job as a reporter on the *Albuquerque Journal* in 1908. He remembered that when the company providing water to the city supposedly failed to follow the rules of its franchise, William S. Burke, editor of the *Journal,* wrote editorials defending the company's position. Another Albuquerque paper, the *Daily Citizen,* published several editorials critical of the water company, and one calling attention to Burke's physical deformity. The editorial accused the editor of the *Journal* of becoming crippled in mind and body because of constant stooping to do dirty work for his political masters. Burke answered the charge in the *Journal,* noting that he had become deformed as the result of wounds sustained in a battle during the Civil War "in defense of his country," while the editor of the *Daily Citizen* had hidden out in the backwoods of Missouri, avoiding military service.

Keleher thought the *Citizen*'s editorial unfair and approached Burke, who replied: "Will, I don't want you to be concerned, and I hope you won't be. I must tell you in confidence that by arrangement with the publishers of the *Citizen,* I am writing the editorials for that paper, and at the same time writing the *Journal* editorials. I wrote the editorial published in the *Citizen* yesterday, directing attention to my physical deformity. It was designed to divert the minds of the people from thinking too much concerning the complaints about the water supply and franchise rights. We wanted the people to think about me and my personal physical affliction, and in this I think we have succeeded."[8]

The dusty old issues of nineteenth-century western papers contain many fine examples of editorials that propose solutions to local problems. Following a destructive fire that swept through many wooden buildings in Virginia City, Montana, the editor of the *Montana Post* undertook an editorial crusade to prevent such fires in the future. On October 29, 1864, he wrote:

FIRE! FIRE!

It appears to us that a night watch should be instituted. One good, sober, vigilant man could be found to patrol from sun to sun, over all the town, and to give the alarm of fire. As we like to see such matters arranged in a business like manner, we have thought over a plan, which should prove very simple; more so than a patrol. Let a watch box be built high on Cemetery Hill, furnished with a window divided into three compartments facing the town. Let one compartment be painted blue, another red and one left plain, representing Cover, Main and Idaho street districts. A light placed east, west or in the middle of the proper compartment, would at once specify the locality of the fire, and five shots in quick succession followed by blasts from a horn, or the roll of a drum, would be a certain and easy alarm.

A few weeks later, on November 12, 1864, the *Montana Post* noted:

Let someone look to the *Water*. Without it, buckets are as useful as thimbles to thirsty men. . . . A few reservoirs could be made along the branch so that water could be had at once. . . . Most important additions to the tools of a fire company without an engine, are two or three troughs, holding about a barrel of water each. Such a trough laid on the ground and worked by a stout fellow throwing up water with a large wooden shovel, can do more than 12 bucket men. . . . A good man can throw water with it on top of almost any house in town, except the two-story buildings, and the side walls of these can be kept safe by water thrown from the ground where no man can stand the heat and smoke on a ladder.

Any subject on readers' minds was fair game for editors. In the first issue of the *Oklahoma Capital,* published at Guthrie, Oklahoma Territory, on August 21, 1889, Frank H. Greer wrote:

THE SAME OLD SNAKE

The council of Guthrie passed another lottery charter Wednesday night. It is the same old snake. It has simply sluffed off and taken on a new skin. The other charter was incubated in the minds of Guthrie men, who thought they saw millions ahead, if they could get the city to go into the business for them. The charter was passed by a vote of six. These six as some of them openly acknowledged, had been properly "approached" and each "donated" from $10,000 to $15,000 of the lottery stock. Some of this stock was assessable and some nonassessable according to the case in hand. One [member] of the council was the chief "approachers" [*sic*] being familiar with the boodle or non-boodle temperament of his brethren and parcelled out the stock according to the needs. The same councilmen voted for the lottery charter Wednesday night. We are informed by one who certainly had ought to know that a councilman was offered, by the Chicago promoter of this scheme, $1,000 in cash and $10,000 of non-assessable stock for his vote and influence for this charter. Is it not reasonable to suppose the councilmen who voted for the charter this time lost their keen eye for business, so well cultivated when the other tempter gobbled them? The Capital, the people, and other members of the council and Mayor Dyer rose up and strangled that first lottery charter in its incipiency. So they will this one. Col. Dyer will no doubt again stand with the people, who do not propose that their servants shall launch Guthrie proper into the lottery business. We the people have full confidence that Mayor Dyer will sit down on that charter so hard it will never rise again, so far as the city is concerned. . . .

It was not uncommon for editors to express their opinions concerning stories appearing in other newspapers. One such example was published on October 23, 1887, in the *Sunday Growler,* a short-lived newspaper at Wichita, Kansas:

GROWLS AND GLANCES:

The Leavenworth Times is responsible for the story that a farmer of that county recently brought a load of smoked meat to town and sold it for money enough to take his family to the circus. After the circus he returned to the merchant and bought some of the same meat on credit for use in the family. There are just that kind of people in this world, and you will find them in almost every community.

Editors of most American Indian newspapers were just as vocal in expressing opinion as were the editors of other papers. In retrospect, the editors of some of the Indian papers seem to have been far more civilized in their opinions than those expressed in papers published by whites during the nineteenth century. When the National Council of the Creek Nation in May 1876 established the weekly *Indian Journal* at Muskogee, in what is now eastern Oklahoma, Myron P. Roberts, a New Yorker and former reporter on the Chicago *Inter-Ocean,* was hired as publisher, and William P.

Ross, a Cherokee, who had earlier served as editor of the *Cherokee Advocate,* was editor. The following year the paper was moved about forty-five miles northeast to the town of Eufaula. The *Indian Journal,* first under Ross's leadership and later under other editors', gave the Creek Nation a public voice. For example, the October 26, 1876, issue of the *Indian Journal* contained the following editorial:

> Has not the government of the United States guaranteed to us our country, as we are now in possession of it, as long as grass grows and water runs? Then if so, let your prosperous and enlightened government act in good faith and stand by her treaties with us, which she should hold sacred.
>
> We have been driven from our homes in Alabama, and here have we found a resting place. Here would we remain and rear our children into a better civilization than we have yet known. If we are forced hence, nothing remains for us but the desert plains. I, therefore . . . beg and pray that honest men that have the interest of the Indian at heart, may protest against any and all measures which would tend to injure that interest.

Beginning in July 1876 the *Indian Journal* carried many reports on General George Armstrong Custer's defeat in the battle at the Little Big Horn. Ross expressed "wrath, humiliation and grief" at what had happened and took the position that "the Sioux must be beaten and brought back to their reservation." Those whites who were calling for extermination of the Sioux, Ross added, should "recall the Chivington massacre, the slaying of man, woman and child in Black Kettle's village, and a hundred other instances in the last 10 years" that showed the cruelty of the white man at least equal to that of the Indian.[9]

Between 1879 and 1880, on three different occasions, Ross wrote editorials calling for handgun control. And in 1881, he wrote about a train robbery in the neighboring state of Missouri and suggested that Indians in the territory "want[ed] more light and civilization and less barbarism on their border."[10]

Indian newspapers, however, were few in number when compared to those operated by whites. There were no Indian papers in the Arizona Territory, where the early editors were critical of what they considered the weak policies of military authorities in dealing with the Indians. In 1871 the *Prescott Miner* published a list of four hundred people murdered by the Apaches between March 1864 and the fall of 1871. The story noted that of the four hundred at least two were known to have been burned alive. Fifty-three others had been wounded and crippled, and five had been carried into captivity. When Geronimo reached the height of his power in 1885, editors pressed the fight against the Indians. The *Phoenix Herald* reported:

> There is only one course to pursue with these San Carlos Apaches, and that is to transport the entire gang. Till that is done, the Southwestern part of the Territory will never be safe. As to where they should be taken, there is not much hesitation on the part of Arizonians in saying that it should be to a graveyard, but in deference to the "eastern notion" we will be satisfied with the Dry Tortugas or some island on the Pacific coast or Boston.[11]

By the late nineteenth century, the practice of separating opinion and news was becoming commonplace in the larger eastern newspapers, but in the West only a few large newspapers were doing it. Most western editors of weekly papers were not greatly influenced by the eastern practice. They continued to tailor their practices to meet the needs of their communities, including the booming of their towns. Their survival came first.

CHAPTER FIVE

TOWN BOOMING

Hell is full of newspapermen who killed themselves blowing for some little one horse town.... We have decided that it is a sin to lie anyway, and in the future we'll be found telling the truth.
—*Watonga* (Oklahoma) *Republican*, December 20, 1893

IT WAS ONLY NATURAL that some new towns in the West became trading and transportation centers. The earliest towns were established along major rivers and the coasts of Texas, California, Washington, and Oregon; others developed along trails that had been followed by explorers, traders, and emigrants. Towns sprang up like weeds near where gold or silver had been discovered, and still others appeared on the desolate plains and prairies, created by promoters seeking to turn a profit. Some of these towns existed only on paper and never attracted a single live resident. The arrival of railroads gave birth to settlements along their tracks to capitalize on the transportation provided by the iron horse. While many early western towns have grown into modern cities, far more have become ghosts: They were born, flourished, and died. They were all born of expectation. The reasons for their deaths varied, but most of those that survived had newspapers with civic-minded printers-turned-editors who were willing to cast their lot with the towns and promote, or boom, the places.

Booming meant that an editor had to proclaim his town's bright future by praising and giving encouragement to residents, businesses, churches, and schools. The editor had to promote reform and civic development to help alleviate his readers' hardships and give them hope. To attract new settlers an editor had to rely on exaggeration. Many did so without hesitation, since the success of their newspapers depended on the growth of their towns. Editors boomed their towns while also dispensing factual news and information, and selling advertising to local merchants as they and their towns fought to survive. To succeed, an editor had to be optimistic and believe that his town was destined to become an important and influential place in the West.

Perhaps the first newspaper in the West to shout up its town was the *Oregon Spectator,* also the first newspaper along the Pacific Coast. The semimonthly was established at Oregon City in 1846 by an association of local promoters who hired its successive editors and printers. To the east, new communities developed in the Nebraska, Kansas, and Dakota Territories as settlers arrived in search of cheap land to buy or homesteads to claim. It was a rare town that did not have at least one weekly newspaper loudly proclaiming its existence.

Congress had made it easy to establish towns on government land in the West. The Federal Townsites Act of 1844 provided 320 acres for a townsite once the first townspeople occupied it, and the land was not subject to the preemption law of 1841, which limited the amount of surveyed government land an individual citizen could buy to 160 acres. Anyone could also start a town by organizing a company that bought the 320 acres for $1.25 an acre, or $400. The town was then cut into lots, and shares were sold, usually on the basis of ten lots per share. The individual company members could preempt adjacent quarter sections and hold them until the town grew and the nearby land was more valuable.

Congress gave states and territories the right to regulate the disposal of townsite lots and the proceeds of the sale. When the territories of Kansas and Nebraska were established in 1854, their legislatures established special acts of incorporation, which gave promoters sound title to a townsite on payment of a small fee. During the first session of the Nebraska territorial legislature, seventeen towns were incorporated, and nearly twenty during the first session of the Kansas territorial legislature. The town promoters proclaimed bright futures for each, since they sought to make money by selling lots.

To attract settlers new towns also needed hotels where potential residents could stay while looking over the area. Some town companies could afford to build a hotel and sell it to a proprietor. Poor town companies tried to attract someone with money to build one, or, as in the case of Brownsville in the Nebraska Territory, the company set up a lottery to raise construction money. With the help of the editor of the local paper, the *Brownsville Advertiser,* they publicized the lottery, which was selling tickets at $5. As the paper reported on September 3, 1857, there were 1,927 prizes, valued at $11,000. They ranged from 147 acres of land adjoining the town, valued at $2,500, several city lots valued at $800, to twenty-five cents in cash.

When Sol Miller came to Kansas from Ohio and established the weekly *Kansas Chief* in the Missouri River town of White Cloud, he boomed his town, but he did not think much of the glib-tongued town promoters. In the first issue of his paper, on June 4, 1857, he printed the following:

> Strangers have no idea how thickly settled Kansas already is. The towns are spread over her surface as thickly as fleas on a dog's back. We said towns—we meant to say cities—for we have nothing but cities out here—and the proprietors are bound to let people know it, too; for they stick city to the name of every town. We venture to say, there is scarcely a store or tavern in the union, in which there is not posted in a conspicuous place, town plats of some large city in Kansas or Nebraska, a majority of which do not contain a single house! Travelers out here are not aware, unless they are told, that they are passing through cities every few miles of their journey—such as Tadpole City, Prairie City, Opossum City, et cetera. Each one, of course, is bound to make the most important place in the West!

Though White Cloud, with a few hundred residents, was *not* called a city, many other towns of that size in Kansas and Nebraska were. Promoters tacked the word "city" onto just about every new town laid out. It was a popular idea that great *cities* would emerge in the West, and if promoters were to sell lots to potential settlers, their lots had to be located in cities. New York newspaperman Horace Greeley, who visited the Kansas Territory in 1859, wrote in his New York *Tribune:* "It takes three log houses to make a city in Kansas, but they begin calling it a city so soon as they have staked out the lots."[1]

Promoters may have been surprised to discover later that towns without the word "city" attached to their names actually *became* cities. Omaha, Nebraska, was one such settlement. Joseph E. Johnson and J. W. Pattison started the first newspaper there soon after the Nebraska Territory was opened to settlement, although before they could set up shop on the townsite, they had to pay the Omaha Indians ten dollars for their claim, since the Indians still occupied the land. They also had to have their paper, the *Omaha Arrow,* printed across the Missouri River at Council Bluffs, Iowa, until a cabin could be built to house the newspaper office and press. In the first issue of the *Arrow,* July 28, 1854, Johnson wrote:

> Well, strangers, friends, patrons, and the good people generally, wherever in the wide world your lot may be cast, and in whatever clime this Arrow may reach you, here we are upon Nebraska soil, seated upon the stump of an ancient oak, which serves for an editorial chair, and the top

of our badly abused beaver for a table, we propose editing a leader for the Omaha Arrow. . . . There sticks our axe in the trunk of an old oak from which we purpose making a log for our cabin and claim.

While the *Arrow* boomed the new Nebraska Territory, the paper did not last. In December 1854, five months after it began, Johnson and Pattison published the paper's last issue.

The *Arrow* was just one of many early papers in the Nebraska and Kansas Territories that extolled their areas. Some were established by town companies eager to promote their communities, and it was not uncommon for town promoters to locate a printer and provide him financial backing to establish a newspaper in their town. Meriwether Lewis had done this at St. Louis, when he asked Joseph Charless to start a paper. However, not all early papers were begun in this fashion. Joseph E. Johnson, who operated the *Omaha Arrow* for five months, moved farther west and established a newspaper called the *Huntsman's Echo* at what became known as Wood River Center in south central Nebraska, about 150 miles west of Omaha. There were no settlers in the area, but Johnson's Ranche, as he called his new combination home and trading post, was located on the Oregon Trail. Johnson boomed the region by circulating copies of his paper among emigrants and wagon freighters traveling the trail. He attracted many settlers to south-central Nebraska Territory with glowing descriptions of the area, but it did not make his newspaper a financial success. He supported his newspaper with profits from operating a bakery, a combination café and saloon, a stock-trading business, and a blacksmith shop where he repaired wagons belonging to travelers.

Johnson operated his trading post and published the *Huntsman's Echo* until the summer of 1861. He then decided to abandon the commercial potential of his paper and businesses, perhaps because he was a Mormon with two wives and numerous children: Prejudice against Mormons and especially against polygamy had intensified. In the last issue of the *Huntsman's Echo,* published on July 4, 1861, Johnson wrote: "Friends and patrons—adieu. We have secessed, and tomorrow shall start westward and probably become a citizen of Utah, and perhaps—soon our Echo may be Re-Echoed from the tops of the mountains. . . . We go from turmoil, strife and bloodshed to seek quiet in the happy, peaceful vales of Utah." Johnson moved to Utah and soon bought some land seventy-five miles south of Salt Lake City, where he established a home he called Spring Lake Villa. There for a while he published a paper called the *Farmer's Oracle.* But in 1868 the cold winters forced him to move to St. George in southern Utah. There he

This is a portion of the front page of one of the surviving copies of the *Huntsman's Echo* (1860), established by Joseph E. Johnson at Wood River Center in south-central Nebraska Territory. *(Author's collection)*

published the *Dixie Times,* and later the *Rio Virgen Times* and the *Utah Pomologist and Gardener.* Later Johnson moved to Arizona, where on December 17, 1882, he died. He was typical of the early itinerant newspapermen of the Old West.[2]

ALTHOUGH THE PANIC of 1857 and the Civil War slowed the establishment of new towns in the West, especially in the Nebraska and Kansas Territories, town promoters resumed their work with new vigor during the late 1860s. When the nation celebrated its centennial in 1876, the event heightened awareness of communities everywhere and gave people, especially those in the West, a new pride in their towns and what they had to offer. Yellowed copies of old newspapers reflect this in their columns. Even in well-established towns, papers continued to boom their communities. W. D. and C. F. Jenkins, owners of the weekly *Kirwin Chief,* published at Kirwin in central Kansas, printed the following front-page story in the February 26, 1876, issue of their paper:

COME TO KANSAS

There are more than usual indications of a heavy flow of immigrants next spring to this country. Hard times in the east and poor crops, have made the people uneasy, and their eyes are turned again to the fertile and productive west. Kansas offers an inviting field for immigration. It is brim full of produce. The settler lives cheaply until he raises his own crops. Land is cheap here. Our state offers to the seeker of a good home and cheap lands, the best of climates, the richest of soils, churches, railroads, and all the equipments and adornments of an advanced civilization already provided. All these advantages, the western bound emigrant will not overlook. They should be kept constantly before his mind. Immigration is the life-blood of the commonwealth. Our eastern friends should be constantly advised of the fact, that all things considered, Kansas is the most desirable of all the western states in which to make a home.

Many other editors also boomed their towns and nearby areas with similar front-page stories, but George H. Head, who started a little weekly called the *Settler* at Ludell in Rawlins County, Kansas, avoided blatant boosterism. In the first issue of his paper, on May 14, 1887, he simply scattered throughout the columns of his four-page paper short items that reflected optimism about the future. They included:

The type for the first number of *The Settler* was set in a sod-house, with the fleas and bed-bugs having a fall round-up on all the territory below our shirt-collar. A wind-mill in town is needed.

The dance in honor of the opening of the Ludell *Settler* building was well attended, and passed off in fine shape. As an index to the morality of the community, we will state that not a drop of anything intoxicating was indulged in; in fact, not a drop was to be had.

There's no grave yard in Ludell, and probably will be no need for one in the next ten years, unless an accident happens.

The mammoth milch cow staked in front of *The Settler* office is an advertisement for the nutritious buffalo grass with which every acre of uncultivated land in Rawlins county is covered. We will soon be compelled to either shorten the rope or feed anti-fat.

Five new buildings put up within two weeks, five more contracted for.

The school bonds have been accepted, and the new frame schoolhouse will be erected as soon as the lumber can be hauled.

Remember, no lots in Ludell are sold for speculation. They are disposed of only to those who intend to build and become residents. The editor of *The Settler* will buy the four lots on which the old sod schoolhouse stands. The object is to secure the old ground for the planting of fine shrubbery.

On Sunday afternoon we counted twenty-seven men in front of one store in Ludell, eighteen of whom were land-seekers. They come in squads. No more sod houses should be allowed inside the town limits. While admissible for stock sheds, they are outrageous in appearance as dwellings in a town like Ludell.

Think of it, ye slaves on [eastern] morning papers! The editor of this paper takes in more fresh air in one minute than is to be found in the composing room of a daily paper in a natural lifetime.

The location of Ludell is lovely . . . with an abundance of good well water at a depth of twenty feet. On the south is the Beaver, with its beautiful banks crowded with timber. The scene to the east of town, the stream making a dozen lovely curves within sight, is bewitchingly beautiful. Add to the above scene countless knolls capped with coveys of bright and shining grain stacks, and some idea can be formed of the richness of the country adjoining the stream. And yet there is vacant land within a mile or two!

The town of Ludell survived, but George Head's *Settler* lasted only three years.

NOT ALL TOWNS in the West needed newspapers to boost them. The railhead cattle towns in Kansas did not need newspapers to attract Texans looking for markets where they could sell their Texas longhorns. They required only a railroad, hotel, cattle buyers, and a few stores. But the cattle towns of Abilene, Newton, Wichita, and Dodge City, among others, all had newspapers established by editors wanting to capitalize on the business prospects brought by the Texas cattle trade. When A. W. Moore established the *Messenger* at Dodge City, Kansas, on February 26, 1874, the town was only about a year old and had about three hundred residents and

sixteen businesses, including several saloons doing a fair trade. In the first
issue of his four-page, six-column paper, Moore wrote:

> Here we are. How do you like us? We dislike a long Salutatory with
> more words than sense—promising great things which cannot be ful-
> filled—(as is too often the case with editors in Kansas)—but we merely
> say that we are here, in Dodge City, Ford County, State of Kansas, for the
> purpose of publishing a newspaper, earning and receiving our "chuck,"
> and doing what we can towards promoting the interests of said county.
> The *Messenger* is an Independent—or Neutral, paper—reserving the
> right, however, to criticize the actions of our public servants both in high
> and low places—to denounce public robbery and wholesale stealing—
> and speaking a good word for those who merit it.

Even though the town's few commercial establishments did not have to
advertise to get business, they supported Moore's paper for some months,
until grasshoppers invaded Kansas during the summer of 1874. As the
town's businesses declined, so did their support of the newspaper. Although Dodge City survived, the paper went out of business in 1875 and

This is the office of the *Mercury* at Kingman, Kansas, about 1879, two years after the
last wild buffalo was killed in the vicinity. The small five-column folio paper, established by J. C. Martin in June 1878, sought to promote the town. When settlement declined, Martin sold the paper to A. E. Saxey in August 1880. Saxey changed the
paper's name to the Kingman *Blade,* but it died three months later. *(Courtesy Kansas
State Historical Society)*

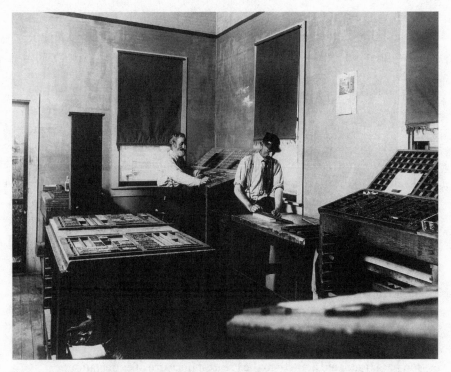

The bewhiskered man at left is Nicholas B. Klaine, who bought the Dodge City (Kansas) *Times* in 1876. By 1906, when this photo was made, Klaine was editor of the Dodge City *Globe-Republican*. (The other man, a printer, is not identified.) Four years after this photo was taken, the newspaper became simply the Dodge City *Globe*. *(Courtesy Kansas State Historical Society)*

Moore moved about 160 miles east to Newton, Kansas, a larger community, and established the weekly *Harvey County News.* Later Moore moved on to Colorado and edited a paper at Gunnison. Within a year after the *Messenger* died, another paper, called the *Times,* was established by Lloyd and Walter Shinn at Dodge City on May 20, 1876. Soon afterward they apparently concluded that the town had no future and sold the *Times* to N. B. Klaine, who thought otherwise. Like many successful editors in the West, Klaine realized that residents had developed common interests, which had created a sense of community. As residents made preparations for the return of Texas cowboys driving herds of longhorns to Dodge City's railhead market, Klaine praised the town for what it was. In the May 4, 1878, issue, he wrote:

> In this delectable city of the plains the winter of discontent is made glorious by the return of the cattle trade. With the countless herds come the

hordes of bipeds. Weeks and months before, through the blasts of winter and the gentle zephyrs of spring, has impecuniosity longed for the opening of the cattle trade, in which Dodge City outshines all envy and rivalry. This "cattle village" and far-famed "wicked city" is decked in gorgeous attire in preparation for the long horn. Like the sweet harbinger of spring, the boot black came, he of white and he of black. Next the barber "with his lather and shave." Too, with all that go to make up the busy throng of life's fitful fever, come the Mary Magdalenes, "selling their souls to whoever'll buy." There is "high, low, jack and the game," all adding to the great expectations so important an event brings about.

The merchant and the "hardware" dealer has filled his store and renovated his "palace." There are goods in profusion in warehouses and on shelves; the best markets were sought, and goods are in store and to arrive. Necessarily, there is great ado, for soon the vast plains will be covered with the long horn, and the "wicked city" is the source from which the great army of herder and driver is fed.

The season promises to be a remarkable one. The drive is reported to be larger, and the first herd will probably reach this point within a couple of weeks. There has been no undue preparation, and the earlier season has stimulated activity to the greatest measure of expectation.

LEGH FREEMAN, a young telegrapher at Fort Kearny, decided to get into journalism during the late 1860s, when the transcontinental railroad was being built across Nebraska. He acquired an abandoned Army printing press and established a newspaper called the *Frontier Index* to serve the construction crews and pleasure providers who accompanied the railroad builders as the line was extended westward. Each time the railroad moved farther west, a temporary town—established to house and entertain the construction crew—moved with it. The towns were known as "Hell on Wheels." Freeman moved with them, publishing his paper and in turn booming each new town. During 1868 Freeman promoted the railroad towns of Laramie, Green River City, and Bear River City in what became Wyoming, although Freeman's booming was different from that performed by editors elsewhere. The towns he boomed were transitory, and his goals, like those of the townspeople, were short-term. Although much of what Freeman printed in his paper promoted the town where he and his press happened to be, his papers did contain stories about crime and other problems, and a few times he called for vigilante action.

.   .   .

Legh Freeman, a telegrapher turned editor, started the *Frontier Index,* a paper that accompanied construction workers westward as the transcontinental railroad was being built during the late 1860s. *(Courtesy American Heritage Center, University of Wyoming)*

THE DISCOVERY OF gold or silver gave birth to a town without the help of a local paper to boom the community. Tents and crude buildings soon appeared in the area of a strike, as merchants and pleasure providers arrived to mine the miners. Soon an editor would arrive on the scene in a wagon, figuring a newspaper was needed. His wagon carried a printing press, type, paper, and associated printing equipment. The editor would search out a place to set up the press and soon would publish the town's first paper. This pattern repeated itself time and again in new mining towns throughout the West, and maintaining the boom would be the editor's first order of business. He would tell his readers what a great future they had because the gold or silver strike was the richest ever found anywhere in the world. At the same time the editor would fill his paper's columns with news of local happenings and anything else he could steal from exchange papers that he believed might be of interest to his readers. The editor, like the local merchants, realized his future depended on the gold or silver strike not playing out. If the strike lasted and the town's future looked bright, the editor would try to make the town a city. The merchants would advertise to give the editor encouragement, and, in turn, he would use every opportunity in his columns to point with pride to the town's

To promote rail travel, officials of the transcontinental railroad took a group of wealthy easterners west on an excursion train, on which they printed a daily newspaper titled the *Trans-Continental*. This illustration from *Frank Leslie's Illustrated* shows typesetters working next to a printer operating an Army press. The daily paper included national and international news received by telegraph at various stops along the route west. *(Courtesy American Heritage Center, University of Wyoming)*

progress. But if the gold or silver played out, the editor usually closed down his paper, loaded his printing equipment on a wagon, and moved on to whatever opportunity called. There he would start another paper, usually giving it a name different from his previous one.

One mining-town newspaper that played a unique role in booming its area was the *Rocky Mountain News* at Denver City, in what was then far western Kansas Territory. The paper was founded in April 1859 by William N. Byers, John L. Dailey, and Thomas Gibson soon after gold was discovered on the eastern slopes of the Rocky Mountains. Gold seekers streamed across the plains, clogging the Oregon, Santa Fe, and Smoky Hill Trails, and others came from the south and the west. But when inexperienced and impatient miners failed to find gold as quickly and easily as expected, many headed east proclaiming the gold boom a hoax. Newspapers to the east echoed their cries, and it appeared that the gold rush might end. Merchants in Denver City, who smelled profit from the rush, realized that a recognized authority was needed to confirm that the gold strikes were real. The authority turned out to be three eastern newspapermen.

Horace Greeley arrived in Denver City on June 6, 1859. The following day Greeley, along with William Byers of the *Rocky Mountain News,* Albert Richardson of the *Boston Journal,* and Henry Villard of the *Cincinnati Commercial,* went to visit diggings near modern Central City, Colorado. There, in Gregory Gulch, they saw perhaps two thousand miners at work. Greeley watched as they took gold from a creek and from the earth nearby. He even washed a pan of dirt and found color. Greeley and the others, convinced that the gold strike was real, returned to Denver City to file a report. On June 11, 1859, Byers printed his paper's first extra, one sheet, with printing on only one side, containing a detailed report signed by Greeley, Richardson, and Villard. It read in part: "We have this day personally visited nearly all the mines or claims already opened in this valley . . . have witnessed the operation of digging, transporting and washing on the veinstone . . . have seen the gold plainly visible in the riffles of nearly every sluice, and in nearly every pan." The *Rocky Mountain News* extra printed by Byers was distributed far and wide, and when copies were read in the East the gold rush began anew. Even gold seekers who had headed home out of frustration turned around and came back. The *Rocky Mountain News,* thanks to Greeley, Richardson, and Villard, had saved the day.

A FEW NEWSPAPERS retained the same name even though they moved from one mining camp to another. One such paper was the *Territorial Enterprise* at Virginia City, Nevada, which was actually started at Genoa in what was then Utah Territory. The few people who had settled in what is now far western Nevada wanted news from the outside world. In fact, the demand for news was so great that two handwritten news sheets were issued before the *Enterprise* was started. One was called the *Gold Canyon Switch* and was produced by Joseph Webb about 1854 at Johntown, then located in the Utah Territory. The second, the *Scorpion,* was written down in pen by Stephen A. Kinsey in February 1857 at a tiny Carson River Valley settlement that had developed as a stopping point for freighters traveling between Salt Lake City and California. First called Mormon Station, it had been renamed Genoa by early 1857, and it was there nearly two years later that the *Territorial Enterprise,* the first printed newspaper in what became the Nevada Territory, was published on December 18, 1858. Alfred James was editor and W. L. Jennegan was business manager. They printed their paper on a Washington handpress that had been hauled over the Sierra by wagon. At the time the whole population of the region was less than a thousand, but that number increased rapidly in 1859 after gold and silver were found in the Washoe country and the famous Comstock Lode was discovered. When nearly everyone around Genoa headed for the strike, Jennegan and James moved the paper to Carson City, about a dozen miles north and a little east of Genoa. Carson City had become a major supply and freighting center for the Comstock Lode. There, on December 17, 1859, one day short of its first anniversary, the paper carried a front-page story relating its brief history. It begins:

OURSELVES.

One year ago to-day, the first number of the TERRITORIAL ENTERPRISE was issued at Genoa. Our publishing room was in Singleton's Hall, Nevada Hotel, a room indiscriminately used by preachers, debating-clubs, secret societies, and once at least, for a prison. Upon the latter occasion we had a man accused of crime chained to our printing press, with a log chain, for two days and a half. What secrets that old Hall might tell, could it, by chance, be endowed with the gift of speech! Our establishment was removed to Carson City, on Thursday, November 10, 1859. We now occupy half of the upper part of Major Ornsby's adobe building, southwest corner of the Plaza. Our volume is not yet completed by seven numbers, owing to the fact that we have twice been compelled to suspend our issue for want of paper. During last winter, most of our paper was brought over on snow shoes, by attaches of this office. Many a time in the past year have we suffered for lack of fuel, and been pinched for want of actual necessaries of life. But so far we have struggled on successfully, and to-day we find ourselves in more comfortable circumstances in many respects. To be sure we still have to descend from the editorial tripod to superintend the cooking of a beefsteak, the seasoning of a bean soup, or the concoction of a pot of coffee, (and in this line, let us indulge our vanity by saying that we yield to none other as a caterer to the *physical* man, whatever our shortcoming in regard to intellectual pabulum). But as we have said, we feel that we have made a step in advance. It has been and still is our aim, to lay the foundation of a reliable newspaper, such as the rapidly increasing population, and the developing interests our pet New Territory demand. So far as literary ability is concerned, we make no claims for the past.

About a year after the above appeared in the *Territorial Enterprise*, the paper was sold to J. B. Wollard and Jonathan Williams and moved several miles northeast of Carson City to the boomtown of Virginia City, which had just been established on the site of the Comstock Lode in 1859. There the *Enterprise* grew, prospered, and became more than just a boomtown newspaper. As one observer later wrote:

> Almost from its first beginnings in Virginia City, the affairs of The Enterprise assumed an accelerated tempo, and the paper itself was destined to become the pattern and archetype of all Western newspapers in pioneer times. Its gunfighting editors, celebrated news beats, authority and power in affairs of state, and its hilarious and uninhibited way of life were to become legendary, the glass of journalistic fashion which was to find its counterpart in every frontier paper from Alder Gulch to Durango and from Bodie to the Black Hills.[3]

However, the editor of another Nevada paper, established a few years after the *Enterprise,* does not seem to have been influenced greatly by the Virginia City paper. When silver was discovered about 135 miles east of Virginia City, the boomtown of Austin was born. There W. C. Phillips established the weekly *Reese River Reveille* on May 16, 1863. In the first issue he told his readers: "Deeming it self-evident that every denizen came here to improve his fortune, we shall act upon the idea that our readers prefer discussion about silver lodes, rather than wrangling about politics, religion or local jealousies." Still, the paper did its share of booming Austin. About two months after it began publication, Phillips told his readers on July 4, 1863: "The rapid increase of our town brings with it the concomitant growth of new cities. Stores, saloons, restaurants, etc. These we already have—we want a school house." Phillips told readers that there were fifty to sixty school-age children in Austin. Townspeople responded, and three weeks later Austin opened a school. The action prompted Phillips to boast: "Fast—ain't we!"[4]

The *Territorial Enterprise* undoubtedly did impact many other papers in the West, but it is not known if it influenced two Colorado men, W. A. Laughlin and A. W. Merrick. They started the *Black Hills Pioneer,* a weekly established in the boomtown of Deadwood, Dakota Territory, soon after gold was discovered there in 1876. Laughlin and Merrick had been printers employed by the *Colorado Farmer* in Denver. On learning of the discovery of gold in the Black Hills, they loaded their printing equipment onto two wagons and headed north toward the area of the gold strike without knowing where they would establish a newspaper. Between Cheyenne and Fort Laramie, one of their wagons overturned and their printing equipment and type were scattered on the ground. When they reached Deadwood, Laughlin was too sick to work, so Merrick set up their office in an unfinished log cabin with a dirt floor. Because the floor turned to mud when it rained, they kept their press and printing equipment in a tent on a nearby hillside. The flavor of the paper's early issues is captured in the following excerpts taken from its first issue, published on June 8, 1876:

> Our material has been in Deadwood less than a week; our house is not up; it has rained two days during the time. . . . Our material to print this paper was transported in the depth of winter, almost 400 miles, and brought through and into a hostile Indian country, and in the first settlements made we have set up our presses and set the type for this number of our paper. . . . Six weeks ago the site of Deadwood City was a heavy

This illustration from *Frank Leslie's Illustrated Weekly* shows the offices of the *Black Hills Champion,* edited by Charles Collins and established on June 2, 1877, at Deadwood, Dakota Territory. The *Champion* was the third newspaper established in Deadwood, nearly two months after Porter Warner established the *Black Hills Times* on April 7, 1877. The first paper in Deadwood was Laughlin and Merrick's *Black Hills Pioneer,* started on June 8, 1876. *(Courtesy American Heritage Center, University of Wyoming)*

forest of pine timber, now it extends nearly a mile along Deadwood and Whitewood [creeks] and contains nearly two thousand of the most energetic, driving people on this continent.

The July 1, 1876, issue included these observations:

Some of the skeptical newspapers of the East are beginning to change their tune in regard to the mineral wealth of the Black Hills. Nuggets weighing $150.00 and claims yielding $1000.00 a day are facts they can't get around.

Our Mines: Last Monday the owners of No. 6 below discovery, on Deadwood, struck the pay streak on their claim and took out $2300.00. This is the largest yield for one day's work yet on record in the hills. From four to seven hundred dollars has been quite common, and the yield has been high as $1500.00, but No. 6 carries off the red ribbon.

Captain Jack left for Omaha last Wednesday taking with him a large assortment of specimens and the good wishes of all the boys.

List of letters remaining in office at Sieppy's Saloon lower Deadwood.

No. 11 below discovery, owned by Mr. Flourman who paid $2,000 for it has taken out $1400.00. Passes on to the famous #2 owned by W. P. Wheeler & Co. They run two set [*sic*] of sluice boxes and have taken out about forty three thousand dollars.

And these are some of the highlights of the July 8, 1876, issue:

Merrick & Gardner Props. Mr. D. Cannon, one of the good boys who own and work #7 Bobtail, has a nugget that weighs $44.50. Picked up in his sluice box at the end of a days run.

Messrs. Seymour and Utter have established a pony express between Deadwood and Fort Laramie and will make round trips weekly thereafter.

The July 22, 1876, issue:

The Theatre—The Langrishe troupe will make their first appearance in their mammoth pavilion theatre, and give the first dramatic rendition ever witnessed in Western Dakota this evening. The attendance we hope will be large, for the company is notorious throughout, able to withstand fair criticism in any part of the country. They will not disappoint the expectations of their friends. We hope the enterprising manager will never have occasion to regret locating in Deadwood.

In reporting the completion of a theater, one of the trappings of culture, the editor seems to have been seeking to instill a sense of community and civic pride in the minds of what were really transient readers. Such stories helped an editor to elevate the moral tone of the community to the perceived level of civilized society in the East. But in that same issue of the *Black Hills Pioneer,* Merrick and Gardner also noted that their newspaper had published an extra edition two days earlier containing details of the "butchery of Gen. Custer" late in the previous month. And less than a month later, the August 5 issue reported the murder of Wild Bill Hickok by Jack McCall in a Deadwood saloon. By then the civilized life of the East may not have seemed as close as the editors had hoped.

WHILE EDITORS WANTING TO start a newspaper were welcomed with open arms by residents of new towns, not all of them met the expectations of the townspeople. One of the best examples is the story of M. J. Cochrane, who early in 1878 decided that the new frontier town of Medicine Lodge, in south-central Kansas, was ripe for a newspaper. Cochrane bought a Washington handpress from W. T. McElroy, who ran the Humboldt (Kansas) *Union,* together with a couple of racks, a few type cases, a well-worn font of long primer type and another font of brevier, and a few job fonts for advertising purposes, and moved the press and equipment to Medicine Lodge.* There, on May 10, 1878, Cochrane started the *Barbour County Mail,* a Republican paper. Since his was the only paper in town, Cochrane may have concluded that it did not make much difference what kind of paper he published, or he may not have known how to keep the worn type clean or how to make a decent impression with the Washington handpress. Cochrane was a man of fair editorial ability, with a rather catchy style of writing, but the townspeople were not particularly enamored of him. While he did a little booming for Medicine Lodge, he became unpopular with women not only because of his flirtatious disposition but because of the worn type he used to print the paper: It was difficult to read.

In February 1879, several months after Cochrane started his paper, a number of townspeople held a meeting and decided that Cochrane was

---

* For descriptions of printing equipment, see Appendix A.

not an asset to the community. They decided further that they wanted him to leave and never return. So these self-appointed regulators took the editor from his humble office, stripped him of his clothing, and then administered a punishment that was entirely unique and unprecedented in the treatment of editors. There was no tar in the town and not a featherbed to be split open, but an enterprising settler had brought in a sorghum molasses mill the year before, and as sorghum generally grew well there, had manufactured a crop into thick, ropy molasses. Owing to the cold weather the molasses was thicker and ropier than usual. The regulators secured a gallon of this, mixed it well with sandburs, which grew with great luxuriance in the sandy bottom of the Medicine, and administered this mixture liberally to the naked person of the editor. With the unwelcome covering of sandburs and sweetness, Cochrane was placed on a cedar rail and carried about on the shoulders of the self-appointed regulators. He privately acknowledged afterward that while this was an elevation and distinction such as no other editor had ever received, he would personally rather have

This small building, constructed from wooden packing cases, housed the *Hardesty Herald* in the Oklahoma Territory when the paper was started in 1890. The man in the doorway may be the paper's founder and editor, Richard Briggs "Dick" Quinn. *(Courtesy Archives and Manuscript Division of the Oklahoma Historical Society)*

remained a private and humble citizen on foot. After carrying the shivering and besmeared editor about to their hearts' content, occasionally adding to his general discomfort by bouncing him up and down on the rough and splintered edges of the rail, the regulators told him that he must leave town within twenty-four hours and never show his face or form there again.

Cochrane was soon rescued by some friends who had armed themselves. They told him that he could remain as long as he wished and they would protect him. Cochrane thanked them, but he quickly concluded he had better move on. He sold the paper to J. W. McNeal and his brother-in-

This old wood-and-metal printing press was used in 1890 by Richard Briggs "Dick" Quinn, editor of the weekly *Hardesty Herald*. Hardesty, a stop on a cattle trail linking Texas to railheads in Kansas, was located in "No Man's Land" (the Oklahoma panhandle). When the railroad arrived nineteen miles away, Hardesty died. Quinn moved his weekly to the new town of Guymon and renamed it the *Guymon Herald*. The paper is now a daily. *(Courtesy Archives and Manuscripts Division of the Oklahoma Historical Society)*

law Ezra W. Iliff and departed. Iliff loved good literature, especially the writings of the English poet Milton. Milton's *Paradise Lost* includes a vivid description of Satan's palace in hell, which was lighted by "cressets"—iron vessels or baskets holding oil that when burned served as torches. Iliff renamed the paper the *Cresset*. McNeal and Iliff were often asked to explain the paper's name. Once a weatherbeaten cowboy ambled into the newspaper office and asked, "What's the meanin' of this here name Cresset?" Iliff carefully explained its meaning. The cowboy thought for a few moments, looked at the latest issue of the rather meager paper, and exclaimed, "Damned fittin' name, I would say. This here is a hell of a paper, isn't it?"[5]

Another form of newspaper boom occurred during the 1880s, when all of what is now Oklahoma remained off limits to settlement except by Indians. While the Missouri, Kansas, and Texas Railroad and the Atlantic and Pacific line had penetrated the sparsely populated Indian lands and linked Kansas and Missouri to Texas in 1880, the leaders of the Five Civilized Tribes* fought every move to organize the territory for statehood. Railroads, banks, wholesale distributors, and farm equipment manufacturers, however, who saw profit if the territory was opened to settlement, hired lawyers who gained the support of the Wichita *Eagle* in Kansas and the *Kansas City Times* in Missouri to do so. To build public interest the lawyers, who became known as boomers, also organized groups of purported settlers in Kansas, Missouri, and Texas, who claimed they wanted to settle in Indian Territory.

Still another group of boomers was headed by David L. Payne, a native of Indiana, who charged each home seeker two dollars for a certificate guaranteeing a quarter section of land, or twenty-five dollars for a town lot in a future town in Indian Territory. Payne tried several times to lead expeditions onto Indian lands, but each time was turned back by federal officials. Payne even published his own newspaper, called the *Oklahoma War-Chief*, started at Caldwell, Kansas, on January 12, 1883. It moved frequently along the southern border of Kansas just north of what is now Oklahoma. Then, in the spring of 1884, Payne and a large number of boomers crossed the Kansas border and established an illegal settlement at Rock Falls on the Chicaskia River, four miles inside Cherokee Indian territory. Grant Harris, a printer earning seven dollars a week at a newspaper in Caldwell, Kansas, went to Rock Falls and was hired at twenty-five dollars a week by Payne to set type for the *Oklahoma War-Chief*. Publishing a paper on Indian land was illegal for white men since the territory had not yet

* The Choctaw, Chickasaw, Creek, Cherokee, and Seminole.

been opened to settlement. Rock Falls consisted of only one frame building, which had been erected for the printing office. Most of the people lived in tents. As Harris later recalled:

> For several days before the actual arrest soldiers surrounded the camp, but they did not interfere with us in any way. Capt. Payne had received a tip in some manner that the arrest would be made when we started to print the next paper, and for a day after the forms were on the press we waited, but finally he gave the word to start. The first paper I pulled off the press I folded up and put in my pocket, and by the time a half dozen were printed soldiers entered the office and arrested all of the officers of the colony. . . . After placing the prisoners under guard, the boomers were lined up and escorted over the state line, four miles away.[6]

In November 1884 Payne died suddenly at a Wellington, Kansas, hotel. He did not live to see about two million acres of Indian Territory opened to settlement in a land run held on April 22, 1889. Three years later, on April 19, 1892, another large area in west-central Oklahoma was likewise opened for settlement.

Since many of the good public lands elsewhere in the West had already been claimed, thousands of people made the runs, seeking the chance to

David L. Payne published the *Oklahoma War-Chief* to propagandize his efforts to open to settlement part of what is now Oklahoma. *(Courtesy Western History Collections, University of Oklahoma)*

claim a quarter section of land on which to homestead, or a lot in a new town. Among the newcomers were newspapermen, who like most settlers proclaimed their new home "God's country," and sought not only to boom their towns but the entire Oklahoma Territory as well. After all, their futures were dependent on the future of what would become the forty-sixth state admitted to the Union in 1907.

Typical of the booming newspapermen who settled in Oklahoma was Walter M. Ellis, who started publishing a paper called the *New World* at Wichita, Kansas, about two weeks before the April 22, 1889, land run. He moved the paper to Kingfisher, Oklahoma Territory, in May 1889 and continued to publish it there until May 1891, when another Kansas newspaperman, Jacob V. Admire, bought the *New World* and the *Kingfisher Journal,* the town's second paper, which had been founded in March 1890. Merging the two papers, Admire established the Kingfisher *Free Press* in June 1891. Having boomed Kansas towns as an editor there, Admire began to echo the spirit of the townspeople, who thought their town had a very bright future. In fact, the *Free Press* printed a great deal of pure booster propaganda, describing Kingfisher as a "young Chicago." Outspoken in his opinions, Admire occasionally became a disenchanted boomer. He complained in the March 31, 1892, issue that—while a correspondent for the *Kansas City Times* could get a hundred dollars for boosting Kingfisher—he was supposed to keep up a boom for the town at all times while being paid in "wind pudding." Still, he continued to defend the role of his paper in booming. In the September 8, 1892, issue he wrote: "A man may blow and bluster on a street corner and it is soon forgotten, but what a newspaper says lives always." During the first year of the *Free Press,* Admire doubled the paper's circulation. By late 1892 he had nearly fifteen hundred subscribers.

When land in west-central Oklahoma was opened for settlement in 1892, the town of Arapaho was founded. Ten days later Frank Fillmore and William Seaman started a weekly paper there called the *Arrow* to boom the region. In their first issue, published on April 29, 1892, the editors promised readers that the paper would be devoted to the upbuilding of Arapaho and County G, now called Custer County:

If you want to settle in one of the most prosperous counties in the territory; if you want one of the best claims in Oklahoma; if you want to get the best at little cost; if you want timber and water in abundance; if you want an ideal home in a law-abiding community, come to County G.

The paper, like others booming their towns, portrayed the residents of Arapaho as having the brains, capital, energy, and business ability needed to "build up a new town." The editor even claimed the town's citizens were so outstanding the sheriff found it difficult to make a living.

Early in the summer of 1892 Frank Fillmore's poor health forced him to go to El Reno for medical treatment. He left the paper in the hands of his partner, William Seaman. When Fillmore returned to Arapaho in the fall of 1892, he learned that Seaman had turned the *Arrow* over to the mortgage holder. Fillmore immediately started another paper called the *Arapaho Bee* and took as his partner Jesse W. Lawton, a former schoolteacher from Indiana. The *Bee* continued to boom the town and region and the security of living in a dugout. On May 4, 1893, the *Bee* noted: "Adversity has its compensation at times. In the case of the western settlers who found lumber too expensive a luxury, their dugouts are safe retreats in these days of warring elements and afford a sense of security that a mansion cannot give." A little more than five months later, on October 19, the *Bee* reported on the wonderful crops in the area, including pumpkins grown by the paper's editor, Fillmore, who wrote: "Ye editor exhibited four pie melons [pump-

When the railroad reached El Paso, Texas, in 1881, there were two newspapers, the *Times* and the *Herald.* The following year S. H. Newman, from New Mexico, arrived and started a third paper, the *Lone Star,* a semiweekly. This photo was taken in 1882, just after the *Lone Star* had moved into new offices. All three papers promoted El Paso. *(Courtesy Western History Collections, University of Oklahoma)*

No newspaper office had been built when the *Freedom Express* was established at Freedom, Oklahoma Territory, in 1906. The printer set up his equipment under a tree until a building could be finished. *(Courtesy Archives and Manuscripts Division of the Oklahoma Historical Society)*

kins] averaging 48½ pounds taken from one vine grown on a lot in Arapahoe. This vine (a volunteer) received no cultivation or manuring and bore 92 melons averaging 25 pounds each—an aggregate yield of 2,300 pounds."

During the late 1880s and early 1890s, new newspapers were being started not only in the Oklahoma Territory but in the panhandle of Texas, where new counties were being organized. Land promoters and boomers were numerous, claiming the superior advantages of the places—all future metropolises—where they set up shop. Newspapers appeared at just about every new town. Some survived; many did not. The *Rivers Hammer,* published at the town of Rivers (later renamed Channing), on the northern breaks of the Canadian River, died after one issue.

In the Texas panhandle and the neighboring Oklahoma Territory to the east, new papers in one form or another boomed not only their communities but their regions. In the Oklahoma Territory, editors of the newly formed Oklahoma Press Association eagerly agreed to boost Oklahoma at their 1895 meeting. They passed a resolution that included these words:

> The Press Association of Oklahoma, having the best interests of the territory at heart and being fully identified with its past, present and future . . . looks with alarm at the many monstrous untruths contained in the associate press reports sent . . . from the various towns of this territory in regard to crimes and misdemeanors which are multiplied in a sensational way until, figuratively speaking, a mouse becomes an elephant, which injures our "land of the Fair God," from the fact that timid capital and more timid human nature refuse to come among us to invest or make homes.[7]

Newspapers continued the practice of booming not only their communities but regions into the twentieth century. When the *Avard* (Oklahoma) *Breeze* began publication on January 15, 1915, H. M. Cooley, editor and publisher, was adamant about the purpose of his little weekly. He exclaimed that putting Avard on the map was the paper's business, and he devoted the front page to signs of progress, including the railroad track on the Atchison, Topeka, and Santa Fe line, a train turntable, and a new bridge over the Red Horse crossing on the Cimmaron River. Cooley was proud that Avard had grown into a "thriving city" of several hundred people by 1915, having been built on the site of what in 1893 was a prairie-dog town. But he emphasized on page 1 that his paper was "strictly nonpartisan. But open to clean discussion of all political partie's [*sic*]."

CHAPTER SIX

PISTOL-PACKIN' EDITORS

Embry, who shot Anthony, editor of the Leavenworth Times, *has been acquitted. That's just the way with some juries – they think it no more harm to shoot an editor than a Jack-rabbit.*

—*Marion County* (Kansas) *Record*

MOST READERS OF early newspapers in the American West were not very discriminating. Certainly some were educated, but most had little concern about the literary mode of the content of their papers. They had come west in search of better lives and opportunities. When they took time to read a local newspaper, they wanted interesting and incisive subject matter produced by editors who commanded their respect. It is not surprising that the most respected early editors were often those who could fight with their fists as well as their pens, in a very personal way. Some of these editors became well known, not necessarily because they were gifted writers but because of the way they lashed out at citizens who were thought to have done wrong, or at other editors in barroom and back-alley terms. If an editor printed a particularly inflammatory story, he could expect to be accosted on the wooden sidewalks or in the local saloon. Since the editor was more often than not a lone wolf, he could seldom blame the words on someone else. Such editors became very thick-skinned, and many carried weapons for their own protection.

The first pistol-packin' editor west of the Mississippi was none other than Joseph Charless, who in 1808 established the *Missouri Gazette* at St. Louis. Charless was fearlessly independent. When he did not give in to political opponents, and they started their own newspaper, Charless called it a "tool," or "hireling," press, controlled by the local politicians who owned it. From then until he retired in 1821, Charless had to confront the prospect of physical violence time and again. Once, outside the post office at St. Louis, William C. Carr, a political opponent, approached Charless

and spat in his face. Charless picked up some stones and threw them at
Carr until he retreated. Another time someone shot and narrowly missed
Charless as he walked in his garden. Probably Charless's most publicized
trouble occurred when he got into a fight with Isaac N. Henry, coeditor
with Thomas Hart Benton of the St. Louis *Enquirer.* Following the fight
Charless wrote about it in his *Gazette,* placing the blame on Henry, whom
he then sued for assault. Henry pleaded guilty and was eventually fined.
Meantime Benton swore out an affidavit against Charless, accusing him of
telling his side of the story in his paper *after* Charless had filed suit against
Henry. Benton claimed that the story contained falsehoods, which—he im-
plied—were designed to influence the court before it had ruled on the case.
Charless was called before the court to show cause why he should not be
fined for contempt. After he failed to show cause, the court fined him
twenty dollars and costs. When he could or would not pay the fine, Charless spent several days in jail, because newspapers had not yet gained the
right to discuss court proceedings without risking judicial reprisal.[1]

SUCH DISPUTES were commonplace on the frontier, where the spirit of
the American Revolution thrived and people were a proud lot. They believed in speaking their minds without fear of the consequences. Many disputes turned violent because weapons were plentiful. Add to that the
tradition brought west by southerners who believed in defending their
honor by dueling or fighting with knives, and it is easy to understand the
rugged environment in which the early newspaper editors lived and
worked.

Southern traditions were particularly strong in Texas, where in August
1847 a feud between two Texas editors ended in the killing of one. The
principals were Henry A. Kendall, who in 1846 founded the *San Augustine
Shield,* a weekly, and James Russell, who with H. M. Kinsey owned the San
Augustine *Red-Lander.* Russell, a Scottish-born Presbyterian minister, had
more scholarly accomplishments than most Texas editors of the day. He
held an M.A. degree from Edinburgh University, and had brought with
him a personal library of about five hundred books. Russell taught at and
then became president of San Augustine University. One writer described
him as fearless and "a man of irascible, impetuous temperament and domi-
neering personality" who was constantly in trouble one way or another.[2]
Russell expressed his opinions without regard for the consequences. The
feud developed after Russell published an article defaming Kendall's sister.
What happened next was reported by another Texas paper:

We learn from a reliable source that the Rev. James Russell, editor of the *Red-Lander,* was killed in San Augustine some days since by Mr. Kendall, publisher of the *Shield.*

This deplorable result grew out of some bitter controversy which had been going on between the two persons for some weeks past. The parties are said to have met the day before the killing and exchanged two shots each, ineffectually. On the day of the occurrence, Kendall, it is said, waylaid Russell as he left his office, and shot him dead.[3]

Kendall quickly fled to New Orleans, where he found work as a printer on the *Picayune,* but within weeks he contracted yellow fever and soon died.

When gold was discovered in California, fortune seekers and those seeking to prey on them hurried west. Many went to San Francisco, which had become the major trading center. By the early 1850s San Francisco had as many as twelve daily newspapers, but hard news was secondary to their content and, when included, was presented in a haphazard fashion. The so-called newspapers were actually opinion papers. Most of them, including the *Alta California,* were primarily used to express their owners' opinions or those of the group he supported. One day Edward Gilbert, senior editor of the *Alta California,* wrote a sarcastic editorial criticizing the state's efforts to care for inexperienced travelers who regularly got trapped in snow crossing the Sierras. Reacting to the criticism, Governor John Bigler ordered General J. W. Denver to take a relief party and rescue the travelers. Denver, who liked pomp, made a production out of it and brought the travelers back to Sacramento alive. Denver gained much notoriety, but Gilbert, who was one of California's first congressmen, charged in the *Alta California* that the rescue was a disgraceful exhibition, making political capital out of misery. Denver responded by writing a letter to a Sacramento newspaper. When Gilbert read the published letter, he found Denver's language objectionable and challenged him to a duel. Rifles at forty paces were chosen. On August 2, 1852, the two men and their parties met at Oak Grove, near the state capital. Forty paces were marked off. Both men then took their places and stepped off the proper number of steps, turned, and faced each other. Gilbert fired his rifle but missed Denver, who turned his rifle away from Gilbert and fired into the air. The seconds asked if the two men were satisfied. Denver said yes. Gilbert said no and demanded a second shot because, he said, Denver had once ridiculed bloodless duels. The seconds returned and reloaded the rifles. By then Denver was getting angry, and when the order to fire was given, Denver fired, the ball striking Gilbert just above the left hip. He said nothing, smiled weakly at his second, and died moments later.[4]

Gilbert and many other editors in early San Francisco took their politics seriously. They were willing to back their opinions and prejudices with their fists, pistols, rifles, knives, or whatever weapon was chosen. A. C. Russell, editor of the *Evening Picayune,* fought a duel with Capt. Joseph Folsom, a West Pointer, but their shots injured neither man. They chose knives in a second duel, and Russell got the best of Folsom by wounding him several times.

Such affairs of honor became so intense that a man identified only as "J. Walker" placed an advertisement in the *Golden Era* on May 15, 1853. It read:

To Editor, Legislator and all whom it may concern: The undersigned, desiring to "turn an honest penny" would respectively inform Editor, Legislators and others, whose moral and religious scruples may prevent their willingness "to stand and face the music," that he will at the shortest notice and on the most liberal terms, engage to fight duels with pistols, rifles or bowie knives, or, if preferable, "strike from the shoulder."
J. Walker, care of the San Francisco Post Office.

One of the better-known disputes between San Francisco editors involved James King of William, who owned the *Evening Bulletin,* and James P. Casey, who edited the *Times.* As background, James King of William grew up in the Georgetown area of Washington, D.C. Because there were many other James Kings in town, he added his father's first name and called himself James King of William. He arrived in San Francisco in 1847, opened a small bank, and during the gold rush became a millionaire, then lost everything during a bank crisis in 1855. Having worked as a printer's devil as a boy, he decided to start a newspaper to fight what he believed was the dishonesty of the larger banks, which he blamed for his small bank's failure. On October 8, 1855, his *Evening Bulletin* began publication.

James King of William's crusade against dishonest bankers brought threats, and in one instance he was challenged to a duel. He responded in the December 6, 1855, issue of the *Evening Bulletin* with the following: "We pass every afternoon about 4½ to 5 o'clock along Market street from Fourth to Fifth street. The road is wide and not so much frequented as those streets farther in town. If we are to be shot or cut to pieces, for Heaven's sake let it be done there. Others will not be injured, and in case we fall our house is but a few hundred yards beyond and the cemetery not much farther." As far as is known, James King of William never fought the

James King of William, who owned the San Francisco *Evening Bulletin,* was shot and wounded in 1856 by James P. Casey, editor of the San Francisco *Times.* Members of the Vigilance Committee sentenced Casey to death by hanging six days later when King died. *(Courtesy California State Library)*

duel, but such items helped to increase his *Evening Bulletin*'s circulation, which was more than five thousand early in 1856. By then James King of William had shifted the focus of his paper's crusading efforts from dishonest bankers to crime. He told his readers that it was more of a crime to steal a mule than to kill a human being in San Francisco, and to prove his claim he noted that there had been 487 murders, including six hangings by the sheriff and forty-six hangings by mobs. When other San Francisco papers failed to join his crusade, he attacked them in print. About then, his older brother, Thomas, sought appointment as a U.S. marshal and lost. James King of William began to editorialize about the lack of ability of the man who was appointed. It was then that James P. Casey, editor of the San Francisco *Times,* printed a letter signed "Caliban," a pen name sometimes used by a judge named McGowan. The letter accused James King of William and his paper of trying to cover up irregularities at the Customs House, where Thomas King worked. King demanded that Casey reveal the identity of the letter writer, but Casey refused. The next day Thomas King again confronted Casey and demanded the name of the letter writer. It was then that Casey claimed he had written the letter, and when Casey picked up the next issue of the *Evening Bulletin,* he found James King of William telling his readers that a future issue of the paper would detail how Casey had served time at Sing Sing prison in New York State for robbing his mistress. The story was true, but the event had occurred many years earlier. Casey went directly to the offices of the *Evening Bulletin* and confronted James King of William. A rival paper gave the following account of what was said:

Casey: What do you mean by this statement?

King: Is it not the truth?

Casey: Yes, but I don't wish my past acts raked up; on that point and as the evidence showed, it was, at the worst, but a case of constructive larceny.

King: I will publish what I see fit, and tomorrow I shall be even more severe.

Casey: Then you must be prepared to defend yourself on the street, for I intend to attack you on sight.

King: Leave my office at once. If you do not, I shall kick you into the street. Go and never darken my door again!

Casey left, went to friends, and put his affairs in order. Some of his friends tried to talk Casey out of attacking King, but to no avail. Late that afternoon, May 14, 1856, Casey was waiting at the corner of Montgomery and Washington Streets, about half a block from the *Evening Bulletin* office, when James King of William walked out of his office. As King neared, Casey called out for him to defend himself, but before King could draw his pistol, Casey fired his weapon and the bullet struck King in the breast. He staggered into a nearby office, where a physician was called. Police arrived and took Casey to the city jail, where he was placed in a cell next to Charles Cora, a gambler who had killed a marshal named Richardson. Meantime thousands of people gathered. Casey's friends discussed how they might rescue him, while friends of James King of William talked of how they could help him. Some of them said they ought to kill Casey. Others thought it time to reorganize the Vigilance Committee first set up in 1851 to deal with troublesome characters. As tempers flared, the sheriff sent a message to the governor in Sacramento, claiming that the situation was out of control. The governor came and soon declared the city in a state of insurrection. Casey was then moved to the county jail. In the meantime the Vigilance Committee began to reorganize, establishing its headquarters in a grain warehouse fortified with sandbags and called Fort Gunnybags.

For three days James King of William remained in critical condition. On the fourth day a doctor reported that he was near death. By then the Vigilance Committee had reorganized, and about 2,600 members, divided into twenty-six companies, marched up Sacramento Street with bayonets set. San Francisco's small police force was helpless and stood by as members of the committee stopped in front of the county jail and formed in lines facing the building. Cannons were brought up and aimed at the jail. Several officers of the Vigilance Committee then went into the jail and demanded the release of Casey and Cora. The sheriff started to argue but quickly gave in and turned the two men over. Once outside, the armed men marched Casey and Cora back to Fort Gunnybags. Committee members also arrested two other men and charged them with being accessories before the fact to the shooting of James King of William. All four men were held by members of the Vigilance Committee.

On May 20, 1856, six days after he was shot, James King of William died. As word spread throughout San Francisco, church and fire bells began tolling, and thousands of men clogged the streets near Fort Gunnybags. Business throughout San Francisco was suspended, but not before dry-goods stores were swamped by men wanting to buy mourning crepe to bind around their arms. About ten thousand mourners marched the body of James King of William to Lone Mountain cemetery for burial. Back at Fort Gunnybags, Casey and Cora were quickly tried, found guilty, and sentenced to death by hanging.

Both men were then taken to a platform in front of Fort Gunnybags, and a noose was placed around each man's neck. Cora was quiet, but Casey asked to speak to the great crowd. One account quoted Casey as saying: "Gentlemen: I hope this will be forever engraved on your minds and hearts. I am no murderer. Let no man call me a murderer or an assassin. Let not the community pronounce me a murderer. Let no editor dare to slander my name or memory. Where I belonged I was taught to fight, and that to resist my own wrong was my province."

When Casey stopped talking, the firehouse bells began to ring. Casey and Cora fell to the ends of the ropes and strangled to death. That night San Francisco was quiet. The streets had cleared for the first time in days.[5]

EDWARD E. CROSS, a journeyman printer, was an editor with a strong will. Cross had been editor of the *Cincinnati Times* and special correspondent for the New York *Herald* before he went to Arizona during the late 1850s. Using a Washington handpress, Cross established the *Weekly Arizonian* in 1859 at Tubac, a center of much mining activity, located on the Santa Cruz River. Tubac had a population of about six hundred people and was one of the four largest settlements in what became the Arizona

Territory. Cross wrote not only for his own paper, but for many eastern papers. He also became a stockholder of the St. Louis and Arizona Mining Company, which was reason enough for him to call for the development of the region's natural resources, as he often did. Sylvester Mowry, an ex–army officer from West Point who had been elected a delegate to Congress for the proposed Territory of Arizona, agreed with Cross, and they also both believed that the Arizona Territory should be established. But Mowry's mining company had quietly been fighting the St. Louis and Arizona Company, in which Cross had an interest.

Although they had never met, Cross and Mowry began to exchange letters, and these were printed in eastern papers including the *Washington States,* a secessionist paper published in Washington, D.C., between 1857 and 1861. When Cross questioned figures given by Mowry about the region's population, Mowry responded: "The person who wrote the letter you publish, has never seen enough of Arizona to write intelligibly about it; and in this item of population, he has stated what is absolutely untrue."[6] Cross responded that he had been a careful reader of Mowry's

voluminous (and, as I now find, *fabulous*) productions regarding the country, and supposed them correct. I found, however, that many of his assertions were not true, and that all were exaggerated. Not only this, but also that his letters and pamphlets were the laughing stock of the western portion of the Territory; that he had never lived in Arizona, and derived most of his information from old Jesuit records and tradition, which are known to be the most unreliable of all authorities. . . . I apprehend that he is eminently more deserving and more in danger of lynch law than myself.[7]

In his next letter, dated July 2, 1859, Mowry defended his own statements and added:

It is a part of the freedom of the press that any man may mapoon another in the papers, and to this fact I am indebted for the blackguardism to which Mr. Cross has resorted. The fact that I have raised him to the level of a gentleman, by demanding of him personal satisfaction for the scurrilous language he has used towards me, prevents my showing him in his true light.[8]

Since the correspondence had been published in many eastern newspapers, the duel that Mowry proposed gained national attention. Mowry returned to Tubac from Washington, D.C., on June 7, 1859, to defend his honor. That morning Mowry selected one T. L. Mercer as his second, and Cross selected a man named Jack Donaldson. Burnside carbines were chosen as the weapons to be used at a distance of forty yards, and it was agreed that the duel would take place in the plaza at Tubac the following morning. Both men spent the afternoon practicing their shooting. The next day a large crowd gathered to witness the duel, and most of the men were armed not only with six-shooters but with bowie knives.

The duel began, and Cross and Mowry each fired three shots. Neither was hit. When Mowry pressed the trigger on his fourth round, his carbine did not go off. His second demanded another shot for his principal. Cross's second protested, but before the matter was settled, Cross handed his weapon to his second and said Mowry should have the shot. Cross folded his arms against his chest and waited. Mowry raised his gun but paused. He realized that if he fired and hit Cross, there might be a general fight among all the armed bystanders, some of whom supported Cross, others who supported Mowry himself. So he simply fired his carbine into the air, handed the weapon to his second, and began walking toward Cross, who walked to meet him. When they met, the two men shook hands as the crowd cheered. Cross and Mowry then led the crowd to a nearby mining-company store, where a barrel of Monongahela whiskey was opened and everyone celebrated.

Later that day Cross and Mowry wrote a letter that was not only published like a business card in Cross's paper at Tubac but also sent to papers in the East. It read:

EDITOR STATES: Mr. Edw. E. Cross withdraws the offensive language used by him, and disclaims any intention to reflect upon Mr. Mowry's veracity, or upon his character as a gentleman, in any publication he has made in reference to Arizona. Mr. Mowry withdraws any statement that he has made in his letter to the press of July 2nd, which in any degree reflects upon Mr. Cross' character as a man and a gentleman.

Any difference of opinion which may exist between them in reference to Arizona is an honest one, to be decided by weight of authority.

(signed) SYLVESTER MOWRY
EDWARD E. CROSS

Tubac, Arizona, July 8, 1859[9]

It has been written that Southerners in the West just before the Civil War "carried themselves as gentlemen and boasted of a taste for cold bour-

bon, hot blood, and jealous honors."[10] Duels, or at least challenges of
honor, were commonplace in nearly all areas where Southerners appeared.
Following one duel in Denver, Colorado Territory, in the fall of 1859,
William N. Byers of the *Rocky Mountain News,* on October 27, 1859, denounced dueling as "another stain cast upon the name of our fair young
city, to be taken up and enlarged upon by the correspondents of the Eastern press." Less than a month later, when the paper published the names
of delinquent debtors, the name of Thomas Warren appeared. Warren, a
ferryman and bricklayer, and a Southerner, took offense and challenged
Byers to a duel. In the November 24, 1859, issue of the *Rocky Mountain
News,* Byers responded: "To anyone who may feel like 'calling us out,' we
have merely to remark that you will only waste your time in inditing and
send[ing] us challenges, or other belligerent espistoles. You may murder
us . . . under the dignified name of a duel. . . . While we do live and conduct a public press, it shall be free and unfettered, fearless to rebuke the
wrong and uphold the right."

Later Byers complained in print about readers who threatened to anni-
hilate editors. On April 2, 1862, he wrote:

> This class of the genus-liped, almost wholly unknown in the Eastern
> States, flourishes . . . in the West. . . . An editor gives publicity to a cur-
> rent rumor on the street [and] the next morning in comes some over-
> grown mustached fellow . . . [who] wants a "retraction." He [the
> editor] publishes a letter reflecting ever so slightly on some individual—
> enter Mr. Man, and threatens blood and thunder, unless the thing is
> "made right." It is certainly wrong to criticize a man in a newspaper ma-
> liciously, but no matter how the case stands, the editor has to bear the
> brunt. . . . They [those objecting] go to law about it in the East which,
> on the whole, is probably the better way. And then, again, every little
> item is not noticed there as here. A good joke is laughed at, and forgot-
> ten. [But here in the West] it is brooded over until the meaning is so dis-
> torted that personality is seen sticking out of every line, and the fancied
> victim starts out with his friends to make a personal matter of it.

Such experiences were not limited to editors in Colorado. The editor of
the *Weekly Arizonan* wrote in his paper on April 23, 1870: "Recent devel-
opments go to show that to be a journalist in Arizona it is necessary to be a
fighting man—a first-class bruiser—unless the editor would have his paper
controlled by every demagogue who might feel disposed to dictate to him."

This illustration of the office of the *Rocky Mountain News* in Denver was taken from Albert D. Richardson's book *Beyond the Mississippi,* published in 1867, and is captioned "Armed neutrality." *(Author's collection)*

The same was true in Kansas, where Cecil Howes, a longtime newspaperman in Kansas, wrote that many editors "represent numerous black eyes, some broken noses; a cracked skull or two, some cauliflower ears and numerous abrasions of the scalp, hands and arms. They preferred a meat ax rather than finesse; direct action rather than deftness, and the record indicates they got the desired results."[11]

Abe Steinberger was such an editor in Kansas during the late nineteenth century. He founded the *Elk City Courant* in 1874 and filled his paper's columns with epithets, innuendos, and uncomplimentary names about people he did not like, including other editors. When his paper did not prove successful, he moved the *Courant* to nearby Longton later the same year. Again his practices failed to attract advertisers, and about a year later he moved the paper to Howard, Kansas. Later he became editor of one of two papers at Pittsburg, in southeast Kansas. One day, W. W. Graves, editor of the *St. Paul* (Kansas) *Journal,* was visiting Steinberger, who frequently attacked the editor of the town's other paper. Graves later wrote:

In 1893 we were accompanying Mr. Steinberger home to supper one evening when a large man jumped onto Steinberger as we passed a corner and soon had him down and was landing knockout punches on his face. Steinberger, like the writer, was tall, and hungry looking and no match for the 225 pound assailant. We grabbed the big fellow by the collar and yanked him off, but soon had to do some good sprinting to keep out of his reach. There was fiery language around there for a few moments, but that ended the fight.[12]

Colonel Dan Anthony was probably the best-known fighting editor in early Kansas. He was a man of strong convictions, and he did not hesitate to express them, much like his sister, Susan B. Anthony, who gained national prominence as a campaigner for women's rights. During his first week in the Kansas Territory, Anthony was attacked three times by proslavery men because he opposed slavery. Anthony first went west to Kansas during the summer of 1854, as a representative of what became the New England Emigrant Aid Society, a group opposing slavery and seeking to settle the Kansas Territory with northerners. He stayed only a short while and then returned to his home in Rochester, New York. Kansas, however, beckoned him back, and in 1857 he settled in Leavenworth, then a hotbed of abolitionist activity across the Missouri River from the slave state of Missouri. With financial help from friends, Anthony established the *Leavenworth Conservative* on January 28, 1861, with Daniel Wilder as editor. The following day the telegraph, which had reached Leavenworth early in 1859, carried the news that Kansas had been granted statehood. Anthony had a special edition of the paper printed and rode on horseback to distribute copies of his paper to territorial lawmakers, then meeting in Lawrence thirty-two miles to the south.

During these troubled times along the border between Kansas and Missouri, Anthony carried two big horse pistols. In the summer of 1861, he learned that a Confederate flag was being flown at a store in Iatan, Platte County, Missouri, just across the river. Anthony and a friend crossed the river to see it and visited the store where it was displayed; he returned to tell of the adventure in the columns of his *Conservative*. A competitor, R. C. Satterlee of the *Leavenworth Herald*, reprinted Anthony's version and then printed his own, concluding: "Whereupon, it is said, Anthony made double-quick time out of the store down the railroad track, with coat-tails extended, and the utmost horror depicted on his countenance." The next day Anthony and a friend called at the *Herald* office to see Satterlee. He was gone. Anthony and his friend left, only to meet Satterlee on the street a short distance away. Anthony demanded that Satterlee print a retraction. Satterlee refused and shots were exchanged. Satterlee was killed and Anthony's friend was wounded. A jury acquitted Anthony.

When the Civil War began, Anthony sold his interest in the paper to Wilder and became a lieutenant colonel in the First Kansas Cavalry, later known as the Seventh Kansas Volunteers. He fought first in Missouri and then in Mississippi and Kentucky, where in June of 1862 he was given temporary command of his brigade. He then ordered his officers and enlisted men not to arrest and deliver any fugitive slaves to their masters. This went contrary to the government's attempt early in the war to keep Kentucky from seceding by downplaying slavery. When asked to countermand the order, Anthony refused and was ousted from command. He remained with the brigade for nearly two months and then on September 3, 1862, resigned and returned to Leavenworth. Within a few months he was appointed postmaster, a position he held for five years. In 1863, while postmaster, he was also elected mayor of Leavenworth. Soon Brigadier General Thomas Ewing Jr., commanding the District of the Border at Kansas City, Missouri, declared martial law at Leavenworth, and some of his men seized some horses belonging to a black man. Mayor Anthony objected to both actions, declaring that Kansas was a loyal state, and that its civil authorities were entirely competent to enforce the laws. He then ordered Leavenworth police to recover the horses, which they did. Mayor Anthony was arrested on orders from General Ewing and escorted, under military guard, to Kansas City. Meantime the citizens of Leavenworth, outraged at what had happened, held a meeting and passed a resolution calling on President Abraham Lincoln to punish or censure those responsible. They then sent the resolution by telegraph to Washington, D.C. Martial law in Leavenworth was cancelled, and Anthony was set free. When he arrived back in Leavenworth the next day, he was cheered by townspeople.

In 1864 Colonel Anthony returned to journalism and purchased the *Evening Bulletin* at Leavenworth, a Republican paper started a few months earlier. Anthony was soon engaged in supporting Captain J. B. Swain, who had been sentenced by a court-martial at nearby Fort Leavenworth for killing rebels. In relating the story Anthony wrote in his paper: "Col. Jennison gave the orders for the killing, and when called on to testify, denied his verbal order." The next day the following advertisement appeared in the *Leavenworth Daily Times,* a competing paper: "D. R. Anthony, in his statement of May 11th, in regard to me, lied, and knew he lied, when making it. [Signed] C. R. Jennison."

Col. Dan Anthony was perhaps the most prominent fighting editor in early Kansas. He often carried two large horse pistols for protection and did not hesitate to use them. *(Courtesy Kansas State Historical Society)*

Jennison, armed with two eight-inch Colt Navy revolvers, met Anthony on the street the following day. Jennison called to Anthony, saying he wanted to talk. Anthony backed away and told Jennison he did not want to talk. In a flash, pistols were drawn and shots exchanged. Jennison was wounded in the leg. Anthony was arrested and charged with assault with intent to kill, but he was acquitted.

In 1871 Colonel Anthony purchased the *Leavenworth Daily Times* and merged it with his *Bulletin.* One day Anthony learned that a group of men had decided to stop the paper from printing the facts about a particular story. He armed an editor with one of his two big guns and took the other himself. The two men stood on the top step of the entryway into the newspaper office as the men came marching along the street. Someone told the mob's leaders that Anthony was ready for them. There was a short meeting of the leaders, after which the crowd melted away.

On a spring evening in 1875, Anthony went to the Leavenworth Opera House to see a show. As he was on a stairway, a rival editor named William W. Embry, publisher of the *Daily Appeal,* fired three shots at him. One of the balls struck Anthony, entering his right breast, just below the collarbone, severing an artery. The wound was thought to be fatal, but as one newspaper reported, "Death was warded off only by the iron constitution of its would-be victim." News of the shooting spread across Kansas, and the Topeka *Commonwealth* reported: "It seems to us that the shooting of Col. Anthony was unprovoked and criminal to the last degree. . . . It was, then, if Col. Anthony survives, a wicked, unnecessary and unprovoked assault; if Col. Anthony dies, a cruel, wicked murder." Colonel Anthony recovered. Embry was charged with assault but a jury acquitted him. Five years later, on New Year's Day 1880, he was shot and killed in a Leavenworth saloon by Thomas C. Thurston, his newspaper partner.

A few days later, on January 8, 1880, Dan Anthony wrote in the *Leavenworth Weekly Times*:

> It is reasonable to believe that the editorial shooting of the Missouri valley is nearly over. This is not a new country; we are no longer on the border. Let Leadville, San Juan, Las Vegas, and Salt Lake settle its politics with knives and revolvers. When swallow tails, plug hats, and white chokers come in, the manners of beats and tramps ought to go out. . . . Next to party passion, whiskey has been the chief provocative of all fights in the South and West. . . . Men who are cool and sober rarely shoot or get shot at. The outside public has less respect for our profession than it would have if we blowed, drank and shot less. Twenty or more years ago they all did it, but it is no longer a necessity. If we expect to be mourned when dead we must be reputable while living.

About the same time the *Kansas City Times* suggested someone should stuff and preserve a specimen Kansas editor before the race became altogether extinct.

Although Colonel Anthony's aggressiveness mellowed a good deal as he grew older, he still kept his two big horse pistols ready to go, laid on (or in the top drawer of) his desk at the newspaper office. H. H. Seckler, who learned the newspaper business under Anthony, recalled: "He was a hard task-master, yet a good one. His likes and dislikes were very marked. If he didn't like you it was best to remain in the background, for he never forgot why he disliked you." Although there was little violence associated with Anthony in his later years, he continued to present his views in print forcefully until he died of natural causes at the age of eighty in 1904.[13]

While Dan Anthony managed to live a long life, another controversial editor, J. Clarke Swayze, did not. He was editor of the *Topeka* (Kansas) *Daily Blade* in 1877. For a long time he had exchanged editorial jabs with

F. P. Baker, editor of the Topeka *Commonwealth,* and John W. and V. P. Wilson, former editors of the Topeka *Times.* Early in 1877 Swayze accused the Wilsons of padding the bills for county printing and otherwise questioned their integrity in the *Blade.* On March 27, 1877, John Wilson got his gun and went looking for Swayze. What happened was reported surrounded by black borders in the *Blade* the following day:

ASSASSINATION!
J. Clarke Swayze Brutally
Murdered at the Thresh-
old of His Own
Office

—

John W. Wilson, a Notorious
Character, the Murderer.

—

The Assassin Arrested and
Lodged in Jail

—

The city was thrown into the wildest excitement last evening by the assassination of J. Clarke Swayze, editor and proprietor of this paper. Mr. Swayze left his office almost half past five in the evening and went to the postoffice, to get the mail. Upon leaving the postoffice he was returning to his office through the alley in the rear. He stopped a few minutes to talk with F. Poppendick, and while engaged in conversation, John W. Wilson, the assassin, came across the avenue to where Mr. Swayze was. Mr. Swayze seeing him approaching and having been warned and advised that Wilson meant to do him harm, he started for his office, the back entrance of which was only but a few feet distant. Wilson called him by name and Mr. Swayze turned and said he wanted nothing to do with or say to him, and noticing that he, Wilson, had his hands behind him suspected mischief, and quickly drew his revolver with which he covered Wilson and could have shot him dead in his tracks but spared him, thinking no doubt, that he, Wilson, would desist and go away. Wilson sprang behind James Blue, who had accompanied him, and while behind this protection the cowardly murderer whipped out his revolver and shot at Mr. Swayze, the ball in all probability being the fatal one. Mr. Swayze then shot at Wilson but the ball only grazed one side of his cheek. As Mr. Swayze was a good shot this may be accredited to the

death-wound he had received. The testimony before the coroner's jury
shows that Wilson fired the first and last shots, and there is some doubt
as to whether four shots were fired, or Mr. Swayze fired only one shot.
After the shooting ceased, Wilson grabbed Mr. Swayze about the neck
and began pounding him over the head with his revolver, and that, too,
after the victim was dead.

The *Blade* then printed word for word the testimony given to the coroner's
jury and reported that Swayze left a widow and five children. Whatever the
merits of the feud, Wilson was tried and acquitted on May 30, 1877.

In Nevada another man named Swayze was involved in a feud with
George W. Derickson, owner of the *Washoe Times.* Although the details
are hazy, H. F. Swayze, a subscriber, apparently submitted a humorous article to the *Washoe Times* early in 1863. Either Derickson or his editor,
James Allen, realized that the article had been lifted from an earlier issue of
their paper. In the January 17, 1863, issue of the *Washoe Times,* they sarcas-
tically noted:

> A tall, gawky greenhorn dressed in a buckskin suit stepped into the
> *Times* office yesterday and handed us an article, which he was very anx-
> ious to have published. He said he had spent a great deal of time in get-
> ting it up, and wanted a dozen . . . copies of the paper containing the
> article . . . to send to his friends. The article was headed, "How I Got
> My Wife," and was signed "Ichabod." The said greenhorn, whose
> name, he informed us, is H. F. Swayze, is hereby informed that he can
> have a dozen copies of the *Times,* containing his article, by calling at this
> office and paying for same. His article, which he says cost him so much
> trouble and study to get up, was published in the second number of the
> *Times,* word for word. . . . The same greenhorn, who seems to think
> printers are as green as himself, brought in a long article several weeks
> since, ridiculing the town of Ophir and its inhabitants, and was very
> much surprised because his literary efforts were not appreciated and
> published. The manuscript copy of the last article of the said H. F.
> Swayze is at his disposal by calling at the *Times* office; and he can also
> purchase, for cash, several copies of the *Times,* containing this notice, to
> send to his friends.

When Swayze read the above, he rushed to the *Washoe Times* office,
crushed his copy of the issue in Derickson's face, and demanded a retraction and apology. Derickson refused and told Swayze the paper only

printed the truth. Swayze supposedly bellowed, "You're a goddamn liar!" and backed away as Derickson drew his derringer and fired. The ball struck Swayze's chin, breaking his jaw and two teeth, which he spit out. As Swayze ran, Derickson fired again but missed; Swayze then stopped, turned, drew his pistol, and fired twice. The first ball struck a bystander in the leg, but the second ball went through Derickson's heart, killing him instantly. Another account claims that Swayze and Derickson fired their weapons at the same moment. In any event, Swayze was arrested, tried, found guilty of manslaughter, and sentenced to three years in the Nevada state penitentiary.

During the Civil War there were other feuds in Nevada involving editors supporting the Union and Southern firebrands. In one instance Edwin A. Sherman, a staunch Union man and owner of the *Esmeralda Star* at Aurora, Nevada, was walking home on September 18, 1862, when Gustave Quinton, a Southern secessionist, beat Sherman with a club and shot him in the leg.[14]

At Carson City, David Sessons, a Princeton-educated reporter on the *Daily Appeal,* had a feud with R. R. "Deacon" Parkinson, editor of the *Nevada Tribune.* In March 1874, Parkinson charged in print that Sessons, who was born in South Carolina, was a "hireling secessionist," and the following day called Sessons "the obscene local reporter of our morning contemporary" and reported that he had been seen "sneaking along like a whipped cur." When Harry Mighels, editor of the *Daily Appeal,* made a trip to San Francisco and turned over his duties to Sessons, the feud heated up. Sessons described the English-born Parkinson as "a chance scribbler of foreign birth who shocks you by committing murder on his Sovereign's English at every breath." Parkinson came looking for Sessons and found him. Words were exchanged; Sessons got angry and struck Parkinson. His son, Edward J. Parkinson, announced publicly that he would get even for his aging father, and on April 9, 1874, young Parkinson and Sessons, both armed with revolvers, met on the street and exchanged shots. Both men were wounded but survived.[15]

Perhaps the most celebrated feud in Nevada involved Joe Goodman, editor of Virginia City's *Territorial Enterprise,* and Tom Fitch, editor of the rival *Virginia Daily Union.* While there are several versions of what happened, it appears their feuding in the columns of their papers reached a new height when Goodman made an attack on Fitch's character. Fitch responded in print with fairly mild words but sent Goodman a challenge demanding satisfaction. Pistols were selected, and on August 1, 1863, both men and their seconds and surgeons headed for Six Mile Canyon outside

Virginia City for the duel. But the sheriff and his deputies arrived on the scene and stopped the duel. Fitch and Goodman posted a five-thousand-dollar bond each and pledged to keep the peace. Both editors, however, were determined to have their duel, and almost a month later, on September 28, Goodman and Fitch with their parties traveled to a ranch in the Stampede Valley near Verdi, about ten miles from Virginia City. An account of what happened may be found in the Sacramento (California) *Union* of October 1, 1863:

> The weapons chosen were Colt's five-shooters, one chamber loaded; distance 15 paces. The two parties were upon the ground at half-past five o'clock, and the duel took place at about a quarter to six o'clock. . . . The word was given as follows: "Ready, fire—one—two—three—stop!" The parties took their places and the word was given. Fitch discharged his pistol at the word "fire," and Goodman almost immediately afterward. Goodman's shot took effect in Fitch's right leg, a little below the knee, producing a bad but not dangerous wound. Goodman was not struck.

The duel received much newspaper coverage, and Mark Twain covered the event for the *Territorial Enterprise.* In his autobiography Twain claimed that Goodman's second advised:

> Take all the risks of getting murdered yourself but don't run any risk of murdering the other man. If you survive a duel you want to survive it in such a way that the memory of it will not linger along with you through the rest of your life and interfere with your sleep. Aim at the man's leg; not at the knee, not above the knee, for those are dangerous spots. Aim below the knee; cripple him but leave the rest of him to his mother.

Twain added: "By grace of these truly wise and excellent instructions, Joe tumbled his man down with a bullet through his lower leg, which furnished him a permanent limp. And Joe lost nothing but a lock of hair."[16]

More than a decade after Mark Twain entered Comstock journalism, a young man named Wells Drury arrived and went to work as a reporter for Alf Doten, editor of the *Gold Hill News,* and was paid $7.50 a day, plus $2.50 a day as "whiskey money" to use for gathering news in saloons, where everyone met. On his first day Drury covered one murder, two fatal mine accidents, and a runaway stagecoach incident and gained a reputation as a gunfighter. When the paper went to press the afternoon of his first day, Drury was told it was custom that the new man on the staff had to stay, look over the first copy of the paper as it came wet off the press, and make any corrections caught in the proofreading. Everyone else went across the street to the Fashion, a saloon owned by Tim Dumar. Drury pulled the first copy from the press and began to read. What happened next is told in Drury's own words:

Standing back scanning a rough proof, I was almost hidden behind the big desk when a great, hulking fellow stormed in and banged his hand down on the desk, demanding to see the editor. On a platform slightly raised above the main floor of the office, I found myself next to the drawer which held the six-shooter. I recalled Alf's parting words, "Be careful—that gun has a hair-trigger." As soon as I saw the big stranger come stalking in I naturally thought of the revolver, and wondered if it was really loaded.

"I'm John Somers," he announced in stentor tones. "I want to see Alf Doten or whoever is in charge. You people have slandered me and I came to get an apology or get satisfaction, I cowhided an editor of this paper once, Conrad Wiegand—you may have heard of that little picnic."

"Did you?" I mildly confessed my ignorance of this episode.

"Well, I had to horsewhip *him,* and I guess I'll have to repeat the dose. Are you an editor?"

"N-no," I faltered. "I'm just one of the reporters—a *new* one. The managing editor is across the street, sir, getting a drink. If you'll wait just a few moments I'll run right across and tell him you want to see him."

"Oh no, you don't," roared Somers. "Not much! If I can't find the editor, by thunder, I've a mind to take the first man here I *can* find."

His hand manifestly was against all scribes, and as he raised it in a menacing manner and made a move in my direction, almost involuntarily I picked up that pistol. It had a hair-trigger, all right; and, sure enough, 'twas *loaded,* for it went off with a terrific bang, almost at my merest touch.

With his face white as chalk, Somers cried, "Hold on! Don't kill me!" turned and ran breaking the glass doors of the office as he slammed his way out. He was never seen again in Gold Hill.

At the sound of the shot and the shattering glass, all the staff of the *News* came running back across the Main street. I told the truth, that the gun went off accidentally.

"Oh yes, it did!" chorused the gang. "But you can't make us believe that you didn't try to wing Somers. Serve him right, too!"

This time *all,* man and boy, went over to the bar. Overnight I found myself pitchforked into a small reputation as a gun-fighter, strenuously as I disclaimed that doubtful honor.[17]

No review of pistol-packin' editors would be complete without including E. C. Boudinot, Jr., editor of the *Cherokee Advocate,* published at Tahlequah, in what is now eastern Oklahoma. In the spring of 1887, B. H. Stone, a fifty-four-year-old Kentuckian who had been a newspaperman in Missouri, arrived with his wife and family and started a competing paper called the *Tahlequah Telephone.* Stone opposed the opening of the Indian Territory to settlement, and he criticized the Cherokee government for spending too much money publishing the *Cherokee Advocate,* which

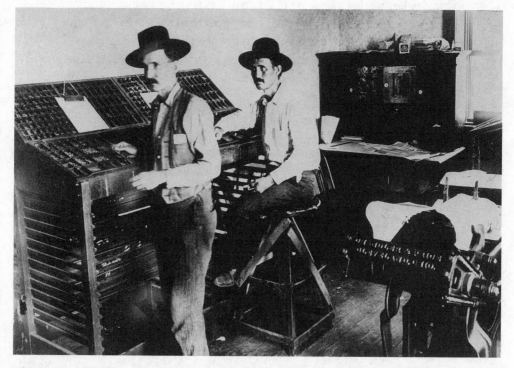

This is the typesetting corner of the printing plant of the *Cherokee Advocate* at Tahlequah, Indian Territory, in the 1890s, a few years after the paper's editor, E. C. Boudinot, Jr., shot and killed B. H. Stone, editor of the rival *Tahlequah Telephone.* The men in the photo are identified as Cale Starr (*left*) and T. Watie Foreman, who managed the paper for twenty-five years until it ceased publication in March 1906. The *Cherokee Advocate* printed in English and Cherokee. Founded in 1844, it was the first paper published in modern Oklahoma. *(Courtesy Archives and Manuscripts Division of the Oklahoma Historical Society)*

Boudinot edited. Stone suggested the Cherokee Council look into the matter. During the next few weeks he also editorialized on other matters about which he and Boudinot disagreed.

On Friday, October 1, 1887, Boudinot walked into Stone's office with a .45-caliber pistol and demanded the retraction of an editorial concerning disputes within the Cherokee tribe. When Stone refused, Boudinot shot him and walked out of the office. Stone died a few hours later. Boudinot was arrested several days afterward and charged with Stone's death; he pled self-defense. The trial was delayed for some time, and Boudinot died before it could take place.[18]

The public's view of newspapermen in the West was perhaps best summarized by Ambrose Bierce in the San Francisco *Argonaut* on August 3, 1878:

> One day last week a journalist of this city was severely beaten for something—I do not know what—that had appeared in a newspaper with which he is connected. . . . Without reference to this particular case, I beg leave to state, in the character of an expert who has a practical experience with both methods of redress, that it is more agreeable to a journalist to be shot than beaten. . . . There is no recorded instance of punishment for shooting a newspaper man. The restrictions of the game law do not apply to this class of game. The newspaper man is a bird that is always in season; sportsmen and pot-hunter alike may with assured impunity crack his bones with a bullet, or fill his skin with buckshot, compiling his carcass in a bag and exposing it for sale. I am quite serious in the statement that nobody in the United States has ever been hanged for killing a journalist; public opinion will not permit it. . . . Although the American public will not deny itself the pleasing pageant of some blameless citizen accomplishing serpentine contortions under the editorial pen, neither will it inhibit the flight of the blithe bullet through the editorial body.

CHAPTER SEVEN

REPORTING THE NEWS

If the Sentinel *is a little thin this morning, just bear in mind that the telegraph office was moving yesterday, the mail from the East didn't come in and there wasn't anybody in town who had enough accommodation to die, get married or have a baby.*

Laramie (Wyoming Territory) *Daily Sentinel*, 1875

UNTIL THE EARLY nineteenth century, the primary purpose of newspapers in America was to disseminate foreign news. The practice dated back to colonial times, when printers along the Atlantic coast reprinted stories from English and European newspapers and news related by sea captains in coffeehouses. One printer who did more was Henry Ingraham Blake, who started the *New England Paladium* in Boston on January 1, 1793. Today considered the father of modern news reporting because instead of going to coffeehouses to get the news retold there by sea captains, he would go down to the wharves, get into a boat, and often go out alone to meeting the incoming vessels. After getting the news from the captain or some member of the crew, he would rush back to the newspaper office and there, by memory and by a few notes written on his cuffs or on his fingernails, he would put the news into type as he sang to himself in a monotone.[1]

Blake may have been influenced by President James Madison, who, during the early 1790s, expressed the belief that government should encourage the extension of knowledge and the exchange of ideas in the new nation. As a result Congress passed the Post Office Act of 1793, permitting newspapers to send exchange issues free of charge to other papers.[2] This established an informal news service system later called by printers "scissors and pastepot" journalism, and it was in place in 1813, when Joseph Charless started the first newspaper west of the Mississippi River at St. Louis.

The content of Charless's *Missouri Gazette* reflected the scissors-and-pastepot approach to news reporting. Occasionally Charless would report the death or marriage of a prominent local person or make passing reference to a social or economic event in St. Louis, but the paper made no effort to chronicle local history as most dailies do today. Such organized local reporting did not develop in Missouri until the late 1850s. Until then editors relied almost solely on exchange papers for hard news, and because of this the *Missouri Gazette* did not always publish on the same day each week. In 1808 the St. Louis mail from the East was due on Tuesdays, the day the paper was supposed to publish. But Charless promised his paper for Tuesday, Wednesday, or Thursday, depending on the arrival of the mail. News from Europe was about three months old by the time Charless printed it. News from the Atlantic coast might take six to eight weeks to arrive in St. Louis; newspapers from Indiana Territory took two or three. Many stories were almost history when Charless reprinted them, but still they were news. For example, the July 26, 1808, issue of the *Missouri Gazette* reported the toasts given at a Fourth of July celebration in Indiana Territory under the headline PATRIOTIC EFFUSIONS.

Like most American newspapers of the day, the *Missouri Gazette* contained little local news that was not opinion. The July 26, 1808, issue included only seven paragraphs of local items, and one of them told readers Samuel Soloman would receive subscriptions and advertisements while Charless was away in Kentucky. The other six paragraphs read more like a gossip column without reference to sources:

At a special court of Oyer and Terminer, held at the court-house of this town, on Saturday last, the two Ioway Indians who were committed to prison some time ago for murder, were tried and found guilty. Sentence of death will be pronounced upon them this day. The trial of the Saukee who killed the white man at Portage de Sioux, will be tried this day.

It is with heart felt pleasure we announce the patriotism displayed by the St. Charles troop of horse, a few days ago; they offered their services to accompany Gen. Clark up the Missouri, in order to protect and assist in the building of the intended Fort, at or near the Osage river.

The Osages have lately committed so many outrages on the frontiers, that government have permitted the Delewar's, Shawnes's, Kickapoos, &s. &c. to go to war with them. We understand from some of the chiefs of the latter, that they will be able to bring 5,000 warriors into the plains, it is probable the Osages will get the Panies to join them; as the invaders must march into the plains, & as the Osages and Panies fight on horseback, there is no doubt of a warm and important campaign.

At the election for trustees for the Town of Saint Louis, on Saturday last, the following gentlemen were chosen: August Chouteau, Edward Hempstead, Bernard Pratte, Peter Chouteau and Alexander M'Nair, Esquires.

It is truly lamentable to observe the infamous calumny, the glaring falsehoods and gross ribaldry, which is daily sent forth by some of the newspapers of New-York, Philadelphia and other places, where the soil is curst by British agents and spies, and where printers are found base enough to prefer an English bribe to the esteem of their fellow citizens. It is generally known that the British merchants or manufacturers who are engaged in the trade of this country, send a partner to reside at some of the Atlantic ports, if he has not been an old tory citizen, he soon gets naturalized, he and his fellows pick up some rascally printer and pay him liberally to defame all those who struggle against British domination.

Three months after the above news items were published, Charless told his readers what subjects he considered newsworthy:

Essays on Morals and government, concise pieces on history, (particularly the early settlement and progressive growth of Louisiana,) Antiquities, Topography, Botony [*sic*] and vegetable Materia Medica, and Mineralogy, with such hints on Husbandry as may tend to induce the planter to embrace those wonderful advantages nature has thrown in his way, Indian manners and customs with their best speeches, Cases argued and determined in our Courts, or any thing that may contribute to enliven the passing moment by an ingenious Tale or Song, [which] will be gratefully received and carefully inserted.[3]

Obviously the *Missouri Gazette* was not a *news*paper in the modern sense.

In those days exchange papers were so important in the West that one unidentified editor wrote:

> He can live without towels
> Live without soap,
> Breakfast on vowels,
> And dine upon hope;
> He can live without galluses,
> Live without shirts,

Keep a-kicking despite
All manner of hurts;
He can manage to get on
Without advertisers,
But the editor cannot
Survive without scissors.[4]

Speeches and communications received by editors were published in
full. News was condensed. Local news received no notice or at best only a
few lines, while a similar event abroad might be given several inches of
space. The printers publishing western papers were not journalists. It was
not unusual for significant local or regional stories to go unreported, because most editors did not go out and gather news; they waited for readers
to bring it to them. An example would be the New Madrid, Missouri,
earthquakes that were centered in southeastern Missouri, along the Mississippi River about two hundred miles from St. Louis, on December 16,
1811. The ground between Cairo, Illinois, and the mouths of the White
and Arkansas Rivers rose and sank in huge undulations, turning uplands
into lakebeds, and heaving up swamps and riverbeds to dry and whiten in
the sun. The ground rolled with great waves, like waves in the sea. Vast fis-
sures opened in the ground, with spouts of muddy water going skyward
carrying fragments of shale and sand. And for miles the great Mississippi
River flowed backward. The stores and houses in the village of New
Madrid disappeared, many falling into the crevasses that had opened in
the earth. The cemetery in the churchyard fell into the river, and bodies
were swept away. Other towns in the region were also destroyed or heavily
damaged.

The *Missouri Gazette* did not carry its first report of the earthquake until
January 18, 1812, more than a month after it occurred, and the story consisted of only twenty-six words. It read: "The earthquakes of December
16th & etc. was [*sic*] felt in the flats of Ohio and Kentucky, some houses
have been thrown down but no lives lost." More than a month later, on
February 29, 1812, the paper published a two-hundred-word account of
the destruction at Cape Girardeau, Missouri, 170 miles south of St. Louis.

Unlike today, there was no sense of urgency in getting news to readers.
Looking through old issues of newspapers, one not uncommonly sees notices to the effect that news received too late for one issue would appear the
next week. When the early weekly papers in the West did report local news,
it usually was about crime. Other news came from exchange papers. Print-

ers clipped stories about politics, odd bits of information, and news tending toward the bizarre, such as a story of a man in London "who ate fire."

Since residents of new western towns came from somewhere else—many from the East—editors liked to clip and reprint stories from eastern exchange papers so that readers could keep up with the news from back home. It was through the exchange papers that western editors learned of changes in eastern journalism, especially those in New York City, where the penny papers had found that people wanted to read police-court reports and other local trivial and flippant news, emphasizing emotion for its own sake. The hiring of reporters to gather local news for the daily penny papers marked a major change in the practice of journalism, but western newspapers were slow to adopt the change, since most were weeklies published in small communities where proprietors could not afford to hire reporters to gather local news.

The distribution of exchange papers was dependent on the mail service, which was slow and often unreliable. Their arrival was contingent on the weather, road conditions, and other factors, and papers were sometimes weeks old when editors received them. When stage lines were established to carry passengers and the mail, they were no faster than steamboats, which also carried the mail. But west of the Missouri there were few rivers that steamboats could traverse, and the mail arrived by stage. In California early newspapers had to rely on steamers going around the Horn to bring them news from the Atlantic coast, and there was sharp competition in meeting the ships and getting condensed stories into the papers and on the streets quickly.

Letters received by readers, who shared them with editors, constituted a great deal of the news published by early California newspapers. It was in this manner that the *California Star* at Yerba Buena (San Francisco's early name) learned the fate of the Donner party, emigrants bound for California from Illinois. In the paper's second issue, January 16, 1847, it reported:

EMIGRANTS IN THE MOUNTAINS

It is probably not generally known to the people, that there is now in the California mountains in a most distressing situation, a party of emigrants from the United States, who were prevented from crossing the mountains by an early heavy fall of snow. The party consists of about sixty persons, men, women, and children. They were, almost entirely out of provisions, when they reached the foot of the mountain, and but for the timely succor afforded them by Capt. J. A. Sutter, one of the most humane and liberal men in California, they must have all perished in a few days. Captain Sutter as soon as he ascertained their situation, sent five mules loaded with provisions to them. A second party was dispatched with provisions for them, but they found the mountain impassable, in consequence of the snow. We hope our citizens will do something for the relief of these unfortunate people.

Three weeks later the paper reported on February 6 that "eight hundred dollars" had been raised at a public meeting to purchase provisions, clothing, horses, and mules to bring the emigrants to Yerba Buena. In the next issue, February 13, the *California Star* had more details and printed a story of almost two columns under the headline

DISTRESSING NEWS.

By Capt. J. A. Sutter's Launch which arrived here a few days since from Fort Sacramento—We received a letter from a friend at that place, containing a most distressing account of the situation of the emigrants in the mountains, who were prevented from crossing them by the snow,—and a party of eleven who attempted to come into the valley on foot. The writer, who is well qualified to judge, is of the opinion that the whole party might have reached the California valley before the first fall of snow, if the men had exerted themselves as they should have done.

The newspaper then printed a lengthy letter in which the writer described the emigrants' journey from the Missouri River, the route they followed toward California, and then:

. . . Scantily clothed and provided with provisions they commenced the horrid journey over the mountains that Napoleon's fete [*sic*] on the Alps was child's play compared with it. After wandering about number of days bewildered in the snow, their provisions gave out, and long hunger made it necessary to resort to that horrid recourse casting lots to see who should give up life, that their bodies might be used for food for the remainder. But at this time the weaker began to die which rendered it unnecessary to take life, and as they died the company went into camp and made meat of the dead bodies of their companions.

In 1847, the year the *California Star* printed the first accounts of the Donner party, the telegraph, which had been perfected by Samuel F. B. Morse in 1844, reached St. Louis from the East. Under the headline THE

MAGNETIC TELEGRAPH, the St. Louis *Republican* reported on December 18, 1847, that "the posts and wires have been put up to the east bank of the river [Mississippi], and in a few days connections will be made into the city. We are told that the wires work well and have been tested up to this point from Vincennes [Indiana]." Two days later, on December 21, the paper reported:

DISPATCHES BY THE LIGHTENING LINE
FOR THE REPUBLICAN

The lightening commenced operating vigorously yesterday at 1 p.m., and from that time there was a constant flow of communications from all cities along the line until a late hour, and many messages from our neighboring cities, as we may style New York, Philadelphia.

Dispatches from the East were three or four days old by the time they were received by and published in the St. Louis newspapers, but within days the service improved, and the papers were printing New York and Washington news of the preceding day. Because Congress refused to assume responsibility for the telegraph, private companies were organized in Missouri and California. As the Missouri company laid lines westward from St. Louis via Boonville to Kansas City, Missouri, which it reached in 1858, a California telegraph company linked San Francisco with San Jose, Stockton, Sacramento, and Marysville in 1853. The following year another California company established lines east of San Francisco to Placerville, Grass Valley, Auburn, and Nevada City. By October 1860 a telegraph line linked San Francisco with Los Angeles.

In June 1860 Congress passed the Pacific Telegraph Act, authorizing forty thousand dollars a year for ten years to any company constructing a telegraph from the western boundary of Missouri to San Francisco. The Pacific Telegraph Company, a subsidiary of the Western Union Telegraph Company, won the government contract and started to build the line west to Salt Lake City through Nebraska, while the Overland Telegraph Company, a subsidiary of the California State Telegraph Company, started to build the line eastward from Fort Churchill, Nevada, to Salt Lake City.

Meanwhile, the Pony Express bridged the gap between the telegraph terminals in the East and West. The mail service improved as riders on fast horses delivered the mail, including exchange papers, in half the time of steamers going around the Horn. The San Francisco *Bulletin* of April 16, 1860, reported:

It took 75 ponies to make the trip from Missouri to California in 10½ days, but the last one . . . had the vicarious glory of them all. Upon him an enthusiastic crowd were disposed to shower all the compliments. He was the veritable Hippogriff who shoved a continent behind his hoofs so easily; who snuffed up sandy plains, sent lakes and mountains, prairies and forests, whizzing behind him, like one great river rushing eastward.

But the Pony Express died soon after the telegraph lines were joined at Salt Lake City on October 24, 1861, and an exuberant editorial in the *New York Times* the next day caught the mood of everyone in the nation, especially newspaper editors. These lines capture the mood:

It is with almost an electric thrill that one reads the words of greeting yesterday flashed instantaneously over the wires from California. The magnificent idea of joining the Atlantic and the Pacific by the magnetic wire is today a realized fact. New York, Queen of the Atlantic, and San Francisco, Queen of the Pacific, are now united by the noblest symbol of our modern civilization.

Readers of western newspapers marveled at dispatches from the East published the following day, and with the arrival of the telegraph came cooperative newsgathering. Editors in communities linked by the telegraph began to rely on press association news reports transmitted by telegraph instead of stories clipped from exchange papers.[5]

In 1850 the only large city in the West was San Francisco, which became a major trading center after the discovery of gold in California. Only then did newspapers begin to report local news in San Francisco. But elsewhere in the West journalism remained in a state of arrested development until the late 1850s, when the storm over slavery forced it to overcome its inertia. Horace Greeley and his weekly New York *Tribune* exerted a considerable influence over many weekly editors in the West. Greeley was well known and respected as a successful newspaper editor and publisher, and he sent his paper to editors who wanted to receive it in exchange for their own. When any of them asked him how to operate a successful weekly, Greeley was free with his advice. In one letter to a weekly editor written on April 3, 1860, Greeley gave the following suggestions about how to cover local news:

Begin with a clear conception that the subject of deepest interest to an average human being is himself; next to that, he is most concerned about his neighbors. . . . If you will . . . secure a wide-awake, judicious correspondent in each village and township of your county,—some young lawyer, doctor, clerk in a store, or assistant in a post-office,—who will promptly send you whatever of moment occurs in his vicinity, and will make up at least half your journal of local matter thus collected, nobody in the county can long do without it. Do not let a new church be organized, or new members be added to one already existing, a farm be sold, a new house be raised, a mill be set in motion, a store be opened, nor anything of interest to a dozen families occur, without having the fact duly though briefly chronicled in your columns. If a farmer cuts a big tree, or grows a mammoth beet, or harvests a bounteous yield of wheat or corn, set forth the fact as concisely and unexceptionably as possible. In due time, obtain and print a brief historical and statistical account of each township,—who first settled in it, who have been its prominent citizens, who attained advanced years therein, &c. Record every birth as well as every marriage and death. In short, make your paper a perfect mirror of everything done in your county that its citizens ought to know. . . .

Take an earnest and active, if not a leading, part in the advancement of home industry. Do your utmost to promote not only an annual county Fair, but town Fairs as well. Persuade each farmer and mechanic to send something to such Fairs, though it be a pair of well-made shoes from the one or a good ear of corn from the other.

In the same letter Greeley also warned the editor:

Don't let the politicians and aspirants of the county own you. They may be clever fellows, as they often are; but, if you keep your eyes open, you will see something that they seem blind to, and must speak out accordingly. Do your best to keep the number of public trusts, the amount of official emoluments, and the consequent rate of taxation other than for common schools as low as may be. Remember that—in addition to the radical righteousness of the thing—the tax-payers take many more papers than the tax-consumers.[6]

By the end of the Civil War even editors of weekly newspapers were paying more attention to local news. They realized the reporting of local news was good for their newspapers' business. Covering local events attracted readers and gave them a sense of community and contributed to better government, transportation, churches, schools, police and fire protection, an adequate water supply and other things to improve their town and in turn their newspapers' business. But editors continued to respond to reader interest in stories of violence, crime, and police-court news. The *Boise* (Idaho) *News,* October 15, 1864, printed the following: "Justice Walker's Court—Oct. 13th. Joseph Enochs fined costs of arrest and trial for breaking and disarranging cigars in Kramer's store. William Jennison fined $20 for hitting John Griffiths a slap in the face, was satisfied with the verdict and inquired what it would cost to whip him all he wanted to."

Editors who could afford to do so hired one or more full-time reporters in an effort to increase their paper's local news coverage. They also encouraged readers to supply them with local news. It was not uncommon for editors to publish notices addressed "TO CORRESPONDENTS"— meaning any reader—asking that they send in news from their neighborhood. One of the earliest requests for news was made by the editor of the Santa Fe (New Mexico) *Gazette* on September 24, 1853. He advised readers that the paper "would be glad to receive every species of information about the territory." The editor of the Hot Springs (Arkansas) *Courier* of August 21, 1874, told his readers he wanted "news of passing incidents, local happenings, the crops, etc." The editor of the *Utah Weekly Miner* published at Salt Lake City, July 24, 1876, asked his readers for "correspondence from every part of the territory on new discoveries of every kind, on the inauguration of new enterprises, such as railroads, irrigating canals, or other public works, on manufactories, and, in fact, anything that has a bear on the growth and material prosperity of our territory." Sometimes an editor would thank readers in print for sending in news. But occasionally an editor would reject such news. The editor of the *Oregon Argus,* published at Oregon City, wrote in the July 28, 1855, issue that he had "received several communications which are admirably well-written, and no doubt contain a great deal of truth, but which we shall be compelled to decline publishing on account of their personal character." The editor of another paper, the *Oregon Spectator,* also published at Oregon City, observed in the May 30, 1850, issue that he had "received two or three rather ill-natured articles" which he declined to publish.

By the late 1870s some newspapers paid correspondents for the news they gathered in their neighborhoods or provided free subscriptions. A correspondent on the Rogue River in Oregon may have received a free subscription to the *Port Orford Post* for reporting local news, such as the following in that paper's June 30, 1881, issue:

The crops are looking well on the river, but I don't know how long they will be so, for the grasshoppers are as thick as graybacks on a bummer's corpse. They are taking the grass as clean as they can.

There is no one logging on the river now except Mr. Huntley, who is logging on a small scale.

The pack train that passed through Port Orford was packing the family of Mr. King to Rogue river to reside. They are not satisfied with this country, but I guess they will have to stay, for they are like the rest of us—they can't get away.

When George H. Hand started a newspaper called the *Settler* on October 18, 1884, in the small town of Ludell, Kansas, he stressed the importance of having correspondents who provided local news from their neighborhoods. He wrote: "When a country editor realizes the fact that he doesn't know it all, and accords merit where it belongs, correspondents will step to the front and assist in making a paper. We are even now looking, and probably won't be compelled to look long, for assistance with more brains than we possess."

In some predominantly rural areas of Texas, the treatment of local news had to be handled very carefully. By merely mentioning certain events, an editor could antagonize advertisers and subscribers or possibly involve himself in other people's personal vendettas. More often than not, an editor sought to maintain detachment from such stories, often using the passive voice. For instance, the *Texas Republican,* published at Marshall, carried an item on May 22, 1858, picked up from the *Texas Telegraph,* published at Sulphur Springs, which simply noted "that a personal rencontre occurred . . . between W. F. Scott and J. M. Brown in which the latter was killed at the time and the former subsequently died." On November 10, 1860, the *Texas Republican* carried the following: "Mr. J. O. Shook, editor and proprietor of the *Democrat,* at Waco, Texas, was killed on the morning of the 25th ult." The report states that he was killed by a printer.

Some western mining towns grew so rapidly that their weekly papers became dailies. The demand for local news increased and reporters were hired to gather it. Mark Twain, who served as city editor of the daily *Territorial Enterprise* at Virginia City, Nevada, during the 1860s, described the reporting responsibilities of his paper:

Our duty is to keep the universe thoroughly posted concerning murders and street fights, and balls, and theaters, and pack-trains, and churches, and lectures, and school-houses, and city military affairs, and highway robberies, and Bible societies, and hay-wagons, and a thousand other things which it is in the province of local reporters to keep track of and magnify into undue importance for the instruction of the readers of this great daily newspaper.[7]

The handling of local news varied from paper to paper and often depended on whether the paper was a daily or a weekly. In small towns a weekly editor might wait until a day or two before the paper was to be published to visit with townspeople to find out the local news. Other editors encouraged people to stop by the newspaper office and relate the news. Still other editors did both. When two men brought news to the editor of the Dodge City (Kansas) *Times,* he included everything he was told in his story on November 23, 1878:

S. B. Williams and C. E. Moore, who have sheep ranches south, called at our office Thursday, and reported having found the dead body of a man, on the big bend of Crooked creek, seven miles east of Ganz's. The body is described as follows: Height 5 feet and 9 inches; light curly hair tinged with gray; thin sandy whiskers; about 50 years; one tooth in upper part of mouth broken. Had on brown cotton coat, cotton shirt, red stoga shoes, common red overalls; black hat, narrow brim. Supposed to have been killed by Indians. Two holes in shirt indicated that shot passed through from side to side. A bullet was found 100 yards from the body. The body laid flat, face down. There was nothing to identify it. Some pieces of Ford county maps and some wheat chaff were found in vest pockets. Mr. Williams wrapped the body, which was nothing more than skin and bones, in some blankets and buried it where it lay. He marked a head board: "Unknown—killed by the Indians."
    Could the plains give up their dead, what tales would be told! How many have died with their "boots on"—"unwept, unhonored, unsung."

For daily newspapers the gathering of local news was usually a full-time task. Dan De Quille, the local news editor of the *Territorial Enterprise,* described what a local editor must do in the paper's June 28, 1868 issue:

The "local" must know to the minute when every meeting of all the religious societies, all the secret societies, gymnastic clubs, political clubs, fire companies, military companies and every other kind of company, club or society takes place. He must know the hours when the several Courts will be in session—what they have done and what they intend

Local news often dominated the front page of the *Caldwell* (Kansas) *Weekly Advance*. In this photo, circa 1895, John E. Wells, editor and publisher, inspects one of the first papers just off the press. *(Courtesy Kansas State Historical Society)*

doing; must attend the meeting of the city authorities and report their proceedings; must find out the names of all the passengers who arrive and depart by the public conveyances; must see all the dog, man, and cock fights—all the runaway teams, fires, funerals, foot races, festivals, picnics, parades, balls and public exhibitions and a thousand other things; for if he should miss seeing any of these things he is obliged to write twice as much about them—in order to make folks believe he saw them—as though he had actually been present. He must not forget while doing all these things to keep a sharp look out for the arrival of Hon. Polliwog Smith and at the same time keep well posted in regard to the movements of Hon. Augustus Bump and Rev. So-and-so and Professor This-and-that—all great men and each worthy of a neat little "Personal."

It was only natural that interviews would take on new importance as more and more newspapers reported local news. Certainly editors had to ask questions of people who knew what had happened, but to write the story as an interview was something new. The interview itself became a

Brigham Young as he appeared in 1877, about eighteen years after Horace Greeley interviewed him in Salt Lake City. *(Courtesy Western History Collections, University of Oklahoma)*

story. Probably the earliest published interview was conducted by Horace Greeley, who in 1859 came west and interviewed Brigham Young in Salt Lake City. Greeley's interview was published in the New York *Tribune* on August 20, 1859. Greeley's story about two hours of interviewing Young began as follows:

My friend Dr. Bernhisel, late delegate in Congress, took me this afternoon [July 13, 1859] to meet Brigham Young, President of the Mormon Church, who had expressed a willingness to receive me at two P.M. We were very cordially welcomed at the door by the president, who led us into the second-story parlor of the largest of his houses (he has three), where I was introduced to Heber C. Kimball, General Wells, General Ferguson, Albert Carrington, Elias Smith, and several other leading men in the church, with two full-grown sons of the president. After some unimportant conversation on general topics, I stated that I had come in quest of fuller knowledge respecting the doctrines and policy of the Mormon Church, and would like to ask some questions bearing directly on these, if there were [*sic*] no objection. President Young avowing his willingness to respond to all pertinent inquiries, the conversation proceeded substantially as follows:

H. G.—Am I to regard Mormonism (so-called) as a new religion, or as simply a new development of Christianity?

B. Y.—We hold that there can be no true Christian Church without a priesthood directly commissioned by, and in immediate communication with the Son of God and Saviour of mankind. Such a church is that of the Latter-Day Saints, called by their enemies Mormons; we know no other that even pretends to have present and direct revelations of God's will.

H. G.—Then I am to understand that you regard all other churches professing to be Christian as the Church of Rome regards all churches not in communion with itself—as schismatic, heretical, and out of the way of salvation?

B. Y.—Yes, substantially.

H. G.—Apart from this, in what respect do your doctrines differ essentially from those of our Orthodox Protestant Churches—the Baptist or Methodist, for example?

B. Y.—We hold the doctrines of Christianity, as revealed in the Old and New Testaments—also in the Book of Mormon, which teaches the same cardinal truths and those only.

Publication day in Salt Lake City for the *Deseret News*. The paper was published in the Deseret Store and Tithing Office, seen in the background. The paper first appeared as a weekly on June 15, 1850. After seventeen years as a weekly and semiweekly, the *Deseret News* became a daily on November 20, 1867. *(Author's collection)*

Other newspapers soon began to publish interview stories containing intimate details of the behavior and the words of well-known persons, but such stories were not welcomed by everyone and were frequently criticized as unwarranted invasions of privacy. One writer called the interview "the most perfect contrivance yet devised to make journalism an offence, a thing of ill savor in all decent nostrils."[8]

Another new development in reporting was the eyewitness account. This story form originated in the West during the Mexican War of 1846. After Texas was annexed by the United States in 1845 and the Mexican government refused to recognize the independence of Texas, or the Rio Grande as an international boundary, Mexico severed its diplomatic ties with the United States, which declared war against Mexico on May 13, 1846. Americans eagerly volunteered for military service, and a few newspapers sent reporters to report the war. In one dispatch, an unidentified reporter wrote:

> While I was stationed with our left wing in one of the forts, on the evening of the 21st, I saw a Mexican woman busily engaged in carrying bread and water to the wounded men of both armies. I saw this ministering angel raise the head of a wounded man, give him water and food, and then carefully bind up his wound with a handkerchief which she took from her own head. After having exhausted her supplies, she went back to her own house to get more bread and water for others. As she was returning on her mission of mercy, to comfort other wounded persons, I heard the report of a gun, and saw the poor innocent creature fall dead! I think it was an accidental shot that struck her. I would not be willing to believe otherwise. It made me sick at heart, and, turning from the scene, I involuntarily raised my eyes toward heaven, and thought, great God! and *is this war?* Passing the spot next day, I saw her body still lying there with the bread by her side, and the broken gourd, with a few drops of water still in it—emblems of her errand. We buried her, and while we were digging her grave cannon balls flew around us like hail.[9]

While eyewitness reporting was more the exception than the rule during the late 1840s and early 1850s, it became more common during the Civil War, when reporters accompanied the soldiers and witnessed battles, including those in the West. Thomas Wallace Knox, reporting for the New York *Herald,* covered the battle of Wilson's Creek, in southwest Missouri south of Springfield, when Union troops lost to Confederate soldiers on August 10, 1861. Two days later, after retreating with the Union forces,

Knox and another reporter stopped at a small country inn on the Gascon-
nade River, southwest of Rolla, Missouri. Knox took his pen and wrote the
following lead to his story:

> Nathaniel Lyon, courageous Yankee from Connecticut, refused to yield
> Southwest Missouri to the Rebels without a fight. Now he lies dead in a
> Springfield funeral parlor, dressed in his new uniform which he never
> wore in life. The Union army in Missouri flies in retreat before the Rebel
> hosts of McCulloch and Price. This is what happened day before yester-
> day along the banks of Wilson's Creek; this is how a force of 5,500
> Union volunteers from Iowa, Kansas, Missouri hurled themselves
> against three times as many Rebels.[10]

During the Civil War readers became accustomed to news about the
war, and by the time peace came, newspapers in the West were no longer
primarily journals of opinion. While opinion still held an important place,
and most newspapers proclaimed allegiance to one political party or another, newspapers were reporting more local, regional, and national news.
The telegraph had made this possible. Editors seemingly sensed for the
first time the power of news in attracting readers, and news began crowd-
ing out editorials and articles of opinion in some newspapers. Foreign
news no longer dominated, and local news especially received its fair share
of attention.

Human interest stories also began to play an important role in attracting
readers. For instance, when showman P. T. Barnum traveled across Kansas
by railroad, he stopped in central Kansas. His experiences were reported
in the *Daily Kansas State Record,* published at Topeka, on October 26,
1870:

> P. T. Barnum, wishing to gratify his taste for curiosities, stopped off at
> Hays City to see the "man-eaters" of that town "eat." He fell in with sev-
> eral of the more carnal-minded youth of the place, who invited him to be
> sociable and take a hand at poker. The cards that were dealt to his com-
> panions literally "knocked the spots off" of anything Mr. Barnum had
> ever "held" in his life, and, when the exercises of the solemn occasion
> were ended, Phineas mourned the departure of $150 that he will never
> see, not any more. "Woolly horses" and "Feejee mermaids" are nice
> things to have, but they don't weigh out much playing poker at Hays
> City. Barnum will probably incorporate his Hays City experience into
> his famous lecture, "How to Make Money."

And then there was the story in the Cawker City (Kansas) *Sentinel* published during the summer of 1872:

> Mrs. Mary C. Hawes, of Crooked creek, four miles north of Bulls City, has this season, with a yoke of oxen driven by herself, broken 25 acres of prairie; drove the oxen to break 25 acres more; has shot two buffalo with her rifle, which she calls "Betsey." Her plowing is very well done and with the rifle she is an expert. She has the best crops of corn, etc., that there are in her neighborhood.

John P. Clum (*center*) purchased the weekly *Tucson Citizen* in 1877 and moved the paper to Florence, where it remained until early 1879. Clum then moved the paper back to Tucson and made it a daily. In 1880, when a rich silver strike was made seventy miles southeast of Tucson, at Tombstone, Clum sold the *Citizen,* moved to the boomtown, and started the *Tombstone Epitaph.* This photo was taken during the 1880s, when Clum was an Apache Indian agent. (*Courtesy Western History Collections, University of Oklahoma*)

Our "devil" [printer's devil] is very anxious to know if Mrs. Hawes is a widow. Says he wouldn't mind settling on that farm!

By the late 1870s most editors did not hesitate to write news stories on events they had witnessed personally. When John P. Clum, editor of the *Citizen,* published at Florence, Arizona Territory, was among the victims in a stagecoach robbery, he gave the following firsthand account in the August 2, 1878, issue of his paper:

BOLD STAGE ROBBERY

The editor has frequently read of the daring deeds of fierce highwaymen and several times within the last six months it has been necessary for us to describe the bold operations of these desperadoes, but never until day before yesterday have we had the good fortune to witness the modus operandi by which these members of the shotgun gentry extract the valuables from a stage coach and passengers by the simple but magical persuasive power of cold lead.

The stage left Tucson on Wednesday at 2 o'clock p.m., the usual hour, Auther Hill was driver and Veterinary Surgeon Wheatley, J. P. Clum and one Chinaman were passengers. The ranch at Point of Mountain, eighteen miles from Tucson, was reached at about 5 p.m., a light rain was falling and our party was correspondingly happy. About ten minutes later we struck the sand at the Point of the Mountain and our horses took a slow walk. Suddenly some one accosted the driver in rather harsh tones to which he made some reply and stopped the coach, but before we could imagine the cause or suspect anything serious a tall form in mask appeared at the left side of the coach and covering us with a Spencer rifle and a six-shooter commanded us not to move at the peril of our lives. THE CITIZEN reporter had a pistol but it lay on the floor of the coach. Mr. Wheatley had one also, but it was on the seat under a blanket. The attack was in open daylight and so unexpected that we were wholly unprepared, and once under the cover of his arms we were quite willing to obey his commands. He remarked, "The first one that moves I'll kill deader than h——l; you may get me but I'll get some of you first and I'd just as soon die as not." He then ordered out the express box and two mail sacks, which orders were promptly executed by driver Hill; he next requested the Heathen to disgorge his loose change, which amounted in all to six dollars. Then with exquisite grace he leveled his rifle on the editorial innocent and demanded the net profits of THE CITIZEN office since its location in Florence. Three Mexican dollars was the best showing we could make and upon these we refused to allow any discount. The bold robber was finally induced to accept this humble contribution as our best effort and the range of his battery was changed so as to cover Surgeon Wheatley's manly form. This was more agreeable to us but less comfortable for Wheatley. The effect of this change of range was an involuntary contribution from Wheatley of $28. After the collection had been taken the robber remarked that some one in our party "looked like a sick man." No doubt he was correct, whoever he intended to address. After scanning the coach for a moment he ordered us to drive on which order we found it quite convenient to obey, and just as we started this persuasive wayfarer extended a very polite invitation for us to come back and fight him as soon as we felt disposed to do so. We were soon beyond the reach of our arbitrary visitor and felt less need of the life insurance companies than we had a few moments previous. Having no guns we concluded to go on to Desert Station, seven miles distant and report.

We have some causes for self-congratulation as we wore on our person a watch and chain which represents to us $225. The chain was exposed on our right side but passed unobserved by the robber.

We learn by dispatches from Tucson that the express box was empty and there was nothing of great value in the mails, hence as he only obtained $37 from the passengers his booty was small and he will no doubt feel it necessary to rob another coach soon, passengers and officers should be correspondingly careful.

Editor John P. Clum, who also studied law in an attorney's office at Florence, later went to the boom mining town of Tombstone, about seventy miles southeast of Tucson, and in 1880 started the weekly *Tombstone Epitaph*. When someone asked him how he came to name the paper, Clum supposedly replied, "Every tombstone needs an epitaph." Before he sold his paper in 1886, Clum had helped to promote civic growth and also rid Tombstone of outlaws. Later he worked for the San Francisco *Examiner* before leaving the newspaper field.

The style used in writing news varied widely in the West during the early years of newspapers. A review of issues of papers published across the West in 1850 shows that editors often did not bother giving the full names of people in the news. It was simply Mr. Jones or Mr. Smith, but by the late 1850s full names were appearing in most stories. Many editors also continued to use the chronological form of storytelling where the reader had to read the full article to learn what happened. Other editors adapted

Geronimo, a medicine man and leader of the southernmost band of Chiricahua Apache, is here being interviewed by an unidentified reporter (*left*). The man on the right is an interpreter. This photo was made in 1908 at Fort Sill, Oklahoma, about a year before Geronimo died. *(Courtesy Archives and Manuscripts Division of the Oklahoma Historical Society)*

to the changed method of story organization that developed during and just after the Civil War, in which the basic elements—who, what, when, where, why, and how—appeared toward the beginning of a story. Nevada editor Wells Drury taught young reporters never to write "It is reported," or "We are informed," or anything like that. He told them to find out the facts and then give them as they actually happened. Drury later wrote that this practice was one reason for the infrequency of retractions in early Nevada newspapers, adding, "It didn't pay to make mistakes in a country where every man was his own judge as to whether his dignity had been offended."[11]

Occasionally in reporting court news, editors resorted to a little humor. The editor of the *Wilson County Citizen* at Fredonia, Kansas, reported the following on May 29, 1874:

The accomplished burglar and thief, Mr. Chase Noble, Esq., who knows how to pick five locks and break jail twice all in one-half hour, has concluded, by unanimous request of twelve of his countrymen, to accompany the sheriff of this county to Leavenworth soon for the purpose of inspecting the public improvements of that place. He contemplates remaining about ten years.

The editor of the *Kansas Reporter* at Louisville, Kansas, entertained his readers with the following on May 3, 1877: "Sheriff Shehi has no use for handcuffs. When he gets a prisoner he just cuts off the fellow's pants buttons and keeps him busy holding up his breeches while the sheriff quietly marches him to jail without any trouble. Necessity is said to be the mother of invention, but in this case it is the father."

Court news and stories about local law and order became a mainstay in most western papers, especially in the wilder towns. On July 13, 1878, the Dodge City (Kansas) *Times* reported:

Friday is said to be an unlucky day. It is hangman's day. Some star having special gravity struck with sporadic force yesterday, and illuminated some of the social phases in the zodiac of Dodge City.

There was a gambling sport who was chaired by a pugilistic concubine.

A drunken prostitute led to the "tannery" by her stocking-leg protector. But it was no go; she broke loose and was again on the street.

A gambler was spittooned on the head by a show-case capper. Some blood.

Another event. The morning air echoed with the cries of "police"—a stranger had come to town and was taken in, verifying the adage that a fool and his money is soon parted. He was from near St. Joe and on his way to the San Juan country. He had a pony he wished to sell, and was lured into an "insurance office" by a seemingly rural youth, who informed him that the "insurance" agent wished to purchase a hoss. It was the lottery agent who engaged the pretended rural youth in a game of chance, which induced the dubious Missourian to stake $81, which suddenly disappeared before two flying coat tails; but which was robbed from him, says the innocent Missourian; as he had no intention of betting on any game or engaging in any lottery scheme.

After this, of course, the pretended rural youth and "insurance" hoss dealer were not visible to the Missourian's optics—they had taken the back door, and old St. Joe, squealing like a stucked pig, rushed frantically into the street and vociferously yelled "police. . . ."

P.S. Since the above was put in type the "show cases," like the Arabs, have folded their tents and silently stole away. They left on the eastern bound train last night. The pressure was bearing a little hard, and they found it convenient to leave for other parts.

And then there was the following item about a new local law that appeared in the *Gridley* (Kansas) *Light* on July 21, 1911:

AN ORDINANCE

Making it unlawful for any person to practice what is known as "Goosing" another person, and fixing a penalty for the same:

Be it proclaimed by the Mayor and Councilmen of the City of Gridley, Kansas:

Section I. That it shall be unlawful for any person to punch another person with thumb, finger, stick or any other thing, in the manner commonly called and known as "goosing."

Section II. Any person convicted of the violation of Section I of this ordinance shall be fined in any sum not to exceed twenty-five dollars and shall stand committed to the city jail until said fine and costs are paid.

Passed by the council and approved by the mayor, in special session, this 20th day of July, 1911.

J. R. ANSPAUGH, Mayor

C. E. Pilcher, City Clerk.

ONE OF THE BEST newspapers in the West during the last two decades of the nineteenth century was William Rockhill Nelson's *Kansas City Evening Star,* founded in 1880 at Kansas City, Missouri. The competition was stiff—two morning and two evening papers in the English language and two German papers—but Nelson, who was thirty-nine years old and had never been a practicing journalist, sensed the future wealth and greatness of Kansas City. He hired seven reporters when the paper began, an unprecedented number for all but the largest newspapers in the West. Nelson's idea of a good reporter was once expressed when he was advising a new member of the staff: "Remember this; the *Star* has a greater purpose in life than merely to print the news. It believes in doing things. I can employ plenty of men merely to write for the paper. The successful reporter is the one who knows how to get results by working to bring about the thing he is trying to do."

The importance of the reporter was constantly emphasized in the *Star's* office. To be useful around a newspaper, Nelson said, a man must have a reporter's instinct. He might report news or he might report ideas. But at bottom he must be a reporter and not a "journalist," a word Nelson had no patience with. He added:

The reporter is the essential man on the newspaper. He is the big toad in the puddle. . . . we could get on pretty well without our various sorts of editors. But we should go to smash if we had no reporters. They are the fellows whose work determines whether the paper shall be dull or interesting, whether it shall attract readers or repel them. . . . It is the reporter with the nose for news. He is the only fellow who has any business around newspapers or magazines. In general their job is not to produce literature but to do reporting. The essential, then, is the nose for news—the instinct to recognize the real story in an event or situation. This, I presume, is inborn. If a man hasn't it let him forsake the newspaper field. He will never make a success of it. With this news instinct must come industry. Often a good pair of legs makes a good reporter. The newspaper man must always be on the job, always hustling, always ready to go to any inconvenience or suffer any fatigue to get the news. And above all, so far as the routine of reporting goes, he must be honest and accurate. At the same time he must never be a machine. Many reporters are ruined by allowing themselves to become messengers of the city editor. They cover assignments, and that is all they do. . . . Finally, the reporter must be, above all, a good citizen in all that term implies. He must be honest; he must be sincere. He must be against shams and frauds. His heart must be right. Mere smartness will never give permanent success.

Nelson, who constantly gave leads to his reporters, crusaded against a monopoly in the local street-railway system, against corruption in municipal affairs, against fraud in elections, and against gambling and vice. The paper not only offered rewards for the arrest and conviction of those trying to bribe city officials, but he employed his own detectives. One of Nelson's longest crusades was for parks and paved boulevards shaded by trees. Nelson even established nurseries of his own and experimented to see what trees and shrubs would grow best along the city's streets.[12]

THE INVESTIGATIVE REPORTING often emphasized by newspapers today is nothing new. It existed in the East during the nineteenth century. It also could be found in the West when a reporter or editor had the time and inclination to dig deeply into a story. In one instance, however, it was a *printer* named Bill, who worked on the *Florence* (Arizona) *Citizen*, who was responsible for exposing a tremendous fraud. It started when James

Addison Reavis came forward with what appeared to be ancient Spanish documents. The government recognized them as legitimate, and he was granted a tract of land in Arizona 236 miles long and 78 miles wide. Reavis quickly became known as the "Baron of Arizona," but Tom Weedin, editor of the *Florence Citizen,* sensed fakery. Weedin's views, however, were soon drowned out when Robert G. Ingersoll, a well-known attorney, declared the claim flawless.

Six years later, however, a printer named Bill, who worked for Weedin, went on vacation and traveled to Phoenix, the capital. While there he took time to look at the printing exhibited in old documents on file in the court-house. When he inspected the documents used by Reavis to acquire his land grant, Bill discovered one very "ancient" deed had been printed in a type that had been invented only a few years before the filing of the claim in 1887. In examining the rest of the documents, Bill discovered that one of the documents plainly bore the mark of a Wisconsin paper mill that had only been in existence about a dozen years. Reporting his finding, his boss, Tom Weedin, was vindicated, and Reavis was convicted of fraud in January 1895 and sentenced to six years in prison.[13]

Getting a scoop or an exclusive on an important national story was only a dream for most small-town editors, but for J. H. Downing in Kansas and his Hays City *Star,* it was a dream that seemed to come true on July 6, 1876. Downing had the forms on his press and had just started to print the afternoon edition, when a messenger brought a telegram from a friend named Cushing at Fort Wallace, about 125 miles west of Hays. Cushing, a telegrapher, had sent an important message from Fort Wallace to Fort Leavenworth. He then sent the same message to Downing, who, after read-ing the telegram stopped the press, picked up a stick and put into type the news he had just received. At 5:00 p.m. he printed and distributed the paper with the following story on the front page:

WAR!!
OUR TROOPS SURPRISED BY
THE SIOUX
GENERAL CUSTER AND HIS ENTIRE COMMAND KILLED.
[SPECIAL DISPATCH TO THE STAR.]

WALLACE, JULY 6, 1876

Editor Star:

News just received that General Custer had a fight with four thou-sand Sioux Indians on June 15. General Custer and his entire command, of five companies, are reported killed. Every member of Custer's family were killed, including his two brothers, nephew and brother-in-law.

The fight took place about 30 or 40 miles below Little Horn Mountain. The troops were nearly all killed by the first volley fired by the Indians.

As Downing later recalled:

The officers at Fort Hays were greatly excited. When they got the news, cavalry officers came galloping over to town and crowded into the *Star* office. They said they didn't believe the story—that it couldn't be true, else the post commander would have received word direct from Fort Leavenworth. I told them I knew every word of it was true but I couldn't divulge the source of my information. To do so would in all likelihood have cost my telegrapher friend his job. Then the post officers telegraphed Fort Leavenworth and a few hours later they received full information of the story we have printed. The next morning, Friday, July 7, the morning paper at Leavenworth printed the news of the massacre. I knew then we had 'beat' every other paper in Kansas in publishing the news of the battle.[14]

The Hays City *Star* was the first paper in Kansas to publish the story, and the same day the *Tribune* at Bismarck, Dakota Territory, published the news in an extra, but neither the *Tribune* nor the *Star* was the first paper with the news. That distinction goes to the *Bozeman* (Montana) *Times,* which published the first scant details of the event on July 3. The following day, the *Helena Daily Herald* published the full story.

Mark Kellogg was the only newspaper reporter with Custer and his men during the battle. He did not survive. Kellogg, a reporter for the *Bismarck Tribune,* had taken the place of Col. C. A. Lounsberry, editor and publisher of the *Tribune* and a correspondent for the *New York Herald,* who had to remain in Bismarck because of sickness in his family. Kellogg's body was found three days after the battle, along with his notes, which served as the foundation for a lengthy story of the battle transmitted by telegraph from Bismarck to the New York *Herald.*[15]

BY THE LATE nineteenth century, reporters for many western papers had incorporated storytelling techniques in writing stories, and editors made effective use of headlines to enhance the stories. A good example is the following story that appeared in the first issue of the weekly *Territorial Topic* at Purcell, Chickasaw Nation, Indian Territory, on August 1, 1889:

FIRST BLOOD FOR LEXINGTON
TWO MEN KILLED AT ONCE

—

THE TRUSTY WINCHESTER AND HANDY
SIX SHOOTER USED WITH
TERRIBLE EFFECT.

—

**Francis Jones shoots the City Marshal
and is in return shot by him.—The
little town all excitement**

—

About 3 o'clock Tuesday evening the report was received here that two men had been shot in the town of Lexington, just across the river. This was presently verified by the arrival of two men from that place in quest of a physician and U.S. Marshal. Having learned this much, a TOPIC reporter lost no time in procuring a spotted pony and making for the scene of the tragedy; where, upon our arrival, we found the people of that quiet little village gathered here and there in squads, discussing the bloody affair. Accosting the first denizen we met we were piloted to a little building, on the south side of Broadway, owned by James Lappin, and occupied as a residence, where, just inside on a cot close to the window, the summer breezes was [*sic*] wafting over the haggard features of Francis S. Jones, one of the principals of the bloody tragedy. He was suffering the most intense agony from a wound made by a ball fired from a 44-calibre Smith & Wesson revolver in the hands of Henry Simmons, city marshal. The ball entered just above the hip on the left side and passed squarely through his body, ranging upward, striking the center of the fourth rib on the right side breaking it and lodging just beneath the skin, where it was found and extracted by Dr. G. O. Johnson.

Leaving here we proceeded just across the street and a few doors to the east to the bakery and restaurant, which was the home of Henry Simmons, and there in the front room, another scene presented itself, sadder than the first, for on another cot lay a man—but all his suffering was over—covered with a shroud and surrounded by a weeping widow and three orphan children, lay the cold body of Lexington's brave marshal, in that placid but eternal sleep. He too had been shot, a ball from a 3S Winchester rifle fired by Francis S. Jones had entered near the pit of his stomach and ranging downward and back, lodged in the heavy bones of the hip or in the pelvis bone, causing death in a very few moments.

When we got to Lexington we found Dr. Johnson and Marshal Carr of this place [Purcell] had both preceded us, but the services of the latter were not needed.

The writer then went on to describe the inquest held by the U.S. commissioner and what each witness said. The writer ended the story with the fact that Jones, the wounded man, "lingered till 5 o'clock Wednesday morning when he was called before a higher tribunal to answer for his crime, if his intention was to commit a crime."

Editors of western newspapers had a great deal of freedom to report what they wanted about people and events in their communities, but most appear to have been responsible. The editor of the *Grand Junction* (Colorado) *News* was one of them, as he told his readers under the headline "Must We Print It?" on June 14, 1893:

How many times for every issue do you suppose the newspaper man asks himself the question which constitutes the heading for this article? For, there is not a single issue of his paper in which he reports everything he is "onto," and which would be genuine and relished news to most of the community.

There are a few innocent denizens of every community who think the newspaper ought to tell everything it finds out. But, Oh My! Just suppose it should try that policy. Before noon the fighting editor would have to lick half the community, and that would give the community a bad reputation.

The newspaper man could keep any community in a stew, if he were a mind to. But would anybody think any more of him for that? And would he be doing his constituents any good by such a course?

There are opportunities in every community to stir up sensations. But would it mend matters to expose "dirty linen"? Or would it give the community credit and standing among strangers, or would it not disgust all decent people at home? Oh, it isn't always because the newspaper man doesn't tell them. It is more often because he has learned to be charitable. If it is possible for a mistake to be corrected, isn't it best to keep still and give the perpetrator a chance to correct it than it would be to fire away at him, and break him down and, with him, break down a dozen innocent people?

The newspaper man may sin sometimes—very likely he does. For he is human, just like the preachers and the saints. And he remembers that the community all around him is made up of human creatures.

This is the first issue of *The Morning Reporter,* a daily established by R. C. Harper and Sam M. Wassam on September 1, 1881, at Independence, Kansas. The paper had a circulation of four hundred. After four months Harper bought out Wassam's interest and published the paper as an independent. Harper was born in 1840 in Ohio, where he began learning the printing trade at the age of thirteen. After serving in the Union army for about two years, he headed west to Kansas and worked as a printer before joining Wassam to start the paper. Containing much local news plus material taken from exchange papers, *The Morning Reporter* was typical of so many small-town dailies in the West during the 1880s. Local advertising was displayed on page one while national advertising, consisting mostly of patent medicine ads, appeared on page four. *(Author's collection)*

CHAPTER EIGHT

PERSONALS AND MISCELLANEOUS

The only qualities for real success in journalism are ratlike
cunning, a plausible manner, and a little literary ability.
The capacity to steal other people's ideas and phrases . . .
is also invaluable.

—Nicholas Tomalin

MANY YEARS AGO in a small northern Texas town, I asked the longtime editor of a weekly newspaper why he was more successful than other weekly editors in his area. The editor replied, "It is very simple. Each week I print the names of as many of my readers as I can. Everyone reads the paper each week to see if their name or the names of people they know are there." While his readers cared about what happened elsewhere, he understood human nature. He knew, as Horace Greeley had so memorably pointed out years before, his readers' first interest was in themselves and their neighbors. Thus the editor made his newspaper a local institution by concentrating on people, places, and things in his community.

The columns of successful weekly and small daily newspapers in the Old West contained brief local items, or *personals,* about people. To the editor and his readers they were news, but to most outsiders they were not. Gathering such local items took more time than collecting information on more important news stories since personals often started as rumors the editor had to confirm. But editors learned quickly the extra work was well worthwhile. Personal items were the backbone of small newspapers. It was as though the editor were talking over the back fence to his or her readers, telling them what he had seen or heard. Personals were very much like gossip, and readers often perused the personals before reading the rest of the newspaper.

Some editors scattered personal items throughout their papers. Others isolated them in columns. Early San Francisco newspapers had such columns reported under bylines such as "Paul Pry" and "Night Owl." W. W. H. Davis, editor of the Santa Fe (New Mexico) *Weekly Gazette*, introduced a column entitled "Local Items" during the early 1850s, and as newspapers were established in the new territories of Kansas and Nebraska in that period, many of them established columns of short local items.

By the 1870s local news columns of many western weeklies had an impressive array of banner lines with such titles as "Local Record of Passing Events," "What We See and Hear," "Hither and Yonder," "Local and Miscellaneous," "Local and Personal," "Local Intelligence," "Local Affairs," and so forth. In the small towns most editors were very informal in the portrayal of purely local happenings, including many personal notes picked up by the editor in conversations along Main Street.

The editor of the *Morning Reporter* published at Sumpter, Baker County, Oregon, ran his paper's personals on the front page. In one issue they included:

Judge J. D. Goss is in Baker.

Mr. and Mrs. Louie Rusk of Bourne were in the city yesterday and went to Baker.

County Commissioner W. H. Gleason is in Baker, attending an adjourned session of the county court.

Col. Tom C. Gray returned to Sumpter yesterday and is greeting his many friends after a several weeks' absence.

Mrs. J. P. Baird left yesterday for Waitsburg, Washington, to visit with her daughters, Mrs. A. H. Brown and Mrs. C. J. Mohr. She will probably be absent for two months.

R. E. Strahorn, owner of the Sumpter water works system, is in the city, having just returned from an extended trip east. Mrs. Strahorn says that it is his intention next spring, as early as possible, to build storage reservoirs with sufficient capacity to guard against any water famine in the dry season.[1]

In producing personals, editors had to make certain what they were told was accurate. At the *Territorial Enterprise* in Virginia City, Nevada, the job of producing the personals, or "locals" as they were called, was the responsibility of Dan De Quille. He recalled:

How often it happens that someone—generally Mr. Jenkins—comes to the hungry, itemless "local" with "Oh, such a rich joke!" on his friend

Slasher, a man with whom you (the "local") have not the slightest acquaintance. Jenkins is very anxious—persistently so—to have you get off his great joke on Slasher. He assures you over and over that he and Slasher are the greatest friends alive, and that he wouldn't for the world say or do a thing to hurt Slasher's feelings—why, Slasher regular dotes on him, and he does the same on Slasher.

The item will tickle Slasher when he sees it—he is such a jolly dog, this Slasher: so good-natured and fond of a joke. Jenkins is sorry you don't know Slasher; he is sure you would like him, and he will introduce you to Slasher the first opportunity.

Finally Jenkins tells you the immense joke on Slasher and laughs— oh, how he laughs. He knows Slasher, and can see him in his mind's eye, and all the circumstances attendant upon the joke are vividly impressed upon his mind. It is a rich thing as he sees it, but to you it has no point, and your make-believe laugh is a sorry effort.

You are at last coaxed into making a promise to publish the joke, as you are assured that the jolly dog, Slasher, has some inkling of the matter and will rather expect to see himself in print. You make a note of the outlines of the joke, and for the remainder of the day are quite miserable every time you see the same.

You don't see how you are to make anything readable out of the flimsy skeleton furnished you. You find in reality the man Jenkins has thrown upon your shoulders nearly the whole responsibility of getting up the joke.

However, the man so much doted upon by Slasher has given you liberty to color the thing up; in fact, said to you several times: "Color it up! color it up! Damn it, you know how to do these things!" You write up the joke and do "color it up" with a vengeance. Finally, you make a passable thing of it.

Next morning you seat yourself in the sanctum and look over the paper. You come to the joke, and as you read it in the big, clear type, it seems to loom up, and looks a great deal bolder than it did in manuscript. You begin to think you may have added a trifle too much color, yet the thing is rather funny and you laugh—laugh just a little, for at the moment there comes a rap at the door—a regular shower of thundering raps.

You are somewhat startled, but by an effort to recover your equanimity, and in a cheerful tone say: "Come in."

The door opens and in comes a huge, broad-shouldered, black-whiskered, six-footer—striding in tremendous boots that have soles two inches thick and tops that reach above his knees. He wears a very slouchy slouched hat, and has awful arms and hands. The giant eyes you over.

"My name is Slasher!"

He might have saved himself the trouble of speaking. You knew the moment you heard the knock at the door that Slasher was coming, and you knew the moment the boots and whiskers marched towards you that Slasher had come—Slasher in all the awfulness and grandeur of his wrath.

"My name is Slasher, and I want to know what in the name of hell this means? This, sir—*this!*" pointing with his big hairy forefinger to that "great joke."

You cough and try to make out you don't see just what he is pointing out.

"Did you write this?" still pointing at the great joke on him, given you by his bosom friend, Jenkins.

"You finally say you did publish the thing—it is only a *thing* now—at the earnest solicitation of his most intimate and particular friend, Joshua P. Jenkins, Esq.

"Him! Jenkins? That damned ass! That squirt! That sneaking, impertinent, bladder-headed puppy! Jenkins? Why, the sneaking low-lived pimple! I'll mash him the first time I meet him; I'll spread his nose all over his face. As for you, sir, you ought to have had better sense. By thunder, I ought to pull your nose! I've half a mind to pull it, anyhow!" but, after eyeing you a moment, he gives a snort, turns on his heel, and departs.[2]

De Quille and other editors who produced personals knew they were important in attracting and keeping readers, but privately they considered them puff. Edgar Wilson "Bill" Nye, who won fame between 1876 and 1883 for his humorous writings as a reporter in the *Laramie Daily Sentinel* and later as editor of the *Laramie Boomerang,* described such newspaper puff as "something which makes you feel bad if you don't get it. The groundwork for a newspaper puff consists of a good, moral character and a good bank account. Writing newspaper puffs is like mixing sherry cobblers and mint juleps all through the summer months, for customers, and quenching your own thirst with rain water," wrote Nye, adding:

Sometimes a man is looking for a puff and don't get it; then he says that the paper is going down hill, and that it is in the hands of a monopoly, and he would stop the paper if he didn't have to pay his bill first.

Writing a newspaper puff is like taking a photograph of a homely baby. If the photograph doesn't represent the child as resembling a beautiful cherub with wings, and halos, and harps, and things, it shows that the artist does not understand his business. So it is with a newspaper puff—if the puffee don't stand out like the bold and fearless exponent of truth and morality, it shows that the puffer doesn't understand human nature.

It is more fun to watch a man read a puff of himself than it is to see a fat man slip up on an orange peel. The narrow-minded man reads it over seven or eight times, and then goes around to the different places in town where the paper is taken, and steals what copies he can. The kind-hearted family man goes home and reads it to his wife, and then pays up his bill on the paper. The successful business man, who advertises and makes money, starts immediately to find the newspaper man and speak a word of grateful acknowledgment and encouragement. Then the two men start out of the sanctum and walk thoughtfully down the street together for a drink, and the successful business man takes sugar in his, and the newspaper man doesn't put anything in his, and then they both eat a clove or two, and life is pleasanter and sweeter, and peace settles down like a turtle dove in their hearts, and after awhile lamp-posts get more plenty, and everybody seems to be more or less intoxicated, but the hearts of these two men are filled with a nameless joy, because they know just where to stop, and not make themselves ridiculous.[3]

For the editor who had to write personals week after week, the task soon became mechanical. Some editors took time to come up with new, bright, and vivid words and phrases. Some may have tried to avoid employing certain favorite words or phrases each week, perhaps alternating their use every other week or two. But not all took the time to do so, and in retrospect these personal items contained what can only be called trite expressions. Here are a few gathered from the columns of western weeklies during the late nineteenth and early twentieth centuries:

blushing bride	crying need
bolt from the clear sky	Dan Cupid
burning issue	dastardly deed
California weather	delicious refreshments
checkered career	divine passion
city fathers	doing as well as can be expected
cool as a cucumber	elegantly gowned

entertained lavishly	one of the most unique
few well chosen words	our noble pioneers
foregone conclusion	poor little tots
gala attire	popular citizen
goes without saying	present-day generation
good time is assured for all	prominent young man
good time was had by all	promising young man
kind and loving	received an ovation
land-office business	red letter day
large and enthusiastic audience	rendered a solo
last but not least	rendered a selection
leave no stone unturned	select few
madly in love	small but appreciative audience
marriage was consummated	social event of the season
milady	Sundayed
musical circles	sweet child
never in the history of	the light fantastic
news leaked out	this fair city
noble work	took things into his own hands
on the sick list	vale of tears

The use of trite words and phrases was not the only problem engendered by careless editors. There were those who had difficulties with spelling, grammar, and punctuation. One such was H. M. Cooley, editor of the *Avard* (Oklahoma) *Breeze,* which was published every Tuesday during the paper's short life. Cooley's column of personals, "Local Mention," often included one-line advertisements. The following gems appeared in his February 16, 1915, column:

John Miller has a beautiful case of mumps (not for sale).

F. W. Passwater is hauling out a bill of lumber from Avard as he can't stand to see his neighbors make improovemets [*sic*] and not help the cause along.

If it takes a four months old woodpecker eight months to peak [*sic*] a hole through a Cypress log that will make 117 bales of shingles 165 shingles to the bale—How long will it take a cross-eyed grasshopper with a rubber leg to kick the seeds out of a dill pickle pickled in Avard.

Cooley did not provide an answer to the riddle.

His February 23, 1915, column had more:

Master Geo. Murray son of John. Murray has the measles.

Red Texas Seed Oats at the Avard Produce Co.

It was reported that the men were on the ground at Goshen with two traction engines and other tools necessary to comence [*sic*] moveing [*sic*] the church to Avard.

For first-class dentist see Dr. Edwards. Waynoka.

Rev. Prentice go [*sic*] the committee together thursday and arranged plans for the location of the M. E. Church buildings. It may be necessary to purchase a new lot to acomadate [*sic*] the new building.

Mr. Roy Lashbaugh was in Avard Friday. on buisness [*sic*] and ordered the BREEZE for a year   Roy says the BREEZE is all Right.

The best news we have this week is the Rain.

Arther Paris two small children for [*sic*] miles south of Hopeton has a very bad case of Diphtheria. both are very serious are expected to recover Dr. Leney is attending them.

Little Virgie Hinderliter is quite sick at this writing with the La.grippe we hope to report him much better, soon.

We are very sorry to state of Loyd Curtris being sick with the meassels [*sic*].

Sometimes editors ran into problems in trying to include personals in the columns of their papers. The following item, written by A. L. Runyan, editor, was included among the personals in the September 17, 1880 issue of the *Enterprise* at Manhattan, Kansas:

How newspaper items are misconstrued sometimes. Now, last week we paid a young man a compliment, we thought, but the next day he came around and said that he had been insulted and talked a good deal about it and felt really injured. This is the third or fourth time we have been hauled over the coals for complimentary items and we are going to cease writing them. The next fellow who wants a compliment must write it himself, and then if it don't suit him he can go out and pound his head against the wall.

When editors came across anything unusual, they often included it in their personal columns. The editor of the Marysville (Kansas) *Enterprise,* found a "notis" on a fencepost somewhere near the northern Kansas town.

He copied it exactly as it was posted and then included it as a short local item in the August 11, 1866, issue of his paper: "ey Due hear Buy for Bid eney purson of cutting eney grass on my plase if thay Due that will loose thar labor and I want them to Bee veary carfull and not cum over the line. July the 30 1866."

Even before personals became the vogue, some editors inserted short sayings in their columns when there was nothing else to fill the space, or when they ran across something they thought their readers would be interested in. Edward Kemble, editor of the *California Star,* used such items in 1847. They included:

There is a lawyer down east so exceedingly honest, that he puts his flower pots out every night, so determined is he that everything shall have its dew. (June 26, 1847)

Better is little where there is love, than a fat ox and a fight. (July 31, 1847)

Believe about a sixteenth part of what you hear, and possibly you may be near the truth. If you believe a quarter, you are green; if a half, you are soft, if the whole, you are a fool. (November 13, 1847)

J. B. Robb, editor of the *Stockton* (California) *Journal,* enjoyed gathering and creating sayings to include in a column entitled "Wit and Sentiment." An example is his January 11, 1851, column:

Children pick up words as pigeons peas – be careful therefore with what you feed them.

An ounce of mother wit is worth a pound of learning.

Boys, if you would be honored men, take care of your conduct now.

To make a drunkard, give him a wife who will scold him every time he comes home.

Never be angry with your neighbor because his religious views differ from yours, for all the branches of a tree do not lean the same way.

Girls, to add a new leaf to the roses on your cheek, all that is necessary is to go to bed at nine and get up at sunrise.

So long as the mind continues uncontaminated, there is small danger that the person will be otherwise.

There is a young man in Washington who thinks the anger which girls show when kissed is real. What a goose!

Man dies, but not *one* of his *actions* ever dies. Each is perpetuated and prolonged for ever by interminable results, affecting some *beings* in every age to come.

As western towns became large, personals gave way to full-blown society columns. The *Kansas City Star* published its first such column on November 6, 1894, and it included the following items:

Mr. and Mrs. Joseph Brey leave to-day for a southern tour.

Mrs. B. D. Jafler of Trace avenue, is entertaining Miss Fletcher of Cincinnati.

Mr. and Mrs. William M. Reed of Central street will give a dancing party to-night.

Miss Florence Wicks, who returned with Miss Nelson from Chicago and was her guest for a few days, left Saturday night for a visit with friends in St. Louis.

Mr. and Mrs. William H. Chipman will celebrate their wedding anniversary with a dancing party to-night.

Humor was something many western editors liked to include in their personals columns to brighten the lives of their readers and to give them a smile while reading the paper. The editors found humor in their own towns, but often created such items from stories in exchange papers, as the following examples show:

Since the saloons at Beloit closed, the residents of that burg are drinking water from the Spirit Springs at Cawker City. (*Independent,* Kirwin, Kansas, January 26, 1881)

A customer in town offered a half eagle for a cigar, but the barkeeper, not having seen a $5 gold piece for so long, mistook it for a nickel, saying he had no "5 cts. cigars for sale." (*Glendale Atlantis,* Montana, September 8, 1880)

Game is abundant in Ellsworth just now. Buffalo, draw poker, antelope, old sledge, venison, faro, quails, billiards, rabbits, euchre, elk and keno are the prevailing varieties. (*Kansas Daily Commonwealth,* Topeka, June 16, 1872)

The newspapers of Kinsley are debating the question as to which is the least harmful at church socials, dancing or kissing games. (*Pioneer,* Atwood, Kansas, January 29, 1880)

Two tramps in a neighboring town hit upon a novel plan to get some whiskey. They went into a saloon with a gallon jug and had it filled with liquor and offered a dollar in payment. Of course the bartender refused the money and emptied the liquor back into the barrel and the tramps took the jug and departed. Later they were seen to break the jug over a stone and squeeze out over a pint of liquor from the sponges which they had placed on the inside of the jug. (*Free Press,* Hays City, Kansas, January 2, 1892)

The other day two oxen passed through Glen Elder, all saddled, one with a lady rider, the other with a gentleman. (*Norton County People,* Norton, Kansas, December 22, 1881)

McCracken "onion socials" are very popular this winter. One of the girls takes a bite out of a raw onion. The boys pay ten cents apiece for guesses. Those who guess correctly get to kiss all the other girls, and those who guess incorrectly must kiss the girl who bit the onion. (*Chieftain,* LaCrosse, Kansas, February 12, 1904)

By the latest reports we see that Gen. Crook has called on the Government for mules and asses for Black Hills transportation. No man is safe in these days. (Hays City, Kansas, *Sentinel,* September 20, 1876)

The *Linn County* [K.T.] *Herald* says that they want in Linn County "one hundred School Marms, who will pledge themselves not to get married within three years." (*Leavenworth Daily Times,* Kansas Territory, June 10, 1859)

A newspaper in Ottawa county, Kansas, has the following: "Last week we announced the marriage of a young friend, and now it becomes our pleasant duty to announce that he is the father of a bouncing boy." (*Reporter,* Ellsworth, Kansas, January 16, 1873)

The lightning struck a Great Bend girl last week. She was not injured in the least, but her corset ribs were sadly demoralized, as was also the arm of a young man who was trying to keep them in place. When asked by his friends why he keeps his arm in a sling he explains that he "didn't know she was loaded." (*Optic,* Larned, Kansas, July 30, 1880)

And then there was this personal published by the *Ellis County Star* at Hays City, Kansas, on July 6, 1876: "Billy King, rushing down the street the other day, asked Billy Patterson if he had seen his black-faced antelope. 'No,' said Patterson, 'who did your blackfaced aunt elope with?' King made no reply, but went on in pursuit of his pet."

This type of material was particularly popular in weekly papers published in rural agricultural areas. The column produced by the editor of the *Wamego* (Kansas) *Weekly Times* was titled "Wayside Gleanings." One issue contained the following:

Beauty, of course, is only skin deep, but sometimes it is over a quarter of an inch thick.

Indiana has followed the example of Texas in regulating the size of bed sheets. So they do use them in Indiana.

Probably, by this time, some of the members of the late, lamented Kansas legislature are again getting used to the idea of work.

An innocent little 5-year-old Wamego child said: "Mama, if flour is so scarce, why do some ladies waste so much on their faces?"[4]

One western editor who became nationally known for his short personal items was E. W. Howe. With two hundred dollars and help from his brother, he began publishing a tiny free daily paper called the *Little Globe,* which eventually became the *Atchison* (Kansas) *Globe* in 1876. Howe began to attract attention as a "paragrapher." His pithy comments were soon copied by editors throughout the nation. Journalism historian Calder Pickett makes it clear in his fine biography of Howe how remarkable it was that the Atchison editor should have achieved the fame he did in God-fearing Kansas while carrying on his unrelenting war against religion and the "weaker sex." People simply had to read what he wrote whether it offended them or not.[5]

Ralph "Doc" Tennal, who worked for Howe, recalled in 1914:

For thirty years Howe wrote matter that was quoted all over the United States. His daily output was about 40 items. The matter was picked up on the streets in talks with people. It was meant for local news or local entertainment, yet it was so replete with general interest that it had an audience that was nation wide.

Mr. Howe always kept a note book on his person. He did not wait for someone to tell him something before writing in it. The best things Mr. Howe wrote were suggested rather than told to him. The suggestions came, not only from conversation, but originated frequently from objects he saw.

Tennal recalled that one day Howe attended the theatre and wrote in his notebook: "The most natural man in a play is the villain." Later he wrote: "What a villain a man is willing to become in making 'a good trade'!"

Ed Howe, editor and publisher of the *Atchison* (Kansas) *Globe,* became nationally known as a "paragrapher." He carried on an unrelenting war against religion and what he described as the "weaker sex." *(Courtesy Kansas State Historical Society)*

One day an advertisement Howe saw in the composing room suggested the following paragraph: "Occasionally we see an article advertised as self-cleaning. Nothing is self-cleaning. Dirt is the enemy of the human race, and constant scouring, and rubbing, and cleaning by hand, is necessary."

Another time a very boring person came into the newspaper office and took up too much of his time. Afterward Howe wrote: "The most worthless man I ever knew is in town, and I believe he has the best collection of letters of recommendation I ever saw. I would be willing to give him a letter of recommendation myself, in order to be rid of him."

Like many editors, he cultivated certain people in the community who suggested stuff for the newspaper. One item resulting from a meeting provided the following: "We know a certain man who is bright, and we hang around him a good deal because of the original things he says. But we have noticed lately that he is beginning to repeat his sayings."

Howe enjoyed running items in his paper that were likely to arouse discussion. For example: "How early do mothers begin spanking their children? So far as we have been able to learn, by inquiring among mothers, it is necessary to begin spanking girl babies when about a year old, and boy babies when about sixteen months old." Two more: "Every successful man I have ever heard of has done the best he could with the conditions as he found them, and not waited till next year for better." "Every great man must realize that he is not as great as the newspapers say he is."

Another useful trick used by Howe was taking his readers into his confidence. For example: "If to-morrow is a dull day, it will be the seventh in succession, and we will be compelled to print more stories of what Joe Schott saw when he was in Europe last summer."

A strong point in Howe's methods lay in writing somewhat mysteriously and in making people guess. Sometimes his paragraphs referred to a real situation, but at other times an idea was attached to a purely imaginary situation, as in the following: "We are much interested in the case of an old gentleman who is ill. Once or twice a week he comes downtown, and, on being asked how he is, replies: 'I am very well, thank you; but my wife is poorly. I am compelled to spend a great deal of time with her.' As a matter of fact, his wife is well. The old gentleman is passing through the Dark Woods, and he whistles to keep up his courage." This item by Howe, however, had a factual basis: "An heiress is about to visit Atchison. The young men should remember that what the town needs now worse than anything else is outside capital."

Ed Howe knew the residents of Atchison so well that he was able to write about them with intimate familiarity, as the following example indicates: "Atchison hasn't a real thoroughbred at this time, but it has a citizen who used to be one. When Fred Giddings lived in London, as a young man, he never went to bed until 7 or 8 o'clock in the morning." Another one: "Every time we see big, fat George Hargrave, we can't help laughing over the fact that when he isn't feeling very well, his wife makes him take Jayne's Vermifuge, a worm medicine for children."

E. W. Howe despised anything that hinted at show-off, sham, or ostentation. He apparently thought all these attributes were combined in Oscar Wilde. When Wilde lectured in Atchison, Howe hired a boy to lead a donkey up and down Commercial Street wearing a banner that read: "I will lecture at the opera house tonight at eight o'clock. Oscar Wilde."[6]

CHAPTER NINE

DEATH AND RELIGION

The average length of a farmer's life is sixty-five years, while that of a printer is thirty-three, hence the necessity of paying for your paper promptly.
—Vermillion (Dakota Territory) *Dakota Republican,* 1886

LIFE WAS PRECIOUS in the Old West, especially among pioneers who came to accept Indian raids, floods, stampedes, accidents, sickness, violent weather, and death as they sought to survive. Editors treated a death as an event because the person who died was usually known to many residents of a community and had many friends. In some instances, a death was the most important event in a town and talked about for days or weeks. Editors therefore usually treated death with reverence and sought to report a person's demise as part of the town's history as well as a personal loss.

In reporting a sudden death, editors often tried to explain to readers how and why death had come. A example of such early reporting is the following story, told chronologically, in the *Northern Standard,* Clarksville, Texas, on January 23, 1845. It was published under the small headline:

DISTRESSING OCCURRENCE

Mr. Alfred Moore, an old and well known resident of our country, started home three or four weeks back, with his family, to move from his late residence on Pine Creek to a new place where he was about settling, upon the head waters of the Sabine. He had with him his household furniture, and stock of cattle, hogs, etc., and was accompanied by three men, who were assisting him in moving.—On the morning of the last day of the journey, they started from their camp, six miles this side of their destination, and after getting along a couple of miles, a negro child fell out of one of the wagons, and the wheel ran over its hand. Mrs. Moore, who was carrying a little son about 14 months old, before her on horseback, put him down and dismounted herself to attend to the negro, proposing to her little son to put him up again with a little girl some three or four years old, whom she placed upon the horse. The little fellow declined, and insisted upon walking along with a man, who was driving the hogs, and she let him go, telling the little girl to keep with him. Some distance beyond there, the hogs took out of the road, into a sort of circular hollow, which ran round into the road again, where the grass was very high, and the driver followed after, telling the little boy to keep on the road with the girl and supposing that he did so. The child however, did not heed him, but followed into the grass and the little girl went on the road, without attending to him. Mrs. Moore in the meantime was far behind with the wagon and Mr. Moore was in advance of all, driving sheep. The man who was driving the hogs, supposed the little fellow was on the road with the girl and the horse, and thought no more about him, but drove on, till he got to the place, where Mr. Moore had arrived before him.

About two miles this side of the place, a wagon turned over, and Mrs. Moore, who was with the hindmost wagon, when she got up, staid by it until the things were put in, and the wagon started again, and arrived at the house about sundown. She immediately inquired after her child, and Mr. Moore who supposed it with her, asked also, and then for the first time it became at once understood that he was missing, the little girl being interrogated and knowing nothing about him.

Mr. Moore and two or three others immediately started back to look for him, and arrived at the point where he was last seen, about dark. They searched about as long as there was any light, fruitlessly. The night was intensely cold. In the morning the search was renewed and continued till dark, but still they could not find him. They found his tracks leading out into the high grass at the place where the hogs turned out, and coming into the road again, where they came in, and then wandering up and down it for a few yards, two or three times, and then leading off into the prairie.

On the morning of the second day, they found the little fellow, in the edge of a prairie road, reclining upon one arm and sleeping the last sleep. It seemed upon further examination that he had left the road a little ways but struck it again at the first creek they crossed; the road winding round to the crossing. It seemed that he did not like the crossing and had gone further up till he found one that suited him better, and there crossed— Keeping on his course which appeared to be due west, as it supposed following the setting sun, he crossed one or two more creeks, each time leaving the place where he first struck them, and seeking a shallow ford, and so keeping on until he found his resting place, and never varying his course, except where it struck some burnt woods contiguous which he avoided. The poor little fellow had persevered for an amazing distance, considering his age, and kept on as he supposed after his parents, until benumbed with cold, he had lain down never to rise again on earth. His countenance when found was placid, and unmarked by a single painful emotion, though one would suppose his childish agony must have been intense, as he wandered on, seeking his mother.

It was and still is a common heritage in the West that people think only of the good things about a person's life after he or she has died. This feeling of reverence toward the dead gave unusual importance to the newspaper obituary. Because most people believed that a dead person should be spoken of creditably and with demonstrations of appreciation, the newspapers were under a certain obligation to convey these feelings. The newspaper was, after all, the instrument that recorded the life happenings of a community. As one newspaper editor once said, "A person hears of a man only three times in his life: namely, when he is born, married, and buried."[1] The same was true for a woman.

An example of the positive nature of an Old West obituary, with its headline, follows:

JAKE MOFFATT GONE SKYWARD

As we feared on hearing that two doctors had been called in, the life of our esteemed fellow-citizen Jake Moffatt ebbed out on Wednesday last, just after we had gone to press. Jake was every inch a scholar and a gentleman, upright in all his dealings, unimpeachable in character, and ran the Front Street Saloon in the very toniest style consistent with order. Jake never fully recovered from the year he spent in the county jail at the time of the Ryan-Sternberg fracas. His health was shattered, and he leaves a sorrowing widow and nary an enemy.[2]

Editors, however, did sometimes make exceptions to the rule of reporting only positive things about people who died. Consider the candor of the following obituary, which appeared in the *Butte* (Montana) *Miner,* January 12, 1899, in reporting the death of one of the proprietors of the Clipper Shade, a dance hall and saloon, well known for its female courtesans:

Pete Hanson, the "King of Galena street," is dead. He was a notorious man. Under his management and that of his partner, J. W. Kenny, the Clipper Shade acquired such a reputation that letters dropped in letter boxes throughout the country addressed merely to "The Clipper

Shade"—without mention of city, county or state, arrived at their destination.

Hanson was reputed to be a "druggist"—that is, he made a practice of
drugging men who came into his saloons with money so that they may
be "rolled" in safety by the horde of pickpockets that clustered about his
place of business.

Pete always denied the drugging. "When a man is determined to get
drunk," he would say, "the safe course is to allow him to get drunk. No
drugs are needed in such instances."

Report has it that when a man with money was found touring the twi-
light zone, a string or wire was pulled that rang a bell in Hanson's. Apparently each house had its own bell because the ring immediately
brought a crook or robber to relieve the visitor of his roll.

Outlaws were another exception to the rule, and stories about their
deaths rarely contained any mention of the individual's positive traits. At
Deadwood, Dakota Territory, the first issue of the *Black Hills Pioneer* was
set in type in a half-built newspaper office still open to the elements. When
the paper appeared on June 8, 1876, one prominent story, which told of
vigilantes hanging a man named Richard Burnett for horse stealing, included the sentence: "We rolled him up in his saddle blanket, and entered
him in the blood red soil of Red Canon [*sic*] with a pine board at his head."
The "we" suggests that the writer may have been one of the vigilantes who
hanged the man.

Less than two months after the *Black Hills Pioneer* reported Richard
Burnett's death, Jack McCall killed Wild Bill Hickok in a Deadwood saloon. Three days later the weekly *Black Hills Pioneer* published the following account:

ASSASSINATION OF WILD BILL.
He is shot through the head
by John McCall while unconscious of
Danger—Arrest, Trial, and Discharge of the Assassin, who
claims to have avenged
a brother's death
in killing Wild Bill.

On Wednesday about three o'clock the report was started that J. B.
Hickok (Wild Bill) was killed. On repairing to the hall of Nuttall &

This photograph of James Butler "Wild Bill" Hickok is believed to have been made by A. P. Trott of Junction City, Kansas, in 1871, a few years before Hickok was killed at Deadwood, Dakota Territory. *(Courtesy Western History Collections, University of Oklahoma)*

Mann it was ascertained that the report was too true. We found the remains of Wild Bill lying on the floor. The murderer, Jack McCall, was captured after a lively chase by many of our citizens, and taken to a building at the lower end of the city and a guard placed over him. As soon as this was accomplished a coroner's jury was summoned, with C. H. Sheldon as foreman who after hearing all the evidence, which was to the effect that while Wild Bill and others were seated at a table playing cards, Jack McCall walked in and around directly back of his victim and when within three feet of him raised his revolver, and exclaiming, "Damn you take that" fired, the ball entering at the back of the head and coming out at the center of the right cheek, causing instant death, rendered a verdict in accordance with the above facts. Preparations for a trial were then made by calling a meeting of citizens at the theatre building. Immediately after the Theatre was over the meeting was called to order, Judge W. L. Kuykendall presiding. After a statement by the president of the object of the meeting, the gentlemen present numbering about 100, elected Judge Kuykendall to preside at the meeting as judge at the trial of the case. Isaac Brown was elected sheriff, and one deputy and twelve guards were appointed. It was then decided to adjourn to meet at 9 o'clock a.m. Thursday, Aug. 3, in order that the gentlemen appointed for the purpose might have time to announce the meeting and its object to the miners of Whitewood and Deadwood mining districts. At nine o'clock Thursday the meeting was called pursuant to adjournment, when the action of the previous meeting was submitted for adoption or rejection, and after some remarks were adopted. Col. May was chosen prosecuting attorney, and A. B. Chapline was selected by the prisoner, but owing to sickness Mr. Chapline was unable to attend, and Judge Miller was chosen in his place.

A committee of three was then appointed by the chair, one from each district, whose duty it was to select the names of 33 residents from each of their respective districts, and from these persons so chosen the jury was afterward obtained. Mr. Reid of Gayville, James Harrington, of this city and Mr. Coin of Montana City were the gentlemen appointed for this purpose. At this time the meeting adjourned. At two o'clock the trial was commenced, and lasted until six. The evidence in the case was the same as that before the coroner's jury, so far as the prosecution was concerned. The defence was that the deceased, at some place in Kansas, killed the prisoner's brother, for which he killed deceased. The Jury after being out an hour and thirty minutes, returned the following verdict.

Deadwood City, August 3, 1876

We the jury find Mr. John McCall not guilty.

(signed)	Charles Whitehead, Foreman
J. J. Bump	L. D. Bookaw
J. H. Tompson	S. S. Hopkins
J. F. Cooper	Alex Travis
K. F. Towle	J. E. Thompson
L. A. Judd	Ed. Burke
	John Mann, Jurors

This ended the scenes of the day that settled a matter of life and death with one living, whose life was in the hands of twelve fellow men whose duty it was to decide upon the guilt or innocence of the accused, charged with the murder of Wild Bill, who while it was in progress, was being laid in the cold, cold, ground: in the valley of Whitewood, by kind hands that were ever ready to administer to his sufferings while living, and ready to perform the painful duty of laying him in his last resting place.

Elsewhere in the same issue of the *Black Hills Pioneer* was the following editorial comment: "Should it ever be our misfortune to kill a man, which we pray God it may not, we would simply ask that our trial may take place in some of the mining camps of these hills."

When Jesse James was killed at St. Joseph, Missouri, the first news story published by the *Kansas City Times,* on April 4, 1882, vividly captured the details. Who wrote the story is not known, since the paper did not use by-lines, but the writer adopted a storytelling approach to capture the reader's interest.

ST. JOSEPH, MO. April 4 – About ten o'clock this morning a hurried report was made in this city that Jesse James had been shot and killed at his home in the south part of this city, where he has been residing for the past six months, under the assumed name of Howard. In a few minutes an immense throng was on its way to the place designated, and on arrival there, found the report verified, and Jesse James dead, he having been assassinated by two members of the gang, Charles and Robert Ford, of Ray county, both of whom immediately surrendered themselves to the authorities. One of them confesses having wounded the express messenger in the Blue Cut robbery.

The home where the great outlaw was killed is a frame building, a story and a half high, sitting in a little grove of fruit trees on one of the round ridges back of the World's hotel. It commands a view of the approaches for a long distance.

The wife of the outlaw first insisted that the name of the dead man was Howard, but later

MADE A FULL CONFESSION

of the whole affair, along with a history of the robberies in which her husband had been engaged. She said they resided last summer in Kansas City, but had removed to this city where Jesse hoped to reside in peace and earn an honest living. They brought with them two Ford boys who had since been living in their house. These boys are mere youths, apparently between 15 and 20 years of age. This morning after breakfast Robert Ford and Jesse went into the sitting room to some work about moving a stove, and Charles was assisting her in the kitchen washing dishes. After a little Charles also went into the room where the two men were; soon after she heard a shot and rushing in she found her husband laying on the floor shot to death, while on a chair lay his pistol, belt and cartridges which he had removed while at work with the stove. The Ford boys both ran from the house, one jumping over the rear fence, the other running around by the front way. They both returned again and then started to the city to deliver themselves up and

CLAIM THE REWARD OFFERED

for Jesse James. They first came to the marshal's office, but finding him out, went direct to the sheriff and gave themselves into custody.

Soon after the shooting the reporters were informed by Coroner Heddens that a man had been shot and killed on thirteenth and Lafayette streets. Reaching the place indicated, and on approaching the door leading into the front room, a man was found lying on the floor cold in death, with blood oozing from his wounds. From the few who had gathered around the door, more from curiosity than anything else, it was inquired what was the cause of the shooting. None of them knew, but said we could find out from the man's wife, who was in the rear room. Walking into the room and passing around the dead man's body, we opened the door leading into the kitchen, where we found the

This woman, identified as Mrs. Jesse James, poses with her dead husband's weapons. *(Courtesy Western History Collection, University of Oklahoma)*

Jesse James was killed in this house at St. Joseph, Missouri, in 1882. The photo was taken after the shooting. *(Courtesy Western History Collections, University of Oklahoma)*

WIFE AND TWO LITTLE CHILDREN

a boy and girl. When she discovered us with notebook in hand, she began to scream and said: Please do not put this in the paper. At first she refused to say anything about the shooting, but after some time she said the boys that had killed her husband had been living with them for some time, and that their names were Johnson, but no relation. Charles, she said, was her nephew, but she had never seen Robert until he came home with her husband a few weeks ago. Robert was an old friend of her husband, and when he met him upon the street he invited him to come and see them. He came home with them that night and had remained ever since. When asked what her husband's name was she said it was Howard and that they had resided here about six months.

"Had your husband and the two Johnson boys ever had any difficulty?"

ON FRIENDLY TERMS

"Never. They have always been on friendly terms."

"Why, then did they do the deed?"

"That is more than I can tell. Oh, the rascals!" And at this she began to cry and ask God to protect her.

"Where were you when the shooting was done?"

"I was in the kitchen, and Charley had been helping me all morning with my work. He entered the first room, and in about three minutes I heard the report of a pistol; and upon opening the door I discovered my husband lying in his own blood upon the floor. I ran to the front door and Charles was getting over the fence, but Robert was standing in the front yard with a pistol in his right hand. I says: Oh you have killed him, and turning around walked into the kitchen and then [he] left with Charles, who was waiting for him outside the fence."

At this juncture the two Johnson boys made their appearance and gave themselves up to the officers, telling them the man they killed was

JESSE JAMES

and now they claim[ed] the reward. Those who were standing nearby drew their breaths in silence at the thought of being so near Jesse James, even if he was dead.

Marshal Craig said: My God, do you mean to tell me this is Jesse James?

Yes, answered the two boys in one breath. That man is Jesse James and we have killed him and don't deny it. We feel proud that we have killed a man who is known all over the world as the most notorious desperado that has ever lived.

THE WIFE'S FINAL CONFESSION

How are we to take your words for this? asked the marshal.

We do not ask you to take our words. There will be proof enough. The confession of the wife will be enough.

The marshal then took Mrs. Howard, as she called herself, into the room, and told her the name of her husband was not Howard, but James. She denied it at first, and when the marshal left her the reporter entered the room in company with three or four other gentlemen and one lady, who was present. Mrs. Howard, it is said your name is not Howard, but James, and you are the wife of Jesse James.

I can't help what they say, I have told the truth.

The boys who killed your husband have come back and given themselves up, and they say that he is Jesse James and your husband.

My God, can it be that they have come back? She was told that they were standing outside the house near the fence, and she should see them with her own eyes. Walking through the room by her dead husband she caught sight of the ones who had killed her husband, and screaming at the top of her voice she called them cowards, and asked them why they had killed the one who had always befriended them. Then turning to the body of Jesse, she prayed that she and her children might be in death's cold embrace by his side. She then left the room, followed by the reporters, who told her that the boys were not mistaken, that it certainly must be Jesse. She uttered not a word, but the little 7 year old boy who stood by her side said: God Almighty may strike me down if it is not pa.

The boys said their names are Ford and not Johnson as you said, continued the reporter.

Do they say so, and what else do they say?

That they killed him to get the reward.

Holding her dear little children closer to her bosom, she said: I can't shield them long. Even after they had shot my husband, who has been trying to live a peaceable life, I protected them and withheld their names, but it is all true. My husband is Jesse James, and a kinder hearted, truer man to his family never lived.

The confession from the wife of the most notorious outlaw known to the annals of criminal history created a profound sensation. The thought that Jesse James has lived among us for the past six months, and walked our streets daily, causes one to shudder with fear.

As we can see, the writer of the Jesse James story used trite words and phrases, apparently to capture emotion. But many editors in frontier towns avoided such language and reported the deaths of criminals in a very straightforward manner. Thomas Dimsdale, who edited the *Montana Post* at Virginia City, did this in providing his readers with an eyewitness account of a hanging by vigilantes in the September 24, 1864, issue of his paper:

Sat. evening, Sept. 17, John Dolan, *alias* Coyle, *alias* The Hat, paid the penalty of his crimes at Nevada.

Shortly after sundown, a strong body of armed citizens marched from Highland, Pine Grove, Junction and Virginia, and joining the force already on the ground, formed on each side of the entrance to the ballroom next to the Jackson House where the prisoner was confined. In a few minutes the culprit, pinioned and guarded, made his appearance, when the procession moved in military array to the place of execution. The prisoner . . . was in the center. At the ground, a circle was instantly formed and the prisoner standing on a board supposed . . . that a touch of the hand only was required to convert it into a drop. The citizens' guard, revolvers ready for instant use, faced outwards, and confronted the crowds, 4000–5000 individuals.

The prisoner admitted he had committed the crime . . . but was drunk when he did it. He requested that some of his friends would bury his body. . . . The plank fell and in a moment, the prisoner was swaying in the night wind. He died without a struggle.

A stern order to fall back, enforced by the click of 5400 revolvers, startled the dense crowd, and a stampede of the wildest description took place. . . . After ascertaining that life was extinct, the body was delivered to Dolan's friends.

If an editor did not happen to be present when vigilantes meted out justice, the story might be short and to the point, as in the case of Dimsdale's report in the September 30, 1865, issue of the *Montana Post:* "A man by the name of Jack Howard was found dangling from a limb of a tree in town. His face was turned toward the east and a paper was pinned upon a leg having a significant inscription, 'Robber.' He was left dangling nearly all day."

Just before the end of the nineteenth century, some newspapers continued to report the death of outlaws with a matter-of-fact "he had it coming" tone. When Bill Doolin died, the *Weekly Elevator* at Fort Smith, Arkansas, August 28, 1896, reported:

BITES THE DUST
BILL DOOLIN, THE OUTLAW, MEETS
DEATH AT HANDS OF HECK THOMAS
AND POSSE

Bill Doolin, the outlaw who broke jail at Guthrie [Indian Territory] a short time ago, was killed Monday night by Deputy Marshal Heck Thomas and his posse.

Doolin was one of the hardest cases that ever afflicted a country. He operated for a time with the Bill Dalton gang, and for a time was thought to be the manager of the now defunct Cook gang. He was one of the crowd upon whose heads the government once placed rewards of $250. Heck and his posse did a praise-worthy act when they put out his light.

Certainly death and acts of violence were familiar to everyone in the West. Editors reported them and readers read their stories, but it was not unusual for an item about a new shipment of goods arriving in a local store or the arrival of a visitor from the East to be of more interest. For example,

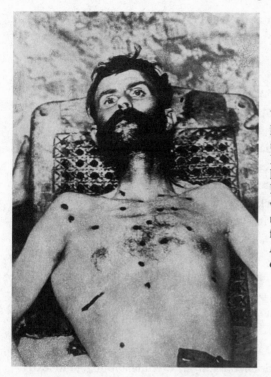

William M. "Bill" Doolin after
he was riddled with bullets from
the guns of a posse in 1896 at
Lawson, in what is now Oklahoma. The photo was made by
Bruce Daugherty after the body
was taken to Guthrie. Copies of
the photo were sold for twenty-
five cents. *(Courtesy Western
History Collections, University
of Oklahoma)*

the *Prescott* (Arizona) *Miner* led one story with the reason a man came to
town rather than the news he carried:

> Charlie Genung is in from Peeples Valley to buy some bacon. The
> weather is cold in his locality and there is little of news. He says that he
> and his neighbors were annoyed last week by a bunch of Yavapais, who
> came into the valley and ran off a couple of mules. Genung and several
> other ranchers pursued and killed several of the redskins. George
> Brown got a bad arrow wound in the shoulder.[3]

Unlike their treatment of the death stories of outlaws, editors wrote with
respect about good people who died in their communities. But they tried
to avoid the word "death" or "died." Instead, phrases such as "the community is saddened at the passing of" or "passed away" or "went to her
[his] final rest" or "passed to the great beyond" or "gone to his [her] reward" were used. In describing the funeral services they were often "sad
rites." Nearly everyone was "a well respected citizen of the community,"
and if the person who had died was a member of a local church, they were
often described as "a pillar of the church."

When my great-grandmother died at Hope, Kansas, April 13, 1893, the Hope *Dispatch* used such phrases in reporting her death at the age of fifty-six:

The citizens of Hope were very much surprised Tuesday morning to learn that Mrs. Thomas Dary, one of our oldest and most respected citizens, had passed the dark portal during the night and had gone to her final rest. She retired Monday night in her usual health but, about one o'clock was attacked with a coughing spell which caused hemorrhage of the lungs and she died before a doctor arrived. Funeral was held this afternoon in the M. E. Church and the remains were buried in Pilgrims Home Cemetery where she has two sons buried.

In small towns where everyone knew everyone else, the accidental death of children almost always merited special treatment by editors. For instance, the *Porter Enterprise* published at Porter in Wagoner County, Oklahoma, reported on the front page of its May 12, 1916, issue:

CHILD DIES SUDDENLY

Porter and vicinity were saddened Saturday evening about 7:30 to learn of the sudden death of Nell, infant daughter of Mr. and Mrs. Ed Howard. She was playing in some water in a 50 pound lard can in the yard, where she had gone just a minute or two before from the front porch, where her parents were and in some unknown way lost her balance and fell in, smothering herself instantly. Drs. Joblin and Carlington called at once and all that skilled physicians' loving minds could do was without avail, as life had been extinguished for several minutes.

Also on the front page was "A Tribute to Little Nell Howard," written by M. W. DeLoach, the family's pastor, who tried to console the family and community. Part of his tribute read:

On February 12, 1915, a little more than a year ago there came into the home of Brother Ed and Sister Pearl Howard a little baby girl to cheer their hearts and to brighten their lives. She was the "Little Sunshine" in their home, a great joy to her father and a precious jewel to her mother. But on May the 7th, 1916, by a strange Providence, she was called away to live in another world and to cheer another home—Our Father's home in Heaven.

It is hard for us to understand God's mysterious dealings with us—how it is He often sends his Angel into our garden to pluck the sweetest rose, the tenderest bud and leave the bush all torn and bleeding. But may we say, "The Lord gave, and the Lord taketh away, blessed be the name of the Lord."

Of all the obituaries published in western newspapers during the nineteenth and early twentieth centuries, one of the most moving and certainly the most reprinted was that written by William Allen White, editor of the Emporia (Kansas) *Gazette* following the accidental death of his seventeen-year-old daughter Mary in May 1921. White wrote:

MARY WHITE

The Associated Press reports carrying the news of Mary White's death declared that it came as the result of a fall from a horse. How she would have hooted at that! She never fell from a horse in her life. Horses have fallen on her and with her—"I'm always trying to hold 'em in my lap," she used to say. But she was proud of few things, and one of them was that she could ride anything that had four legs and hair. Her death resulted not from a fall but from a blow on the head which fractured her skull, and the blow came from the limb of an overhanging tree on the parking.

The last hour of her life was typical of its happiness. She came home from a day's work at school, topped off by a hard grind with the copy on the High School Annual, and felt that a ride would refresh her. She climbed into her khakis, chattering to her mother about the work she was doing, and hurried to get her horse and be out on the dirt roads for the country air and the radiant green fields of the spring. As she rode through the town on an easy gallop, she kept waving at passers-by. She knew everyone in town. For a decade the little figure in the long pigtail and the red hair ribbon has been familiar on the streets of Emporia, and she got in the way of speaking to those who nodded at her. She passed the Kerrs, walking the horse in front of the Normal Library, and waved at them; passed another friend a few hundred feet farther on, and waved at her.

The horse was walking, and as she turned into North Merchant Street she took off her cowboy hat, and the horse swung into a lope. She passed the Tripletts and waved her cowboy hat at them, still moving gayly north on Merchant Street. A Gazette carrier passed—a High

This photograph of Mary White was made shortly before her death in May 1921. Her mother said it was made after Mary had been in some mischief and was trying to look innocent. *(Courtesy Special Collections, William Allen White Library, Emporia State University, Kansas)*

School boy friend—and she waved at him, but with her bridle hand; the horse veered quickly, plunged into the parking where the low-hanging limb faced her and, while she still looked back waving, the blow came. But she did not fall from the horse; she slipped off, dazed a bit, staggered, and fell in a faint. She never quite recovered consciousness.

But she did not fall from the horse, neither was she riding fast. A year or so ago she used to go like the wind. But that habit was broken, and she used the horse to get into the open, to get fresh, hard exercise, and to work off a certain surplus energy that welled up in her and needed a physical outlet. The need has [*sic*] been in her heart for years. It was back of the impulse that kept the dauntless little brown-clad figure on the streets and country roads of the community and built into a strong, muscular body what had been a frail and sickly frame during the first years of her life. But the riding gave her more than a body. It released a gay and hardy soul. She was the happiest thing in the world. And she was happy because she was enlarging her horizon. She came to know all sorts of conditions of men; Charley O'Brien, the traffic cop, was one of her best friends. W. L. Holtz, the Latin teacher, was another. Tom O'Connor, farmer-politician, and the Rev. J. H. Rice, preacher and police judge, and Frank Beach, music master, were her special friends; and all the girls, black and white, above the track and below the track, in Pepville and Stringtown, were among her acquaintances. And she brought home riotous stories of her adventures. She loved to rollick; persiflage was her natural expression at home. Her humor was a continual bubble of joy. She seemed to think in hyperbole and metaphor. She was mischievous without malice, as full of faults as an old shoe. No angel was Mary White, but an easy girl to live with for she never nursed a grouch five minutes in her life.

With all her eagerness for the out-of-doors, she loved books. On her table when she left her room were a book by Conrad, one by Galsworthy, "Creative Chemistry" by E. E. Slosson, and a Kipling book. She read Mark Twain, Dickens and Kipling before she was ten—all of their writings. Wells and Arnold Bennett particularly amused and diverted her. She was entered as a student in Wellesley for 1922; was assistant editor of the High School Annual this year, and in line for election to the editorship next year. She was a member of the executive committee of the High School Y.W.C.A.

Within the last two years she had begun to be moved by an ambition to draw. She began as most children do by scribbling in her school books, funny pictures. She bought cartoon magazines and took a course—rather casually, naturally, for she was, after all, a child with no strong purposes—and this year she tasted the first fruits of success by having her pictures accepted by the High School Annual. But the thrill of delight she got when Mr. Ecord, of the Normal Annual, asked her to do the cartooning for that book this spring, was too beautiful for words. She fell to her work with all her enthusiastic heart. Her drawings were accepted, and her pride—always repressed by a lively sense of the ridiculous figure she was cutting—was a really gorgeous thing to see. No successful artist ever drank a deeper draft of satisfaction than she took from the little fame her work was getting among her schoolfellows. In her glory, she almost forgot her horse—but never her car.

For she used the car as a jitney bus. It was her social life. She never had a "party" in all her nearly seventeen years—wouldn't have one; but she never drove a block in her life that she didn't begin to fill the car with pick-ups! Everybody rode with Mary White—white and black, old and young, rich and poor, men and women. She liked nothing better than to fill the car with long-legged High School boys and an occasional girl, and parade the town. She never had a "date," nor went to a dance, except once with her brother Bill, and the "boy proposition" didn't interest her—yet. But young people—great, spring-breaking, varnish-cracking, fender-bending, door-sagging carloads of "kids"—gave her great pleasure. Her zests were keen. But the most fun she ever had in her life was acting as chairman of the committee that got up the big turkey dinner for the poor folks at the county home; scores of pies, gallons of slaw, jam, cakes, preserves, oranges, and a wilderness of turkey were loaded into the car and taken to the county home. And, being of a practical turn of mind, she risked her own Christmas dinner to see that the poor folks actually got it all. Not that she was a cynic; she just disliked to tempt folks. While there, she found a blind colored uncle, very old, who could do nothing but make rag rugs, and she rustled up from her school friends rags enough to keep him busy for a season. The last engagement she tried to make was to take the guests at the county home out for a car ride. And the last endeavor of her life was to try to get a rest room for colored girls in the High School. She found one girl reading in the toilet, because there was no better place for a colored girl to loaf, and it inflamed her sense of injustice and she became a nagging harpy to those who she thought could remedy the evil. The poor she always had with her and was glad of it. She hungered and thirsted for righteousness; and was the most impious creature in the world. She joined the church without consulting her parents, not particularly for her soul's good. She never had a thrill of piety in her life, and would have hooted at a "testimony." But even as a little child, she felt the church was an agency for helping people to more of life's abundance, and she wanted to help. She never wanted the help for herself. Clothes meant little to her. It was a fight to get a new rig on her; but eventually a harder fight to get it off. She never wore a jewel and had no ring but her High School class ring and never asked for anything but a wrist watch. She refused to have her hair up, though she was nearly seventeen. "Mother," she protested, "you don't know how much I get by with, in my braided pigtails, that I could not with my hair up." Above every other passion of her life was her passion not to grow up, to be a child. The tomboy in her, which was big, seemed loath to be put away forever in skirts. She was a Peter Pan who refused to grow up.

Her funeral yesterday at the Congregational Church was as she would have wished it; no singing, no flowers except a big bunch of red roses from her brother Bill's Harvard classmen—heavens, how proud that would have made her!—and the red roses from the Gazette forces, in vases, at her head and feet. A short prayer: Paul's beautiful essay on "Love" from the Thirteenth Chapter of First Corinthians; some remarks about her by her friend, Carl Nau; and, opening the service, the slow, poignant movement from Beethoven's Moonlight Sonata, which she loved; and closing the service a cutting from the joyously melancholy first movement of Tchaikovsky's Pathetic Symphony, which she liked to hear, in certain moods, on the phonograph, then the Lord's Prayer by her friends in High School.

That was all.

For her pallbearers only her friends were chosen: her Latin teacher, W. L. Holtz; her High School principal, Rice Brown; her doctor, Frank Foncannon; her friend, W. W. Finey; her pal at the *Gazette* office, Walter Hughes; and her brother Bill. It would have made her smile to know that her friend Charley O'Brien, the traffic cop, had been transferred from Sixth and Commercial to the corner near the church to direct her friends who came to bid her good-by.

A rift in the clouds in a gray day threw a shaft of sunlight upon her coffin as her nervous, energetic little body sank to its last sleep. But the soul of her, the glowing gorgeous, fervent soul of her, surely was flaming in eager joy upon some other dawn.[4]

WHEN FRONTIER TOWNS were founded, organized religion did not exist, and Sundays were treated like any other day. Thomas Dimsdale recalled there was "habitual Sabbath breaking" during the early days. "This sin is so general in newly discovered diggings in the mountains that a remonstrance usually produces no more fruit than a few jocular oaths and a laugh. Religion is said to be 'played out,' and a professing Christian must keep straight, indeed, or he will be suspected of being a hypercritical member of a tribe, to whom it would be very disagreeable to talk about hemp."[5]

Because organized religion was viewed as a mark of civilization in a growing town, and therefore of permanence and prosperity, newspaper editors frequently encouraged it. During 1862 and 1863, Alfred Thomson, editor of the *Tri-Weekly Miners' Register*, at Central City, Colorado, called upon businessmen to close their stores on Sunday to encourage residents to attend church. At Prescott, Arizona, the editor of the *Arizona Miner* told his readers on May 9, 1866: "We doubt if there is in the whole land a place of equal size and prominence with Prescott, and settled by Americans, so utterly destitute of religious privileges. The Sabbath brings no invitation to public worship, the sound of the church bell is not heard, and the Sabbath school, the nursery of the church, is unknown, albeit children are numerous."

In 1870 the editor of the *Laramie* (Wyoming) *Daily Sentinel* proposed a solution to the problem in his community. In the September 26, 1870, issue of his paper, he wrote: "If we refuse to purchase goods on Sunday, there will be none sold! If we refuse to employ men on Sunday, there will be very little unnecessary labor done that day! If we keep away from the dram shops, we will save our hard earned money, our health, and our characters; and at the same time, aid materially in enforcing the Sunday Laws."

When organized religion finally arrived in the wild Kansas cattle town of Dodge City, the editor of the *Times* reported on June 8, 1878:

The 'wicked city of Dodge' can at last boast of a Christian organization—a Presbyterian church. It was organized last Sunday week. We would have mentioned the matter last week but we thought it best to break the news gently to the outside world. The tender bud of Christianity is only just beginning to sprout, but as tall oaks from little acorns grow, so this infant, under the guide and care of Brother Wright, may grow and spread its foliage like the manly oak of the forest. Years ago John the Baptist preached in the wilderness of Judea, and his meat was locusts and wild honey, but he baptized many converts in the river of Jordan. Who can tell but that years hence another Luke may write a book about our minister preaching in the wilderness of Dodge City and baptizing in the river Arkansaw?

Once organized religion arrived, editors reported weekly on their town's religious activities. At Ruby City, Idaho Territory, where services had been held in a vacant building since the new town had no church, the *Olwyhee Avalanche,* on September 16, 1865, reported:

Preaching in a mining camp, as far as my observation goes, is an up-hill business. It is a question with so many, after roughing it in the mines for years, whether they have any soul at all, let alone the idea of a soul to save. It is all well enough for a few of the more idle and easy-going to talk about absorbing a few hours of sermon of a Sunday, but the honest miner can't be made to see it; preaching to him would be about as unpenetrating as water to a gum boot. It is about all he can do to live in this world, without having to lay in a supply of religious grub for the next. He is too well versed in practical mineralogy to be interested in word pictures of brimstone localities.

After organized religion became fully established in their communities, editors occasionally took potshots at those not fully observing Sunday as a day of rest. For example, the editor of the *Idaho World* at Idaho City wrote in his April 18, 1872 issue: "There is a fellow in Silver City who makes a 'stand off' between God and the devil by attending Sunday School on Sunday forenoon and running a faro game in the afternoon." When a protracted meeting in a church produced results, an editor might rejoice and report in print that certain old hard and crusty sinners had succumbed to the spiritual onslaught of the hosts of righteousness. Or an editor might find some pleasure in printing items like the following: "The Methodist folks have tacked cards on the walls of their church calling attention to the fact that you are not expected to spit on the walls of the building or throw nut hulls around promiscuously. They intend to break up this practice if it takes all winter."[6]

Organized religion, however, was not supported by all editors. Perhaps the most outspoken editor in the West was Edgar Watson Howe, editor and publisher of the Atchison (Kansas) *Globe*. He frequently announced in print that he was intolerant of liars, hypocrites, and religion. Howe's biographer noted: "He did this in a time of intense national piety, and in a section of America often regarded (and so referring to itself) as the Bible belt. In retrospect his comments on religion seem tame, calm, and reasoned, and, considering his lack of formal education, reasonably intellectual."[7] Howe frequently attacked religion with humor. In the October 16, 1876, issue of the *Globe,* he made fun of the Sunday laws, observing:

A farmer called at this office in great indignation to-day to protest against church members going out to his farm on the Sabbath to shoot quail and chickens. He says they come out with lean and hungry dogs to chase his sheep, and endanger the life of his stock by careless shooting. We suggested with considerable sternness that this practice be stopped. Hereafter go to Missouri to shoot on Sunday, where the people are neither religious nor particular.

One of the most unusual experiments involving a newspaper and religion occurred at Topeka, Kansas, where on November 3, 1899, Frederick O. Popenoe, the thirty-seven-year-old publisher of the *Topeka Daily Capital,* was sitting on the front porch of his mother-in-law's home watching a parade. One of the guests sitting nearby was Rev. Charles M. Sheldon, the forty-one-year-old minister of Topeka's Congregational church. A few years earlier Sheldon had gained national fame for his book *In His Steps, or What Would Jesus Do?* Because Sheldon's publisher had failed to copyright the book properly it was in the public domain, and scores of publishers had brought it out in paperback. The book soon became a best-seller with millions of copies sold. As the two men talked, Popenoe asked Sheldon how he would like to edit a newspaper. Sheldon reportedly responded that he had never thought of himself as a newspaper editor, although the theme of a truly Christian daily newspaper had appeared in his book. Popenoe then offered to let Sheldon edit the *Capital* for at least a week as Sheldon thought Jesus would. Sheldon accepted.

Popenoe chose the period from Tuesday, March 13, through the following Saturday, March 17, 1900, and agreed that Sheldon's version of the *Capital* would be eight pages, issued each morning, plus an extra issue Saturday afternoon as a substitute for the regular Sunday paper.

Just before Sheldon began his editorial stint, at least forty newspapermen from major dailies as far away as Boston and San Francisco converged on Topeka. Sheldon announced that he was annoyed by the uninvited correspondents and their misleading reports. He then assembled his own staff, telling his reporters not to smoke and not to swear. He said they should avoid the use of slang—both words and phrases—in writing reports; they were to submit all interviews to the person interviewed; and if a reporter was assigned to interview a person and the person did not wish to talk, the reporter was not to insist on it. Sheldon gave specific orders that the paper was not to publish theatrical news of any kind, and only clean sports were to be reported. He told his reporters that, in reporting crime, they were to go into the causes but avoid the horrible details. Political stories, he said, must be nonpartisan. And reporters were told to avoid reporting scandals: They would not be printed.

Sheldon ignored the newspaper's advertising contracts regarding the placement of ads in the paper and even changed some of the advertising copy. The Topeka Laundry Company had a standing declaration in its ad that read: "Strictly High Grade Work." During Sheldon's week as editor, the declaration was changed to read: "Claims to do Strictly High Grade Work."

Sheldon's paper was a journalistic failure, not only in Topeka but in Chicago and New York City, where special editions were also published. The paper's circulation nationally was more than 360,000 each day during the week, but it was not well received. E. L. Bertrand, a correspondent for the Chicago *Tribune,* sent a story to his paper on March 13, the day the first Sheldon issue appeared. Bertrand's article began:

No guns were fired at sunrise this morning. The newspaper created by the Rev. Charles M. Sheldon on the lines suggested in 'In His Steps,' proved a disappointment, even to townspeople, who love him for himself and revere him for the genius which they consider he possesses. Those of Mr. Sheldon's Topeka admirers who looked for news in the first issue . . . had hard work finding it, and those who hoped to find homilies and sermons and lessons were rather annoyed because matter of that kind set before them had already been read by them in religious publications of uncertain and remote dates.

A reporter for the Rochester (New York) *Post-Express* described Sheldon's paper as being "closely akin to a number of newspapers issued from an office when a sudden strike has taken place. The editors are worried and cannot write anything of value."

On the evening before Sheldon's final day as editor, Popenoe entered the *Capital* newsroom and announced that he and the stockholders had decided to continue publishing the paper as a Christian daily. But not all the stockholders agreed, and when Popenoe tried to get Sheldon's support, the minister was silent. He had had enough of newspaper editing. The change never took place, and the *Capital* resumed publishing as a secular paper and soon had a new owner.[8]

CHAPTER TEN

MAKING A LIVING

*Some women knead dough with gloves on; if subscriptions
don't come faster, I will need dough without anything on.
. . . Your editor.*
—R. B. Darlington, *Molson* (Washington) *Leader*

WHEN JOSEPH CHARLESS established the *Missouri Gazette* at St. Louis in
1808, American newspapers had been respectable for less than a hundred
years. Before 1729 the American pioneers of journalism produced dull
papers, and they were generally dull people with little business sense who
had trouble meeting expenses, but in that year Benjamin Franklin took over
management of the *Pennsylvania Gazette* in Philadelphia, and Franklin
changed all that. He was not only a good journalist but a good businessman,
and by showing that journalism could make money, Franklin made newspapers respectable. But the success of the papers that followed depended
on the acumen of the proprietor.

By the time Charless began publishing the *Gazette,* most owners of papers were deriving their income from three sources—advertising, subscriptions, and job work, or the printing of cards, posters, stationery, and
other such things for individual customers. Subscriptions and advertising
yielded little income. To make ends meet, some printers even sold stationery and books. Still, the sources of income were meager. Had there
been no job work or public printing, and no politicians or town promoters
who felt the need of newspapers and supported them, few early papers
would have survived more than a year.

Starting a weekly in the West did not require a great deal of money. For
as little as two hundred dollars, a printer could acquire a used printing
press, a font or two of type, a composing stick with which to marshal the
letters, galleys to hold the columns of type before they were arranged in
forms, an imposing stone to keep the type level while being readied for the
press, wedges of various shapes to lock the forms into the master frame,
known as the chase, and ink balls to smear the type between impressions.

The cost of maintaining this equipment was small. The indispensable supplies were ink powder and paper, preferably genuine newsprint, while better paper was stocked for other printing jobs, ranging from advertising throwaways to books and pamphlets.

After the Washington handpress was perfected during the late 1820s, it became very popular in the West because it gave printers more mobility. The press was compact and solidly built. It needed no steadying wooden struts. In fact, it needed no installation whatever. Once unloaded from a wagon, the Washington handpress could be operated efficiently anywhere, including in the open while a building was being constructed.

In most early weekly papers one person did all the work. Seldom were more than two people employed. In many instances a lawyer or other ambitious person who wished to start a paper would find a printer, furnish the necessary equipment, write the editorials and some of the news, and let the printer solicit advertising, gather other news items, and select other news and miscellaneous material from exchange papers, set the type, and print and deliver the paper. Putting out a weekly newspaper required a great deal of work. It took an unusual amount of perseverance, physical strength, and moral courage. There was often little time to sell advertising.

One of the earliest descriptions of the numerous tasks performed by a newspaper editor in the West was published by Godwin Cotten in his *Texas Gazette* at San Felipe, on May 15, 1830:

A Country Editor—Is one who reads newspapers, selects miscellany, writes articles on all subjects; sets type, reads proof, works at press, folds papers; and sometimes carries them; prints jobs, runs on errands; cuts wood; toats water; talks to all his patrons who call; patiently receives blame for things that never were nor can be done; gets little money; has scarce time or materials to satisfy his hunger, or to enjoy the quiet of "nature's grand restorer" sleep; and esteems himself peculiar happy, if he is not assaulted and battered, (or bulletted and his ears cut off) by some unprincipled demagogue, who loves puppet shows, and hires the rabble with a treat of corn whiskey, (and that burnt), to vote him into some petty office,—A man who does all this and much more, not here recorded, you well know is rather a busy animal: and as he performs the work of so many different persons, he may justly be supposed their representative, and to have an indisputable right, when speaking of himself, to use the plural number, and to say "we," on all occasions and in all places.

Most newspapers asked that subscriptions be paid in advance. As an incentive the price was usually a dollar lower than if paid at the end of the year, but from the number of published appeals for money in the early papers, one can only conclude many subscribers found a way to save more than one dollar. Subscribers who did not pay were cajoled, praised, lectured, and denounced by editors in prose and verse. In one instance the editor of the *Western News,* published at Marion, Kansas, told his readers: "If our employees were cannibals, we'd feed 'em awhile on delinquent subscribers." When money was not available, an editor would turn to bartering and appeal for cordwood, potatoes, chickens, and other commodities. Many editors not only accepted such things for subscriptions but for advertising space as well. A full list of what the printers offered to receive would be an inventory of the daily needs of the pioneer.

In the first issue of the *Settler,* published October 18, 1884, at Ludell on the plains of western Kansas, editor George H. Hand told his readers:

> We buy, sell or trade anything that walks on four legs and eats buffalo grass. No papers sent out of the county unless paid for in advance, Oberlin excepted. We want one hundred shocks of sorghum, on subscription. Wood of any length, green or dry, is just as good as cash on subscription—in fact, better. Rye, corn, hay, millet, potatoes, eggs, chickens, etc., will be credited on subscription to *The Settler.* We want to place the paper within the reach of all, and shall endeavor to make it sufficiently interesting as a local paper to cause a healthy demand for it. Any one with a dollar and a half can act as a special agent.

Occasionally a potential subscriber might make a ridiculous request. In one instance the editor of the *Kansas News* published at Emporia, Kansas Territory, informed his readers on January 8, 1859:

> Cool. – A gentleman entered our office a few days since, and stated that he would like to subscribe for the paper for *forty days,* provided we would change the day of publication and "print his'n on Monday," and also provided he could pay his subscription in instalments [*sic*] of ten cents at a time, as he did not wish to risk a large amount of cash in our hands. We thought that "rather cool."
>
> P.S. Since writing the above, we found out that the individual alluded to, wanted to pay his subscription in frozen pumpkins.

One printer who started his weekly on a shoestring was Emerson Purcell. He decided to start his paper at Merina near Broken Bow in western Nebraska. Purcell got a bank loan for $120 and set up the *Merina Record* in an "unfinished" rent-free room, partially open to the elements, behind a photographer's gallery. Purcell was not yet of voting age when he printed the paper's first issue, while the photographer burned ten-cent corn in a pot-bellied stove to warm the wind-whipped newspaper office. In the larger community of Broken Bow, the *Broken Bow Republican* was printed on crude equipment in a sod house. Its news coverage was slim, but residents eagerly awaited each week's issue. Revenue was meager. The editor survived by bartering. When he accepted a horse in payment from a subscriber, the editor gave it to his young typesetter in lieu of a month's wages.

Some newspaper editors experienced more than financial problems. Samuel J. Albright, chief clerk of the Minnesota legislature and its official printer, took a Washington handpress and associated equipment in 1858 to the Dakota Territory. There, by the summer of the following year, he was publishing the *Democrat,* a weekly, at what became Sioux Falls, South Dakota. Making a living was difficult, and the difficulties got worse in 1862 when hostile Sioux Indians raided the settlement and among other things broke up Albright's press and other printing equipment. The settlers abandoned their townsite.[1]

As towns grew in population and new businesses arrived, it was only natural that someone would start a second newspaper. Usually the better paper survived because of journalistic reasons. Such was not the case in Salt Lake City, Utah, where the Latter-day Saints, or Mormons, established the weekly *Deseret News* on June 15, 1850. Brigham Young was publisher, Dr. Willard Richards, editor, and Horace K. Whitney, printer. Then, in May 1868, another weekly, the *Salt Lake Reporter,* was started. About a year later John Hanson Beadle, an attorney and native of Indiana who had given up his law practice and turned to journalism, arrived in Salt Lake City en route to California. With only three dollars in his pocket and waiting for money to arrive from the east, he visited the *Salt Lake Reporter* and wrote a few lines of editorial material for S. S. Saul, the paper's editor and publisher. Impressed, Saul offered Beadle twenty dollars a week to edit the weekly while he, Saul, went east to sell advertising. Beadle accepted the job.

The *Salt Lake Reporter* was small in format, only about a foot square, and had only sixty-nine paying subscribers. The first thing Beadle did was enlarge the size of the paper. Then while A. Aulbach, the paper's foreman, handled the business, Beadle wrote and edited the little weekly. The num-

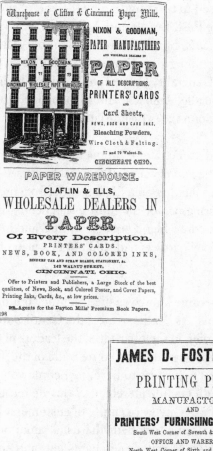

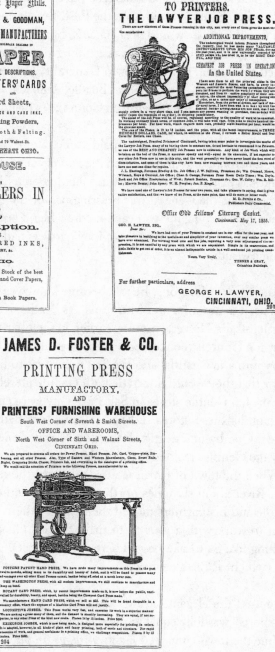

Cincinnati, Ohio, became a leading trading center by the late 1840s for presses and printing supplies, including type and paper. Many western editors obtained their printing equipment from Cincinnati firms. These illustrations were taken from mid-nineteenth-century national newspaper trade publications. *(Author's collection)*

ber of paid subscribers had increased to two hundred by the end of seven weeks when Saul returned from the East. Beadle and Aulbach were confident that the paper would be a success, but Saul returned without selling any advertising. His money was running out. Depressed, Saul soon returned ownership of the paper to General P. Connor, from whom he had bought it on terms. At that point Beadle, Aulbach, and a man named John Barrett purchased the paper from Connor. As Beadle later wrote:

> The price was $2,500, to be paid at the rate of $300 a month. By the most heroic exertions we raised the first payment of $100 each; the second was paid, I believe, some three months later. Eight months from the day of sale the General was pressing us, for the third installment, six months over due; but you cannot "draw blood out of a turnip," and he never did get his money till both my partners had sold out to a man of some wealth.

Among the Mormons, Beadle became known as the "Gentile" editor, a term used to describe non-Mormons. As Beadle wrote, "the Gentiles were in cruel straits." Several months earlier, in October 1868, the leaders of the Mormon Church "concocted a plan for getting the entire trade of the Territory into a few hands, and the first move was to have the people vote *en masse* that they would not trade with Gentile merchants." Beadle recalled that the ten Gentile stores in Salt Lake City were empty of customers. For six months these stores did not sell one-twentieth the usual amount of goods. One by one nearly all the non-Mormon merchants left, and soon only 150 Gentiles resided in Salt Lake City.

When the town of Corinne was laid out at the railroad crossing on the Bear River about six miles north of the north end of the Great Salt Lake, Beadle and his partners moved the *Reporter* there, and in April 1869 "all went to work with a *hurrah* to make a great Gentile city." Corinne was nothing like Salt Lake City. There were nineteen saloons and two dance halls which, as Beadle wrote,

> amused the elegant leisure of the evening hours, and the supply of "sports" was fully equal to the requirements of a railroad town. At one time the town contained eighty *nymphs du pave,* popularly known in Mountain-English as "soiled doves." Being the last railroad town it enjoyed "flush times" during the closing weeks of building the Pacific Railway. The junction of the Union and Central was then at Promon-

tory, twenty-eight miles west, and Corinne was the retiring place for rest and recreation of all the employees. . . . Legitimate business was good for the first two months of the city's existence; for the railroad was just being completed, and everybody supposed that the harvest of gain was about to begin. We had public meetings in abundance. Two or three times a week flaming posters called the citizens together, to consult on "improvements for the benefit of Corinne." Bonfires were lighted, a stand improvised by turning up a dry-goods box, and a number of florid speeches delivered; the crowd then voted unanimously for various heroic resolutions, and dispersed to read their proceedings in the next morning's *Reporter*.

Beadle remained in Corinne for some time and then took time off to travel. When he returned, he found that his two partners had sold out and hired a new editor. Beadle soon sold his share in the *Reporter* and in September 1869 took a train west.[2]

IT WAS NOT UNCOMMON in some western towns for merchants to buy advertising in their local papers as charity rather than as an investment on which they would receive returns. The merchants recognized the importance of having a local newspaper. In such cases merchants often ran the same advertisements week after week. This helped the newspaper, since the advertisements did not have to be reset. On the other hand, editors did everything they could to encourage all merchants to advertise. H. L. Weston, publisher of the *Sentinel* in the Nevada mining town of Como in 1864, tried to motivate merchants to advertise with the following verse:

> Come, you who burn the midnight taper,
> Contribute something for the paper;
> Come all, support the enterprise
> And in the paper advertise.
> Merchants, tailors, doctors, lawyers,
> Landlords, blacksmiths, teamsters, sawyers,
> Bakers, too, of bread, cake, pies,
> Come one, come all, and advertise.[3]

A New Mexico editor, John P. Hyland, published similar verse in his weekly, the *Weekly Shaft*, at Rincon. The following appeared in 1893:

He had traveled through Sahara,
   Braved the dangers of the Nile,
Defeated enraged Musselmen
   And dined on crocodile;
Knew everything of politics,
   Religion and the law,
Could box and fence and scull and race
   And please his mother-in-law,
In short had all accomplishments
   Of men both great and wise,
But he couldn't run a business,
   For he wouldn't advertise.[4]

   National advertising was pretty much nonexistent in the early papers of the West, for many reasons. Communication and transportation were poor. The birth and quick death of many papers was notorious. Then too, many newspaper proprietors were not good businessmen. They were not

A newspaper's success depended on its distribution. Even in small western towns, boys were used to distribute papers to subscribers. The three boys in this early 1900s photo are waiting to receive their consignments of copies of the weekly *Dispatch* published at Woodward, Oklahoma. *(Courtesy Western History Collections, University of Oklahoma)*

reliable about sending copies of their papers to national advertisers so that they could confirm that ads had actually been published. Some papers even failed to send bills to eastern advertising firms who placed the ads.

Many advertisements in western papers were unique. Advertisers told the editors what they wanted to say, and that is what was set in type. One of the earliest such ads appeared in the *Missouri Republican* during the 1820s. It read:

LOOK HERE!!

Fred Yeiser, on Main Street, next door to Dougan's Silver Smith shop has on hand a "great heap of whiskey," plenty of peach brandy, linsey, country linen, shoes, nails, cotton, bed cords, etc., etc., low for cash or hides. N.B. No credit as I have never learnt to write.—Fred Yeiser.[5]

Advertisements for saloons can be found in most early western papers. Some of the more interesting ones include:

William Parker's Saloon
Blacktail, Near Watson, Montana
Travelers Invited to Drop In
No Sheep Dip Dispensed
A jovial party of hilarious fellows
May usually be found congregated at this shrine
of Bacchus
(*Atlantis*, Glendale, Wyoming)

Ice Cream Saloon. We call attention of our citizens to the preparation made for their entertainment at "The Counts." A fine lunch is provided in the evening for the benefit of frequenters of the saloon. That rarest of stimulants, a good cup of coffee, is there to be had, in perfection. A trial will convince the most skeptical.

(*Montana Post*, Virginia City)

HARMONIC SALOON AND SHOOTING GALLERY
J. K. Reitze, proprietor
The very best of Wines, Liquors and Cigars
Call and See for Yourselves
John K. Reitze will Furnish Brass and String Music
for balls, parties, picnics and parades

Lessons given on the piano, organ and melodeon
Pianos tuned on liberal terms.
(*Union Democrat,* Tuolumne County, California)

And then there is the following advertisement taken from the Fresno (California) *Expositor:*

Attention! Sinners!
Hot Stuff Coffins
Asbestos! Asbestos!
My factory is turning out a line
of Asbestos Coffins that are rapidly
going out of sight. No need fear
the hereafter, as I guarantee to see a
corpse through without singeing a hair
W. Parker Lyon
Philanthropist and Furniture King

Sometimes advertisements were disguised as news stories to get readers to pay attention, forerunners of today's advertorials. The following example appeared on June 14, 1860, in the *Huntsman's Echo,* published at Wood River Center Ranch in central Nebraska:

AN ACCIDENT

Whilst in Omaha the other day, we were startled by a cry in the street of – stop thief! stop thief! . . . We rushed out and saw a "peaker" [a gold hunter en route to the Pike's Peak region] with a huge load of goods, making off in hot haste with a whole train in his wake, re-echoing the shout. The man in the lead being very heavily loaded, was soon brought to, and upon asking the cause of the fuss, was informed that he was suspected of having stolen the goods with which he was so rapidly making off. The fellow laid down his load and gave vent to the following exclamations:

"You d——d fools—you are as soft as toadstools and green as squash! Think I'd be such a ninny and simpleton as to spend my time stealing goods when I can buy them so cheap as McGeath's! Why, a fellow would be a blamed fool to steal under such circumstances."

The crowd dispersed, and we ran down to McGeath's to see, and went away satisfied the "peaker" was right.

Some advertisers chose verse as their vehicle for advertising. A dentist at Chetopa, Kansas, inserted the following in the town's weekly *Advance* on December 22, 1869:

Persons whose teeth are decaying
Should go to a dentist without delaying,
And have them cleaned, then filled in
With good gold, amalgam or tin.
If your teeth have ached unto distraction,
Then, for a short time you will wait,
And get a new set on a corral plate.
Artificial teeth are extremely fair,
They are everlasting—with care.
For a set of teeth that are number one,
Be sure to go to Dr. Patterson.

Once it came time for homesteaders to prove their claims staked on the prairie and plains, Federal law required that each one run his final proof notice six times in the newspaper nearest to his claim. The proof notice was a published statement proclaiming that the homesteader had faithfully lived up to the government rules and was expecting to give final proof of this and receive a patent from the government, which would give him full ownership of the land he had homesteaded. Newspapers looked forward to publishing such proof notices since they meant more revenue. Papers usually charged between $6.50 and $10.00 to print a proof notice. The charge depended on what the editor thought a fair price and whether there was another newspaper in the town competing for the business. Since homesteaders usually staked claims in one area within a few months of each other, the publishing of proof notices came close together. These were boom periods for local editors, who, after filling their pockets with cash, sometimes packed up their presses and printing equipment and moved farther west to areas where homesteaders were about to proof up on their homesteads. In Sully County, Dakota Territory, nine papers were published during final proof days, and after the Big Sioux reservation was opened to homesteading, E. L. Senn set up thirty presses, each in a different area, ready to capture the proof-notice business.[6]

With improvements in communication and transportation, and as western newspapers became better organized and adopted better business practices, advertising revenues improved. They came from four sources:

W. E. Showen, editor of the *Minco* (Oklahoma) *Minstrel,* cut a dapper figure dressed in his Sunday best for this 1900 photo, showing him checking the back page of his four-page weekly. But Showen's daily dress (see below) was that of a printer. Most editors in small towns printed their own papers. *(Courtesy Western History Collections, University of Oklahoma)*

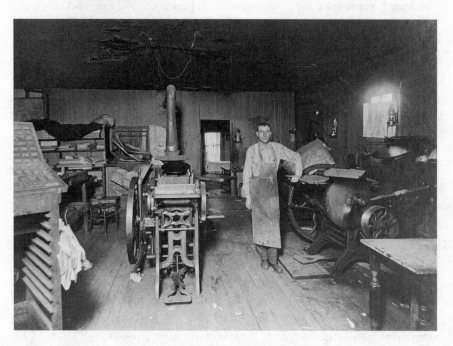

W. E. Showen in the backshop of his Maysville, Oklahoma, weekly *News* in 1917. Showen had sold his Minco paper and was publishing the Maysville paper when this photo was taken. Showen's only other employee was Hattie Griffen, a typesetter, not shown here. Showen's living quarters were in the back of the newspaper office. A bed and rocking chair are visible through the door in the back of the room. *(Courtesy Western History Collections, University of Oklahoma)*

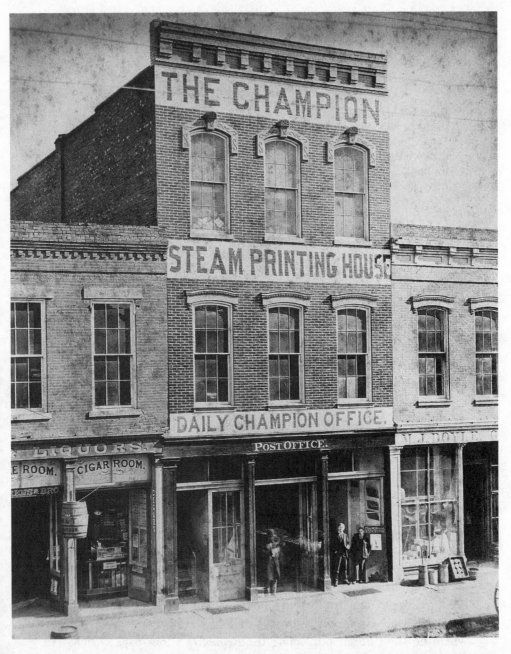

After the Civil War the most modern newspapers in the West used steam to power their printing presses. Steam power was a sign of progress. The *Daily Champion* at Atchison, Kansas, announced its pride in being a "steam printing house" with the sign on its building. Steam-powered presses were first used in the East during the 1820s. This photo was taken about 1866, after proprietor Col. John A. Martin made the weekly a daily. Three years later the building, which housed the post office on the first floor, was destroyed by fire. *(Author's collection)*

Ansel Nash Kellogg founded the A. N. Kellogg Newspaper Company in Chicago just after the Civil War and produced the first preprinted sheets for newspapers in the West and elsewhere. *(Author's collection)*

local merchants and farmers, business concerns, national advertisers seeking to establish and sell some particular brand or line of goods, and legal advertising. Legal advertising included notices to creditors, mortgage sales, and all the other legal notices that the local and state laws required to be published. If a newspaper was located in a county seat, legal advertising often provided considerable income to a publisher. In towns where there was more than one newspaper, the competition was great, and obtaining the business of publishing the town's legal notices often depended on the politics of the paper's proprietor.

One of the biggest boons for western newspapers came following the Civil War. Type was still set by hand much as it had been by Gutenberg more than four hundred years earlier. Hand composition of type was slow. It was costly, took much time, and delayed the publication of news. A partial solution to these problems was the creation of pre-printed sheets by Ansel Nash Kellogg, a native of Reading, Pennsylvania, and a graduate of Columbia College in New York City. In 1855 Kellogg went to Baraboo, Wisconsin, where he soon began publishing the *Republic,* a four-page weekly. His paper was printed on a Washington handpress that turned out 150 sheets per hour, one side at a time. When Kellogg's assistant went off to fight in the Civil War, Kellogg realized that he could not set all the type necessary to publish his paper without help, and arranged to get the war news in half-sheet supplements, printed on both sides, from the *Wisconsin State Journal* at Madison. These he folded inside his own printed half sheets. It then occurred to Kellogg that the awkwardness of handling a paper consisting of two separate pieces could be removed if he purchased full sheets, printed on one side, instead of half sheets printed on both sides. In the summer of 1861, Kellogg's weekly appeared as a four-page paper with two pages printed in his shop and two pages printed at Madison. Other weekly editors, also short of typesetters, followed Kellogg and did the same thing. By the end of the Civil War fifty Wisconsin weeklies were involved in the practice.

Sensing a business opportunity, Kellogg sold his Baraboo weekly in 1865 and, with his proceeds, moved to Chicago and formed the A. N. Kellogg Newspaper Company, which was devoted exclusively to producing preprinted newspaper sheets. At that time, however, the appearance of newspapers varied widely in layout and type style. Columns varied in length and width. The only standard was the size of the sheet, which had to fit the presses then in use. To overcome this problem and to create a large market for his product, Kellogg set about standardizing newspaper appearance so that it would match his preprinted or "ready print" sheets. Kellogg let editors of weeklies trade in their old type in exchange for fonts that matched what he used on his preprinted pages.

Within a few short years Kellogg was responsible for what became the standard look of weekly newspapers. When the sheets printed only on one side arrived at a weekly, the editor usually printed the first and fourth pages on the blank side. Kellogg sold his readyprints for five dollars or less a week, which he could do because he made money from the advertising on his side of the sheets. Editors were able to cut costs since someone else did half their work. Typesetting time was halved. Using preprinted pages also cut an editor's paper costs and provided more profit.

As papers began to use readyprint, many readers must have been surprised by the appearance of well-written yet folksy material in their local papers. Kellogg hired a bright editorial staff to produce stories and literary material for his side of the readyprint. Among the guidelines he prepared for his writers and editors were:

Spare no pains or expense to get the best and freshest of news and literary matter.

It is as much the mark of a good editor to know what not to print as to be able to select good and appropriate matter.

When in doubt about the propriety of printing an article, leave it out; there is plenty of that which is unquestionably good and desirable.

In the news columns avoid, as far as possible, the giving of details of scandals and crimes—confining the accounts to mere statements of facts of general interest or importance.

There is always room for improvement and betterment. The Best is none too good for the Kellogg service.[7]

Most weekly editors did not tell their readers that half of their four-page paper had been written, edited, illustrated, headlined, and printed by un-named persons. Instead they took credit for everything that appeared. In time Kellogg had editors send their long-running local business notices from lawyers, funeral parlors, and the like to Chicago. They were im-printed with matching typefaces on the same pages as the readyprint mate-rial, along with advertisements obtained in Chicago from patent medicine companies and other businesses. On January 1, 1872, a trade publication called *American Newspaper Reporter* ran an advertisement for Kellogg's company that reflected the wide range of services offered, including these:

Insides, Outsides, Exteriors and Supplements.
Republican, Neutral and Democratic.
Six, Seven, Eight and Nine Column Folios.
Headings changed free. No interferences.
Thirty-six Regular Editions Weekly.
Save a Thousand Dollars a Year.

Kellogg soon exercised enormous influence on what Americans read, especially those in the West, where the cost of books was out of most peo-ple's reach, and most homes had only a Bible and perhaps an English novel and a medical self-help book. The preprinted pages constituted what was really a national newspaper, something like the modern *USA Today*.[8]

The content of weekly newspapers using preprinted pages helped to shape the national character from just after the Civil War into the twentieth century. For instance, the editors responsible for producing the content of the preprinted sheets recognized only two national political parties—the Republican and the Democratic. The editors also stressed conformity in matters of manners, dress, writing, speech, and ideas on moral beliefs and patriotism—even recipes. Not only were readers influenced by what they read, but many journalists who learned their craft on weekly papers, espe-cially in the West, were undoubtedly influenced by what they learned in the preprinted pages. When many of them moved on to larger newspapers, in some cases magazines, located in cities from coast to coast, they carried

THE PRESS FOR THE TIMES!

NEW NONPAREIL PRESS.

SUPERLATIVELY STRONG,
SIMPLE IN MANAGEMENT,
CAPABLE OF THE FINEST WORK.

Every part of the machine is accessible to the hand of the Operator, and easy to oil and clean. The Sectional Roller for saving ink, and adjustable distribution for Printing in various

COLORS

at one impression are very simple and quickly adjusted, adding nothing to the cost or complication of the Press, nor detracting in any manner from its usefulness for one-colored

PLAIN WORK.

This is not only the *best*, but No. 4 is also the *largest* Bed and Platen Jobber built. All Presses sold warranted satisfactory.

Cincinnati Type Foundry Co.,
201 Vine Street.

(Printed on the Nonpareil Job Press at one impression.)

This is a page from an 1870 Cincinnati Type Foundry Company catalog, promoting their "nonpareil" press. The press was operated by treadle and capable of printing different colors. It was used to print job work by larger papers in the West. *(Author's collection)*

A. N. Kellogg took advantage of technological advances and offered papers with stereotype plates containing a wide range of prepared stories and features. This advertisement was taken from an 1875 issue of the *American Newspaper Reporter. (Author's collection)* with them notions about the United States that were shaped in part by Kellogg's readyprints. Their role in creating the American culture has largely been ignored by historians. More recently, however, Page Smith, who wrote *The Rise of Industrial America,* published in 1984, noted:

> It has been observed that the first generation of young exposé journalists and editors was, almost without exception, from the Midwest and Far West, although the meaning of this has been less generally commented on . . . they signified the displacement of the New England literary establishment by a wholly new and fundamentally more "American" type. . . . They stood outside what we would call today the old-boy network. . . . As outsiders they saw everything freshly.[9]

The success of Kellogg's company inspired imitators to move into the field. By the 1880s the companies producing preprinted pages supplied more than 3,000 of the nation's 8,600 weekly papers. The national circulation of preprinted pages was greater than that of today's circulation of

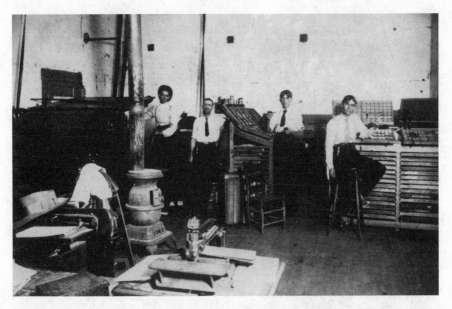

The backshops of many western newspapers looked much like this 1901 photo taken at the *Duncan* (Oklahoma) *Banner.* The paper was founded in 1892 by James P. Sampson of Greeville, Texas. In 1893 Sampson brought his son, Fred (*left*), into the business. The Sampsons later sold their interests in the paper to Ed J. Leeman (*second from left*), who eventually made the paper a daily. The other men in the photo are not identified. *(Courtesy Western History Collections, University of Oklahoma)*

national papers, including *USA Today,* the *Washington Post,* and the *New York Times.* When significant changes in printing technology occurred during the 1880s, Kellogg and the other readyprint firms began using type-casting machines, cheaper methods of producing illustrations, high-speed presses, and improvements in the stereotyping process to send out stories, illustrations, and advertising on precast metal plates so a newspaper could print without having to set type. Gradually preprinted sheets gave way to stereotype or "boilerplates," as they became known. As late as 1915, however, nearly 2,500 weekly papers in the West were still using preprinted pages.[10]

WHEN A GROUP OF Republican businessmen in Laramie, Wyoming, decided to start a new daily to compete against the Democratic *Daily Times,* Edgar Wilson "Bill" Nye became editor. A stock company was formed, and Nye named the new paper the *Boomerang,* after a mule that one day had wandered into town, ambled up to Nye, and, rubbing its nose against

Edgar Wilson "Bill" Nye started the *Laramie Boomerang* in March 1881. *(Courtesy American Heritage Center, University of Wyoming)*

his sleeve, brayed earnestly in his ear. The mule became Nye's mascot. The *Boomerang*'s first office was located on the second floor of a business building, and a press was installed that could produce no more than 250 papers an hour, two pages at a time. The first issue was published on March 11, 1881. Years later Nye recalled:

It wasn't much of a paper, but it cost $16,000 a year to run, and it came out six days in the week, no matter what the weather. We took the Associated Press news by telegraph part of the time, and part of the time we relied on the Cheyenne morning papers, which we procured from the conductor on the early morning freight. We received a great many special telegrams from Washington in that way. And when the freight train got in late, I had to guess at what Congress was doing and fix up a column of telegraph the best I could. There was a rival paper . . . and sometimes it would send a smart boy down to the train and get hold of our special telegrams. Sometimes the conductor would go away on a picnic and take our Cheyenne paper with him. . . .

There were two daily and three weekly papers published in Laramie City at that time. There were between two and three thousand people and our local circulation ran from 150 to 250, counting dead-heads. In our prospectus we stated that we would spare no expense whatever in ransacking the universe for fresh news, but there were times when it was all we could do to get our paper out on time. Out of the express office, I mean.

One of the rival editors used to write his editorials for the paper in the evening, jerk the Washington hand press to work them off, go home and wrestle with juvenile colic in his family until daylight and then deliver his papers on the street. It was not surprising that the great mental strain incident to his life made an old man of him, and gave a tinge of extreme sadness to the funny column of his paper.

In an unguarded moment, this man once wrote an editorial that got all his subscribers mad at him, and the same afternoon he came around and wanted to sell his paper to us for $10,000. I told him that the whole outfit wasn't worth ten thousand cents.

"I know that," said he, "but it is not the material that I am talking about. It is the *good will* of the paper."[11]

Nye's own health was not good, and he had to leave the *Boomerang* after a few years.

A majority of the newspapers in the West during the nineteenth and

The office of the *Laramie Boomerang*, a paper started by Edgar Wilson "Bill" Nye in 1881. *(Courtesy American Heritage Center, University of Wyoming)*

early twentieth centuries were started on a shoestring. Most were established by printers like J. Marvin Hunter, who was born on March 18, 1880, in Loyal Valley, Texas. His father was a schoolteacher until 1891, when he purchased the *Menardville* (Texas) *Record*. There young Hunter learned the printing trade from his father. In 1904, J. Marvin Hunter started his own paper at London in Kimble County, Texas. Fifty years later he provided one of the most vivid first-person accounts of how a weekly newspaper was started very early in the twentieth century:

> I believe I can safely say there is not one man in a thousand who would have started a newspaper under the same conditions and circumstances that I faced when I launched the *Kimble County Crony*. Practically without funds, but with plenty of grit and determination I made a real success of the venture. I bought a little 6-column Army press for $31.00. Then I borrowed a small amount of type from my father's [printing] office in Mason. My printing plant was shockingly small. I did not have the proverbial "shirt-tail full" of type. No slugs or leads; no job type. In

fact, I had barely enough type to set up two of four short columns to the page. But I brought out the first issue of the *Kimble County Crony* on June 7, 1904. . . .

When we moved our household effects over from Menardville and paid the man who moved us $12.00 for his service, we rented two rooms in the old Lewis hotel for $3.00 per month in advance, and I secured a small room in an old house on Main Street for my printing office for $3.00 a month. After paying out this $18.00 "right off the reel," I had mighty little change left in my pocket, and the next day when a box of type came up on the stage from Mason, to be delivered to the "printing office," there was fifty cents charges on the package. The stage driver was none other than Bush Collins, the same fellow who once hauled me from London to Junction in a gulley jumper for a can of peaches and a box of sweet crackers. The stage arrived at 12 o'clock, and when I saw a man pointing out the "printing office" to Bush Collins, I made myself scarce, figuring correctly that Bush could not wait long to collect his

J. Marvin Hunter founded the *Kimble County Crony* in 1904 at London, Texas. *(Courtesy Western History Collections, University of Oklahoma)*

four bits, as he had to be on his way with the mail. He drove up, unloaded the box of type on the front porch, and after waiting some ten or fifteen minutes, got in his hack and drove on toward Junction. I came out of my "retreat" and carried the box inside, and proceeded to get ready for the printing of the little newspaper. Four days in succession I had to dodge that mail carrier, but when the *Crony* came from the press I soon had money to pay up what I owed.

London at that time had the following business houses: B. P. Woody, drug store; G. T. May, general merchandise; R. C. McCollum, general merchandise; E. W. Brewer, general merchandise; Frank McKean, hardware; Mrs. Alice Bannowsky, general merchandise; W. L. Smith, blacksmith shop; Seth Lewis, saloon; Jack Brewer, hotel,—and now a newspaper. The stores were all small, and so was the newspaper. I secured $11.00 worth of advertising patronage, monthly, in the town. My subscription price was $1.00 a year. But there was Mason, 25 miles to the east; Menardville, 25 miles to the North; Junction, 22 miles to the southwest; and Brady, the nearest railroad point, was 45 miles away. All of these towns were reaching out for the trade of that London country. London was located in the corner of Kimble county, next to Menard and Mason counties. There is a strip of territory there about ten miles wide by about twenty miles long which is the cream of productiveness of that whole region – a rich farming and stock-raising region.

I hustled early and late for advertising patronage and subscriptions. I would trade advertising space in my paper and subscriptions to it for anything we could consume, butter, eggs, chickens, produce of any kind, and for dry goods and groceries, for I believe strictly in the system of barter and trade. About two weeks after I started the *Crony* a big barbecue was held in one of the fine groves at London, and fully 1,500 people were there. I hustled for subscriptions on that occasion, and when the day ended I had thirty silver dollars jingling in my pockets. I would meet a man, introduce myself to him, and tell him he ought to take the *Kimble County Crony,* and if he said he did not have the money I would tell him he could pay me in the fall when he sold his cotton, and of course I got him. I remember I introduced myself to a man and told him I wanted him to subscribe for my paper. He handed me a dollar, and said: "I have already told you three times that I would take your paper, and pay you this fall, but you must have forgotten it. So here's your dollar. Don't forget to send me the *Crony.*"

Within a month I had taken in enough cash to order one hundred pounds of new type, and so I made the *Crony* a six-column paper, the

William Allen White was born in 1868 at Emporia, Kansas. After attending college and working in all aspects of newspapering elsewhere, he returned to Emporia in 1895 to purchase the weekly *Gazette*. This photo of White was taken two years before he gave Rolla Clymer, another Kansas editor, advice on running a newspaper. White became nationally known as a small-town editor. He made the *Gazette* one of the most successful small-town papers in America before his death in 1946. *(Courtesy Kansas State Historical Society)*

best in that section. Soon I bought a larger press, a seven column Washington hand press, a job press, and built a three-room house, doing much of the carpentering myself. On November 11, 1904, our first child, a boy, was born, and we named him for his grandfather, John Warren Hunter. In February, 1906, our second child was born, a fine little baby girl, and we named her Myra Jennette. By this time my *Kimble County Crony* had reached its peak as a newspaper, and I fully realized it. I was like a frog in a well, going round and round, and getting nowhere.[12]

Hunter sold the *Kimble County Crony* and soon started a new paper at Garden City, Texas.

By the early twentieth century, publishing a successful newspaper had become something of a science. Successful publishers knew certain things had to be in place if a paper was to succeed. In 1918 Rolla Clymer, who was editor and manager of the *Olathe* (Kansas) *Register*, wanted to buy the El Dorado (Kansas) *Republican* from the Murdock family of Wichita, Kansas. Clymer, however, wanted an experienced publisher to look over the paper and to give him advice on making it a success. Clymer asked his friend William Allen White to do this. White visited the paper and then wrote Clymer a four-page letter. White's candid letter provides a fascinating look at the inner workings of the newspaper business. It reads:

Dear Rolla:

In El Dorado I found the situation splendidly hopeful for you. Their new equipment will be all in and settled before you get there and you will find an absolutely virgin field before you. The paper is chaos; chaos in the business department; chaos in the news department. I think the bookkeeping is the first place to begin . . . put in a new system of books. . . . Next, in the advertising department you will find that they are charging stupidly cheap rates. The first thing to do is to bring every merchant under a contract, and to charge thirty cents an inch for all transient advertising, no matter what the other paper charges. When you get around to this point, I may be able to do something with Mr. J. B. Adam, the owner of the other paper. I will be glad to confer with him either personally over the phone, or by letter; and whether he agrees or not, whether he cuts prices secretly or openly, there is but one course for the *Republican* to follow and that is to compel merchants who do not have the contract to pay the highest rate and to put every merchant on a contract. That will take time, and it will take diplomacy, and it will take lots of legs, but you have got to do it. And of course you cannot do it in a day. If you complete the job in six months, I will think you are a wonder. But you must make the announcement as soon as you get there and first of all take all the advertising off the first page. Then kill all patent medicine advertising as fast as the contracts expire. They won't pay the price and the merchants will. Then after you have established your rates, you must see that the collections are promptly and thoroughly made. And in that connection you will have your chief trouble in the circulation department. You must insist that the carrier boys buy the papers and sell them to the subscribers. Go right to the High School and get a hold of the Senior and Junior boys, pick out your carriers, and go to it. Raise the rate of the paper to fifty cents a month and sell the papers to the carriers at one cent a copy and at the end of the month ten cents additional for each subscriber. We do that here and it pays. There is plenty of money in El Dorado and you can make it pay. Get the office in the habit of paying all their bills between the first and the tenth of the month. Have no old personal bills of the Murdocks [former owners] hanging over it. They [the Murdocks] have always been great hands to let the bills run, and settle them semi-annually or semi-occasionally. Stop that if you never do anything else. Go borrow money to pay all the bills outstanding for at least a month, and in borrowing the money, make three notes for thirty, sixty, and ninety days to cover that amount and take these notes up as they come due, so that every month you will clean up all the debts of the office, and know exactly how you stand, and have a settlement with every merchant every month.

Now as to the news policy. Of course the first job of the newspaper is to print the news, but on the other hand after you have piled your paper full of names, you must have a policy, and I should say that policy should be the material and spiritual improvement of El Dorado; and do not forget the spiritual improvement stands for dozens of things. You may have to tear up your city printing contract, but do it; and you may have to tear up your county printing contract; but do it, and do it in a cold-blooded way. You will find that the confidence of the community in the paper's integrity is worth three times as much as the contracts which you lose. And you will only lose those contracts temporarily, for when your integrity is established they will come back, and then they will stay with you. A newspaper's good name is its chief asset, it brings not only circulation, but power and prosperity.

There isn't anything else in the newspaper business as sure as that axiom. You will find it hard to preach spiritual things in a material minded town. You do not want to be longfaced about it and sanctimonious, but you do want to stand for brotherhood and the Golden Rule. And the best way to get brotherhood and the Golden Rule in that community is to preach a municipal band and auditorium where it can give free concerts; and a park system where the band can give concerts; and a Y.M.C.A. with gymnasium and swimming pool and dormitories to make it self-sustaining; a trolley line going to the various oil camps of the county and running into El Dorado; a welfare association with a free employment bureau and a scientific care of the poor of the community, and many other such propositions as will give the poor devil who has not much of a home a chance to move around in the community to enjoy himself and to live decently upon his wages; and stand for a clean town. Insist on law enforcement. Make them drive out the prostitutes and the gamblers no matter whose building they occupy. Brace up your courage and do not be afraid that a small loss of today is going to weigh against the great good of the paper by having it proved to be loyal and brave and fair.[13]

Clymer took over the El Dorado *Republican* in April 1918 and followed White's advice. The following year Clymer purchased the *Walnut Valley Times*, published at El Dorado, merged it with the *Republican*, and re-named the paper the *El Dorado Times*. He went on to publish and edit it until his death in 1975.

EXACTLY HOW MANY newspapers lived and died in the West during the nineteenth and early twentieth centuries is not known. A majority failed because their owners did not follow sound business practices. When the *Daily Appeal* faded in Leavenworth, Kansas, on July 3, 1879, the following day the editor of the *Leavenworth Daily Times* published what could have served as the obituary of countless other papers in the West. The editor wrote: "The *Daily Appeal* died yesterday morning. It has been running about two months. It lived about one month longer than anybody supposed it would. It was a bankrupt concern in every sense of the word, from the first. It was without capital, ability or integrity."

But many early newspapers in competent hands did survive. They employed good business practices and able journalists and some continue to be published by descendants of the early proprietors today. One is the *Los Angeles Times*, which was established by local printers in 1881 when Los Angeles had a population of only twelve thousand people and two other papers, the *Express* and the *Herald*. The following year Harrison Gray Otis bought into the *Times*. Otis was a forty-five-year-old Civil War veteran with colonel's rank who had some previous experience in newspapering. By 1886 Otis had full control of the morning paper, which had a circulation of seven thousand. He also invested in real estate, and a boom increased his profits. By 1900 the *Times* had a circulation of twenty-six thousand and boasted the country's largest advertising linage. Later it claimed to devote more space to editorial matter than any other paper in the nation. In spite of labor disputes in the late nineteenth and early twentieth centuries, the *Times* continued to grow in circulation as Otis's

Col. Harrison Gray Otis bought an interest in the *Los Angeles Times* in 1882 and by 1886 had gained full control. The paper has since become a leading daily on the West Coast, with a national reputation. *(Courtesy California State Library)*

son-in-law, Harry Chandler, and later other family members became publishers. By the 1970s the paper's circulation passed the one million mark. Today, what started as a pioneer paper is a leading daily on the West Coast with a national reputation.[14]

Up the Pacific coast in Portland, the *Oregonian,* established as a weekly in 1850 and first printed on an old Ramage screw press, became a daily in 1861 and well known because of Harvey W. Scott, a very competent journalist, who became editor in 1865. Twelve years later he bought the paper and operated it until his death in 1910. Scott's writings, especially his editorials, made the paper a leader in the Pacific Northwest. The *Oregonian* was successfully managed by Henry L. Pittock until his death in 1919. Today the paper is published by the Newhouse Group.[15]

In San Francisco, the *Chronicle* was started by two brothers from Missouri, Charles and Michael H. De Young, in 1865 as a free theater-program sheet called *Dramatic Chronicle*. In 1868 the paper dropped the word "Dramatic" from its title and soon became the city's leading paper. On April 23, 1880, Charles De Young was shot and killed in the *Chronicle* office by the son of a political enemy whom De Young had shot and wounded earlier. Michael H. De Young took over the entire management of the paper and continued to supervise its operation until his death in 1925.[16]

North of San Francisco, the *Sacramento Bee*, founded in 1857, became well known during the 1880s, when C. K. McClatchy became publisher and editor. Eleanor McClatchy continued to operate it after her father's death in 1936, and the family still owns and publishes the *Bee* along with several other papers.[17]

Another long-lived pioneer paper is the *Dallas Morning News*, started by Colonel A. H. Belo, who enjoyed the distinction of having been the youngest colonel in the Confederate army. Following the Civil War, he went to Galveston, Texas, where in late 1865 he got a job as a bookkeeper on the *Daily News*, a paper established in 1842, during the days of the Republic of Texas. By March 1866 he was part-owner, and he took full control of the paper in 1875. Anticipating a bright future for the then small town of Dallas in northern Texas, Belo started the *Dallas Morning News* as a twin paper carrying many of the same articles as his Galveston paper. With the help of George B. Dealey, who had served as his business manager in Galveston, Belo made the Dallas paper a success. Colonel Belo was an enthusiastic Texas booster and an enterprising publisher until his death in 1901. Family members, along with George Dealey and others, then took over operation of the paper. As Dallas grew, so did the *Dallas Morning News*. In 1926 Dealey purchased a controlling interest in the paper, and his son E. M. "Ted" Dealey inherited it in 1946. Today it is the largest daily in Texas and still operated by descendants of the pioneers who started it.[18]

North of Texas across the Red River is another family-owned daily with its roots firmly entrenched in the heritage of pioneer times. In December 1902 Edward King Gaylord, a twenty-nine-year-old Kansan who had grown up in Colorado, arrived in Oklahoma City looking for a newspaper in which to invest. He found the *Daily Oklahoman*, published by Roy E. Stafford, who liked Gaylord's ideas about newspapers. Together they formed the Oklahoma Publishing Company early in 1903, and Gaylord began the process of improving the paper. In 1916 the *Oklahoman* bought the bankrupted evening *Oklahoma City Times* at public auction, and in 1918 Stafford sold his interests. E. K. Gaylord took control of the business and editorial policies and transformed the paper into the largest and most prominent daily in Oklahoma. With the help of his family, Gaylord continued to operate the paper until his death in 1974 at the age of 101, when his son, Edward L. Gaylord, and other family members took over its operation, which continues today.[19]

In St. Louis, where the first newspaper west of the Mississippi was

Col. A. H. Belo, born at Salem, North Carolina, in 1839, went to Texas following the Civil War and soon gained control of the *Galveston News*. In 1885, he started what is today the *Dallas Morning News*. Belo died in 1901. *(Courtesy A. H. Belo Corporation Foundation)*

Edward King Gaylord visited Oklahoma City late in 1902, liked what he saw, and invested in the *Daily Oklahoman* early in 1903. By 1918 he had taken control of the paper, which became the largest and most prominent daily in Oklahoma. Gaylord continued to operate the paper until his death in 1974 at the age of 101. His son, Edward L. Gaylord, and other family members took over the operation of the paper. This photo was made during the 1930s. *(Courtesy Oklahoma Publishing Company)*

established in 1808, another family-run newspaper, the *Post-Dispatch*, founded by Joseph Pulitzer, still flourishes. While he is perhaps best known as the publisher of the New York *World* and for his circulation battles with William Randolph Hearst's New York *Journal* late in the nineteenth century, Pulitzer bought the distressed St. Louis *Dispatch* at a sheriff's sale in 1878. Later he absorbed the St. Louis *Union* and then combined the *Dispatch* with the St. Louis *Post*. Following his father's death in 1911, Joseph Pulitzer, Jr., took the reins and managed the paper until 1955, when Joseph Pulitzer III took over, until his retirement in 1982. The family continues to operate the *Post-Dispatch*.[20]

Other large western papers continue to be operated by descendants of either their founders or early owners, and countless other, smaller journals across the West are still in the hands of the families who either established papers or bought weak ones and built them into viable businesses while reporting news and providing strong editorial voices in their communities. The early traditions continue.

CHAPTER ELEVEN

——◆——

HYPERBOLIZING

Newspapers, like toads shut up in a dark cellar,
are characterized by a wonderful amount of vitality,
and live upon nothing for an almost incredible period.
—*Western Mountaineer,* 1859 Golden, Colorado Territory

IF THERE IS ANYTHING unique about the character of humor in the Old West, it is the tendency to exaggerate. The humor of exaggeration gave people an opportunity to forget their hardships and problems, and it was only natural for many newspaper editors to stretch the truth and spice up their columns to attract and entertain readers. But editors also used humor to escape from writing about politics, slavery, or some other topic they wished to avoid. They wrote on subjects they felt comfortable with, and with assurance that suggested they knew what they were talking about. Editors lacking education may have felt inferior, but they tried not to show it. Like other pioneers who had come west, they were optimistic that the future would solve such problems.

In particular, western editors did not hesitate to stretch the truth when responding to statements made by easterners, who believed people in the West were nothing more than a collection of misfits or refugees from justice. Much of the hyperbolizing was simply satire suggesting that editors and their readers were more amused than offended by the way easterners viewed westerners. When English travelers visited the West during the 1840s and 1850s, their comments about their experiences often generated indignant retorts. Charles Dickens, who came west during the early 1840s, wrote of his experiences in his book *American Notes,* and criticized not only the climate but the way people lived. In response to Dickens, one Texas editor wrote in the LaGrange weekly, *Texas Monument,* on July 9, 1851:

They have a little town out West, which appears to have been overlooked by Dickens and the other English travelers, and which is "all sorts of a stirring place." In one day they recently had two street fights, hung a man, rode three men out of town on a rail, got up a quarter race, a turkey shooting, a gander pulling, a match dog fight, and preaching by a circuit rider, who afterwards ran a foot race for apple jack all around, and, as if this was not enough, the judge of the court, after losing his year's salary at single-handed poker, and whipping a person who said he did not understand the game, went out and helped lynch his grandfather for hog stealing.

Readers in the West viewed such material as entertaining, even when an editor exaggerated about his own or nearby communities. In one instance an editor criticized a rival town about forty miles away, where the soil and climate were identical to those of his. He wrote:

It takes several of their pigs to pull up a blade of grass, and they are so poor that the foremost seizes the spear in his mouth, the balance having taken each other by the tail, when they give a pull, a strong pull, and a pull all together, and if it breaks, the whole tumble to the ground for want of sufficient strength to support themselves. It takes three or four of them to cast a shadow.[1]

Consider the following mockingly boastful item, written by the editor of the Leon (Texas) *Pioneer* and published on July 14, 1852:

A friend of ours who lives in the eastern part of this country, near the Trinity River, remarked to us the other day, that he had an excellent, a very excellent crop. And said he, "I have two fine boys, smart and indus- trious fellows, who have worked very hard to make this crop." And said he, "I was in hopes that when we laid the crop by, that there would be some rest for the little fellows—not so little either, very nigh grown." But said he with a sigh, "I was mistaken, for now and then we want some corn, and we send the boys after it; and to see them lugging along, stag- gering under the weight of an ear of corn, one at each end of it, I can not help but feel sorry for the boys."

And there is this item found in the Bastrop (Texas) *Advertiser,* citing a story that appeared earlier in the October 29, 1853, issue of the Seguin (Texas) *Mercury:*

The Mercury makes mention of a tremendous cabbage on the farm of Colonel Pitts of Hays County. It rejoices in the possession of twenty-two heads and extends over an area of eight feet in diameter. The Mercury also speaks of having been presented with potatoes of a larger size. Now, we dislike exaggeration in any body, but John Johnson gave us a sweet potato about a week since, which, by dint of a good deal of prying and rolling, we managed to land at our boarding house. We generously remarked to our esteemed landlady that she might as well chop away upon it for the "bull" family, as it didn't cost us a cent. From time to time for about five days, "slaced tatur" was no rarity to "our folks." But, alas, how often is it that even a good action is followed by unfortunate consequences. A favorite cow belonging to our hostess, having by some chance gotten into the yard during the night, looked upon this potato as lawful prey. She was discovered in the morning, but too late to be saved. She died of surfeit before an hour. A part of the potato was left.

N.B.—The notice we gave of that twenty-seven pound baby the other day, we are sorry to say, was the result of a mistake. The child weighed only thirteen and one-half pounds. The good people in weighing, mistook half-pound for pound notches. As we deal only in facts, we are extremely sorry the mistake occurred, but we are willing to correct it.

In California a favorite topic for hyperbolizing was the climate. Historian John P. Young, writing in 1915, observed:

Articles of this sort seemed to breathe a consciousness on the part of the editor that he was addressing himself to people in the old home, a belief which was justified by the well developed practice of mailing papers to friends in the East and in other parts of the world. It was this custom, begun while the gold-hunting fever was at its height, that laid the foundation on which the boosters of Los Angeles later raised their climate superstructure. The pioneer editor was so accustomed to speaking of California as "God's country," and urged the claim so persistently, that the world soon accepted it without dispute.[2]

The English language as used by some pretend or truly unlettered editors in the West helped to contribute to exaggeration. Such editors ignored dictionary definitions of words and even created new words to meet their needs. Eastern writer Samuel S. Cox observed in 1876:

John Bull growls at what he calls new-fangled terms from America; and he calls on his children to tolerate no longer that which, commencing in humorous aberration, has continued till it has become a nuisance. In the

United States, he says, if a half-dozen newspaper editors, postmasters, and dissenting ministers, two or three revolvers, a bowie-knife, a toothpick, and a plug of tobacco, get together, the meeting is called a monster mass-meeting. If Joel Wainright blows out General Ruffle's brains on the New Orleans levee, it is not a murder, but a "difficulty." Our civil war even is called the "late unpleasantness." . . . The backwoodsman prefers his tea "barfoot," meaning without cream and sugar; a rocky piece of land is heavily mortgaged; hell is a place where they don't cover up their fires o'nights; a hill is so steep that, in the language of the stage-driver, lightning couldn't go down it without being shod. . . . A Colorado man began to tell of a barn on his ranch 190 × 280 feet, seven stories high, and bay-windows. He was at once overtopped by a chicken-coop, 550 × 832 feet, and a cupola on top for the roosters. The roosters died from the high, light atmosphere! The word *roostar,* in fact, is American. He is the *star* that never *sits!*"[3]

Cox added that most editors knew better than anyone else of the "ridiculousness" of their "rhetorical gasconade" in stretching the truth, but still they did it, some newspapers better than others and without butchering the English language. Virginia City's *Territorial Enterprise* was one that did it well, and its Dan De Quille, usually the most painstaking and accurate of reporters, could, when faced with a dry news day, invent a good story. Wells Drury recalled that De Quille would "shine. His invention was inexhaustible. Out of the merest trifles he produced columns of solid type. From filmy threads of unreality he evolved postulates and spun theories that startled scientists and set the Barnums of the country by the ears." Drury recalled one De Quille story entitled "The Traveling Stones of Pahranagat Valley." As Drury wrote:

With feigned scientific minuteness he showed how these traveling stones were by some mysterious power drawn together and then scattered wide apart, only to be returned in moving, quivering masses to what appeared to be the magnetic center of the valley. Upon these pretended observations he predicted a new doctrine concerning electrical propulsion and repulsion.

These curious pebbles, he averred, "appear to be formed of lodestone or magnetic iron ore. A single stone removed to a distance of a yard, upon being released at once started off with wonderful and somewhat comical celerity to rejoin its fellows."

Dan called this kind of a production a "quaint," and when this "quaint" reached Germany it caused a furore among a select set of men who were dabbling in the study of electro-magnetic currents. Their secretary wrote to Dan demanding further details. In vain he disclaimed the verity of his skit. His denial was treated as an unprofessional attempt to keep his brother scientists in ignorance of the truth concerning natural laws, the effects of which they were convinced had been first observed and recorded by "Herr Dan De Quille, the eminent physicist of Virginiastadt, Nevada."[4]

Another De Quille "quaint" was a story about "solar armor." The contraption, he wrote, consisted of a suit of India rubber equipped with a compact air compressor operated by a pocket battery. According to De Quille, when the wearer found himself uncomfortably warm he had but to touch a button to get air-conditioning, and when sufficiently cooled he could touch another button to turn off the power. The inventor, according to the story, undertook to test the suit one afternoon when the thermometer was registering 117 degrees in the shade. Putting on the outfit, he started across Death Valley. After he failed to return, a party started to search for him. Four or five miles out on the desert they found his body. He had apparently started the compressor but, unable to stop it, had frozen to death. The machine was still running, and an icicle eighteen inches long hung from the dead man's nose. Newspapers as far away as England believed the story and heartily endorsed the invention.[5]

Another writer on the *Territorial Enterprise* who stretched the truth was Mark Twain. In fact, one historian observed recently: "Almost nothing Mark Twain wrote is to be trusted. It may be the truth. It may not be. But it is risky to quote it as fact. . . . Twain was a literary giant, the first great, authentic, indigenous American writer. But Twain seldom was a good reporter in the sense of getting the facts and writing them up straight. Twain rarely let the facts get in the way of a good story."[6]

About three weeks after joining the *Territorial Enterprise* in 1862, Twain wrote a story called "The Petrified Man," describing how a mummified man with a wooden leg had been found in perfect condition. Twain wrote that the body was sitting upright, "the right thumb resting against the side of the nose . . . and the fingers of the right spread apart." Twain went on to write how the region's new coroner and justice of the peace rushed to the scene, held an inquest, concluded the man died from protracted exposure, and ruled that burial was out of the question because it would be "little less than sacrilege" to blast out the mummy. Twain's story, of course, was a hoax written to ridicule other hoaxes written by journalists, and to make fun of the justice of the peace.[7]

Twain may have picked up some pointers on storytelling from James E. W. Townsend, better known as "Lying Jim." Twain apparently was attracted to Townsend because he was a talker, a storyteller, and a good drinking companion. Townsend's mere presence was entertaining. There is even a story that Townsend first told the tale that inspired Twain to write "The Celebrated Jumping Frog of Calaveras County." Townsend had worked as a compositor setting type for the *Golden Era,* alongside other compositors, including Bret Harte, who later became the highest-paid author in America. Harte used Townsend as the model for the title character of his *Truthful James.*

In 1862 Townsend headed for Nevada and found a job on the *Territorial Enterprise* at Virginia City, where he wrote stories in his head as he set them in type. Unlike other newspapermen who first composed their pieces in manuscript, Townsend wrote at the type case. He simply set type when he felt like expressing an idea, and he worried constantly because he could not set type as fast as he could think. In time Lyin' Jim became known far and wide for his fictitious stories. His hoaxes were so plausible that even his fellow writers on the paper were fooled. One of his stories told of the invention of an earthmoving windmill to lift sand and gravel. It was so convincing that some engineers began to calculate the mill's horsepower and capacity in cubic yards per diem.[8]

Townsend remained at the *Enterprise* about a year and then left to work at the *Daily Union,* also in Virginia City, where he stayed until late 1864. From there he moved to Grass Valley, California, to edit a paper during a political campaign. During the years that followed he moved from one newspaper to another in California, setting type and writing stories, the usual pattern of itinerant printers who chose not to stay in any town too long. Sometimes Townsend even served as editor of a paper, continuing his inventive and hoax-filled stories. Of his work as an editor Wells Drury later wrote:

> To read his paper you would think that it was published in a city of ten thousand inhabitants. He had a mayor and a city council, whose proceedings he reported once a week, although they never existed, and enlivened his columns with killings, law suits, murder trials and railroad accidents, and a thousand incidents of daily life in a humming, growing town—every one of which he coined out of his own active brain.

Among the most exciting things with which he kept churning up his readers were a shooting scrape and divorce proceedings arising from a scandal in which the mayor's wife and a member of the city council figured. It dragged along through his columns for nearly six months. It was very interesting to read and implicitly believed—except by persons who knew there was no mayor and no council at any time in the town where Jim's paper was published. He was called "Lying Jim" Townsend to the day of his death and could he have had his way it would have been graven on his tombstone.[9]

After working eighteen years for various papers in California, Townsend walked into the office of the *Gazette* in Reno, Nevada, in the spring of 1882. Although Townsend's reputation had preceded him, Robert L. Fulton, editor and copublisher, hired him to write locals. A few months later Townsend left and for a few years spent his winters in Washoe County and his summers in the Sierra. He occasionally returned to the *Gazette* for short stints of work, and in 1886 he went to Virginia City and rejoined the *Territorial Enterprise* as a reporter and editor. Then, in November 1886, Townsend bought the Carson City (Nevada) *Daily Index*. Less than three months later he sold the newspaper. It was too much work, and the prospects for making money were poor. Townsend died in 1900 at the age of sixty-two, rheumatic, nearly deaf, and suffering from liver problems caused by drinking too much frontier whiskey.[10]

Another master of stretching the truth, one who received more national attention than "Lyin' Jim," was Bill Nye. While the following could have been included in the earlier chapter, it is also appropriate here as an example of Nye's approach to storytelling. It appeared in the *Laramie* (Wyoming) *Sentinel,* May 6, 1882:

OBITUARY FOR CAPTAIN JACK

Many of our people have been pained to hear of the sudden death of Captain Jack, of the Ute nation, and none more so than the writer of this.

He was sick but a short time, and even he hardly realized that he was going to die. It is said that five minutes before his demise he was strong and well. In fact, he was a man of unusually strong physique and had a digestion like a corn-sheller. He never felt a pain and rarely employed a physician.

On Saturday last he retired to his tepee, little dreaming that he would be carried out of it in a salt bag.

It seems that he had defied the paleface at the post and in a moment of irritability had killed one of the soldiers. The officer in charge then procured a howitzer and fired a shell into the warrior's tent. This shell, owing to some fault in its construction, no doubt, burst with great havoc near Captain Jack's bosom and a few inches north of his liver. So great was the shock to his system that the only feature that could be recognized was a copper-colored seed wart which he had acquired three years ago.

It was the most severe case of concussion that the history of surgery has ever known. The officer gathered up what could be secured and reported at headquarters the injuries that had been sustained by the great warrior.

While the post surgeon was changing the remains from the salt bag to a baking powder can, Captain Jack breathed his last. His death, however, was not officially announced until a cavalry officer brought in a lobe of liver that he had found in a tree near by. It was then stated authoritatively that Captain Jack was dead. The military department never jumps to conclusions. When a vital organ is found in the limb of a neighboring tree, and the remains under discussion seem to be lacking the particular organ, the military authorities jump at the conclusion that the man is hopelessly injured.

Jack was not educated, but he was great in some respects. He was a self-made man, starting out with no money, no clothes and no friends. He soon, however, acquired distinction as a warrior and a liar which was the envy and admiration of the Ute nation. Now his active brain is still. It has ceased to act. It is congested and scattered over four acres of sage brush.

Still it were better, if he were to die, that he should die in such a manner that we would have no doubts about it. We feel more secure when we know that an Indian has passed away in this manner. Some of his friends, too, may have been cursed through all their lives with the vague fear that Jack had been buried alive. Now it will not be that way. Those who saw his remains will always feel certain that death was instantaneous and painless. His body will lie in state in a cigar box, until the time set for his burial, when he will be interred with proper ceremonies and a corn-planter. We believe that the mountain howitzer is destined at no distant day to become an important factor in the civilization of the Indian and the amelioration of mankind.

The negative attitude held by whites toward the Indians appears frequently in many frontier papers. It was not uncommon for editors to concoct stories about Indians to provide humor for their readers. For instance, the editor of the *Smoky Hill and Republican Union* at Junction City, Kansas, printed the following in his September 3, 1864, issue: "A 'big injun' having strayed from the camp, found himself lost on trying to return to it. After looking about, he drew himself up and exclaimed, 'Injun lost!' but recovering himself, and feeling unwilling to acknowledge such shortsightedness, 'No, Injun no lost—wigwam lost—(striking his breast), Injun here.' "

John G. Maher was one western newspaperman who did more than stretch the truth. He wanted his creations to be believed, and to do so, he provided physical evidence to make them believable. Maher grew up in Nebraska, where his father was a state senator during the late 1880s. After young Maher completed his education at Fremont, Nebraska, he taught school a few years and then went to work for the government, first in the mail service, and then operating a government land office at Chadron, near the sandhill region of northern Nebraska. He studied law and was admitted to the bar just before the Seventh Cavalry attempted in December 1890 to disarm Sioux Indians on their reservation in northwest Nebraska. The Sioux had been performing the Ghost Dance believing it would return their dead. The "Wounded Knee Massacre" saw 146 Indians killed, including 44 women and 18 children. When it occurred, Maher went along with U.S. troops as a special correspondent of James Gordon Bennett's New York *Herald*. Afterwards he continued to send stories to the *Herald*. Whether Maher had read Mark Twain's story about a petrified man published in 1862 in the *Territorial Enterprise* at Virginia City, Nevada, is not

Nebraska newspaperman John G. Maher created the "ossified man" hoax in 1892, and another involving a giant monster in Lake Walgren near Hay Springs, Nebraska, early in the twentieth century. *(Courtesy Nebraska State Historical Society)*

known. Maher did read a story about an eastern archaeologist who found dinosaur remains "a million years old" somewhere in the West. The story generated much national attention. Maher got the idea of planting an "ossified man" for scientists to find. During the summer of 1892, Maher and some cronies made a plaster cast of a large black soldier from the Ninth Cavalry at nearby Fort Robinson, poured concrete into the cast, and created a stonelike figure of a man. Maher even used shingles to flatten the figure's feet because he had read that prehistoric men were flatfooted. In secrecy, Maher and his conspirators hauled the concrete figure by wagon to a spot near where some local science buffs were digging for fossils and buried it in some clay.

On a rainy Sunday morning some days later, the buffs discovered the figure half uncovered in the clay. Astounded, they declared it an ossified man and on the spot classified him as prehistoric. Four days after the figure was uncovered, the *Dawes County Journal* at Chadron reported the find and noted:

> The two Rossiter brothers were collecting fossils about 3 miles from town in a strip of bad lands at the Natural Wall when Ed discovered what he at first thought to be a bone projecting from a bank of clay. A little digging brought him to what he found to be the hand of a man. He called his brother Clyde to watch the treasure while he came to the city for help. That evening the valuable find was safe at the Rossiter hotel and after the clay was partially removed from the body it was placed on exhibition. . . . The face resembles that of a Negro . . . but his shapely heels indicate Caucasian blood. . . . The medical fraternity and all others who have seen the specimen laugh at the idea that it is not genuine. It is undoubtedly the most perfect specimen of the kind ever discovered, and is worth many thousands of dollars. Mr. Rossiter intends taking it to the Chicago World's Fair.

Naturally Maher, as western correspondent for the New York *Herald,* sent dispatches about the find to the paper. His stories were welcomed and given wide coverage. Another time Maher and some friends decided to stop people in Chadron from going to Thermopolis, Wyoming, or Hot Springs, South Dakota, for the alleged cures offered by boiling natural springs. Maher thought people ought to come to Chadron, which had two such springs near town. Maher and his cronies sank sacks of soda in the bottom of the Chadron springs and then promoted them. By the time people came to try the water, Maher had already made up testimonials from people who had drunk from the springs and thrown away their crutches.[11]

Before Maher's death in 1939, at the age of seventy, he created another hoax by sending stories to the New York *Herald* reporting a gigantic monster living in Lake Walgren near Hay Springs in Sheridan County, Nebraska. Other papers in the East picked them up. Even the London *Times* ran a story about the monster in 1923, which was described as having a head "like an oil barrel shiny black in the moonlight. . . . Its flashing green eyes spit fire. . . . When it roars and flips its powerful tail the farmers are made seasick. . . . It eats a dozen calves when it comes ashore. . . . It flattens the cornfields. . . . The gnashing of its teeth sounds like a clap of thunder."[12]

The pages of countless old newspapers contain stories that today seem so far-fetched that one wonders if readers back then believed them. In retrospect some can be checked for accuracy, but it is impossible to determine whether others are fact or fiction. One such story appeared in the second issue of the *Yaquina Bay Post* published at Newport, Oregon, June 7, 1882. Printed on the front page was the following article, credited to the *Whitehall* (Oregon) *Times:*

A FISH STORY

A man has an artificial pond with at least 3,000 fish, each weighing from half a pound to two pounds, more or less. He also has a little girl, 5 years old, who has succeeded in training the fish so that she can go to the edge of the pond, and with a handful of crumbs feed them from her chubby hand. They have learned to jump out of the water and snatch worms from her fingers, and they are extremely fond of their little mistress. One day she lost her balance, and pitched headlong into the water where it was deep. She says that when she went "away down," she called lustily for help. Her cries quickly attracted her parents, and they were horrified at seeing the little girl floating upon the surface of the pond. The father rushed to the water's edge and reached out for his pet, and as he raised her from the water a perfectly solid mass of trout was found beneath her. These faithful subjects of the little queen, as she fell, quickly gathered beneath her, and thus showed their love for their mistress by holding up her body until aid arrived, thus preventing her from meeting a watery grave.

Another story that may or may not have had some truth appeared in the *Leavenworth* (Kansas) *Weekly Herald* on April 21, 1860. It read:

The following amusing incident took place upon one of the Missouri river steamboats, and was reported to us by an eye-witness. While the boat was lying at Kansas City, just ready to start for Leavenworth, a young man came on board leading a blushing damsel by the hand and approaching the polite clerk, in a suppressed voice, said:

"I say," he exclaimed, "me and my wife have just got married over at Westport, and I'm looking for accommodations."

"Looking for a berth?" hastily inquired the clerk—passing tickets on to another passenger.

"A *birth!* thunder and lightning, no!" gasped the astonished man, "*we haven't but just got married;* we want a place to stay all night, you know, and—and a bed."

Whether the editor of the *Mesilla News* in New Mexico was simply trying to remind subscribers and advertisers to pay their bills or really intended to hire a bill collector is not known, but in 1874 he inserted the following item in his paper: "Wanted, at this office, an able-bodied, hard-featured, bad-tempered, not-to-be-put-off and not-to-be-backed-down, freckle-faced young man, to collect for this paper; must furnish his own horse, saddle-bags, pistols, whiskey, bowie-knife and cowhide. We will furnish accounts. To such we promise constant and laborious employment."[13]

There were, of course, stories that local readers knew were nothing but satire. S. W. Taylor and R. H. Mitchell established the Lakin (Kansas) *Eagle,* May 20, 1879, and in their first issue they provided their readers with the following:

DOES IT BLOW IN KANSAS?

As a truth and no fabrication, Kansas is not a windy country. We have here during twelve months of the year an imperceptible circulation of air from the south, west, north and east, (varied to suit one's taste and inconvenience) that in other states as in Colorado, Illinois and Nebraska, might be called high wind, but here it is considered nothing but a gentle zephyr. In some states they have high winds but NEVER in Kansas.

A two gallon funnel turned flaring end windward and gimlet end downward could collect enough of Kansas zephyrs in seven hours to drill a hole in solid sand rock one hundred and eight feet deep. We never dig wells in Kansas. Condensed air does the work most successfully.

It is terrible windy just across the line in Colorado but it never or we might say seldom ever blows in Kansas.

The men here are all pigeon-toed and bow-legged. This is caused from an unceasing effort to stick the toes into the earth and trying to keep a strong foothold on terra firma. The gentlemen carry a pound of shot in each breaches leg to keep them (the gentlemen) right side up.

The editor of the Coolidge (Kansas) *Border Ruffian* really used his imagination when he published the following on Kansas agriculture July 10, 1886:

Think of the Kansas pumpkins! Gentlemen, when I was on a farm . . . I once lost three valuable cows. For three weeks I searched for them in vain and was returning home in disgust when I suddenly heard the tinkle of a cowbell.

Investigation showed that the cows were inside of a pumpkin, eating calmly and enjoying their commodious quarters. How did they get in, you say? Well, the pumpkin vines grew rapidly there, and dragged a pumpkin over the rough ground until a hole was worn in the side, through which the cows entered. I afterwards had it cured and used it for a wagon shed.

Is it a good country for corn, you ask? Stranger, you'll never know what a corn country is until you go to Kansas.

When the husking is done in the fall the men go out with mallets and wedges and split up the cornstalks for shipment to the East as telegraph poles or saw them off in lengths to be used as car wheels.

When the men are husking they carry along stepladders, which they place near the cornstalk. Two men then climb up and cut off the ears with a crosscut saw, letting them fall to the ground. Fourhorses are then hitched to each ear, and it is dragged to the crib.

Exchange papers, of course, provided many editors with fresh stories to entertain their readers. Whether true or not, editors often published them and added their own comments. A good example is the following item gleaned from the weekly *Avard* (Oklahoma) *Breeze* on February 9, 1915:

KILLED BY RUNAWAY BARREL

We see an article in one of our exchanges of a runaway Beer barrel killing a woman. This is the first time on record where a barrel of beer killed a person running away. It is generally the Barrel that stands tied that is killed.

Satire was a favorite of Don Hamilton Biggers, who was born in 1868 at Meridian, Texas. He was the son of a Confederate veteran who moved to Texas from Georgia. In 1876 Bigger's family moved to Stephens County, where as a boy of nine he went buffalo hunting with a friend of his father's. (Young Biggers never saw a buffalo.) At the age of sixteen he went to work for the *Clipper,* a newspaper at Colorado City, where he learned to set type and run a printing press. He went on to start or work on several papers in Texas and New Mexico, moving frequently from job to job until he returned to Colorado City, Texas. There, late in 1899, Biggers started publishing a four-page paper called the *Josher,* containing his own brand of humor and political satire. The first issue, on December 22, 1899, was listed as Volume 300, No. 52, and carried the masthead motto: "Avoid the truth and Prohibition whisky; one is fatal; the other more so." His paper included a few homemade cartoons, Biggers's poetry, and jokes on local affairs. Later issues of his little paper carried the banner statement: "A Very Weakly Paper—Issued Monthly—Devoted to Trouble." His forceful style apparently appealed to many readers on the Texas frontier, for by the spring of 1902 his paid subscribers numbered 1,639. By late summer of 1902, the paper's place of publication had changed to Abilene, Texas, where Biggers apparently operated a printshop and may have worked as a part-time reporter for the Abilene *Reporter.* With the move the *Josher* became bimonthly but then disappeared. In its place appeared the *Texas Clever,* issued twice a month. Its format was similar in terms of humor and satire, but could be described as one big editorial page. Biggers verbally hit anything and everything, and the paper lasted until 1905. Meantime, Biggers wrote local and regional history that was published in book form, and in 1906, he established a new protest paper called the *Coyote,* the "official Howler of the American Desert." He described the paper as being "first class" but with a very limited circulation. It was published on an irregular basis, as was the *Lone Coyote,* its successor, published after Biggers moved to Rotan, Texas. There the town's promoters paid Biggers to establish the Rotan *Advance,* and it was there in 1908 that Biggers started another irregular publication called *Billy Goat Always Buttin' In,* in which he frequently wrote of the mythical "Wampus Cat."

Many years later Biggers's son Earl recalled that the mythical Wampus Cat

evaded all attempts to be killed or captured. It was a ferocious beast—a cross between a wildcat, a badger, and a lobo wolf, with fangs two inches long and claws that could peel the bark off of a mesquite tree. It showed up in the light of the moon, or when the Spirits (imported from Stamford [Texas]) moved Tom [a friend] and the barber to organize a hunt— a hunt they deserted before it got out of town to return to the barber shop and compile a vivid eye witness account. Usually the Wampus Cat was cornered but had killed all of the dogs and escaped before any of the hunters got to the dogs' assistance. I don't know what caused the Wampus Cat series to stop in the *Billy Goat* unless dad decided Tom and the barber were killing off more dogs than could have been supported in Rotan.

In 1909 Biggers moved to the new town of Lubbock, Texas, and became secretary of its Commercial Club. There Biggers remained for a decade, eventually earning his living by farming and freelance writing. In 1914 Biggers ran for the state legislature on the platform: "Don't waste a good man by sending him to Austin. The country needs good men too much. Send me; I'm already ruined." Biggers won and went to Austin but resigned before the session ended. He returned to newspaper work, writing, and a roving life until his death in 1952, about a month after that of his wife.[14]

CHAPTER TWELVE

---•---

WOMEN AND PRINTER'S INK

Since this mortal is of the weaker sex, it is with no little trepidation that I take up the new work. . . . [The] newspaper business is entirely to my liking and I hope to succeed by patient work and unfailing energy.

—Annie H. Martin, *Carson* (Nevada) *Daily News*

UNTIL FAIRLY RECENT TIMES little attention was paid to women newspaper editors in the West. While details about some are known, mystery remains about others, including Caroline Romney. Why she decided to start the *Durango* (Colorado) *Record* late in 1880 is not known, but she had a printing press hauled over the snow-covered trails from Leadville to Durango and set up a newspaper office in a tent with a sawdust floor. She hired at least one printer and on December 29, 1880, published the first issue of the *Record*. Caroline Romney supposedly was shot at by outlaws, and during troubled times her printer worked fully armed with rifles and revolvers. When the editor of another paper suggested she ought to get married, she responded, "We can't afford to support a husband yet." She gave up the paper in 1881 for unknown reasons, and by 1884 she had joined the *Trinidad Review,* a weekly in southern Colorado.[1]

Caroline Romney was just one of many women who took to newspapering in the Old West during the second half of the nineteenth century, following in the footsteps of eastern women during the late eighteenth and early nineteenth centuries. During colonial times at least seventeen women worked in newspapers, some carrying on the trade after their printer husbands died. This continued to be true in the nineteenth century, and by the 1840s Cornelia Walter was serving as editor of the *Boston Transcript* (1842–47). Margaret Fuller became a well-known writer on the New York *Tribune* between 1844 and 1846, and in Washington, D.C., Mrs. Anne Royal published the weekly *Paul Pry,* and later the *Huntress,* for twenty-five years.

In the West few women were involved in newspapering during the first half of the nineteenth century except in Texas and California. In Texas, Samuel Bangs established the *Commercial Intelligencer* at Galveston late in 1838. His wife, Caroline French Bangs, wrote articles under the pen name "Cora." Nine years later Robert B. Wells founded the *Texas Christian Advocate and Brenham Advertiser* at Brenham, Texas. Wells and his wife, Mary, produced the paper, which was half religious and half secular, but they experienced many difficulties. Mary Wells later recalled: "When we came to the work, and tried to get printers to set type and hands to work off the papers we were at a loss to know what to do—a long ways from market, and news of interest was scarce. . . . Houston was our nearest market, and in rainy weather the road was almost impassable. We would have trouble with our press, and it was hard to get paper." The paper lasted not quite a year. Mary Wells's father took it over and moved the paper from Brenham to Houston, where it became the official organ of the Methodist General Conference in 1850.[2]

In California Mrs. Sarah Moore Clarke edited her own newspaper and appears to have been the first woman editor west of the Mississippi. Details of Sarah Clarke's early life are sketchy, but it is known that she was born in Maine about 1821. By the early 1850s she had married Henry Kirk White Clarke, a rancher, journalist, and lawyer, and was living in Oakland, California, where she gave birth to a son. In September 1854, only eight years after the first English-language newspaper was established in California, Sarah Clarke started the *Contra Costa,* a four-page weekly, at Oakland, which provided not only news and information of interest to women but general news as well. Because there was then no printing press in Oakland, she had her paper printed in the offices of the *San Francisco Evening Journal.* There printers apparently resented a woman as editor and inserted small news items in her paper—items Clarke had not given them. Most of the items were in bad taste, and she had to apologize for them to her readers in the next issue. Perhaps because of this, her husband bought the *Evening Journal,* which she helped to run while putting out her own paper. Although Sarah Clarke produced a well-edited paper, it died in scarcely a year because it found few readers and in turn few advertisers. Then, too, Clarke suffered from health problems. After her paper folded, she continued to help her husband edit the *Evening Journal* until he died in March 1856. During her remaining years she contributed to publications in and around San Francisco until her death in 1880 at the age of fifty-nine.[3]

As permanent settlements began to appear west of Missouri, more newspapers were founded. By economic necessity the wives of many printers took an active role in helping their husbands publish their papers. In many instances the husbands taught their wives how to set type, which took great dexterity in picking the tiny lead characters from the typecase. In fact, many women could set type faster than men but seemed to have less enthusiasm for working with the crude inks made of oil and lampblack used by most printers or for pulling impressions on a handpress.

Scattered and incomplete records suggest that more than four hundred women were actively engaged with their husbands in newspaper work in the West between 1854 and 1900. Many of these women also began to gather local news and write stories to help their husbands. It was not unusual for a wife to take over the operation of a paper when her husband became ill or died, and by the 1870s others were establishing their own newspapers. One such woman was Laura De Force Gordon. From what is known of her, she bought an old printing press and associated equipment and established the *Daily Leader* at Stockton, California, about 1873 or

This illustration depicting a female editor of a frontier newspaper appeared in an 1882 issue of the *National Police Gazette. (Author's collection)*

early 1874. The paper was later published at Sacramento until it ceased operation in 1876. Laura Gordon was probably the first woman in the West to publish a daily newspaper.[4]

Another woman who did so was Abigail Scott Duniway, born in Illinois in 1834. She started west for Oregon with her family in 1852, but during the journey her mother and younger brother died. Once in Oregon she taught school briefly in a small town near Salem and then married Benjamin Duniway, another emigrant from Illinois, and raised four children. But when the family lost their farm, Abigail Scott Duniway opened a millinery shop at Albany, Oregon, and earned enough money to move the family to Portland, where her brother, Harvey Scott, was editor of the *Oregonian*.

Through her brother's influence, Abigail's husband got a job at the customs house, and she worked briefly as Oregon editor of the *Pioneer*. After having two more children, Abigail left her husband, set out on her own, and in 1871 established the *New Northwest*, a weekly paper devoted to political, financial, and social equality for women. While her paper supported woman suffrage through articles, editorials, poetry, and fiction, it also published general news and accepted advertising. Her children and younger sister helped to publish the paper by setting type, running errands, and doing other needed chores. She continued to operate the paper until she sold it in 1887. She went on to become editor of the *Pacific Empire*, a weekly published at Portland devoted to suffrage, which had been established by Miss Frances Gotshall. Abigail Duniway retired from journalism in 1897. In failing health and confined to a wheelchair, she wrote the state suffrage proclamation and signed it jointly with the governor of Oregon after voters approved women's right to vote in 1912. About three years later the "mother of equal suffrage in Oregon," an accomplished writer and newspaperwoman, died.

Abigail Duniway's younger sister, Catherine Amanda Scott Coburn, who had worked on the *New Northwest*, also made something of a name for herself. She left her sister's paper in 1883 to edit the Portland *Evening Telegram*, where she remained until 1888. She then joined the Portland *Oregonian* and rose through the ranks to become associate editor at the time of her death a quarter of a century later.[5]

Woman suffrage also brought Caroline Maria Nichols Churchill into newspaper work. Born to American parents living near Toronto, Canada, in 1833, she later married a man named Churchill. Widowed about a dozen years later, Caroline Churchill moved with her only child, a daughter, to Minnesota and opened a millinery and dressmaking business that she operated until 1862. A strong supporter of woman suffrage, she then traveled extensively speaking and supporting suffrage. The year 1879 found her visiting in Denver. Now forty-six years old, she liked the climate and decided to settle in Colorado. There she established a monthly publication called the *Colorado Antelope* in October 1879. She told her readers that she chose the name because she "wanted a name never before given to any paper under the sun; we wanted something that had the least feminine suggestion; something graceful and beautiful, and above all something that was alive and had some 'git up' to it."[6]

Some weeks later Caroline Churchill told her readers why her paper had advantages over all others. Her list included the following:

Its editor is the oldest and handsomest in the United States.

It has the only lady editor who wears a seven by nine boot and dares tell her own age.

It has the only lady editor who dares so far defy underlying principles of political subjection as to write and publish a joke perpetrated upon herself.

It is the most original paper published in the United States, . . . it is the wittiest, spiciest, most radical little sheet published in the United States.[7]

Although the monthly *Antelope* did well and contained much advertising, its eighteen-page format was expensive to produce. In 1882 Churchill decided to change to a four-page weekly and renamed it *Queen Bee*. The masthead read: "Devoted to the Interests of Humanity, Women's Political Equality and Individuality." Churchill soon became known by the name of her paper. In its October 31, 1888, issue, she claimed her weekly had a larger circulation than any daily paper between Kansas City, Missouri, and San Francisco. The paper regularly contained many advertisements and undoubtedly was a financial success, but it never made Churchill wealthy. She was about sixty-two years old in 1895 when the paper ceased publication. She died not long after.[8]

Not all women editors supported woman suffrage. Annie Hudnall Martin was one who did not. Born in Memphis, Missouri, in 1857, she was sent west to Carson City, Nevada, to live with relatives during the Civil War. There she grew up, was educated, and became a schoolteacher. In 1892 she left teaching and purchased the *Carson Daily Morning News,* a successful four-page paper, and announced it would be Republican in its politics. She opposed woman suffrage and only occasionally published material on the subject. Instead she reprinted stories that called on women not to squander their energies on activities outside the home, or advised that a woman's first loyalty was to her children. Her opposition to suffrage does not seem to have strengthened the respect for her held by Samuel P. Davis, editor of the *Carson Daily Appeal,* with whom she frequently feuded.

Davis was an aggressive editor who not only battled against closed meetings of governmental bodies and fought for the freedom of the press but once went to jail for refusing to reveal to a grand jury his sources for stories regarding kickbacks to county officials. Davis called Martin's paper a "Sunday School Journal" and a "Petticoat Paper." Whenever they met they usually engaged in heated arguments on circulation. Davis claimed a preposterous figure and scoffed when Martin said it was much too high. One day, because of a freight embargo, a San Francisco supplier failed to make a paper delivery. Martin's paper had received the last large order. Davis was frantic and asked to borrow enough to run off one issue of his *Appeal.* Martin agreed, *if* he would take only enough paper for his true circulation needs. Davis took far less paper than Martin used to print one issue, proving at last that her paper had a larger circulation.

Triumph was sweet for Annie Martin, who in the early 1890s may have been the only woman editing a daily newspaper west of the Rocky Mountains. In the fall of 1895, however, Martin sold the *Carson Daily News* to H. C. Dunn and Hal A. Lemmon. For seven years she managed retail businesses in Carson City and then, in 1908, became a clerk at the U.S. Mint in Carson City. In 1921 she was appointed superintendent, the first woman to supervise a U.S. mint. When she died in February 1928, the American flag over the mint flew at half mast and Carson City schools closed for her funeral.[9]

IN THE MID-NINETEENTH CENTURY, women were used as strikebreakers to set type for newspapers in New York City. Male printers, as might be expected, objected to the women, but *Tribune* editor Horace Greeley, who had been the first president of the New York Typographical Union, formed in 1850, supported them. Greeley told the male printers:

> If you find yourselves troubled with too strong a competition from female workers, just prove yourselves worthy to be their husbands; provide good homes and earn the means of living comfortable, and we'll warrant them never to annoy you thereafter by insisting on spending their days at the printing office setting type. But waxing theologic and pious, you tell us of the sphere of action God designed woman to occupy—of her "purity" and of the "immorality and vice" she must in-

evitably sink into should she be admitted to the composing room to set type beside you. We feel the force of these suggestions. We admit the bad company into which unregulated typesetting would sometimes throw her—but did it ever occur to you that this is her lookout rather than yours? It is perfectly fair of you to apprise her beforehand of the moral atmosphere to which promiscuous typesetting will expose her, but when you virtually say she shan't set type because if she did your society and conversation would corrupt her you carry the joke a little too far.[10]

Years later, in the 1860s, when printers struck the San Francisco *Call* for better pay, publisher Loring Pickering took a lesson from Greeley and hired women and taught them typesetting. The union printers began to court the women and, Pickering complained later, "The 'Call' office became a matrimonial agency. Every woman we had got married."[11]

By the 1880s many of the larger daily newspapers in the West were hiring women as typesetters. For instance, there were eleven female typesetters on the Salt Lake *Tribune* in the 1880s, two of them the daughters of an owner. John Edward Hicks, a printer who worked alongside the women, recalled: "We frequently saw girl typesetters in the West, especially on

The backshop of the *Minco* (Oklahoma) *Minstrel* about 1900. The man is W. E. Showen, editor and printer. The woman is Hattie Griffen, typesetter. By 1900 women were actively involved in most aspects of newspaper journalism. *(Courtesy Western History Collections, University of Oklahoma)*

the weekly papers. These girls were always treated with the greatest respect. . . . The girl typesetters were becoming accepted in the trade."[12]

By then women were becoming more prominent generally in newspapers. As many as five hundred women worked on the editorial side of American newspapers by 1886, perhaps a third in the West. After Elizabeth Cochran, the famed "Nellie Bly" of the New York *Herald,* made her wild trip around the world in 1889, more women were attracted to newspaper work. One woman already working on the editorial side was Teresa Dean, who as a young girl in 1855 moved with her family from New York to Appleton, Wisconsin. She attended Lawrence College and then began to submit essays to newspapers in both Chicago and Milwaukee. She was eventually hired as a reporter on the Chicago *Herald,* where she covered weddings and church news. When the Ghost Dance troubles among the Sioux Indians developed late in 1890, she wrote some articles blaming the troubles on the Indians' "native" laziness and indolence. About two weeks after the bloody climax at Wounded Knee, *Herald* editor Jimmie Scott sent Dean to the scene in western Nebraska. He gave her a small revolver, which she carried in a large handbag as she took a train from Chicago to Omaha and west to Rushville, Nebraska. There she spent a day interview-

The office of the Saratoga (Wyoming) *Sun,* the paper that competed against Gertrude and Laura Huntington's *Platte Valley Lyre,* also in Saratoga. *(Courtesy American Heritage Center, University of Wyoming)*

ing residents before catching a ride to the Pine Ridge Agency on the daily army courier wagon. Dean was appalled at the Indians' living conditions—smoke-stained canvas lodges—in nearly treeless country with little grass. While male members of the press frowned on her presence, General Nelson Miles and his staff treated her with respect. She was given quarters at the nearby Indian school, and it was there that her affection for Indian children grew. In time she began to send dispatches back to her Chicago newspaper detailing the dreadful treatment of the Sioux and describing how the lack of money from Congress had created hunger and how land given the Sioux for farming was not farmable.

In one of her last stories from the Pine Ridge Reservation, Dean wrote of an Indian woman and three children who had been killed a short distance from the Wounded Knee battle site. Given a horse by General Miles, she accompanied Capt. Frank Baldwin and a party of about fifty troopers, a few Sioux scouts, and a squad of Indian policemen dispatched to recover the bodies. They were located after about a four-hour ride from the Pine Ridge Agency. The woman and three children had been shot sometime subsequent to the fight at Wounded Knee. Captain Baldwin, an interpreter, a few scouts, and Teresa Dean dismounted and stood around the bodies. Nearby was Red Hawk, a Sioux policeman, who had identified the victims. The dead woman was his sister. Dean later wrote: "As I passed Red Hawk, I said, 'I am sorry.' He could not understand the words, but he looked at me with an expression that was unmistakable agony and his lips quivered. For the first time, I realized that the soul of a Sioux might possibly in its primitive state have started out on the same road as the soul of a white man."[13]

Two of the most interesting women in western newspapering were Gertrude and Laura Huntington, who supposedly learned the printing trade in 1889 from J. S. C. Thompson while they attended Kansas State Agricultural College at Manhattan. The college had introduced vocational training in printing for women several years before. With financial help from their father, they purchased the *Platte Valley Lyre* at Saratoga, Wyoming. Gertrude, twenty-four, became editor and publisher, and Laura, twenty-two, was business manager. Their four-page paper was lively and contained not only material from exchange papers but local news, legal notices, and advertisements. The sisters set their own type and printed the paper themselves. The rivalry with the competing paper, the *Saratoga Sun,* was friendly, but when a *Sun* writer labeled the town a "drunkard settlement," the Huntingtons created a "Mrs. Annie Bush" to defend the town's honest, industrious citizens. And when the *Lyre* adopted a new typeface, the *Sun* described the change as "a tramp fresh washed." The two papers were so different that many residents subscribed to both to "see what the editors chose to argue over each week."[14]

The Huntington sisters' paper was politically Republican, and soon after they bought it, they published the following item on page 4: "The Cheyenne *Sun* says: 'Gertrude has joined the g.o.p.' That the *Platte Valley Lyre* has done so, is true, but 'Gertrude' has not 'joined the g.o.p.' for the reason that she has been a member of that party from her cradle."[15] Laura Huntington married in August 1898 and turned her share of the *Lyre* over to her sister Gertrude, who continued to publish the paper until 1902, when she sold it. Later the paper was merged with the *Saratoga Sun*. Gertrude married and lived in Rawlins until her death in 1925. Laura also lived in Rawlins, where her husband died in 1903, but she became actively involved in community affairs, serving as a deputy court clerk, deputy assessor, deputy treasurer, and then county treasurer before her death in 1962.[16]

While many women entered newspaper work on their own, others got into the field by marrying newspapermen. E. Josephine Brawley Hughes was copublisher with her husband of the *Arizona Star* and served as business manager, bookkeeper, and circulation director until 1883, when—after her husband became governor—she took over publishing the paper herself.

Another woman who got into the newspaper business by marriage was Minnie A. Taylor. After she married George Lawless in 1898, she found herself associate editor of her husband's paper, the *Kansas Eagle,* published in the small town of St. Francis on the high plains of western Kansas. Together they struggled to keep the weekly afloat. They shared all the work and printed their paper on an old Army press until 1905, when George Lawless organized a company with the help of six St. Francis businessmen, bought the only other paper in town, the *Cheyenne County Rustler,* and combined it with the *Eagle*. Minnie Lawless was given the honor of naming the new paper, the *Herald*. She and her husband then erected the first brick business building in town and got a new press and equipment. In 1912, however, George Lawless died after a lingering illness. Minnie took over as editor and manager and ran the newspaper, which by 1916 had a circulation of twelve hundred.[17]

Mamie Alexander Boyd was yet another woman who entered journalism by marrying a newspaperman—in her case, Frank W. Boyd, in 1905, when he was working for the *Phillips County Post,* a weekly published at Phillipsburg in northwest Kansas. Years later, at the age of ninety, Mamie Boyd recalled what it had been like to work with an editor husband:

Frank and I started our married life in Phillipsburg. Frank was getting $5.00 a week. Phillipsburg was then a town of 1,200 inhabitants and blessed with four newspapers. We got tired of working for the other fellow and two years later we signed a note for $5,000 and became owner of our own newspaper. Because I had an acute case of Consumption (TB now) it was thought best for me to be out of doors as much as possible and I started my newspaper career, gathering news and locals. However, I deny being a career woman. My husband, my sons, and my home were my first consideration—before many years the boys were helping in the newspaper office and helping me at home.

We had a Washington hand press, and set type by hand. Then we had a Jackrabbit press, turned by hand with a crank. Next we had a gasoline engine for power, and finally electricity. . . .

During the late 20's and early 30's, being in an agricultural area, we had some trying times. Crops failed, advertising fell off, and our subscribers could not pay and we carried them on our books. Two banks failed within a week and our small savings were gone. McDill [the oldest son] quit college and came home, Frank Jr. helped after school and Saturdays, and the four Boyds kept going. A paper salesman said to Frank one day:

"Several western Kansas newspapers have closed their doors. How do you keep going?"

Frank answered:

"Oh, we get up a little earlier, go to bed a little later, buckle our belts tighter so we don't need much."

I believe the same ingredients of the community newspapers have endured from the horse and buggy days to the new look in journalism. The men and women of today are community builders. They have the same yard sticks—how does it affect our town and community? Preach unity at all times. Play up areas of unity and play down areas of dissension— working together for the educational, spiritual, cultural and economical benefits for the community and for America.[18]

One woman who preached "peace on earth, good will to men" published a newspaper to help achieve her aim, which was to gain peace by breaking up every saloon in the West with her trusty hatchet. She was, of course, Carry Amelia Moore Nation, a native of Kentucky, who decided a newspaper would help further her cause—temperance and women's rights. In 1856, at the age of ten, Carry moved with her family to Missouri and in 1867 to Texas. There she married Charles Gloyd, a young physician who was an alcoholic. Failing to reform him, she ended the marriage and returned to Missouri, where she became a schoolteacher. In 1877 she married David A. Nation, a preacher, editor, lawyer, and Civil War veteran, and they soon moved to Texas to farm. Life was difficult as her husband sought to make a success of farming. He finally failed as a farmer and sold out, and in 1889 they moved to Medicine Lodge, Kansas, where she became a member of the Women's Christian Temperance Union. She and other members soon closed Medicine Lodge's illegal saloons. She next smashed saloons in Kiowa, Kansas, in 1900, using a hatchet for the first time. Later that year she wrecked the bar at the Carey Hotel in nearby Wichita. By then she had decided to publish a newspaper to take the temperance issue directly to the people. The paper, the *Smasher's Mail*, a weekly, was published at Topeka, Kansas, each Saturday. Under the masthead she proudly displayed the words "peace on earth, good will toward men" and described herself as "a home defender who defends." By late 1901, however, her own home had problems. Her husband was granted a divorce; he received the homestead and was exonerated of charges of cruelty.

Although Carry Nation continued to carry her crusade across Kansas into Missouri, and to Texas, Michigan, Montana, California, and Washington, D.C., and appeared at Chautauqua gatherings, county fairs, and even in burlesque shows, her newspaper found few advertisers and failed. In 1911, after suffering a stroke, she was admitted to a sanatorium at Leavenworth, Kansas, where she died. She was buried in the Moore family plot near Belton, Missouri, not far from the town of Peculiar. Virtually forgotten when Prohibition came in in 1920, she is primarily remembered today as a larger-than-life figure who promoted the cause not only with a hatchet but with her own newspaper, founded solely to push temperance.[19]

Exactly how many women were involved in western newspapers during the latter half of the nineteenth century is not known. Although Sherilyn Cox Bennion identified more than two hundred women editors in her book *Equal to the Occasion: Women Editors of the Nineteenth-Century West*, published in 1990, there were undoubtedly many more women working on newspapers. Some helped their husbands put out family-owned papers, and others held jobs working as reporters, writers, typesetters, and proofreaders. All of them were continuing a tradition established during colonial times, when women helped their husbands in printshops produce weekly newspapers.

CHAPTER THIRTEEN

TRAMP PRINTERS

Hazlitt, the "Pilgrim," is in town. The Pilgrim is known in every printing office in the United States and comes here from Washington Territory. It is his habit to work for a few days and then start off on his travels again. Tilden, reform and whiskey occupy the Pilgrim's intellect at present.

—*Gold Hill* (Nevada) *News*, September 12, 1876

THE DICTIONARY defines a tramp as a vagrant traveling aimlessly about. The traveling part of this definition applies to the tramp printer, but he was not a vagrant. He had a trade—he usually was a proficient printer and could fill various positions on a paper, including compositor, press operator, and often reporter and writer. It was just that he had acquired a thirst for wandering; he had become something of a typographical tourist. The first tramp printer west of the Mississippi River was Jacob Hinkle, brought to St. Louis in 1808 by Joseph Charless, who started the *Missouri Gazette*. When Hinkle left the paper suddenly after only four months, Charless discovered that Hinkle was a gambler. In November 1808 Charless used his columns to warn other printers reading exchange copies of his paper, and the public in general, about him.

After Hinkle's sudden departure, Charless learned that his previous gambling debts had caused him to move from Virginia to Kentucky and to Missouri. In St. Louis, Hinkle left debts of about six hundred dollars plus the two hundred dollars Charless had advanced him to get settled. Charless warned readers that Hinkle's earlier activities centered around proposing to establish newspapers in various communities, collecting funds in advance for subscriptions, and then disappearing. Hinkle would also buy goods, including watches and horses, giving notes for their purchase. He would then sell these articles for cash before he vanished. In an era before photographs, Charless described Hinkle as twenty-four years of age, five feet nine or ten in height, with a shuffling walk; sallow complexion; curly black hair; crossed, very nearsighted eyes; and "plainly stamped *The Villain* in every lineament thereof."[1]

Most tramp printers began their wandering days after completing an apprenticeship somewhere and then being told to leave and get some experience. In fact, many journeymen printers did not consider a printer's education complete until he had done some wandering. Since jobs were not always plentiful, printers would hit the road looking for work. After the National Typographical Union was established in 1852, traveling cards were issued to all members, giving journeymen printers admission to a local without payment of initiation fees or dues as long as their stay was less than a month. For the tramp printer, the traveling card was indispensable. It was proof to a prospective employer that the cardholder was a printer.

Certainly tramp printers experienced many hardships going from town to town, but for many it was an exciting, even romantic way of life. It was so fascinating that once the wanderlust set in, it was difficult to quit roaming and settle down. There are accounts of tramp printers trying to give up the nomadic life, but wanderlust would grip them and off they would go.

How many tramp printers crisscrossed the West during the latter half of the nineteenth and early twentieth centuries is not known, but there must have been a few hundred if scattered accounts are true. John Hicks, who claimed to have been a tramp printer late in the nineteenth century, recalled:

> Two or three days' work in each town was all that the tramp printer wanted or would expect. Offers of permanent or semi-permanent jobs were turned down. He was always on the move—going nowhere in particular—but moving, nevertheless. He usually reached a town on an early morning freight train, and left the same way, under cover of darkness, a few nights later.
>
> Many of them were intelligent and brilliant conversationalists on many subjects, but they usually avoided personal history other than a brief resume of their travels, and perhaps to relate an experience or two that gave a hint as to why they preferred the road to a steady job. They were reluctant to tell a great deal about themselves. . . . They accepted the world day by day and proceeded on the theory that tomorrow would take care of itself. They lived an easy going life. . . . They could discuss politics, religion, art, music, history, literature of most modern and ancient cultural subjects with such erudition that frequently the editor would be found sitting at their round-table discussions by the office

stove after work hours in the dim light of a flickering coal-oil lamp. The home guards, as the stay-at-homes were called, were ever glad to see the tramp printer, for he brought many a new story and told of his work on the great daily newspapers. . . . He was, as a rule, fairly well educated; acquainted with the topics of the day; good company either in editorial sanctum, tavern, boarding house or saloon. The thoughts that fashioned commonwealths flowed through his mind and fingers to the public.

The printer, as a usual thing, did not marry early, but if married, he had things so arranged that he could make his departure from town without delay, and when things became disagreeable he left quickly, without even a good-by. As for home, home was where he happened to be, and a situation was merely a matter of convenience. He didn't own anything, never expected to, and wouldn't know what to do with it if he had.[2]

One man who wandered for a time as a tramp printer but was able to eventually settle down was Fremont Older, who became prominent as editor of the *San Francisco Call-Bulletin.* As a tramp printer he got a job on the *Territorial Enterprise* in Virginia City, Nevada. Years later he recalled a man named Babbitt, who became known as the "star" tramp printer of America. Older recalled that Babbitt was by far "the most colorful member of the fraternity that I had ever met." Babbitt walked into the office of the *Territorial Enterprise* one afternoon. As Older wrote:

He had 'beaten' his way from New York, and was covered with dirt, grime, grease and coal dust. He was, of course, hungry and broke, and wanted a day's work. . . . Not much attention was paid to Babbitt when he first went to work on the Enterprise. He was regarded as just another ordinary tramp printer. But he was more than that, as we all soon learned. I found his conversation most unusual. Apparently, he had read everything and knew everything. He spoke and wrote fluently in both French and German. Whisky was responsible for his becoming a wanderer. His mad passion for drink had affected him physically [so] that he staggered even when he was sober. He would start for the door and miss it by two or three feet. He had a wandering blind eye. It rolled about in his head as if it were entirely unrelated to the other eye. He was also very hard of hearing. Probably, he was most repellant, hollow chested, stoop shouldered, with a high pitched falsetto voice, but with a mind that attracted every one who met him. No one seemed able to resist him.

A few days after Babbitt arrived in town he appeared at the office in new apparel from hat to shoes. He was perfectly dressed, but too drunk to work.

"How did you get the clothes?" I asked him.

"On credit at Roos Brothers."

Roos Brothers had a thriving clothing store at that time directly across from the Enterprise office.

"I told Mr. Roos my story in French," said Babbitt, "and he was so moved by my plight that he trusted me."

Within a week he had borrowed money from nearly every one in the office, including myself; had charge accounts in saloons, and had worked himself into the good graces of a German restaurant keeper by talking German to him, and representing himself as a secret agent of the German government. To the women of the underworld, who had fallen for him, he was the traveling correspondent of Frank Leslie's magazine, in town incognito to write and illustrate a series of articles for that publication.[3]

Many tramp printers like Babbitt enjoyed drinking, some to excess, and their drinking was often responsible for their losing jobs and moving on. About 1900 at least one tramp printer who liked to drink found the ideal working environment at the *Evening Intermountain,* a daily newspaper in Butte, Montana. The paper's pressroom, for a time, was as close to heaven as any drinker might want. It was located in the basement of a building on North Main Street. Next door was the cellar of a large saloon, which held countless full beer kegs. For some reason, perhaps through an error in construction, the saloonkeeper ran the beer lines of the saloon across the ceiling in one corner of the paper's composing room. The pipes had been there for some time when, one day, an inquisitive worker, perhaps the tramp printer, discovered that beer was flowing through the pipes. A hand drill was obtained and a hole was bored and corked tight with a small steel plug known as a "dutchman." From then on, it was one continual party for the *Intermountain* printers:

> The bartenders in the saloon above thought that something was amiss, but on investigation failed to see the tapped pipe, as the printers had it well camouflaged. They didn't dare press the search too closely for fear that if the printers hadn't discovered the beer lines, any suspicious action might disclose the secret to the ink slingers.

Just after the Butte-Anaconda printer's annual mulligan, a moist affair that lasted several days, many of the boys suffered from parched throats. As a result they began "hitting the dutchman" pretty heavily, and soon several of them were laid out in varying degrees of drunkenness. One printer either forgot to replace the plug or didn't screw it in tight enough with the result that the beer leaked out onto the floor of the print shop. Soon the kegs in the saloon ran dry, and investigation showed where the beer had been going.

Before the discovery of the tapped beer line, however, the printers had magnanimously acted as host at a beer bust for the owner of the saloon, recently elected as county commissioner. The county commissioner, not to be outdone, reciprocated with a party of his own. Later, to his chagrin, he discovered that he had been treated with his own beer.[4]

Quite a few tramp printers eventually became prominent in journalism and literature. Horace Greeley, who first served his apprenticeship as a printer at Poultney, Vermont, at the age of fifteen, spent about a dozen years as a tramp printer before founding the New York *Tribune*. Walt Whitman spent part of his youth working as a tramp printer, an experience hinted at in his poem "Song of the Open Road." Erskine Caldwell worked an entire summer turning a handpress and setting type on a weekly newspaper, and novelist Sherwood Anderson set type and edited two weekly newspapers.

Another tramp was Damon Runyon, whose grandfather, William Renoyan, was a printer. In April 1855 Renoyan and his wife headed west from Cincinnati aboard the steamboat *Hartford* bound for the new territory of Kansas, established the year before. Their route was via the Ohio, Mississippi, Missouri, and Kansas Rivers. At St. Louis the steamer was thought to be an abolition boat, and authorities delayed it some days. Eventually a pilot was hired at the extravagant price of $750 to take the boat to Kansas City, Missouri. Then cholera broke out on the steamer and several people died, but the Renoyans did not. Next the *Hartford* was delayed at Kansas City because of low water on the Kansas River, until it was able to continue westward, passing the mouth of the Big Blue, where in about half a mile it went aground again because of low water. The Renoyans and other passengers were forced to take their belongings and land at a new settlement called Boston on June 1, 1855. Soon the Renoyans and others in the party joined the new residents of Boston, renamed the settlement Manhattan, and began to build a community.

In Manhattan the Renoyans began to spell their name Runyon. The father farmed and eventually opened a printshop. The mother soon gave birth to a son, Alfred Lee Runyon, who as a boy worked in his father's printshop learning to set type. Alfred was too young to fight in the Civil War, but later he enlisted in the U.S. Cavalry at nearby Fort Riley, Kansas, and served under Custer fighting Indians. For Alfred, his six-month enlistment did not end too soon. He passionately disliked Custer and later wrote that while Custer defeated the Indians, he cost more cavalrymen their lives than the Indians did. Out of the army, Alfred went to work for Henry Farey and Theodore Alvord, who had started a newspaper at Junction City, just southwest of Fort Riley. The first issue of the *Junction City Tribune* appeared August 14, 1873. Three years later, in 1876, Alfred married Libbie Damon of Abilene, the railhead cattle town west of Junction City, which only a few years earlier had been wild. The newlyweds moved to nearby Manhattan, where Runyon and a man named C. M. Patee established a newspaper called the Manhattan *Enterprise* on May 3, 1876. After five months—unable to get along with Alfred—Patee quit. Runyon, however, found another partner with money, and the prospects appeared good. Soon the second partner quit for the same reason, and Runyon became the sole proprietor—conducting business, serving as editor, and doing the printing.

By 1880 the Runyons were settled in a small frame house located at Fourth and Osage Streets in Manhattan, and it was in that house on October 8, 1880, that Damon Runyon was born. Alfred tried to make his paper pay, but in 1882 he was forced to sell it to G. A. Atwood, who changed the paper's name to the Manhattan *Republic*. Runyon then took his wife and two-year-old son, Damon, and moved to Clay Center, Kansas, where he formed a new partnership and started the *Clay Center Times* in October 1882. The paper was unsuccessful, but Runyon found still another partner with money and started the *Clay Center Dispatch*. It too failed. With failure seemingly dogging him at every step, and unable to work amicably with any of his partners, Runyon took his family and moved to Wellington in south-central Kansas. There in 1886 he became editor of the *Wellington Daily Press*, a new paper owned and operated by Press Printing Company. Runyon tried to make a big splash when he arrived in Wellington by renting a large house and moving into it in grand style. But again he encountered problems, including libel suits that soon ruined him financially.

Runyon's family had grown to include three daughters. His wife, Libbie, had suffered through a near-fatal case of diphtheria and also had developed consumption. Doctors recommended the high, dry climate of Colorado to restore her health, and Runyon moved his wife, son Damon, and three daughters to Pueblo, then a boomtown in eastern Colorado. The only work he could find was as a typesetter on a local newspaper. Frustrated and angry at the world, Runyon worked nights while spending most days drinking in the Arkansas Saloon. Family conditions worsened, and Libbie took the three daughters east to stay with family at Abilene, Kansas. Months later she returned to Pueblo, only to die. The three daughters were sent back to Kansas to live with relatives. Alfred Lee Runyon and his son, Damon, remained in Pueblo.

While his father continued to work nights and drink days, Damon pretty much survived on his own, avoiding school whenever possible to join his father in the saloon. Young Runyon intently listened to every story his father told and gleaned everything he could from other customers, gobbling up both the yarns and the free lunches tossed his way. Young Runyon's schooling, such as it was, lasted only through the sixth grade. He ran errands for the newspaper where his father worked, probably served as a substitute typesetter, and soon began covering stories for the paper. On the side he wrote verse. Damon Runyon's first big story as a reporter was a lynching, which he handled well. It was the start of a newspaper career that would last more than three decades and would include work as a reporter in Denver and for William Randolph Hearst in New York City, where the byline Damon Runyon became famous.[5]

E. W. Howe was another tramp printer who settled down. His fame as a "paragrapher" has already been related but not his wandering days. Howe learned to set type on his father's newspaper at Bethany, Missouri, and then got a job doing so on the *North Missourian* at Gallatin, Missouri, for five dollars a week and board. He worked as a substitute typesetter on the St. Joseph (Missouri) *Herald* and the Council Bluffs (Iowa) *Nonpareil,* and then went to Chicago with the intention of setting type on the *Tribune,* but saw so many printers that he got cold feet and left. Howe came back west to Omaha and worked on the *Republican,* later moving to Cheyenne, Wyoming, where he got a dollar a thousand ems for setting type. Next he went to the *News* in Salt Lake City, thence back to Falls City, Nebraska. His last fling as a wandering printer was on the *Rocky Mountain News* in Denver. After that he bought the weekly *Eagle* at Golden, Colorado, but failed as a newspaper publisher and editor. It was then that he returned to Atchison, Kansas, and started the *Globe,* which became a successful small-town daily while Howe became nationally known for his writings.

John Hicks remembered Howe. When Hicks arrived in Atchison, he first sought work at the *Champion*. The paper was not hiring, but referred Hicks to a new little paper, Howe's *Globe*. When Hicks went to the *Globe* office, Howe said he did not need a printer for the newspaper, but might use him for book work. Hicks recalled that Howe "had written a book several publishers had rejected. So he had determined to print the book himself, having ordered cases of new minion [popular] type to that end. He engaged me to lay the cases of the new type and then I proceeded to set in type *The Story of a Country Town*, which Howe printed, four pages at a time, on the job press."[6]

Another tramp printer who became nationally known for his writings was Walt Mason, born in Canada in 1862. His father was killed in an accident when young Walt was only four years old. His mother and five other brothers found times hard, but Mason's mother was fond of books, poetry, and old songs and instilled an appreciation of such things in her sons. But when he was fifteen years old, Mason's mother died too, and he set out on his own, eventually going to New York City and then west, taking what work he could find. When Mason arrived in St. Louis, he found a job with a printing company and wrote humorous material on the side. One day he decided to send some examples of his work to a weekly St. Louis paper called the *Hornet*. The paper published his pieces and offered him five dollars a week to work at the newspaper and write gems of wisdom, read proofs, sweep the floors, and otherwise make himself useful. Mason remained with the paper until it went broke. He then headed to Nebraska, where he worked as a hired man for three years. As Mason later recalled: "From that time forward I was chasing myself over the country, and was connected with newspapers in a dozen cities, but always had the idea that the next town would be a little better, and kept moving around. I was mixing up farming with newspaper work in Nebraska for a good many years, and making a failure of both. It took me a good while to discover that pigs and poetry won't mix."[7]

Disgusted with living hand to mouth, Mason moved to Kansas and asked for a job on the *Leavenworth Daily Times*. About 1885 he became a reporter on E. W. Howe's Atchison *Globe*, where he remained until early in the 1900s. Although he had developed a problem with demon rum, in July 1907 Mason and a man named Reese started the Atchison *Sunday Star*. The paper, however, was short-lived, and Mason left Atchison an almost beaten man with a growing drinking problem. On the road he walked into the office of the Emporia (Kansas) *Gazette* and asked the owner and editor, William Allen White, for a job. Already aware of Mason's talents as

Tramp printer, writer, and editor Walt Mason (*right*), posed with William Allen White in this early-twentieth-century photo. *(Courtesy Special Collections, William Allen White Library, Emporia State University, Kansas)*

Walt Mason writing at a typewriter at the Emporia (Kansas) *Gazette* early in the twentieth century. *(Courtesy Special Collections, William Allen White Library, Emporia State University, Kansas)*

a writer and editor, as well as of his drinking problem, White hired Mason and patiently helped him win his battle against alcohol. Mason went on to write news items, editorials, headlines, and proof copy.

When White hired Mason, the *Gazette* had a long-standing rule that it would never publish any homemade verse. White did not want to attract the verse with which rural bards often deluged country papers in those days. But one Saturday in 1907 there was no important local news to fill a place on the front page reserved for it. Mason wrote a short "prose poem"—rhymes run without division of lines and stanzas—which exhorted readers to attend church the next day. Mason gave it to Miss Laura French, city editor. Although she recognized it as poetry, she defied the paper's rule not to publish verse and ran it. Readers liked it and many exchange papers reprinted it. White decided to make an exception for Mason, who went on to syndicate his poems to more than a hundred newspapers in the U.S. and Mexico, delighting millions of readers.[8]

John Hicks, who learned the printing trade on a small weekly before spending a decade wandering from job to job, spent a little time working for Dan Anthony on the *Leavenworth* (Kansas) *Daily Times* about 1880. Anthony had many printers working for him and occasionally hired tramp printers, but he was very strict and even had printed seventeen rules for employees in the composing room to follow. Established during the 1870s and in force when Hicks went to work for Anthony, they read:

OFFICE RULES AND REGULATIONS
No. 1

It shall be the duty of the boy in charge immediately after opening up the office in the morning to pick up all type on the floor and under the stands, and put the same in each compositor's stick who is required to distribute the same immediately on going to his case. He will then sweep the rooms neatly, clean the sinks, trim and fill the lamps. He will keep fresh water in the bucket, keep the fire and sink in good order, and at other leisure time distribute type and work under the direction of the Foreman.

No. 2

Compositors will be prompt on time ready for work at one o'clock P.M. It is required that they walk quietly up stairs into the office, hang up hats and coats and proceed quietly to work distributing cases. Composition to commence at 3 o'clock and work until 5 o'clock P.M., and from 7 o'clock P.M., until the paper is up.

No. 3

No conversation other than that pertaining to the work of the office will be allowed under any circumstances during working hours, and all discussions and controversies are strictly prohibited.

No. 4

No visitors are permitted in the Composing Room. Parties having visitors will meet them in the office.

No. 5

When a case is taken from the rack the compositor will return it to its proper place immediately after he is done with it.

No. 6

Window frames, fat galleys and all other places to be kept free from pi or loose type.

No. 7

Any one throwing type at another or throwing type or material around the room will be discharged at once.

No. 8

All employes of THE TIMES are expected to give their undivided attention to the business of the office during business hours.

No. 9

All loud talking is strictly prohibited; all playing, scuffling and noisy demonstrations are also expressly prohibited.

No. 10

Employes in their necessary conversation with each other on business are requested to speak in a subdued tone and make as little noise as possible.

No. 11

All type and material used to be distributed and cleared away as soon as dead.

No. 12

In putting away material leave it better than you found it. Do not make the quad box a museum; always empty the water basin when done with it. Never throw water on the floor. Don't smoke or use profane language, or drink whisky.

No. 13

All ads. when temporarily set aside must be carefully tied up to prevent same being pied.

No. 14

The Foreman and compositors are prohibited from writing any article and publishing in the paper. Any news which they may have must in all cases be submitted to the City Editor. Should any legitimate news come to the office after the editor has left it should be published by the Foreman.

No. 15

The Foreman will report in writing the time he or any of the employes are absent during the working hours.

No. 16

The Foreman is particularly instructed to enforce the foregoing rules and promptly report any violation of them.

No. 17

The paper must go to press promptly at 3 o'clock a.m., unless important telegraph or local news compels delay.

D. R. Anthony, Proprietor.[9]

Perhaps the rules were too rigid for Hicks, or he simply did not like working for Anthony. Whatever the case, Hicks spent only a few weeks working on the *Leavenworth Daily Times* and left to join a large printing house in Leavenworth owned by a man named Ketchison. There Hicks met a tramp printer called George W. Matchett. One day he told Hicks he was going to Topeka and invited Hicks to join him. "It was spring and I was young with a normal desire to see the otherwhere. That siren, the open road, was beckoning me to follow her."[10]

Before settling down in Kansas City, Missouri, and working for the *Kansas City Star,* Hicks found jobs as a tramp printer in Kansas, Nebraska, Colorado, South Dakota, and Arkansas, where he worked on the Fort Smith *Elevator.* But Fort Smith, located on the east bank of the Arkansas River, opposite the Indian Territory, was not to his taste. Hicks recalled it was then known as the "Swinging Doors to Hell," because outlaws infested the nearby Indian nation. "One day I stepped out of the Hole-in-the-Wall saloon and saw Belle Starr, the noted female bandit, riding down wide Garrison Avenue full tilt, with deputy marshals in pursuit. When she reached the middle of the bridge over the [Arkansas] river, she stopped briefly and patted her rump at the deputies in a gesture of defiance and contempt. They did not pursue her into 'the Nation.' "[11]

Hicks soon left Fort Smith by stagecoach for Baxter Springs, Kansas, where he could catch a train to Kansas City. When the stage stopped at Tahlequah, the old Cherokee national capital, he met

a short, slight, red-haired young man with the map of Ireland all over his face. He was a printer, he said, working at a near-by huddle of huts called Muskogee. He had learned the trade in a South Carolina office and had got this far on his way to see the world. His name was Andrew J. Redmond. Two years later . . . [he] started that peripatetic career which made him one of the most famous tramp printers in America under the nickname of "Muskogee Red." For more than half a century he saw the inside of more print shops and jails than any other man in the trade. On one occasion he burned down a jail of which he was an inmate. He sustained a broken nose when he plunged head first down three flights of iron steps in the building of the Topeka *Capital*. A friend once advised him that he should, when feeling the desire for strong drink coming on, eat an apple. "Who the hell," inquired Red, "wants to run around with a bushel of apples on his shoulder?" He became a great friend of Jay House, writer on the Topeka *Capital*, mayor of the city, and in his early days himself a tramp printer. When the word came up from Oklahoma that "Muskogee Red" had been found dead with a half-empty whiskey bottle in his pocket, Mr. House wrote a touching tribute for his paper in which, among other things, he said: "For forty years he fought a demon appetite that brought him nothing but misery and woe. He never had a home or reasonable assurance of a coming meal. No child ever laid its soft face against his bearded cheek. No woman ever watched at the window or listened for his footsteps. And because there is no other to do it,

Carl Engel, a German immigrant, learned the printing trade from Carl Schurz at Watertown, Wisconsin, and then took to the road as a tramp printer. In 1864, while he was setting type on the *Journal* at Leavenworth, Kansas, Engel decided to quit the printing trade and settle down. A year later he opened a general store at Manhattan, Kansas, and spent the remainder of his life there as a family man. *(Author's collection)*

the writer drops a tear on his neglected grave." A few months later "Red" drifted into Topeka and gently reproved House for the premature obituary. "You might have known it wasn't me," he chided: "didn't the report say the bottle was only half-emptied?"[12]

One of my regrets is that I never met my great-grandfather Carl Engel, who worked as a tramp printer before settling down and living out his life in one community. Engel was born in 1844 in Zorndorf, Neumarkt, Germany. After attending the village school for six years, he immigrated with his family to the United States at New Orleans, but the climate was too humid, so they moved north and settled at Watertown, Wisconsin. In 1856, at the age of twelve, Carl Engel was apprenticed to Carl Schurz, who at the time was editor and owner of the Watertown *Volkszeitung* and later secretary of the interior. About the time young Engel completed his apprenticeship, Fort Sumter was fired on, and he tried to enlist in the First Wisconsin Infantry. But being under age he was not accepted. Instead he took to the road and was hired by a German newspaper at Milwaukee, and later again worked for Carl Schurz, who had become editor of the St. Louis *Westliche Post*. But he left once more and headed west. Toward the end of the Civil War he found himself strapped for funds at Leavenworth, Kansas. The German-language newspaper was not hiring, but the Leavenworth *Journal* was and signed him on as a typesetter. He worked hard and six months later was promoted to foreman at a salary of thirty dollars a week. By then he was saving his money, having decided to leave the printing trade and go into business for himself. This he did in the spring of 1865, when he moved to Manhattan, Kansas, and established a mercantile business that he conducted until his death in 1908.

Tramp printers continued to crisscross the West well into the twentieth century seeking jobs on small newspapers and in printshops. Beginning in the 1920s, however, the number of tramp printers began declining because changing technology, namely the Linotype machine that mechanically cast a line of type, no longer required setting by hand. Slowly the use of the Linotype spread westward, first into daily papers and then gradually into weeklies, although there were many weeklies that could not afford a Linotype until well into the twentieth century. Hal Borland, who became well known as a writer with the *New York Times* and then as a novelist, learned to set type by hand between 1915 and 1917 from his father, who owned and operated the weekly *News* at Flagler, Colorado. Borland later recalled that tramp printers would frequently appear in the office of the *News,* usually after they were thrown off a train "by a hardhearted brakeman or conductor." Few itinerant printers would have stopped in Flagler otherwise, Borland wrote, adding that each tramp printer

would come shuffling down the steps, hesitant, dirty if not ragged, unshaven and often bleary-eyed. He would pause at the doorway, stiffen his shoulders, fight off the hangdog look, and come inside. If Mother was at the desk she would give him one cold look—she seemed to sense a tramp printer's identity even before he opened his mouth—and say, "If you're looking for a handout you can look somewhere else." That usually turned the man on his heel and got rid of him. But now and then it backfired.

One afternoon a seedy-looking man in old dusty clothes and with several days' beard came in, and she gave him the cold look and the curt dismissal. But this man stood his ground, smiled at her, then looked around for Father. Father saw him, called out, "Hello, John!" and came to the front of the office to shake hands. He introduced the man to Mother, who still watched him with cold suspicion, and the seedy-looking visitor gave Father an order for twenty-five dollars' worth of printing. He was, Father explained after he had left, a sheep rancher from thirty miles south of town, and he and his herders had just trailed a flock of fifteen hundred lambs to town to ship to Kansas City, a consignment that probably would net him around twelve thousand dollars.

But now and then a tramp printer appeared when Mother wasn't in the office. He would come in, look around, see Father at the stone or the job press, and ask, "Need a printer?" Father would stop what he was doing, talk for a few minutes, point out that his was a one-man shop, and suggest that there might be work in Limon or Burlington. And always he gave the man either money or a credit slip for a meal and a bath and shave, then tried to hurry him out before Mother returned.

The day came, inevitably, when Mother came back just as the seedy printer was pocketing the money and thanking Father. She stood bristling while the man, sensing trouble, hurried out. Then she turned to Father. "So, you gave him a handout." There was both anger and bitterness in her voice.

"Yes, I gave him the price of a meal."

"If you're so free with your money—" Mother hesitated, seeing the set of Father's jaw. He seldom crossed her, but when he did he couldn't be budged. Now he reached into his pocket, drew out a half dollar, and held it out to her. She refused to take it, turned away, and went to the desk, flushed and bristling. He followed her, tossed the coin onto the desk in front of her, and went back to work at the stone.

"That's not what I meant!" Mother exclaimed.

Father didn't answer.

"He's just another booze-fighting tramp printer!"

Father looked at her and asked, his voice low but tense, "How do you know what he is? You didn't even talk to him."

Father shook his head. He worked quietly for a few minutes, then asked, "Remember where it says in the Bible, 'Cast thy bread upon the waters'?"

"What do you mean by that?"

"I mean that some day my own son may be hungry and out of a job. I hope that if he goes into a print shop and asks for work and there isn't any work for him, the boss will give *him* the price of a meal. That's what I mean."

"Oh," Mother bit her lip, fighting back the angry words. She probably had just paid the interest on the loan at the bank and knew how little money there was in that tin box in the vault. She may have been wishing she could afford a new dress, or that Father could buy a new suit. I know there wasn't any extra money that summer for new clothes, sometimes barely enough to buy groceries. She fought down the angry words, blinked back the tears, and began to type, furiously banging the old Oliver's keys. Slowly she worked out her anger.

Half an hour later Father went to the desk, picked up the half dollar still lying there, and handed it to her. "I wish you'd get some round steak for supper," he said quietly. "We haven't had a good piece of steak in quite a while. Steak and gravy and fried potatoes would taste awfully good."

He went back to work, and a few minutes later Mother put on her coat and left. We had fried steak and milk gravy and fried potatoes for supper, and not another word was said about tramp printers.[13]

Not all editors treated tramp printers as did Hal Borland's father. One who did not was H. M. Cooley, editor and publisher of the *Avard Breeze* at Avard, Oklahoma. As the era of tramp printers was nearing an end, Cooley wrote the following story, which was published on the front page of his paper on February 9, 1915:

WEARY WILLIE DAY

Wednesday was Avard's weary willie day the way it looked. First we were asked to help out a poor unfortunate, a Printer. Came next a court plaster Willie, then the Weary Willie with the card telling how hard the world was using him.

It is very unfortunate that there is not some way whereby the deserving can be distinguished from the unworthy.

But this bunch of Willies was Bums pure and simple and would not work if they had a chance. We offered the printer work and it looked as if we would have to call a Doctor. It was not work he was looking for.

The best way is to pass them along.

Many newspapers in the West benefited from the tramp printers, and even from the tramp editors who never remained long in any one place. Their instability does not appear to have hurt the newspapers seriously or to have altered their role in the frontier community. For the stay-at-homes, the editors and printers who settled down in one place, the tramp printers often brought welcome relief from the daily routine with stories about their experiences on other papers and new ideas about newspaper work and printing that they had picked up. Tramp printers served a role in an institution capable of influencing social change in the West.

AFTERWORD

I would rather live in a country with newspapers
and without a government, than in a country with
a government but without newspapers.
—Thomas Jefferson

Now you have read something of the story of journalism in the West from the founding of the first newspaper at St. Louis in 1808 to the early twentieth century, when every city and just about every town in the West had one or more newspapers. You have read about printers who for a few hundred dollars could acquire a used printing press with a shirttail of type and start a weekly newspaper, how editors freely expressed their opinions in news stories, how they used the English language—sometimes even creating words not previously in that language—to lambast people and things. You have read how some editors helped to promote new settlements, how some editors carried revolvers and occasionally had to use them to defend their right to free speech, and how editors began to separate opinion from news and tailor their columns to the happenings in their towns, from births to deaths. You have read how many editors struggled to make a living, and how women worked alongside men—sometimes without them—to publish newspapers, and how preprinted sheets introduced after the Civil War helped to shape American ideas, and how tramp printers moved about the West until technology reduced the need for their skills.

This story of newspaper journalism in the Old West is more than just a colorful page of American history or a sentimental journey back to an exciting but less complicated time. Nowhere in the history of any other nation has a free press ever played the role it did in settling the American West. Newspapers served as catalysts for social change. They served as a bridge between the West and the more settled East: Reflecting eastern culture, they usually were the first such transplant in each new western town. The establishment of a newspaper gave hope that the community would soon erase its frontier status. Many editors strived to bring stability to their communities along with moral improvements, including better government, fire and police protection, strong businesses, schools, churches, and other institutions that mirrored the image in the West of civilized life in the East.

No two papers were exactly alike. Each paper's objectives and purposes varied, usually depending on its editor and the environment of the community in which it operated. The proprietors of newspapers covered the spectrum from brilliant to dull and incompetent, from those of good character to bad, from very successful to absolute failures in business. As newspapers helped to bring about change, editors who did not adjust to the new conditions they helped to create either saw their papers die or sold them and moved on in search of another frontier town or a new career.

No one is certain how many men and women were involved in newspapering in the Old West, or how many newspapers really existed. Census figures reflect only the number of papers every ten years, and even those figures are incomplete. Many papers were founded and died in between. In fact, newspapers came and went so rapidly that even the records of state press associations do not reflect the exact numbers during the nineteenth and early twentieth centuries. Copies of hitherto unknown papers are still being discovered, much to the delight of archivists watching over newspaper collections in state historical societies west of the Mississippi, in major western collections at universities and colleges across the nation, and at the American Antiquarian Society at Worcester, Massachusetts.

The files of old western newspapers contain a wealth of information, much of which has been untapped, especially by professional historians, most of whom seem to have downplayed the role of newspapers in settling the West and, as a result, shied away from studying old copies. As early as 1908 James Ford Rhodes criticized historians for not using newspapers as historical material. Speaking before a meeting of the American Historical Association on December 29, 1908, in Washington, D.C., he said: "The duty of the historian is, not to decide if the newspapers are as good as they ought to be, but to measure their influence on the present, and to recognize their importance as an ample and contemporary record of the past."[1]

Unfortunately too many historians of the American West seem to have ignored Rhodes and, with only a few exceptions in more recent years, they continue to ignore the role played by newspapers in the Old West, especially the importance of the preprinted newspaper pages produced in Chicago and elsewhere that helped to shape the national character of the United States from just after the Civil War. Many historians and even social and political scientists are still unaware of preprints and boilerplates and how they helped to teach and to standardize American political movements, religions, customs, and social ideas well into the twentieth century.

The well-known historian Frederick Jackson Turner ignored newspapers when, in 1893, he set forth his theory that the westward-moving American frontier was a unique historical phenomenon that gave a special tincture to the development of American society. Turner, who read much but did little formal research, called for a revision of U.S. history, which up to then had credited American democracy and local self-government with being rooted in Anglo-Saxon political institutions. Turner stated that waves of frontier advances by Indian traders, miners, cattle raisers, and farmers provided a "record of social evolution," and that American intellect owed its striking characteristics of democracy and individualism to the frontier. While Turner's thesis was vague, nowhere did he suggest that newspapers in the West reflected that "record," documented the social evolution, or played a significant role in bringing about change. Turner, however, was more of a thinker than a researcher. He may well have lumped newspapers with other institutions transplanted on the frontier. Still, their importance and role should have merited at least slight mention.

The same is true of Frederick Merk, a student of Turner, who taught with him at Harvard. When Turner retired, Merk took over his teaching responsibilities. The index to Merk's *History of the Westward Movement*, published three years after his death in 1980, does not even include a reference to newspapers. Nor does the index in Richard White's *A New History of the American West*, published eleven years later. But then, it is not surprising that White ignores the role of newspapers in the history of the West. He is one of a small group of academic historians who have tried to rewrite history apparently intent on destroying the American dream, of which the Old West is an integral part. Such historians have ignored the role played by newspapers in settling the West perhaps because they reflect the West's tradition of individualism, economic and political opportunity, and the blending of cultures. They have sought to erase these things from our history by accusing those who settled the West of being mercenary, thoughtless, lecherous, cruel, genocidal, heartless, and liars. White and the others, including Patricia Nelson Limerick, have focused on what they consider the failures of the United States and condemn the long-dead pioneers for not adhering to today's standards of political correctness.

Generally, academic historians studying the American West have failed to use newspapers as historical sources perhaps because they viewed them as inaccurate, partisan, and dishonest. Yet historians readily use personal letters and other documents that display similar defects. Perhaps the sheer numbers of papers and their issues put too great a demand on the historians' time and resources. Still, the files of old newspapers are readily available, and they satisfy so many canons of historical evidence. The people who produced them reported daily events without knowledge of the end. Even when the content is colored by honest or dishonest partisanship, historians could place such material in perspective by checking it against other historical evidence.

Certainly the historical contributions of western newspapers vary from one to the next. Many papers that helped to civilize towns and obliterate the frontier survive to this day; others died in the process. Papers located in rough mining or cattle towns engaged in social issues, supporting the more respectable community elements against gamblers, prostitutes, crooks, and drinkers. Still other papers became tools for town promoters or politicians defying all economic and social forces to foster a cause. With a little effort, the credibility of each paper and its editor can be determined: They cannot be stereotyped.

Many modern journalists have seemingly ignored the legacy of frontier editors. Today technology has changed the way news and information is disseminated. There are newspapers distributed daily across the nation and overseas with the help of satellites, and technology has created more competition for newspapers by making it possible to deliver news and information faster not only in print but over the airwaves and through cable and cyberspace. Soon there will be other delivery systems, and Americans will have to adjust to the presence of even other forms of delivering news and information that will know no boundaries. The proliferation of journalism outlets has already given Americans more choices for news, information, and entertainment than at any time in history, while seemingly shrinking the nation—and the world.

But the competitive rush to deliver news and information has greatly deemphasized accuracy, thoughtful analysis, and explanation in favor of speed. Newspapers and other forms of the media have learned that the vast majority of the public tend to become excited about one thing at a time. As a result it is understandable that reporting the leading event of the day, whatever it might be, was the key to attracting public interest and, in turn, more advertising. The result has been that when something happened that promised to appeal to the popular mind, every bit and piece of information was disseminated again and again. Such coverage is sensational and often contains unconfirmed rumors. The event or subject is picked up by columnists, publicity-seeking orators, and preachers who also compound its coverage. Everyone seems to enjoy the sensation of vibrating to the same chord that thrills a vast populace until they finally tire of the subject and seek something else.

While some editors of newspapers in the Old West followed this practice, the legacy of the better western newspapers is that they reflected the total image of their towns and cities. Editors sought to report on the important events that affected the lives and welfare of their readers. Newspapers provided community life with cohesion and direction and purpose by agitating, by creating demands, and by establishing and preserving standards of public morals. Then, too, they provided a written record of the lives of their communities.

Modern journalists have a great deal of freedom, but they have the freedom to be responsible. As we move into the twenty-first century, journalists in all forms of media should reflect on the contributions of the better newspapers in the Old West. They should remember, as Plato supposedly said, that "he who does not appreciate history is still a child."

APPENDIXES

APPENDIX A

PRINTING EQUIPMENT USED IN THE OLD WEST

ACME NEWSPAPER AND JOB PRESS. A press invented by C. W. S. Montague, manufactured mostly in Boston, and intended mainly to meet the requirements of country newspapers. Hand power could be practically and profitably substituted for steam. The construction of the press was simple, and any printer of reasonable intelligence could keep it in order. The press was capable of speed and fine work, and at a very reasonable cost; it made a profitable investment.

ADAMS PRESS. A bed-and-platen press, invented by Isaac Adams of Boston in 1830, and subsequently improved by Adams, his brother, Seth, and its manufacturers, R. Hoe & Co. of New York City. Adams presses differed widely from other power presses in that they used a flat, or platen, instead of a cylinder impression.

ARMY PRESS. A small portable press manufactured by the Cincinnati Type Foundry. Although generally known as an Adams Press, it became known as an "Army Press" when it was used extensively in printing offices attached to military units during the Civil War.

BED-AND-PLATEN JOB PRINTING PRESS. Patented by Seth Adams and manufactured by R. Hoe & Co. of New York City in several small sizes. It was operated with either a treadle or steam-power; the platen could be thrown out of action in an instant by a hand lever, without having to stop the press. The paper, on which the printing impression is made, is aligned with adjustable guides on the platen, which lies in a convenient inclined position, and is lifted up to the bed by means of a cam on the main shaft. The distribution of the ink, which is taken from the fountain by a ductor roller and communicated to a metal cylinder on which a vibratory roller is kept continually traversing, is very good. The inking rollers, which are held in a sliding frame, are supplied from the metal cylinder and then pass and repass smoothly over the form.

BRONSTRUP PRESS. A handpress manufactured by F. Bronstrup of Philadelphia, Pennsylvania, in three sizes; platen 16 by 22 inches, 20 by 26 inches, 22¾ by 29½ inches. The press was constructed principally of wrought iron and stood securely. It could easily be moved and put up quickly.

BULLOCK PERFECTING PRESS. This was one of the first perfecting presses on the market. A perfecting press is one that prints both sides of the paper with one passage through the machine. The Bullock was fed by a paper web. Its cylinders were two pages wide and of sufficient circumference to accommodate two sets of forms, or stereotypes, end to end. With the two cylinders an eight-page paper could be printed in one press run. The papers were delivered unfolded.

CABINET. A stand or frame so arranged that cases of type put in it were protected from dust. Cabinets were made of various sizes and materials.

CASES. A set of boxes embraced in a frame in which type was kept for use in composition. Cases generally were in pairs, consisting of an upper case, in which capitals, small capitals, fractions, braces, and so on, were kept, and a lower case, used for the small letters, points, spaces, quadrats, and the like.

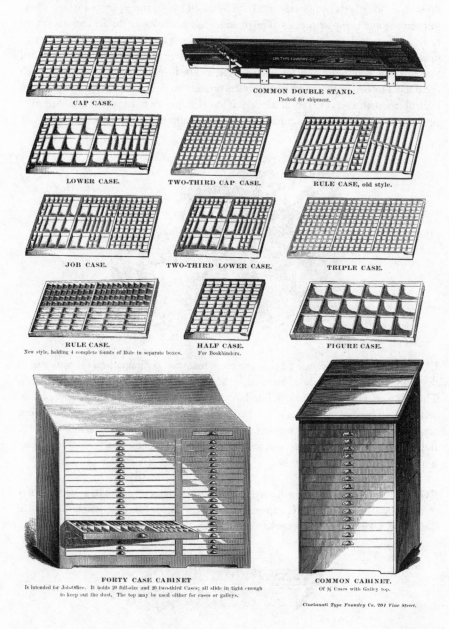

CAP CASE.

COMMON DOUBLE STAND.
Packed for shipment.

LOWER CASE.

TWO-THIRD CAP CASE.

RULE CASE, old style.

JOB CASE.

TWO-THIRD LOWER CASE.

TRIPLE CASE.

RULE CASE.
New style, holding 4 complete founts of Rule in separate boxes.

HALF CASE.
For Bookbinders.

FIGURE CASE.

FORTY CASE CABINET
Is intended for Job-Office. It holds 20 full-size and 20 two-third Cases; all slide in tight enough to keep out the dust. The top may be used either for cases or galleys.

COMMON CABINET.
Of ⅔ Cases with Galley top.

Cincinnati Type Foundry Co. 201 Vine Street.

CHICAGO TAYLOR PRESS. A cylinder press of various sizes manufactured in Chicago and used extensively in the West. It resembles the Taylor presses manufactured by A. B. Taylor Printing Press and Machine Company, established in New York City in 1842. Taylor Presses came in nine different sizes and included a country news and job press, a small-job press, and rapid single- and double-cylinder newspaper presses.

CINCINNATI CYLINDER PRESS. Manufactured by the Cincinnati Type Foundry in three sizes, their beds being respectively 28 by 40, 31 by 46, and 34 by 52 inches. These were strong and compact presses. The press distributed from a cylinder and not from a table, so the rollers were always in motion providing fresh service to the type. The front of press was open and easy to access. The feed guides were newly patented after the Civil War and provided great utility for making register. The fly piles printed sheets with much accuracy. The bed was shod with steel rollers on steel ways. It contained spiral springs to control momentum and to return the bed. It took less power to run at the same speed of similar presses—from seven hundred to a thousand impressions per hour.

COLUMBIAN PRESS. A hand printing press that was the first radical departure from the old Gutenberg-type press, invented by George Clymer of Philadelphia about 1813. The first model was constructed in London in 1818. It abandoned the screw principle and substituted pressure by a series of levels. Built entirely of iron, it had power, durability, ease of pull, and quality of impression. It cost about four hundred dollars, more than the Rampage. A few Columbian presses were used along the Atlantic Coast, but whether any were used in the West is not known.

COMPOSING-STICK. An instrument made of iron, brass, or gunmetal in which letters were set, or arranged in lines. Composing sticks were made of various designs. The usual depth of American composing sticks was about two inches.

COUNTRY PRESSES. This general term was used to designate cylinder presses made by different manufacturers for use by country newspapers, and they could be driven by hand-power rather than steam power if necessary. The Campbell Country Press was made by Andrew Campbell of New York, who was the first American press-maker to engage actively in the manufacture of country presses.

CYLINDER PRESSES. Power printing presses developed by Frederick Koenig in England. The first newspaper to use a cylinder press was the London *Times,* November 29, 1814.

DEGENER & WEILER'S LIBERTY CARD AND JOB PRESS. Developed in three sizes during the middle 1860s. The press provided clear and distinct impressions, simplicity, strength, and durability, plus convenience in making ready a printing job, adjusting, cleaning, and correcting.

EAGLE CABINET. A cabinet for holding cases of type manufactured by Vanderburgh, Wells & Co.

EXCELSIOR CARD AND JOB PRESS. Patented and manufactured by William Braidwood of New York for small-job work. A strong press with good ink distribution, which offered easy and complete supervision of all the principal parts while in motion, it was used by many weekly newspapers for job work.

FOUNTAIN. On power presses, the receptacle for ink before it is conveyed to the press form by distributing and composition rollers.

FURNITURE. Square or oblong pieces of metal, known as labor-saving quotation furniture, and hollow quadrats used in filling up blank space when a form of type was locked up before printing.

GAGE PAPER-CUTTER. A machine for cutting paper, manufactured by S. C. Forsaith of Manchester, New Hampshire. It was a cheap and reliable paper cutter that cut with great ease, smoothness, and accuracy through a depth of four to five inches.

GALLEY. A thin movable frame or tray used to hold types after they are set up, until they are made up into forms, jobs, columns, pages, and so on. Galleys are made of various patterns and materials. Early American galleys, made of wood, were not uncommon in the American West before the Civil War, but by the latter half of the nineteenth century brass galleys were generally in use in western newspaper offices.

GLOBE JOB PRINTING PRESS. Manufactured by the Jones Manufacturing Company at Palmyra, New York, for job work. Among the advantages claimed for it was great strength, ease of running, perfect register and distribution, and superior devices for throwing off and for dwelling on the impression.

GORDON PRESS. Manufactured by George P. Gordon of New York for job work.

HALF CASE. A case whose width is about half that of an ordinary upper case. They were used to hold title letters or fancy fonts of type. A half case contained forty-nine boxes.

HENRY PATENT PRESS. Invented by John Henry and manufactured by the American Power-Press Manufacturing Company at Newark, New Jersey. Produced in various sizes and used to print weekly and daily newspapers in the West. Its advantages included cheapness, simplicity, solidity, strength, and durability.

HOE PRESSES. R. Hoe & Co. of New York City manufactured presses of many varieties, sizes, and descriptions. The most famous was the Patent Type-Revolving Printing Machine, used primarily by daily newspapers in larger cities. The speed of the press was limited only by how fast printers could feed sheets of paper onto it. The company also produced a Single Small Cylinder Press that could deliver from two thousand to three thousand impressions per hour; a Single Large Cylinder Press, adapted to fine newspaper and job-work; a Single Large Cylinder Press that could be run either by hand or steam power; and a Railway Newspaper Printing Press, designed to supply newspapers of moderate circulation with a cheap but serviceable press.

INK. The coloring substance applied to type, engravings, or forms by a roller, and subsequently transferred to paper through impression. Printing ink had to be a mutable preparation, passing from a soft, adhesive state to a perfectly hard and dry substance. In newspaper work black ink was and is the standard color. Some printers made their own black ink. An 1871 recipe for a superior black ink that would not run was:

> Proportions for one pound. Balsam of copaiva 9 oz., Lampblack 3 oz., Indigo, or Prusian-blue, or equal quantities of both, 1¼ oz., Indian-red ¾ oz. Turpentine soap, dry, 3 oz.; to be ground upon a stone with a muller to an impalpable fineness, when it will be fit for use. The objectionable smell which balsam of copaiva has may be entirely removed by putting three or four drops of kreosote in the above quantity of ink. (J. Luther Ringwalt, editor. *American Encyclopaedia of Printing* [Philadelphia, 1871].)

LEAD-CUTTER. An implement used to cut leads, thin pieces of metal composed mostly of lead, which are placed between the lines of matter, or composed type, to provide more space between lines. Hence the term "leading," still in use today, even when most "type" is "set" by computers.

LYE BRUSH. A brush nine or ten inches long by three inches wide, used to apply lye to clean the ink from the form and chase.

MALLET. A wooden hammer used to drive the quoins that lock and unlock forms.

NEWBURY COUNTRY PRESS. A cheap press, with a 31-by-46-inch bed, used for country newspaper and job work, manufactured by A. & B. Newbury of Coxsackie, New York. It could be run by hand or steam power.

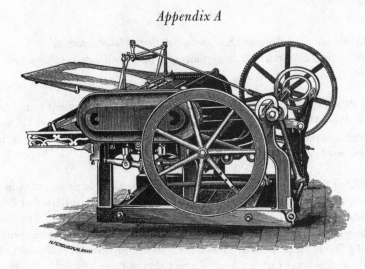

POTTER PRESS. Manufactured by C. Potter Jr., & Co. in various sizes, one size intended for country newspaper work. More than five hundred of these presses were in use by early 1871.

PROOF PRESS. A press for obtaining proofs from matter locked up in galleys. Sometimes called a READY PROOF PRESS.

RAMAGE PRESS. A small handpress, originally made of wood, developed by Adam Ramage, a Scottish immigrant and the most celebrated of the early U.S. press makers. First models introduced a stronger and faster screw press with an iron bed and platen. Later, Ramage presses were constructed and used for proof presses and for various kinds of small work not requiring speed. During the 1870s a greater number of impressions could be obtained in a given time from the Ramage than from any other hand press.

SHOOTING STICK. An implement used with a mallet to drive the quoins while locking and unlocking forms containing type.

STAND. A frame on which cases of type were placed. A single stand was one at which only a sole compositor could work, while a double stand provided sufficient space for two sets of cases and two compositors. Stands were usually made of wood, but improved iron stands were used in the printing shops of larger papers.

STEREOTYPES. The word is derived from the Greek words *stereos,* "fixed," and "*typos,*" form or type; the literal meaning signifies a fixed form of metal. The stereotyping process was introduced by the government in Washington, D.C., during the early 1860s. Pages of type, imposed in the composing room in an iron stereotype chase, were sent to the casting room and placed on a moulding stone. Impressions were made of the type on: plaster, clay, or paper or papier-mâché. A mould of the type faces was then created, checked, prepared, and securely placed on a press. The printing impression was made from the mould and not directly from the type.

TAYLOR PRESSES. *See* CHICAGO TAYLOR PRESS.

TYPE. A raised character, such as a letter, mark, or sign, cast in metal or cut in wood of such dimensions and proportions that it is adapted for use in printing. Type is also described as type in general, as the whole quantity of letters in a font, collectively. Type was kept in cases.

TYPECASE. Perhaps the most popular case to hold type after the California gold rush is called the California Job Case, which holds 89 boxes divided into three parts, the first two parts (left to right) containing the lowercase or small letters, figures, punctuation marks, spaces, quads, and most of the ligatures that the case or font contained. These sections are not arranged in alphabetical order. Rather the lay of the case is such that the most frequently used letters are in the most convenient and largest boxes. The largest box holds the lowercase *e*, with such letters as *q, x,* and *k* occupying the smaller boxes. The third section of the case contains the uppercase, or capital, letters. Because the caps are not used often, they are arranged in alphabetical order with the exception of *J* and *U,* which are found at the end of the alphabet. At the time the case was planned in Europe, Latin was universally used in printing. The Latin alphabet contained only twenty-four characters, so when printing was begun in languages having twenty-six characters, the *J* and *U* were added at the end. Special characters, such as $, -, (), *&, ffl, æ,* and *œ,* were placed in extra boxes in the cap section.

 Until the California gold rush, printers found it necessary to have large quantities of type. Because of this two cases were used. One was called the news case, the other the book case. One was placed on a rack or type cabinet above the other. The lower case contained only the lowercase letters, numerals, and other items found in the first two sections of the California Job Case. The upper case contained the capitals, small capitals, and such special characters as might be needed for the particular type of work being set. From this arrangement we derive the commonly used terms "lowercase" for small letters and "uppercase" for capitals. Using two cases was common until the California gold rush. The need for transporting type across the continent by wagon demanded a more compact case. Thus the California Job Case came into being, with all of them made in standard sizes so they were interchangeable.

UNIVERSAL PRINTING MACHINE. A half-medium job press manufactured by Gally, McNeal & Hamilton of Rochester, New York, with great strength, durability, compactness, and simplicity, and the capacity to speedily produce the best-quality job work.

WALTER PRESS. A fast newspaper press developed in London and manufactured by J. C. MacDonald. This press was soon adopted by larger newspapers in the United States, including some in the West. It had an hourly capacity of twelve thousand sheets printed on both sides. Only two men were required to operate it. The paper was fed from a reel and passed between four cylinders, two printing cylinders, and two platens. Each of the printing cylinders held two type forms. The sheets were delivered unfolded.

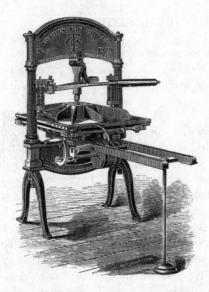

WASHINGTON HANDPRESS. In 1822 Peter Smith of New York introduced a cast-iron press, which used instead of either the screw or lever system a simple toggle joint. Another New Yorker, Samuel Rust, improved on the system and by 1827 was producing a press called the Washington. The frame, instead of being cast iron, had hollow uprights that contained wrought-iron bars securely fastened at the top and bottom of each. These gave the press added strength but greatly reduced the weight and the amount of metal used in construction. Springs above either side of the platen lifted the platen off the impression when the toggle joint was released. The patent for this press was purchased by R. Hoe & Co. of New York City, which made seven sizes of the Washington press and sold more than six thousand throughout the world. Printers purchasing the press were given the following instructions for setting it up:

All the connecting parts being marked, or indented by points, if these be observed carefully, the press may be put together without difficulty.

After setting the frame upon its legs, and putting on the ribs and bed, lay the platen on the bed, placing under it two bears almost type high. Then put the springs in their places, and the nuts over them, and pass the suspending-rods through them, observing to place the rods so that the number of indentations on them correspond with those on the platen. Give the nuts two or three turns, then run in the bed so as to bring the platen under the rods, and screw them fast to the platen; after which, put in the bar-handle, standard, and lever (or wedge and knees, if a Smith press). Turn the nuts on the suspending-rods, so as to compress the springs just enough to give the platen a quick retrograde motion, observing at the same time to get the surface of the platen parallel with the surface of the bed.

After having put the press together level it by means of a spirit-level, be particular not to raise the end of the ribs by the gallows, but let it go under rather loose, which will have a tendency to make the bed slide with more ease on the ribs.

APPENDIX B

GLOSSARY OF PRINTERS' TERMS

The terms and phrases below were used by printers in the Old West. Many of them were used well into the twentieth century, and some adopted for use in ordinary English. Some of these terms have since been adapted to the new printing technology.

AD. Abbreviation for advertisement.

ALIVE. Type matter that is saved for future use.

ALLEY. An aisle in a composing room between type cabinets.

BAD COPY. Manuscript material not carefully prepared, hard to read, or full of errors.

BACK-BOXES. The boxes in the upper case not appropriated to either capitals, small capitals, or figures.

BACKING. In press work, working the second side of a sheet.

BAKED. Type that is caked or sticks together and is hard to separate.

BANK. A wooden table, usually about four feet long, two feet wide, and three and a half feet high, used by hand-pressmen to keep their paper on.

BANNER. A headline, usually in large type, extending across or nearly across a whole page.

BEARD OF A LETTER. That part of a piece of type between the shoulder of the shank and the face.

BEAT. Getting a story ahead of a rival newspaper.

BED OF THE PRESS. The flat, smooth surface on which the form is laid.

BLACKSMITH. A term sometimes used to describe a printer too lazy or too inept to justify a line or a form.

BLANK BOOKS. Bound sheets of blank writing paper in which records are kept; as, day books or ledgers.

BLEED. To run off the edge of a page.

BODKIN. A pointed steel instrument, of various sizes and shapes, used to pick wrong or imperfect letters out of a page, and to push down spaces in correcting material set in type.

BODY. A term applied to the sizes of type, such as Brevier body, Pica body, and so on.

BOILERPLATE. Stereotype plates containing material ready to be printed.

BOOM. To promote something.

BOOMERS. A term used to identify people who continued to call for Oklahoma's homestead settlement during the 1880s. Many were illegal white squatters forced to move around a great deal. Some printers were called boomers during the 1880s and 1890s.

BOXED. Any figure or other work included within a border of brass rules.

BOXES. The compartments in a case in which several varieties of a letter are kept. Thus the compartment in which the *A* is kept is called the A box, and so on.

BRASS RULE. Strips of brass, the height of type, used for forming lines in print.

BREAK LINE. A short line, usually at the end of a paragraph.

BRING UP. To place overlays on those parts in which the impression is defective.

BROADSIDE. A large sheet printed on one side only.

BROKEN MATTER. Discarded and somewhat intermingled pages of type.

BURY A STORY. To place a story on an inside page.

BYLINE. Name of the journalist who wrote a story, usually printed just below the headline.

CASE. A general term used to designate the operations required to prepare type for the press; composition, makeup, imposition, correction, distribution, and the like. The two major divisions in printing were case work and press work; employment in the former was indicated by the phrase "He works at case."

CASING THE LETTER. When the types were to be used continually, as on newspapers, it was necessary to have a pair of cases for every fifty pounds of type in the font because the capitals, figures, and the rest might be required at any moment and needed to be easily available.

CHASE. An iron frame in which type is placed and locked for printing.

CIRCULARS. Advertisements or promotional sheets produced in quantity and usually passed out by hand.

CIRCUS TYPE. The largest type owned by a newspaper, so named because circus promoters would order posters printed in the largest type available.

CLEARING PI. Separating various sizes or kinds of type from a confused mass, and placing each letter in its proper case and box. *See also* PI.

CLEARING THE STONE. A phrase used on some larger newspapers to mean the return of type to cases and all other equipment to their proper places after use—"to clear the stone" for the next printing job.

COMPOSITION. Typesetting.

COPY. Written or typed material to be printed.

COVER. To report news about an event.

CROP. To trim or cut off the edge.

DEAD. Type that has been printed and is ready for distribution in typecases.

DEADHEAD. Any person who obtains something of commercial value without special charge. The term was often applied to those members of the press who received tickets free of charge to places of public entertainment, free passage in public conveyances, and free use of telegraph and express facilities.

DEAD HORSE. Matter billed before it is set, or work for which a printer has been paid before the labor is actually performed.

DEVIL. Sometimes called a printer's devil; the boy who did the drudge work in a newspaper office or printing plant. Tradition has it that the term dates back to the seventeenth century, when young African Americans were apprenticed to printers. When they lifted the printed sheets from the tympan, they would often get ink on their hands, face, and clothing. Printers jokingly called them "devils."

EAR. A small box in the upper corner of the front page that might contain the newspaper's slogan or a weather report.

EDITION. The number of copies printed at the same time or for one publication. Some daily newspapers issued successive editions of each number at stated hours, adding additional news items and sometimes altering other departments of the paper.

EDITORIAL. Material written by the editor expressing opinion and so labeled in a newspaper.

EM. The square dimension of a type body of any size, so called because the capital *M* most nearly approximates this measure.

EMPTY CASE. When some type in a case is exhausted so that the compositor can set no more letters from it, it is said to be empty, although it may still contain type of many other sorts.

FACE OF THE LETTER. The surface of the end of the type that contains the letter.

FACE OF THE PAGE. The upper side of the page from which the impression is taken.

FEET OF THE PRESS. The part of a handpress that is in contact with the floor.

FILLER. Miscellaneous matter set in type and kept ready to fill space whenever needed. On most papers the printer responsible for the makeup usually kept a galley of fillers already set in type.

FIRST PROOF. A proof pulled immediately after matter is composed, used for the purpose of comparing it with the copy to detect errors.

FLOOR PI. Type dropped on the floor during the operation of composition or distribution.

FOLIO. A sheet of paper folded once.

FONT. Type characters of one size of a given series, along with spacing material in the same size.

FOOLSCAP. A folded writing paper, usually 12 by 15 inches or 12½ by 16 inches. The name is supposed to have derived from a watermark representing the cap bells of ancient jesters.

FOOTSTICK. A piece of furniture, sloped or beveled from one end to the other, placed against the foot of the page.

FORM. Type completely assembled and locked in a chase ready for the press.

FORM LIFTS. The condition of the form, when, on being raised from the stone or press, nothing drops out.

FURNITURE. Square or oblong pieces of metal or hard cherrywood used to fill up blank space.

GALLEY. A shallow metal tray used for holding type after it is removed from the composing stick.

GALLEY PROOF. A proof taken from composed type in a galley.

GET IN, TAKE IN. Terms used when more matter is put into a line, page, or form than is in the printed copy the compositor sets from.

GET THE LEAD OUT. This phrase apparently resulted from typesetters who wore pants with cuffs that caught pieces of lead. The phrase, after becoming part of ordinary English, means "hurry up."

GONE TO BED. A phrase meaning that the paper had gone to press. It may have originated from the bed of the press.

GRAF. Paragraph.

HANDBILLS. Comparatively small printed bills, used chiefly to advertise auctions or real or personal property.

HELLBOX. A container in the composing room where used type to be remelted is thrown.

HORSING IT. A phrase used to describe a printer who charges more in his weekly bill than he has earned, or anyone who habitually resorts to tricky devices to secure advances from his employer.

IMPOSING STONE. The stone or plate of various sizes on which forms are imposed and corrected.

IMPRESSION. Pressure made by an inked form of type on a sheet of paper.

JEFFING. When printers had a little time on their hands they would gamble—not with money but with quads. Jeffing was a game in which five 18-point quads were tossed. Whoever got the most nicks up won, whoever got the fewest bought beer.

JOB WORK. All kinds of letterpress printing, except that of books and newspapers.

KEEP IN. To crowd matter into a limited space by using thin spacing.

LAYING TYPE. Putting new type into the cases.

LEAD. Thin pieces of metal, lead being the chief ingredient, which were placed between the lines of matter, or composed type, to open it up. Leads were also used to blank out titles, jobs, and forms of various descriptions.

LIVE MATTER. Type composition or pages that have not yet been printed.

LOCALS. Short items of local news.

LOW CASE. A case that is short of its proper complement of type, or in which the quantities in the different boxes are low.

MAKEUP. Creating each part of a newspaper; placing stories, advertisements, and other material set in type within the page frame.

MAKING MARGIN. The act of placing matter or pages in a position so that, when printed, they fall in their proper places on the sheet.

MAKING READY. The act of getting a form ready to be printed.

MIND YOUR P'S AND Q'S. A printer's phrase that just as easily could have been "mind your d's and b's, 6's and 9's, I's and 1's, or o's and 0's." A beginning typesetter found these letters confusing. This is another printer's phrase that has entered the ranks of ordinary English.

MISPRINT. An error in printing caused either by accident during the progress of press work, by incorrect composition, or by mistakes in making up a form.

NICK. The curved indentation on the lower end of a piece of type or quad indicating the bottom of the letter or quad.

NOM DE PLUME. A French phrase meaning, literally, "pen name." A fictitious name assumed by an author who, unwilling to disclose his real name, wants to distinguish his publications from the mass of anonymous literature.

NUMBER. The number within the volume of the newspaper being printed.

OBIT. The death notice of an individual, whether a mere announcement or accompanied by added material.

OFF THE HOOK. In printing, this phrase means to take things as they come. Typesetters pulled the copy to be set in type off the shop hook and never knew what they would have to set in type next.

ON ITS FEET. A letter that stood perfectly upright was said to be on its feet.

OUT OF HIS TIME. A youth was said to be out of his time when he had completed his apprenticeship.

PAGE. One side of a leaf of paper, a sheet of writing paper, or a folio newspaper containing two leaves or four pages.

PAPER HORSE. A wooden table, usually about four feet long, two feet wide, and three and a half feet high, arranged so as to slant at an angle of about thirty degrees. It is placed on the end of a bank nearest the tympan, and is used for supporting the paper immediately before it is worked off.

PAPER STRETCHER. As a joke printers would sometimes ask an unwary apprentice to fetch a paper stretcher if a job did not fit. No such device existed.

PI. A mass of disarranged type (letters, numbers, and so on). If a printer dropped a case of type, it was said to be nothing but pi. Its genesis is not known, but it is most likely related to the term "humble pie."

PICA POLE. The pica ruler or line gauge, with measurements in picas, inches, and agate lines. It was usually a foot long, but two-foot pica poles were sometimes used for newspaper makeup.

PLATEN. That part of the press which descends on the form and effects the impression.

PONY SERVICE. A brief summary of news obtained from a press association by telegraph or mail.

PRINT. An impression from type.

PROOF. A trial impression of type to verify the correctness of the composition.

PROOFREADING. The detection and designation of composition errors.

PUBLISH. To prepare and issue printed material for public distribution or sale.

PUT TO BED. To complete the operations preparatory to printing a newspaper.

QUADS OR QUADRATS. Pieces of type metal, without letters or numbers, used to leave blank spaces for indentations at the beginning of sentences, for larger space between sentences, and for spacing out the ends of line that do not fill a full paragraph.

RAG. Slang for a newspaper.

RATTING. Working for less than the established wages.

READYPRINT. Preprinted sections of newspapers ready to be incorporated into the rest of the paper.

REGLETS. Wooden furniture of various thicknesses used to fill out blank spaces in forms and to make margin.

RULES. Strips of brass or wood made type height, so as to represent lines of various thicknesses on a printed page.

SCOOP. To get a story ahead of a rival newspaper.

SHEEP'S-FOOT. An iron hammer, with a claw at one end, used in locking up forms, and also by pressmen to tap forms into place.

SHEET. A piece of paper of any of the regular sizes, which, by folding in folio, is prepared for writing upon, as a sheet of letter paper; or which is printed with one impression, and may afterward be folded into any of various sizes.

SHOW CARDS. Cards of a comparatively large size to be put up in public places to describe a business, articles offered for sale; or entertainment including circuses, theatricals, and any other unusual event.

STRING. There were no time cards for printers. They would arrive on the job, grab the proofs from the last day's work, paste them together, and get paid for the length of the string of words set into type.

STRIPED INK. Sometimes if a printer got a job with an American flag on it, the apprentice would be sent in quest of striped ink. Most apprentices soon got wise and took the rest of the day off.

STYLE. The mode of expressing thought in language, whether oral or written; rhetorical expression. Also the custom of a newspaper in regards to unsettled or disputed points relating to orthography, division of words, spacing, compound words, capitalization and display of certain classes of words, and so on.

TAG. A closing, something at the end.

TEARSHEET. A sheet torn from a newspaper.

(THIRTY) 30. The ending symbol on a story. There are two explanations of the use of the numeral "30." One explanation stems from printers' use of a thirty-point slug, cast by the Linotype machine, measuring approximately $\frac{7}{16}$ inches in height, at the bottom of a galley to indicate the end of a take. The other explanation is tied to telegraphers who sent "30" in code on their keys to mean "the end" when they were shutting down for the night. Some accounts say the numerals had to do with "Rule 30," which spelled out a temporary shutting down of telegraph operations. Instead of citing the full rule, telegraphers simply transmitted three x's—*XXX,* or 30—to let other telegraphers know they were closing down, thus "30" became the journalists' symbol for "the end."

TO JUSTIFY. Means spacing out a line of type so that it will fit firmly in the composing stick.

TYMPAN. That part of a press on which the paper to be printed is laid.

TYPE LOUSE. Before solvents came into being, a form was left in a shallow dish of soapy water to soak. As a prank a printer would open the form a bit and invite the apprentice to inspect it for type lice. As the apprentice bent over, the printer slid the type together, causing dirty water to splash into the apprentice's face.

TYPO. Typographical error.

UPPER CASE. The case having the highest elevation on a stand, and containing capital and small-capital letters, references, and so on, which are called uppercase sorts.

WASHING THE FORM. Cleaning type immediately after it has been printed, or during the process of printing, to keep the ink from drying and clogging the type.

APPENDIX C

EARLY NEWSPAPERS IN STATES AND
TERRITORIES WEST OF THE MISSISSIPPI

ARIZONA

The first paper, the *Weekly Arizonian,* was owned by the Salero Mining Company at Tubac, with William Wrightson, printer, and Edward E. Cross and Charles D. Poston, editors. The Washington handpress on which the paper was printed came from Cincinnati in 1858, was taken across Panama; up the Gulf of California to Guaymas, Mexico; and brought by wagon to Tubac, where the paper was first published on March 3, 1859. In 1860 the paper was moved to Tucson, where it was published by J. Howard Wells until the outbreak of the Civil War. In 1867 the paper was revived by W. S. Oury and eventually became the *Tucson Citizen.* The second paper in Arizona was the Mesilla *Times,* established in 1860 by B. C. Murray and Company, with Frank Higgins, editor. Arizona's third paper was the *Arizona Miner,* established at Postle's Ranch near Fort Whipple, March 9, 1864, with Tisdale A. Hand, editor. The paper was moved to Prescott when the town became the capital. The *Arizona Miner* was printed on a Ramage press supposedly manufactured in Cincinnati, Ohio, in 1825.

ARKANSAS

The first paper was the *Arkansas Gazette,* established at Arkansas Post on November 20, 1819, by William Edward Woodruff, a native of Bellport, Long Island. Woodruff learned the printing trade as an apprentice at the *Suffolk Gazette,* Sag Harbor, Long Island. Later he worked on newspapers at Franklin and Nashville in Tennessee. At Arkansas Post, Robert Briggs became Woodruff's partner in March 1820. When Little Rock became the permanent capital, the *Arkansas Gazette* was moved there, the first issue being released on December 29, 1821. A second paper, called the *Arkansas Advocate,* was established at Little Rock in March 1830 with Charles P. Bertrand as editor.

CALIFORNIA

The first paper was the *Californian,* published at Monterey, August 15, 1846, by Rev. Walter Colton, chaplain of the U.S. frigate *Congress,* assisted by two printers, Joseph Dockrill and Robert Semple. Colton had at one time been editor of the Philadelphia *North American.* One-half of the paper was in English, the other in Spanish. The first issue contained the declaration of war between the United States and Mexico, with an account of a debate in the Senate. On April 24, 1847, Robert Semple became sole publisher of the *Californian* and two weeks later moved it to Yerba Buena (San Francisco), where Mormon colonists had established the *California Star,* whose first regular number appeared January 9, 1847. When gold was discovered, so many San Franciscans left to join the gold rush that the *Californian* stopped publishing on June 2, 1848, and the *California Star* with its June 14 issue. Within months San Francisco became a boom town and the two papers were merged in November 1848 and on January 4, 1849, became the *Alta California,* which became a daily on January 23, 1850. The *Pacific News* was started at San Francisco on August 25, 1849, by William Faulkner and Warren Leland. Leland sold his interest within a few months to R. T. P. Allen, who in turn sold it to Jonas Winchester, who had been Horace Greeley's partner in New York. Sacramento's first newspaper was the *Placer Times,* started by E. C. Kemble & Company, April 28, 1849, only a few months after the sale of its town lots had begun.

COLORADO

The first paper was William N. Byers's *Rocky Mountain News,* printed on brown wrapping paper, April 23, 1859, at Denver. The *News* was printed on an old Washington handpress brought overland by wagon from Omaha, Nebraska, and set up in a log cabin. About twenty minutes after the first issue of the *Rocky Mountain News,* John L. Merrick's *Cherry Creek Pioneer* was printed, but only one issue was ever published. The following day Merrick sold his press and equipment to William N. Byers. The first daily newspaper in Colorado was the *Daily Herald and Rocky Mountain Advertiser,* published at Denver on May 1, 1860, edited by Thomas Gibson. The *Rocky Mountain News* became a daily on August 27, 1860.

IDAHO

Although a missionary press had been established near what became Lewiston in 1839 to serve the Nez Percé Indians, the first newspaper was the *Golden Age,* established in August 1862 at Lewiston (named for the explorer Meriwether Lewis) by A. S. Gould, who had worked as a newspaperman in Portland, Oregon. Gould soon sold the paper to John H. Scranton, who published it until August 1863, when he sold it to Frank Kenyon. When the Idaho Territory was organized March 4, 1863, Kenyon was appointed territorial printer. Kenyon continued to publish the *Golden Age* until January 1865, when the paper was discontinued. Two years later Kenyon started the *Mining News* at Leesburg, Idaho Territory, but it lasted only eight months. The first paper published in the new Idaho Territory was the *Boise News,* started at Bannock City—now called Idaho City—September 29, 1863, by Thomas J. and John S. Butler, former California newspapermen. On July 26, 1864, three brothers, James S., Thomas B., and Richard W. Reynolds, started the *Idaho Tri-Weekly Statesman* at Boise. The paper became a daily called the *Idaho Statesman* in 1888. The *Owyhee Avalanche* was established at Silver City on August 15, 1865, by J. L. Hardin and Joseph Wasson.

IOWA

The first paper was the Dubuque *Visitor,* established by John King at the Dubuque Lead Mines in Wisconsin Territory on May 11, 1836. King had founded the Dubuque Lead Mine in 1834. He had purchased a Smith handpress in Cincinnati and hired two Ohio printers, William Carey Jones and Andrew Keesecker, to print the paper, whose primary purpose was to boost the small community into a prosperous city. The second paper in what is now Iowa was the *Western Adventurer and Herald of the Upper Mississippi,* published in 1836 by Dr. Isaac Galland at Montrose. The paper was suspended after a few months and the equipment sold to James G. Edwards, who took it to Fort Madison, where, on March 24, 1838, he issued the first number of the Fort Madison *Patriot.* After a little more than a year at Fort Madison, Edwards moved his paper to Burlington, where on June 6, 1839, he published it as the *Iowa Patriot.*

KANSAS

The first paper published in what became Kansas was a missionary sheet printed in an Indian language. It was called the *Shawnee Sun* in English and was published in 1835 by Isaac McCoy, edited by Rev. Johnston Lykins, at the Shawnee Baptist Mission, near the Missouri border. After the Kansas Territory was established in 1854, the first paper was the *Kansas Weekly Herald,* printed on September 15, 1854, by William J. Osborn and William H. Adams. S. M. Myers set the type. The paper was composed and printed under an elm tree on the townsite before there was a permanent building in Leavenworth. Another newspaper started in Kansas Territory in 1854 was called the *Pioneer,* published at Kickapoo by A. B. Hazzard and a man named Sexton. Three newspapers began in Lawrence in 1855. The first was the *Herald of Freedom,* published by George W. Brown. Next came the *Kansas Tribune,* published by John Speer, and the *Kansas Free State,* established by Robert G. Elliott and Josiah Miller. The first newspaper at Topeka was the *Kansas Freeman,* established by E. C. K. Harvey on July 4, 1855.

LOUISIANA

The first newspaper published in what is now Louisiana was the French-language *Moniteur de la Louisiane,* begun by Louis Duclot on March 3, 1794. A second paper was started there in 1785, called *Le Courrier du Vendredi,* and a third one was founded by Beleurgey et Renard in December 1803 and called *Le Télégraphe, et le Commercial Adver-*

tiser. Later it was published in French and English. All three papers were published in the portion of New Orleans that lay on the east side of the Mississippi. The first newspaper published in New Orleans after the Louisiana Territory was purchased by the United States was the *New Orleans Gazette and Commercial Advertiser,* published by James M. Bradford, whose father had established the first paper in Lexington, Kentucky. Bradford was also the first person to publish a newspaper in the territory adjacent to New Orleans. He had established the weekly *Time Piece* in 1811 at what was then St. Francisville, between the Pearl and Mississippi Rivers.

MINNESOTA

The first paper was the *Minnesota Pioneer,* printed at St. Paul on April 28, 1849, by James M. Goodhue, a lawyer. The second was the *Minnesota Chronicle,* established on May 31, 1849, by James Hughes. It was short-lived, and Hughes sold out to John Phillips Owens and Nathaniel McLean, who combined the *Chronicle* with the *Minnesota Register,* a paper begun by Dr. Andrew Randall. Only one issue of Randall's *Minnesota Register* exists, and it was printed in Cincinnati with extant copies bearing different dates, April 7 and 27, 1849. Randall bought printing equipment in Cincinnati but then decided not to become a printer in Minnesota. He sold his paper and equipment to Owens and McLean, who printed the first issue of the *Minnesota Register* on July 14, 1849, at St. Paul. After purchasing the *Chronicle,* Owens and McLean merged the papers and on August 25, 1849, published the first issue of the *Chronicle and Register* at St. Paul.

MISSOURI

The first newspaper printed in Missouri and west of the Mississippi was the *Missouri Gazette,* published at St. Louis by Joseph Charless and printed by Jacob Hinkle on July 12, 1808. There were 170 subscribers, many of whom agreed to pay the annual subscription price of three dollars in flour, corn, beef, or pork. Charless urged subscribers to pay in advance since it cost upwards of twenty dollars to publish each issue. In 1809 Charless changed the name of his newspaper to the *Louisiana Gazette,* but after Congress created Missouri Territory in 1812, the paper again became the *Missouri Gazette.* The paper prospered but in 1813 suffered from the lack of paper. On December 17, 1813, Charless suspended publication for several weeks, but he promised that every Saturday a handbill, giving a summary of the news, would be distributed free until publication was resumed. Although Charless retired in 1820 and sold the *Gazette* to James C. Cummins, Charless's son, Edward, and Josiah Spalding became joint owners in 1822 and changed the paper's name to the *Missouri Republican.* On September 20, 1835, it became a daily. A second paper, the *Western Journal,* was established at St. Louis in 1815 and printed by Joshua Norvell. It failed but was revived by Sergeant Hall, who changed the paper's name to the *Western Emigrant* on May 17, 1817. Two years later the paper was sold again. The new owners were Isaac N. Henry, Evarist Maury, and Colonel Thomas Hart Benton, and they changed the paper's name to the *Enquirer.* In 1824 the paper was sold to Gen. Duff Green, who later became Superintendent of Printing in Washington, D.C., and publisher of the *United States Telegraph.*

MONTANA

Some evidence suggests that Wilbur F. Sanders and John A. Creighton, a Virginia City businessman who later founded Creighton University at Omaha, Nebraska, printed a few issues of a newsletter at Virginia City during early 1864, but it was not a true newspaper. A few weeks later Francis M. Thompson printed what he called the *East Bannack News Letter* at Bannack, the temporary territorial capital, but no copies are known to exist. The first true newspaper was the *Montana Post,* started by John Buchanan and Marion M. Manners in the cellar of a log cabin at Virginia City on August 27, 1864. Buchanan had brought his press and materials by boat from St. Louis to Fort Benton. After two issues he sold the paper to D. W. Tilton and Benjamin R. Dittes. In May 1868 Dittes bought Tilton's interest but subsequently sold it to a man named Pinney. When Helena became the state's capital in 1868, the paper moved its operation there, the first number appearing on August 25, 1868. After Helena was swept by fire on April 23, 1869, business was paralyzed and the paper ceased publication with the June 11, 1869, issue. Montana's second paper was the *Montana Democrat,* published at Virginia City in 1865.

NEBRASKA

The *Nebraska Palladium* was the first paper published in Nebraska, but its first issue was printed on July 15, 1854, at St. Mary's, Iowa, just across the Missouri River from the Nebraska Territory. Daniel E. Reed and J. M. Latham were the editors and printers. By November the printing equipment had been moved across the Missouri River and set up in Bellevue, Nebraska Territory. There, on November 15, 1854, the first issue was printed on Nebraska soil. The *Arrow,* Omaha's first paper, was printed at Council Bluffs, Iowa, July 28, 1854, by Joseph E. Johnson and John W. Pattison. It lasted until the end of the year. The first paper actually printed in Omaha was the *Nebraskian,* started on January 17, 1855, by Bird B. Chapman. The first daily newspaper in Nebraska was the *Telegraph,* started at Omaha by Maj. Henry Z. Curtis on December 11, 1860.

NEVADA

The first newspaper was *Golden Switch,* written with pen and ink on paper by Joseph Webb, at the Carson River Crossing, where Dayton now stands. It was started in 1854 and lasted no later than 1858. A rival handwritten paper, the *Scorpion,* was soon begun by Stephen A. Kensey in the small settlement of Genoa, at the eastern foot of the Sierra Nevada Mountains. The first printed paper, however, was the *Territorial Enterprise,* issued at Genoa on December 18, 1858, by Alfred Jones and William L. Jernegan. On November 5, 1859, the *Territorial Enterprise* was purchased by Jonathan Williams and J. B. Woolard and moved to Carson City, the territorial capital. Later it was purchased by Joseph T. Goodman and Dennis E. McCarthy and in 1860 moved to Virginia City. The second paper was the *Daily Independent,* started at Carson City in 1863.

NEW MEXICO

The first paper was *El Crepusculo de la Libertad* (Dawn of Liberty), established at Taos by Antonio Jose Martinez on November 29, 1835. The paper failed to pay expenses and was suspended after four issues. The second paper was *La Verdad,* issued at Santa Fe for sixteen months in 1844 and 1845. Later in 1845 *El Payo de Nuevo Mejico* was published at Santa Fe and lasted several months. The founding of the first English-language paper, the *Santa Fe Republican,* occurred on September 4, 1847. The printing equipment was owned by the U.S. Army, and soldiers printed the paper. The paper and equipment were later sold to the founders of the Santa Fe *New Mexican,* who published the paper intermittently in 1849 and 1850.

NORTH DAKOTA

The first paper was the *Frontier Scout,* published in July 1864 at Fort Union by two soldiers, Ira F. Goodwin and Robert Winegar, for the troops of Company I, 30th Wisconsin Volunteers. After a few issues the paper was moved to Fort Rice, with Capt. E. G. Adams as editor and Lt. C. H. Champney as publisher. The paper is not known to have continued publication after 1865. In 1873 Col. Clement A. Lounsberry left the associate editorship of the Minneapolis *Tribune* and took the necessary printing outfit to Bismarck, where he established the *Tribune* on July 6, 1873. The first issue, dated July 11, contains an advertisement for every business establishment in Bismarck. The second newspaper in North Dakota was the *Express,* published at Fargo, January 1, 1874, by A. J. Harwood and Gordon J. Keeney. The third newspaper was the *Plaindealer,* established at Grand Forks in 1874 by George H. Walsh.

OKLAHOMA

Some historians consider that the first newspaper in what is now Oklahoma was a Baptist missionary organ called the *Cherokee Messenger,* printed in August 1844 at Cherokee Baptist Mission near modern Westville, Oklahoma. That paper, however, was published irregularly in an Indian dialect, emphasized religious material, and was not a true newspaper. Oklahoma's first real newspaper was the national organ of the Cherokee Nation, entitled the *Cherokee Advocate* and published on September 26, 1844, at Tahlequah. William P. Ross, a mixed-blood Cherokee educated at Princeton, was the first editor and is today called the "father of Oklahoma journalism." A paper called the *Choctaw Telegraph* was published at Doaksville in the Choctaw Nation during the latter part of 1848. Edited by Daniel Folsom and printed by D. G. Ball, it died after about a year but was revived in 1870 and continued after an interruption in 1876 until 1907. The *Cherokee Rosebud* was started in 1848 by students of Park Hill Female Seminary at Tahlequah.

OREGON

The first paper was the *Oregon Spectator,* printed at Oregon City on February 5, 1846. Its first editor was Colonel William G. T'Vault, a lawyer, who was then postmaster general of the provisional government, and its first printer was John Fleming, who had emigrated to Oregon in 1844. On April 16, 1846, Henry A. G. Lee, a descendant of Richard Lee, of Virginia, became editor. He severed his relations after the August 6, 1846, issue. John Fleming, the printer, served as editor until George L. Curry moved into the position in October 1846. Curry resigned in 1848 to start a rival paper, the *Free Press,* which had a short life. On December 4, 1850, Thomas J. Dryer, who had edited a California newspaper, and A. M. Berry, a native of New Hampshire, started the *Weekly Oregonian,* printing it on a Ramage press brought from California. Henry L. Pittock became proprietor in 1860, and on February 4, 1861, the *Oregonian* became a daily.

SOUTH DAKOTA

The first paper published in what is now South Dakota was the *Dakota Democrat,* established at Sioux Falls City, now Sioux Falls, September 20, 1858. Its owner was Samuel J. Albright, who published the paper irregularly until July 2, 1859. After that date he published the paper regularly until the fall of 1860, when a man named Stewart took over and changed the paper's name to the *Northwestern Democrat.* The paper ceased publication when the Indian war broke out in 1862 and Sioux Falls was abandoned. Indians sacked the town, destroyed the paper's printing plant, and carried away most of the type to make ornaments used to decorate their smoking pipes.

TEXAS

The earliest newspaper of record in what is now Texas was one sheet, seven by thirteen inches, printed in Spanish on both sides and called *Gaceta de Texas.* It was edited by William Shaler and José Alvarez de Toledo and appeared in May 1813. It was followed one month later by *El Mejicano,* another Spanish-language paper, published at Nacogdoches in 1813 and edited by Shaler and Toledo. Only a few issues of each paper were printed. Another early paper was the *Texas Republican,* brought out on August 14, 1819, in Nacogdoches by Horatio Bigelow, editor, and Eli Harris, printer, who had joined Dr. James Long's efforts to "Americanize" Texas. Long wanted the paper to preserve a printed record of his expedition to establish a Texas republic, but less than two months after it was started, Mexicans destroyed its printing plant. When Texas independence was established in 1836, only the *Telegraph and Texas Register* was being published in Texas. It was first issued at San Felice, October 10, 1835, and produced by Gail Borden, Joseph Baker, and Thomas H. Borden. It was the foremost paper devoted to the revolutionary cause and was practically the official organ of the provincial government.

UTAH

The first paper in Utah was the *Deseret News,* started by the Mormon church on June 15, 1850, about three years after the arrival of the first Mormons with Brigham H. Young. Dr. Willard Richards was the editor, and Horace K. Whitney was the printer. Whitney was assisted by Brigham H. Young, a nephew of the Mormon leader, who had been trained as a pressman. Thomas Bullock was the proofreader. The paper continued publication until August 19, 1851, when it was suspended for lack of paper until November 15. After being issued as a weekly for four months, the *Deseret News* was published as a semimonthly until 1854, when it again became a weekly. Kirk Anderson started a paper titled the *Valley Tan* at Salt Lake City, November 6, 1858. The paper lasted under various unsuccessful owners until February 1860, and then died. Another paper, the *Mountaineer,* was started at Salt Lake City, August 27, 1859, by Seth M. Blair, James Ferguson, and Hosea Stout. It lasted until the summer of 1861.

WASHINGTON

The first paper in Washington was called the *Columbian,* published on September 11, 1852, at Olympia on Puget Sound. The paper was owned and edited by James W. Wiley and Thornton F. McElroy. On March 2, 1853, when the Washington Territory was established, Wiley and McElroy changed the paper's name to the *Washington Pioneer.* When the paper was sold, the new owners renamed it the *Pioneer and Democrat,* and it lasted until 1861. The second paper in Washington was the *Puget Sound Courier,* started at Steilacoom on May 19, 1855, by William B. Affleck and E. T. Gunn. It stayed in business about a year. The *Puget Sound Express,* Washington's third paper, was begun at Steilacoom on March 12, 1858, by Charles Prosch, a printer from San Francisco. It continued for about six years, when Prosch sold out. In 1867 the paper was moved to Olympia. The first paper published at Seattle was the *Intelligencer,* on August 5, 1867, by Samuel L. Maxwell.

WYOMING

The first paper in what became Wyoming was the *Daily Telegraph,* published by Hiram Brundage on June 24, 1863, at Fort Bridger. After the Wyoming Territory was organized in May 1869, the first paper published within the present boundaries of Wyoming was the *Cheyenne Leader,* September 16, 1867, by Nathan A. Baker and J. E. Gates. The paper was the first weekly with a subscription price of twelve dollars a year and later successively an evening and a morning daily. Baker established three papers in Wyoming: the *Cheyenne Leader,* the Laramie *Sentinel,* and the South Pass *News.* Early in 1868 a printing office was started at Fort Bridger by Warren and Hastings, who in February of that year published a paper titled the *Sweetwater Miner* to promote immigration. In the spring of 1868 A. E. Slack started the *News* at South Pass. Another paper, the *Wyoming Weekly Tribune,* was established in 1869 at Cheyenne by Edward M. Lee and edited by Samuel A. Bristol.

NOTES

CHAPTER 1   THE STAGE IS SET

1. John Clyde Oswald, *Printing in the Americas* (New York: Gregg Publishing Co., 1937), p. 26. The first quarto Bible to be printed in America in English was an edition of the "Doway" version, issued in 1790 by Carey, Stewart & Company of Philadelphia. In 1801 the same firm issued another quarto Bible; on the title page, in small type beneath the name of the publishers, appears the name of Joseph Charless, who was employed by the firm at the time and later became the pioneer printer of Missouri.

2. Ibid., pp. 175–76.

3. Ibid., pp. 310–13.

4. Ibid., pp. 325–27. See also Osman Castle Hooper, *History of Ohio Journalism, 1793–1933* (Columbus: Spahr & Glenn Co., 1933).

5. Oswald, *Printing in the Americas*, p. 355.

6. William H. Taft, *Missouri Newspapers* (Columbia: University of Missouri Press, 1964), p. 17.

7. Albert Watkins, ed., *Publications of the Nebraska State Historical Society*, vol. 20 (Lincoln: Nebraska State Historical Society, 1922), pp. 19, 22.

8. Oswald, *Printing in the Americas*, pp. 388–90.

9. The story of the printing press brought to Texas by Jose Alvarez de Toledo is detailed in Marilyn McAdams Sibley's *Lone Stars and State Gazettes: Texas Newspapers Before the Civil War* (College Station: Texas A&M University Press, 1983), pp. 15–27.

10. Ibid., pp. 48–51.

11. Ibid., p. 62.

12. Oswald, *Printing in the Americas*, pp. 383–84. Gail Borden, Jr., later originated a method of condensing milk and made a fortune. He also tried unsuccessfully to invent a wagon propelled by sails, but it was difficult to steer. However, his efforts gave rise to the phrase "prairie schooner," later used to describe emigrant wagons crossing

the plains and prairies. For a biography of Borden, see Joe B. Frantz, *Gail Borden, Dairyman to a Nation* (Norman: University of Oklahoma Press, 1951).

13. Douglas C. McMurtrie and Albert H. Allen, *Jotham Meeker: Pioneer Printer of Kansas* (Chicago: Eyncourt Press, 1930), p. 59.

14. Ibid. See also Douglas C. McMurtrie, "The Shawnee Sun," *Kansas Historical Quarterly* 2, no. 4 (1933), pp. 339–42.

15. Oswald, *Printing in the Americas*, p. 418. The *Cherokee Messenger* and the *Cherokee Advocate* were not the first newspapers to be printed for the Cherokee Indians. Elias Boudinot, editor, and Isaac N. Harris, printer, published the *Cherokee Phoenix*, printed partly in Cherokee and partly in English, beginning in 1828 at New Echota, Georgia, after George Guess (Gist)—said to have been the son of Nathaniel Gist and a Cherokee woman—who took the Indian name of Sequoya, took the verbal Cherokee syllables and devised eighty-six characters, or symbols, creating the Cherokee alphabet. The giant redwood tree of California is named for Sequoya. See Grant Foreman, *Sequoyah* (Norman: University of Oklahoma Press, 1938).

16. Rev. Walter Colton, U.S.N., *Three Years in California* (New York: A. S. Barnes and Co., 1850), pp. 32–33.

17. *California Star* (Yerba Buena), January 9, 1847.

18. *Californian* (Monterey), January 23, 1847.

19. *The California Star, Yerba Buena and San Francisco, vol. 1, 1847–1848: A Reproduction in Facsimile* (Berkeley: Howell-North Books, 1965). This work includes a valuable introduction by Fred Blackburn Rogers containing much historical detail.

CHAPTER 2 NO WEASEL WORDS

1. Frederic Hudson, *Journalism in the United States from 1630 to 1872* (New York: Harper & Brothers, 1873), p. 467.

2. The *Kansas Constitutionalist*, at Doniphan, went out of business in July 1858, and its printing equipment was taken to start another weekly, at Iowa Point, Kansas. Solomon Miller's *Kansas Chief* was published at White Cloud until 1872 and was then moved to Troy, Kansas, where it was published until his death in 1897. Thomas J. Key was a Democrat and Sol Miller a Republican.

3. Cecil Howes, "Pistol-Packin' Pencil Pushers," *Kansas Historical Quarterly* 13, no. 2 (1944), p. 115.

4. *Leavenworth* (Kansas) *Times*, May 28, 1880.

5. *Kansas City* (Missouri) *Times*, May 30, 1880.

6. Hudson, *Journalism in the United States from 1630 to 1872*, p. 747.

7. For a full discussion of the history of libel law, see Norman L. Rosenberg, *Protecting the Best Men: An Interpretive History of the Law of Libel* (Chapel Hill: University of North Carolina Press, 1986). Rosenberg examines the complex and historically rooted nature of legal concepts and legal consciousness in the United States. Libel is generally defined as untrue printed information that exposes a person or people to public hatred, contempt, or ridicule and unjustly defames the character of an individual or hurts his or her business.

8. Wells Drury, *An Editor on the Comstock Lode* (New York: Farrar & Rinehart, Inc., 1936), p. 181.

9. Quoted in the *Kansas City* (Missouri) *Star,* May 21, 1942.

10. Howes, "Pistol-Packin' Pencil Pushers," p. 124.

11. Emporia (Kansas) *Gazette,* November 6, 1907.

CHAPTER 3 POLITICS

1. Original prospectus, Pierre Chouteau Collection, Missouri Historical Society, Library and Collections Center, St. Louis.

2. *Missouri Gazette* (n.d., 1809).

3. Nyle Miller, Edgar Langsdorf, and Robert W. Richmond, *Kansas in Newspapers* (Topeka: Kansas State Historical Society, 1963), p. iii.

4. C. B. Boynton and T. B. Mason, *A Journey Through Kansas . . .* (Cincinnati: Moore, Wilstach, Keys & Co., 1855), pp. 23–24.

5. A. T. Andreas, *History of the State of Kansas . . .* (Chicago: A. T. Andreas, 1883), p. 430.

6. Cecil Howes, "Pistol-Packin' Pencil Pushers," *Kansas Historical Quarterly,* p. 117.

7. *Leavenworth Weekly Herald,* quoted in *Freedom's Champion* (Atchison, Kansas Territory), June 4, 1859.

8. Albert D. Richardson, quoted in "Lincoln in Kansas," *Transactions of the Kansas State Historical Society,* Vol. VII (Topeka: W. Y. Morgan, State Printer, 1902), p. 538.

9. H. G. Hawler, Diary, August 6, 1860, Document Resources Department, State Historical Society of Colorado, Denver.

10. David Fridtjof Halaas, *Boom Town Newspapers: Journalism on the Rocky Mountain Mining Frontier, 1859–1881* (Albuquerque: University of New Mexico Press, 1981), pp. 40–41.

11. Porter A. Stratton. *The Territorial Press of New Mexico, 1834–1912* (Albuquerque: University of New Mexico Press, 1969), pp. 3–10, 81–97.

12. Aside from the Hinsdale County, Colorado, district court records of the first Packer trial in April 1883, and the newspaper accounts cited in the text, the *Denver Times,* on February 18, 1900, carried a full-page account of the Alferd Packer story, including court records. This was less than a year before Fred Bonfils and Harry Tammen sought to get Packer pardoned. Several other publications also contain material about Packer. Fred and Jo Mazzulla's forty-eight-page pamphlet *Al Packer: A Colorado Cannibal* (Denver: n.p., 1968), is a well-illustrated account. See also Robert L. Perkin, *The First Hundred Years: An Informal History of Denver and the Rocky Mountain News* (New York: Doubleday & Co., 1959), and Gene Fowler, *Timber Line: A Story of Bonfils and Tammen* (New York: Covici Friede Publishers, 1933).

13. *Denver* (Colorado) *Daily Gazette,* January 4, 1868.

14. William A. Keleher, *Memoirs: 1892–1969: A New Mexico Item* (Santa Fe: Rydal Press, 1969), pp. 72–76.

15. Don Schellie, *The Tucson Citizen: A Century of Arizona Journalism* (Tucson: Tucson Daily Citizen, 1970), pp. 25–33.

CHAPTER 4   EXPRESSING OPINION

1. A sketch of the *Telegraph and Texas Register* is included in Marilyn McAdams Sibley, *Lone Stars and State Gazettes: Texas Newspapers before the Civil War* (College Station: Texas A&M University Press, 1983), pp. 65–84. Additional material can be found in Donna Lee Dickerson, *A Typestick of Texas History* (Austin: Department of Journalism, University of Texas, 1971), pp. 27–33.
2. James Ford Rhodes, *Historical Essays* (New York: Macmillan Co., 1909), pp. 90–91.
3. Walter P. Webb, ed., *Handbook of Texas*, vol. 1 (Austin: Texas State Historical Association, 1952), p. 275.
4. *North American Review*, vol. 102 (April 1866), pp. 375–76.
5. The newspapers reviewed on microfilm were published between 1888 and 1890 in Kansas City, Omaha, Denver, Albuquerque, Salt Lake City, El Paso, San Antonio, Portland, Seattle, and San Francisco.
6. *Chase County Leader,* Cottonwood Falls, Kansas, January 17, 1878.
7. Work Projects Administration, *Nevada: A Guide to the Silver State,* p. 87.
8. William A. Keleher, *Memoirs: 1892–1969: A New Mexico Item,* pp. 69–70.
9. *Indian Journal,* Muskogee, Iowa Territory, July 18, 1876.
10. *Indian Journal,* May 1, 1879; November 13, 1879; August 24, 1880; August 17, 1881. The *Indian Journal* was published at Muskogee, Indian Territory, until its plant was destroyed by fire on December 25, 1876. The paper then moved to Eufaula, Indian Territory. During the early 1880s it moved back to Muskogee but later returned to Eufaula.
11. Work Projects Administration, *Arizona: A State Guide* (New York: Hastings House, 1949), p. 127.

CHAPTER 5   TOWN BOOMING

1. Horace Greeley, *An Overland Journey, From New York to San Francisco, in the Summer of 1859* (New York: C. M. Saxton, Barker & Co., 1860), pp. 36, 39. Greeley supposedly coined the phrase "Go west, young man," but it actually originated with John Babsone Soule, writing in an 1851 issue of the *Terra Haute* (Indiana) *Express.* Greeley reprinted Soule's article in the *New York Tribune,* giving full credit to the latter, but readers of the *Tribune* attributed the statement to Greeley, who so personified everything printed in his paper that people assumed he wrote that, too.
2. Benjamin Pfeiffer, "The Role of Joseph E. Johnson and His Pioneer Newspapers in the Development of Territorial Nebraska," *Nebraska History* 40 (1959), pp. 119–36.
3. Lucius Beebe, *Comstock Commotion: The Story of the Territorial Enterprise and the Virginia City News* (Stanford, Calif.: Stanford University Press, 1954), p. 29.
4. Jake Highton. *Nevada Newspaper Days: A History of Journalism in the Silver State* (Stockton, Calif.: Heritage West Books, 1990), p. 41. For a historical sketch of the *Reese River Reveille,* see Richard E. Lingenfelter, *1858–1958, The Newspapers of Nevada: A History and Bibliography* (San Francisco: John Howell—Books, 1964), pp. 10–11.

5. T. A. McNeal, *When Kansas Was Young* (New York: Macmillan Co., 1922), pp. 80–92.

6. Grace Ernestine Ray, *Early Oklahoma Newspapers* (Norman: University of Oklahoma Bulletin, 1928), pp. 82–86.

7. *Official Report of the Semi-Annual Meeting of the Oklahoma Press Association*, El Reno: Oklahoma Press Association, August 16–17, 1895, p. 11.

CHAPTER 6   PISTOL-PACKIN' EDITORS

1. William H. Lyon, *The Pioneer Editor in Missouri* (Columbia: University of Missouri Press, 1964), pp. 83–84, 766–77.

2. George Louis Crockett, *Two Centuries in East Texas* (Dallas: Southwest Press, 1932), p. 305.

3. *Northern Standard* (Clarksville, Tex.), August 28, 1847.

4. John Bruce, *Gaudy Century, 1848–1949: San Francisco's One Hundred Years of Robust Journalism* (New York: Random House, 1948), pp. 25–26.

5. Ibid., pp. 34–52.

6. *Washington States* (Washington, D.C.), March 1, 1859.

7. Ibid., May 24, 1859.

8. Ibid., July 23, 1859. The duel had been fought by the time the newspaper published Mowry's letter challenging Cross.

9. Jo Ann Schmitt, *Fighting Editors: The Story of Editors Who Faced Six-Shooters with Pens and Won* (San Antonio: Naylor Co., 1958), pp. 1–25. Cross fought in the Civil War as a colonel in the New Hampshire Infantry and was wounded in several battles; he died at Gettysburg. Mowry remained in Arizona. After the Confederacy recognized Arizona as a separate territory, and Southern troops set up a garrison at Tucson, Mowry decided to back the Southern cause. Later he was arrested as a Southern sympathizer.

10. Perkin, *The First Hundred Years*, p. 174.

11. Howes, "Pistol-Packin' Pencil Pushers," p. 138.

12. W. W. Graves, *History of Neosho County Newspapers* (St. Paul, Kans.: St. Paul Journal, 1938), p. 42.

13. Daniel W. Wilder, *The Annals of Kansas* (Topeka: T. Dwight Thacher, Kansas Publishing House, 1886), p. 681. See also A. T. Andreas, *History of the State of Kansas . . .*, pp. 430, 437; Howes, "Pistol-Packin' Pencil Pushers," pp. 118–21.

14. Highton, *Nevada Newspaper Days . . .*, pp. 60–1.

15. Ibid., p. 68.

16. Mark Twain, *The Autobiography of Mark Twain Including Chapters Now Published for the First Time* (New York: Harper & Brothers, 1959), p. 114–15.

17. Wells Drury, *An Editor on the Comstock Lode* (New York: Farrar & Rinehart, Inc., 1936), pp. 6–7.

18. Grace Ernestine Ray, *Early Oklahoma Newspapers*, pp. 102–03.

CHAPTER 7   REPORTING THE NEWS

1. James Melvin Lee, *History of American Journalism* (Garden City, N.Y.: Garden City Publishing Co., 1923), pp. 154–55.

2. When the Postal Act of 1793 became law, nearly every newspaper in America was a four-page sheet of four or five columns. The act established a rate of one cent to send each paper to subscribers anywhere within the state of publication, or to a point not more than one hundred miles from the city of publication. Beyond these limits the rate was one and one-half cents for each paper. These rates were materially less than the rates for letters, and were made so on the theory that newspapers were necessary for the formation of governmental policies and the enlightenment of the people.

    By the 1830s there was agitation for the abolition of special newspaper postage rates to further encourage newspaper reading, but the plan was opposed by the postmaster general on the grounds that some metropolitan papers, especially those in New York City, had grown in size and thereby enjoyed a distinct advantage over the smaller newspapers. The postmaster general argued that if special postage were abolished, the smaller papers would be forced out of business. The Postal Act of 1845 recognized the differences in newspaper sizes and provided one rate for newspapers of not more than nineteen hundred square inches, and another rate for those exceeding nineteen hundred inches. It also raised rates on weight as well as on distance.

    The Postal Act of 1852 established the prepayment of postage by newspapers, and the Postal Act of 1874 abolished zone rates and based rates entirely on the weight of a newspaper. Without the cooperation of the post office, it is doubtful if newspapers in the United States would have had anything like the growth in number and circulation they enjoyed.

3. *Missouri Gazette* (St. Louis), January 4, 1809.

4. Taft, *Missouri Newspapers*, p. 158.

5. The Associated Press was the dominant news service of the period. The cooperative news-gathering organization grew out of the old Harbor News Association, set up by six New York newspapers in 1848 to operate a news boat to obtain newspapers from England and Europe before the ships carrying them had docked. With the advent of the telegraph, what was first called the New York Associated Press (NYAP) made agreements with the Western Union Telegraph Company, giving the NYAP a virtual monopoly of wire news, which was in turn sold to nonmember newspapers. In 1862, however, midwestern newspapers rebelled and formed the Western Associated Press (WAP). By 1866 the WAP was strong enough to defy the NYAP and threaten to establish a competitive newsgathering agency. Soon the organizations came to an agreement and regional news reports were instituted at more equitable charges. Other regional associations soon joined the cooperative.

6. Lee, *History of American Journalism*, pp. 405–06.

7. Albert Bigelow Paine, *Mark Twain, a Biography: The Personal and Literary Life of Samuel Langhorne Clemens* (New York and London: Harper & Brothers, 1912), vol. 1, p. 228.

8. *Galaxy* 18 (December 1874), p. 827.

9. *Louisville Courier*, 1846, cited in Lee, *History of American Journalism*, p. 260.

10. Emmet Crozier, *Yankee Reporters 1861–65* (New York: Oxford University Press, 1956), p. 153.

11. Drury, *An Editor on the Comstock Lode,* p. 186.

12. Icie F. Johnson, *William Rockhill Nelson and the Kansas City Star* (Kansas City, Mo.: Burton Publishing Co., 1935), pp. 125–26.

13. Work Projects Administration, *Arizona: A State Guide* (New York: Hastings House, 1949), p. 127.

14. *Hays City* (Kansas) *Star,* July 13, 1876, and *Hays Daily News,* October 14, 1937.

15. Robert M. Utley, "The Custer Battle in the Contemporary Press," *North Dakota History* 22, no. 1 (January–April, 1995), pp. 75–88. See also Oliver Knight, *Following the Indian Wars: The Story of the Newspaper Correspondents Among the Indian Campaigners* (1960; reprint, Norman: University of Oklahoma Press, 1993), pp. 211–19.

CHAPTER 8   PERSONALS AND MISCELLANEOUS

1. *Morning Reporter* (Sumpter, Oregon), January 9, 1902.

2. Drury, *An Editor on the Comstock Lode,* pp. 170–72.

3. *Laramie* (Wyoming) *Daily Sentinel,* January 6, 1877. For other examples of Bill Nye's writings, see *Bill Nye's Western Humor* (Lincoln: University of Nebraska Press, 1975), containing examples selected by T. A. Larson. See also Frank Wilson Nye, *Bill Nye: His Own Life Story* (New York: Century Co., 1926).

4. *Wamego* (Kansas) *Times,* April 9, 1915.

5. Calder Pickett, *Ed Howe: Country Town Philosopher* (Lawrence: University Press of Kansas, 1968).

6. Ralph Tennal, "A Modern Type of Country Journalism . . ." *University of Kansas News-Bulletin* 14, no. 17 (1914), and John Edward Hicks, *Adventures of a Tramp Printer* (Kansas City, Mo.: MidAmericana Press, 1950, p. 57.

CHAPTER 9   DEATH AND RELIGION

1. Charles Laurel Allen, *Country Journalism* (New York: Thomas Nelson and Sons, 1928), p. 74.

2. Lee, *History of American Journalism,* p. 384. Lee does not provide a source for the obituary.

3. *Prescott* (Arizona) *Miner* as quoted in Work Projects Administration, *Arizona: A State Guide,* p. 124.

4. White, *The Autobiography of William Allen White* (New York: Macmillan Company, 1946), pp. 606–9.

5. Thomas J. Dimsdale, *The Vigilantes of Montana* (1866; reprint, Butte, Mont.: McKenn Printing Co., 1945), p. 14. Dimsdale, editor of the *Montana Post,* reprinted many of his newspaper accounts in this first book printed in Montana.

6. Hope (Kansas) *Dispatch,* November 12, 1886.

7. Pickett, *Ed Howe: Country Town Philosopher,* p. 33.

8. John W. Ripley, "Another Look at the Rev. Mr. Charles M. Sheldon's Christian Daily Newspaper," *Kansas Historical Quarterly* 31, no. 1 (1965), pp. 1–40.

CHAPTER 10   MAKING A LIVING

1. Oswald, *Printing in the Americas,* p. 457. The platen of Samuel Albright's Washington hand press was later recovered and is preserved in the Pittigrew Museum at Sioux Falls.
2. J. H. Beadle, *The Undeveloped West; Or, Five Years in the Territories . . .* (Philadelphia: National Publishing Co., 1873), pp. 115–22, 153.
3. John Myers Myers. *Print in a Wild Land* (Garden City, N.Y.: Doubleday & Co., 1967), p. 39.
4. Ibid., pp. 39–40.
5. Thomas Benedict Hammond, "The Development of Journalism in Missouri: The Newspaper" (M.A. thesis, University of Missouri, 1922), p. 20.
6. Everett Dick, *The Sod-House Frontier, 1854–1890* (Lincoln, Neb.: Johnsen Publishing Co., 1954), pp. 426–27.
7. Elmo Scott Watson. *A History of Newspaper Syndicates in the United States 1865–1935* (Chicago: N.p., 1936), p. 24.
8. For the history of preprinted papers, patent insides, and boilerplates, see Eugene C. Harter, *Boilerplating America: The Hidden Newspaper* (Lanham, Md.: University Press of America, 1991). Preprinted papers were often referred to as "patent insides" because of the patent medicine advertisements they contained. By the late nineteenth century, however, the term "patent insides" became a negative connotation because of public complaints about noxious and poisonous patent medicines advertised in the preprinted papers. The Western Newspaper Union (WNU) began to call the preprinted papers "readyprint" about 1900. In 1920 the WNU called them an "auxiliary service."
9. Page Smith, *The Rise of Industrial America* (New York: McGraw-Hill Co., 1984), p. 403.
10. Western Newspaper Union's 1915 list of preprinted newspapers is reproduced as an appendix on p. 225 in Harter, *Boilerplating America.*
11. Nye, *Bill Nye: His Own Life Story,* pp. 80–82.
12. J. Marvin Hunter, Sr., *Peregrinations of a Pioneer Printer: An Autobiography* (Grand Prairie, Tex.: Frontier Times Publishing House, 1954), pp. 131–33.
13. Letter from William Allen White, *Emporia* (Kansas) *Gazette,* to Rolla Clymer, *Olathe* (Kansas) *Register,* March 29, 1918, copy in the author's collection.
14. Michael and Edwin Emery, *The Press and America* (Englewood Cliffs, N.J.: Prentice-Hall, 1988), pp. 602–4. See also William G. Bonnelli, *Billion Dollar Blackjack: The Story of Corruption and the Los Angeles Times* (Beverly Hills: Civic Research Press, 1954), and Frank Luther Mott, *American Journalism: History of Newspapers in the United States, 1650 to 1940* (New York: Macmillan Co., 1949), p. 602.

15. Emery, *The Press and America,* p. 620. See also Mott, *American Journalism,* pp. 288, 475–76.

16. Emery, *The Press and America,* p. 620. See also Mott, *American Journalism,* pp. 572–73, 532.

17. Emery, *The Press and America,* p. 621. See also Mott, *American Journalism,* p. 680.

18. See Sam Acheson, *35,000 Days in Texas: A History of the Dallas News and Its Fore-bears* (New York: Macmillan Co., 1938). See also Ernest Sharpe, *G. B. Dealey of The Dallas News* (New York: Henry Holt and Co., 1955).

19. Author's files of newspaper clippings relating to E. K. Gaylord. See also L. Edward Carter, *The Story of Oklahoma Newspapers* (Muskogee: Oklahoma Western Heritage Association, 1984), pp. 45, 117, 212–13, 215.

20. Emery, *The Press and America,* pp. 203–6, 613–14. See also Mott, *American Journal-ism,* pp. 432–33. Biographies of Pulitzer include Julian S. Rammelkamp, *Pulitzer's Post-Dispatch, 1878–1833* (Princeton, N.J.: Princeton University Press, 1966); James W. Barrett, *Joseph Pulitzer and His World* (New York: Vanguard, 1941), and George Juergens, *Joseph Pulitzer and the New York World* (Princeton, N.J.: Princeton University Press, 1966).

CHAPTER 11   HYPERBOLIZING

1. O. Henry, *The Voice of the City* (New York: Doubleday, Page & Co., 1919), pp. 109–10.

2. Samuel S. Cox, *Why We Laugh* (New York and London: Benjamin Blom, 1969), pp. 52–55.

3. John P. Young, *Journalism in California* (San Francisco: Chronicle Publishing Co., 1915), p. 40.

4. Drury, *An Editor on the Comstock Lode,* p. 212.

5. Ibid., p. 213. See also Work Projects Administration, *Nevada: A Guide to the Silver State* (Portland, Ore.: Binfords & Mort, 1940), p. 81.

6. Highton, *Nevada Newspaper Days,* p. 19.

7. Ibid., pp. 49–50. No copy of the *Territorial Enterprise* containing Mark Twain's original story of "The Petrified Man" can be found, but the *San Francisco Call,* October 15, 1862, reprinted the article under the headline "A Washoe Joke."

8. Lucius Beebe, *Comstock Commotion: The Story of the Territorial Enterprise and Vir-ginia City News* (Stanford, Calif.: Stanford University Press, 1954), p. 58.

9. Drury, *An Editor on the Comstock Lode,* pp. 197–98.

10. Highton, *Nevada Newspaper Days,* pp. 89–93.

11. Louise Pound, "The John G. Maher Hoaxes," *Nebraska History* 33 (1952), pp. 203–19.

12. Ibid., pp. 212–14.

13. *Mesilla* (New Mexico) *News,* June 9, 1874, cited in Peter Hertzog, *Frontier Humor* (Santa Fe: Press of the Territorian, 1966), p. 16.

14. Lan Franks and Seymour V. Connor, *A Biggers Chronicle . . .* (Lubbock, Texas: Texas Technological College, Southwest Collection, 1961), pp. 87–128.

CHAPTER 12   WOMEN AND PRINTER'S INK

1. Robert F. Karolevitz, *Newspapering in the Old West: A Pictorial History of Journalism and Printing on the Frontier* (Seattle: Superior Publishing Co., 1965), p. 176.

2. Sibley, *Lone Stars and State Gazettes*, pp. 224–25.

3. Edward C. Kemble, *A History of California Newspapers, 1846–1858* (Los Gatos, Calif.: Talisman Press, 1962), p. 223. See also Sherilyn Cox Bennion, *Equal to the Occasion* (Reno and Las Vegas: University of Nevada Press, 1990), pp. 2, 12, 14–17, 25. Only one copy of Sarah Clarke's paper is known to exist. It is in the archives at the State Library of Pennsylvania. Interestingly, during the 1850s there were six women editors in California, nine by the 1860s, fifteen by the 1870s, twenty-five by the 1880s, and seventy-four by the 1890s.

4. Karolevitz, *Newspapering in the Old West*, p. 176.

5. Bennion, *Equal to the Occasion*, pp. 57, 62–66, 102, 141–42.

6. Ibid., p. 87, citing *Colorado Antelope*, November 1879. Colorado claimed three women editors in the 1870s, thirteen by the 1880s, and thirty-nine by the 1890s.

7. Ibid., citing *Colorado Antelope*, January 1880.

8. Ibid., pp. 6, 65, 84–93, 105, 149, 155, 158.

9. Ibid., pp. 145–47. See also Work Projects Administration, *Nevada: A Guide to the Silver State*, pp. 87–88, and Highton, *Nevada Newspaper Days*, pp. 31–32, 187–89. Annie Hudall Martin is not to be confused with Nevada suffragette Anne Martin, who ran unsuccessfully for the U.S. Senate in 1918.

10. John Edward Hicks, *Adventures of a Tramp Printer, 1880–1890* (Kansas City, Mo.: MidAmericana Press, 1950, pp. 215–16.

11. John Bruce, *Gaudy Century, 1848–1948*, pp. 76–77.

12. Hicks, *Adventures of a Tramp Printer*, p. 215.

13. Douglas C. Jones, "Teresa Dean: Lady Correspondent Among the Sioux Indians," *Journalism Quarterly* 49 (Winter 1972), pp. 656–62.

14. Bennion, *Equal to the Occasion*, pp. 38–40.

15. *Platte Valley Lyre* (Saratoga, Wyo.), July 10, 1890.

16. Bennion, *Equal to the Occasion*, pp. 38–40.

17. William E. Connelley, *History of Kansas Newspapers* (Topeka: Kansas State Printing Plant, 1916), p. 87.

18. Remarks by Mrs. Frank W. (Mamie Alexander) Boyd, delivered at the University of Kansas, February 10, 1967, on receipt of the William Allen White Foundation Award for Journalistic Merit. Copy in the author's collection.

19. Herbert Asbury, *Carry Nation: The Woman with the Hatchet* (New York: Alfred A. Knopf, 1929), is one of the better sources for information on Carry Nation. Her own book, *The Use and Need of the Life of Carry A. Nation* (Topeka: F. M. Steves & Sons, 1904), is self-serving. Copies of the *Smasher's Mail* in the author's collection.

CHAPTER 13   TRAMP PRINTERS

1. *Missouri Gazette* (St. Louis), November 23 and 30, 1808.

2. Hicks, *Adventures of a Tramp Printer*, pp. 20–21.

3. Fremont Older, *Growing Up* (San Francisco: San Francisco Call-Bulletin, 1931), pp. 80–81.

4. Work Projects Administration, *Cooper Camp: Stories of the World's Greatest Mining Town, Butte, Montana* (New York: Hastings House, 1943), pp. 93–94.

5. Bill Colvin, "A Local Boy Made Good—Or Did He?" *Manhattan* (Kansas) *Mercury*, December 13, 1964.

6. Hicks, *Adventures of a Tramp Printer*, p. 57.

7. William E. Connelley, *History of Kansas Newspapers*, pp. 114–16.

8. David Hinshaw, *A Man from Kansas: The Story of William Allen White* (New York: G. P. Putnam's Sons, 1945), pp. 154–55.

9. Copy in author's collection.

10. Hicks, *Adventures of a Tramp Printer*, p. 18.

11. Ibid., p. 152.

12. Ibid., pp. 153–54.

13. Hal Borland, *Country Editor's Boy* (Philadelphia and New York: J. B. Lippincott Company, 1970), pp. 62–63.

AFTERWORD

1. James Ford Rhodes, "Newspapers as Historical Sources," *Atlantic Monthly*, May 1909.

BIBLIOGRAPHY

NEWSPAPERS

Advance (Chetopa, Kansas)
Advertiser (Bastrop, Texas)
Advisor (Voltaire, Kansas)
Albuquerque Journal
Albuquerque Sun
Alta California (Yerba Buena/San Francisco)
Amarillo (Texas) *Northwest*
Antelope (Denver, Colorado)
Arapahoe Bee (Oklahoma Territory)
Argonaut (San Francisco)
Arizona Miner (Fort Whipple)
Arizona Sentinel (Yuma)
Arkansas Gazette (Arkansas Post and Little Rock)
Atlantis (Glendale, Wyoming)
Avard (Oklahoma) *Breeze*
Barbour County Mail (Medicine Lodge, Kansas)
Black Hills Pioneer (Deadwood, Dakota Territory)
Boise (Idaho) *News*
Border Ruffian (Coolidge, Kansas)
Borderer (Santa Fe, New Mexico)
Broad-Axe (Los Angeles, California)
Brownsville (Nebraska Territory) *Advertiser*

Bulletin (St. Louis)
Butte (Montana) *Miner*
Californian (Monterey)
California Star (Yerba Buena)
Carson (Nevada) *Daily News*
Centinel of the North-Western Territory (Cincinnati)
Chase County Leader (Cottonwood Falls, Kansas)
Cherokee Advocate (Tahlequah, Indian Territory)
Cherokee Messenger (Westville, Indian Territory)
Chieftain (LaCrosse, Kansas)
Citizen (Florence, Arizona Territory)
Colorado Miner (Georgetown, Colo.)
Commonwealth (Topeka, Kansas)
Courier (Hot Springs, Arkansas)
Cresset (Medicine Lodge, Kansas)
Daily Citizen (Albuquerque)
Daily Kansas State Record (Topeka)
Daily Miner (Anaconda, Montana)
Daily News (Gold Hill, Nevada)
Daily News (Hays, Kansas)
Daily Sentinel (Laramie, Wyoming Territory)
Dakota Republican (Vermillion, Dakota Territory)

Dawes County Journal (Chadron, Nebraska)

Democratic Platform (Marysville, Kansas Territory)

Denver (Colorado) *Daily Gazette*

Denver (Colorado) *Post*

Denver (Colorado) *Times*

Denver (Colorado) *Tribune*

Deseret News (Salt Lake City)

Dispatch (Hope, Kansas)

Dispatch (Iowa Point, Kansas Territory)

Eagle (Lakin, Kansas)

Ellis County Star (Hays City, Kansas)

El Mejicano (Nacogdoches, Texas)

Elwood (Kansas Territory) *Free Press*

Emigrant and General Advertiser (St. Louis)

Enquirer (St. Louis)

Enterprise (Logan, Kansas)

Enterprise (Manhattan, Kansas)

Enterprise (Marysville, Kansas)

Evening Bulletin (Leavenworth, Kansas)

Evening Bulletin (San Francisco)

Evening Kansas City (Missouri) *Star*

Expositor (Fresno, California)

Free Press (Hays City, Kansas)

Free Press (Kingfisher, Oklahoma Territory)

Frontier Index (various locations in Nebraska and Wyoming)

Freedom's Champion (Atchison, Kansas Territory)

Gazette (Emporia, Kansas)

Gazette (Pittsburgh, Pennsylvania)

Gazette (St. Joseph, Missouri)

Gazette (Santa Fe, New Mexico)

Gazette and Western Advertiser (Louisville, Kentucky)

Glendale (Montana) *Atlantis*

Globe (Atchison, Kansas)

Gold Hill (Nevada) *News*

Golden Era (San Francisco)

Grand Junction (Colorado) *News*

Grant County Herald (Silver City, New Mexico)

Gridley (Kansas) *Light*

Herald (Helena, Montana)

Herald (New York City)

Herald of Freedom (Lawrence, Kansas Territory)

Hugoton (Kansas) *Herald*

Huntsman's Echo (Wood River Center, Nebraska Territory)

Idaho World (Idaho City)

Independent (Kirwin, Kansas)

Independent Gazetteer (Lexington, Kentucky)

Indian Journal (Muskogee and Eufaula, Indian Territory)

Indiana Gazette (Vincennes)

Jacksonian (Cimarron, Kansas)

Kansas Chief (White Cloud, Kansas Territory)

Kansas City (Missouri) *Evening Star*

Kansas City (Missouri) *Times*

Kansas Constitutionalist (Doniphan, Kansas Territory)

Kansas Daily Commonwealth (Topeka)

Kansas Free State (Lawrence, Kansas Territory)

Kansas News (Emporia, Kansas Territory)

Kansas Pioneer (Kickapoo, Kansas Territory)

Kansas Reporter (Louisville)

Kansas Tribune (Lawrence, Kansas Territory)

Kansas Weekly Herald (Leavenworth, Kansas Territory)

Kentucke Gazette (Harrodsburg, Kentucky)

Kirwin (Kansas) *Chief*

Knoxville (Tennessee) *Gazette*

Laramie (Wyoming Territory) *Boomerang*

Laramie (Wyoming) *Daily Sentinel*

Leavenworth (Kansas) *Conservative*

Leavenworth (Kansas) *Weekly Herald*

Leavenworth Daily (Kansas) *Times*

Los Angeles (California) *Daily Independent*

Louisville (Kentucky) *Courier*

Marion County Record (Marion, Kansas)

Mesilla (New Mexico Territory) *News*

Messenger (Dodge City, Kansas)

Mexican Advocate (Nacogdoches, Texas)

Missouri Gazette (St. Louis)

Missouri Intelligencer and Boon's Lick Advertiser (Franklin)

Missouri Republican (St. Louis)

Molson (Washington) *Leader*

Montana Post (Virginia City)

Morning Reporter (Independence, Kansas)

Morning Reporter (Sumpter, Oregon)

Nationalist (Manhattan, Kansas)

New Mexican (Santa Fe)

New World (Wichita, Kansas)

New York Times

Northern Standard (Clarksville, Texas)

Norton County People (Norton, Kansas)

Oklahoma Capital (Guthrie, Oklahoma Territory)

Oklahoma War-Chief (various points in southern Kansas and Indian Territory)

Olwyhee (Idaho Territory) *Avalanche*

Omaha (Nebraska Territory) *Arrow*

Optic (Larned, Kansas)

Oregon Argus (Oregon City)

Oregon Spectator (Oregon City)

Platte Valley Lyre (Saratoga, Wyoming)

Phoenix (Arizona) *Herald*

Pioneer (Atwood, Kansas)

Pioneer (Leon, Texas)

Porter (Oklahoma) *Enterprise*

Port Orford (Oregon) *Post*

Prescott (Arizona) *Miner*

Queen Bee (Denver, Colorado)

Reese River Reveille (Virginia City, Nevada)

Reporter (Ellsworth, Kansas)

Reporter (Lexington, Kentucky)

Republic (Manhattan, Kansas)

Riley County Democrat (Manhattan, Kansas)

Rocky Mountain News (Denver)

Rustler (Watonga, Oklahoma Territory)

St. Louis Republican

San Francisco Call

Saratoga (Wyoming Territory) *Sun*

Sentinel (Cawker City, Kansas)

Sentinel (Como, Nevada)

Sentinel (Hays City, Kansas)

Settler (Luddell, Kansas)

Shawnee Sun (Indian Territory)

Smoky Hill and Republican Union (Junction City, Kansas)

Squatter Sovereign (Atchison, Kansas Territory)

Standard (Anaconda, Montana)

Star (Hays, Kansas)

Statesman (Boise City, Idaho)

Stockton (California) *Journal*

Sun (New York City)

Sunday Growler (Wichita, Kansas)

Telegraph and Texas Register (San Felipe and Harrisburg, Texas)

Terre Haute (Indiana) *Express*

Territorial Enterprise (Virginia City, Nevada)

Territorial Topic (Purcell, Indian Territory)

Texas Gazette (San Felipe)

Texas Monument (LaGrange)

Texas Republican (Marshall)

Texas Republican (Nacogdoches)

Texas State Gazette (Austin)

Times (Dodge City, Kansas)

Tombstone (Arizona Territory) *Epitaph*

Topeka (Kansas) *Daily Blade*

Topeka (Kansas) *Daily Capital*

Traveler (Arkansas City, Kansas)

Tribune (Chicago)

Tribune (New York City)

Tri-Weekly Miner's Register (Central City, Colorado)

Union (Sacramento, California)

Union Democrat (Tuolumne County, California)

Utah Weekly Miner (Salt Lake City)

Virginia Evening Bulletin (Virginia City, Nevada)

Wamego (Kansas) *Weekly Times*

Washington States (Washington, D.C.)

Washoe (Nevada) *Times*

Watonga (Oklahoma Territory) *Republican*

Weekly Arizon[i]an (Tubac)

Weekly Chronoscope (Larned, Kansas)

Weekly Elevator (Fort Smith, Arkansas)

Weekly Gazette (Santa Fe, New Mexico)

Weekly Shaft (Rincon, New Mexico Territory)

Western Journal (St. Louis)

Western Mountaineer (Golden, Colorado Territory)

Western Sun (Cincinnati)

Whitehall (Oregon) *Times*

Wilson County Citizen (Fredonia, Kansas)

BOOKS

Acheson, Sam. *35,000 Days in Texas: A History of the Dallas News and Its Forebears.* New York: Macmillan Co., 1938.

Allen, Charles Laurel. *Country Journalism.* New York: Thomas Nelson and Sons, 1928.

Allsop, Fred W. *History of the Arkansas Press for a Hundred Years and More.* Little Rock: Parke-Harper, 1922.

Alter, J. Cecil. *Early Utah Journalism: A Half Century of Forensic Warfare, Waged by the West's Most Militant Press.* Salt Lake City: Utah Historical Society, 1938.

Andreas, A. T. *History of the State of Kansas: A Full Account of its Growth From an Uninhabited Territory to a Wealthy and Important State; of its Early Settlements; its Rapid Increase in Population and the Marvelous Development of its Great Natural Resources. Also a Supplementary History and Description of its Counties, Cities, Towns and Villages, their Advantages, Industries, Manufactures and Commerce; to which are added Biographical Sketches and Portraits of Prominent Men and Early Settlers.* Chicago: A. T. Andreas, 1883.

Asbury, Herbert. *Carry Nation: The Woman with the Hatchet.* New York: Alfred A. Knopf, 1929.

Ashton, Wendell J. *Voice in the West: Biography of a Pioneer Newspaper.* New York: Duell, Sloan & Pearce, 1950. (A history of the *Deseret News* at Salt Lake City.)

Atwood, Millard VanMarter. *The Country Newspaper.* Chicago: A. C. McClurg & Co., 1923.

Ault, Phil. *Wires West: The Story of the Talking Wires.* New York: Dodd, Mead and Co., 1974.

Barrett, James W. *Joseph Pulitzer and His World.* New York: Vanguard, 1941.

Beadle, J. H. *The Undeveloped West; Or, Five Years in the Territories: Being A Complete History of That Vast Region Between the Mississippi and the Pacific, Its Resources, Climate, Inhabitants, Natural Curiosities, Etc., Etc. Life and Adventure on Prairies, Mountains, and the Pacific Coast. With Two Hundred and Forty Illustrations, From Original Sketches and Photographic Views of the Scenery, Cities, Lands, Mines, People, and Curiosities of the Great West.* Philadelphia: National Publishing Co., 1873.

Bleyer, Willard Grosvenor. *Main Currents in the History of American Journalism.* Boston: Houghton Mifflin Co., 1927.

Bonnelli, William G. *Billion Dollar Blackjack: The Story of Corruption and the Los Angeles Times.* Beverly Hills, Calif.: Civic Research Press, 1954.

Borland, Hal. *Country Editor's Boy.* Philadelphia and New York: J. B. Lippincott and Co., 1970.

Boynton, C. B., and T. B. Mason. *A Journey Through Kansas; with Sketches of Nebraska: Describing the Country,*

Climate, Soil, Mineral, Manufacturing, and Other Resources. The Results of a Tour Made in the Autumn of 1854. Cincinnati: Moore, Wilstach, Keys & Co., 1855.

Carter, L. Edward. *The Story of Oklahoma Newspapers.* Muskogee: Oklahoma Western Heritage Association, 1984.

Chidester, Otis H. *First Year Graphic Arts.* Tucson: Graphic Arts Press, Tuscon High School, 1949.

Cincinnati Type Foundry Co.: *Specimen Book.* Cincinnati: Cincinnati Type Foundry Co., 1870. (Illustrated large-format book containing presses and printing equipment including printing cuts and type styles available for sale.)

Cloud, Barbara. *The Business of Newspapers on the Western Frontier.* Reno: University of Nevada Press, 1992.

Coggeshall, W. T. *The Newspaper Record, Containing A Complete List of Newspapers and Periodicals in the United States and Great Britain.* Philadelphia: Lay & Brothers, 1856.

Colton, Rev. Walter. *Three Years in California.* New York: A. S. Barnes and Co., 1850.

Connors, Seymour V. *A Biggers Chronicle Consisting of A Reprint of the Extremely Rare History That Will Never Be Repeated by Lan Franks (pseud) and a Biography of its Author.* Lubbock: Texas Technological College (Southwest Collection), 1961.

Cox, Samuel S. *Why We Laugh.* New York and London: Benjamin Blom, 1969.

Crockett, George Louis. *Two Centuries in East Texas.* Dallas: Southwest Press, 1932.

Crozier, Emmet. *Yankee Reporters 1861–65.* New York: Oxford University Press, 1956.

Dick, Everett. *The Sod-House Frontier, 1854–1890.* Lincoln, Nebr.: Johnsen Publishing Co., 1954.

Dickerson, Donna Lee. *A Typestick of Texas History.* Austin: Dept. of Journalism, University of Texas, 1971.

Dimsdale, Thomas J. *The Vigilantes of Montana.* 1866. Reprint, Butte, Mont.: McKenn Printing Co., 1945. (The rare first edition was printed by the author at Virginia City.)

Drury, Wells. *An Editor on the Comstock Lode.* New York: Farrar & Rinehart, Inc., 1936.

Emery, Edwin. *The Story of America as Reported by Its Newspapers, 1690–1965.* New York: Simon & Schuster, 1965.

Emery, Michael, and Edwin Emery. *The Press and America.* Englewood Cliffs, N.J.: Prentice Hall, 1988.

Folkes, John Gregg. *Nevada's Newspapers: A Bibliography.* Reno: University of Nevada Press, 1964.

Fowler, Gene. *Timber Line: A Story of Bonfils and Tammen.* New York: Covici Friede Publishers, 1933.

Frantz, Joe B. *Gail Borden, Dairyman to a Nation.* Norman: University of Oklahoma Press, 1951.

Graves, W. W. *History of Neosho County Newspapers.* St. Paul, Kans: St. Paul Journal, 1938.

Greeley, Horace. *An Overland Journey, From New York to San Francisco, in the Summer of 1859.* New York: Saxton, Baker & Co., 1860.

Gregory, Winifred, ed. *American Newspapers, 1821–1936: A Union List of Files Available in the United States and Canada.* 1937. Reprint, New York: Kraus Reprint Corp., 1967.

Halaas, David Fridtjof. *Boom Town Newspapers: Journalism on the Rocky Mountain Mining Frontier, 1859–1881.* Albuquerque: University of New Mexico Press, 1981.

Harter, Eugene C. *Boilerplating America: The Hidden Newspaper.* Lanham, Md.: University Press of America, Inc., 1991.

Hertzog, Peter. *Frontier Humor.* Santa Fe, N.M.: Press of the Territorian, 1966.

Heuterman, Thomas H. *Movable Type: Biography of Legh R. Freeman.* Ames: Iowa State University Press, 1979.

Hicks, John Edward. *Adventures of a Tramp Printer, 1880–1890.* Kansas City, Mo.: MidAmericana Press, 1950.

Highton, Jake. *Nevada Newspaper Days: A History of Journalism in the Silver State.* Stockton, Calif.: Heritage West Books, 1990.

Hinshaw, David. *A Man from Kansas: The Story of William Allen White.* New York: G. P. Putnam's Sons, 1945.

Holmes, Charles, and Isom Shepard. *History of the Physical Growth and Technological Advance of the San Francisco Press.* San Francisco: Work Projects Administration, 1940.

Hooper, Osman Castle. *History of Ohio Journalism.* Columbus: Spahr & Glenn Co., 1933.

Howes, Charles C. *This Place Called Kansas.* Norman: University of Oklahoma Press, 1952.

Hudson, Frederic. *Journalism in the United States from 1600 to 1872.* New York: Harper & Brothers, 1873.

Hunter, J. Marvin. *Peregrinations of a Pioneer Printer: An Autobiography.* Grand Prairie, Tex.: Frontier Times Publishing House, 1954.

Jenkins, John H. *Printer in Three Republics: A Bibliography of Samuel Bangs, First Printer in Texas, and First Printer West of the Louisiana Purchase.* Austin, Tex.: Jenkins Publishing Co., 1981.

Johnson, Icie F. *William Rockhill Nelson and the Kansas City Star.* Kansas City, Mo.: Burton Publishing Co., 1935.

Juergens, George. *Joseph Pulitzer and the New York World.* Princeton, N.J.: Princeton University Press, 1966.

Kainen, Jacob. *George Clymer and the Columbian Press.* San Francisco: Book Club of California, 1950.

Karolevitz, Robert F. *Newspapering in the Old West: A Pictorial History of Journalism and Printing on the Frontier.* Seattle: Superior Publishing Co., 1965.

Keleher, William A. *Memoirs: 1892–1969: A New Mexico Item.* Santa Fe: Rydal Press, 1969.

Kemble, Edward C., and Helen Harding Bretnor. *A History of California Newspapers, 1846–1858.* 1858. Reprint, Los Gatos, Calif.: Talisman Press, 1962. (This work is an 1858 supplement to the *Sacramento Union.*)

Knight, Oliver. *Following the Indian Wars: The Story of the Newspaper Correspondents Among the Indian Campaigners.* Norman: University of Oklahoma Press, 1993.

Larson, T. A., ed. *Bill Nye's Western Humor.* Lincoln: University of Nebraska Press, 1975.

Lee, James Melvin. *History of American Journalism.* Garden City, N.Y.: Garden City Publishing Co., 1923. Rev. ed.

Lingenfelter, Richard E. *1858–1958. The Newspapers of Nevada: A History and Bibliography.* San Francisco: John Howell-Books, 1964.

Linton, Calvin D. *American Headlines Year by Year.* Nashville, Tenn.: Thomas Nelson Publishers, 1985.

Lloyd, Lester, and Alix Christie. *A Printer's Ollapodrida.* Lafayette, Calif.: n.p. (A privately printed edition of 175 copies.)

Macy, Katherine Young. *Notes on the History of Iowa Newspapers, 1836–1870.* University of Iowa Extension Bulletin no. 175, 1927.

Marzio, Peter C. *The Men and Machines of American Journalism: A Pictorial Essay from the Henry R. Luce Hall of News Reporting.* Washington: National Museum of History and Technology, Smithsonian Institution, 1973.

McEnteer, James. *Fighting Words: Independent Journalists in Texas.* Austin: University of Texas Press, 1992.

McMurtrie, Douglas C., and Albert H. Allen. *Jotham Meeker: Pioneer Printer of Kansas.* Chicago: Eyncourt Press, 1930.

McNeal, T. A. *When Kansas Was Young.* New York: Macmillan Co., 1922.

Middagh, John. *Frontier Newspaper: The El Paso Times.* El Paso: Texas Western Press, 1958.

Miller, Joseph. *The Arizona Story.* New York: Hastings House, 1952.

Miller, Nyle, Edgar Langsdorf, and Robert W. Richmond. *Kansas in Newspapers.* Topeka: Kansas State Historical Society, 1963.

Moran, James. *Printing Presses: History and Development from the Fifteenth Century to Modern Times.* Berkeley and Los Angeles: University of California Press, 1973.

Mott, Frank Luther. *American Journalism: A History of Newspapers in the United States Through 250 Years, 1690 to 1940.* New York: Macmillan Co., 1949.

———. *The Old Printing Office.* Council Bluffs, Iowa: Yellow Barn Press, 1985.

Myers, John Myers. *Print in a Wild Land.* Garden City, N.Y.: Doubleday, 1967.

Nation, Carry. *The Use and Need of the Life of Carry A. Nation.* Topeka, Kans.: F. M. Steves & Sons, 1904.

Nerone, John. *The Cutlure of the Press in the Early Republic: Cincinnati, 1793–1848.* New York and London: Garland Publishing, Inc., 1989.

Nye, Frank Wilson. *Bill Nye: His Own Story.* New York: Century Co., 1926.

O. Henry. *The Voice of the City* (New York: Doubleday, Page & Co., 1919).

Older, Fremont. *Growing Up.* San Francisco: San Francisco Call–Bulletin, 1931.

Oswald, John Clyde. *Printing in the Americas.* New York: Gregg Publishing Co., 1937.

Paine, Albert Bigelow. *Mark Twain, A Biography: The Personal and Literary Life of Samuel Longhorne Clemens.* 3 vols. New York: Harper & Brothers, 1912.

Perkin, Robert L. *The First Hundred Years: An Informal History of Denver and the Rocky Mountain News.* New York: Doubleday & Co., 1959.

Perrin, William Henry. *The Pioneer Press of Kentucky: From the Printing of the First Paper West of the Alleghenies, August 11, 1787, to the Establishment of the Daily Press in 1830.* Louisville: John P. Morton, 1888.

Pickett, Calder. *Ed Howe: Country Town Philosopher.* Lawrence: University Press of Kansas, 1968.

Rammelkamp, Julian S. *Pulitzer's Post-Dispatch, 1878–1883.* Princeton, N.J.: Princeton University Press, 1966.

Rex, Wallace Hayden. *Colorado Newspapers Bibliography, 1858–1935.* Denver: Center for Bibliographic Studies, 1939.

Rhodes, James Ford. *Historical Essays.* New York: Macmillan Co., 1909.

Rice, William B. *The Los Angeles Star, 1851–1864.* Berkeley and Los Angeles: University of California Press, 1947.

Ringwalt, J. Luther. *American Encyclopaedia of Printing.* Philadelphia: Menamin & Ringwalt/J. B. Lippincott & Co., 1871.

Rosenberg, Norman L. *Protecting the Best Men: An Interpretive History of the Law of Libel.* Chapel Hill: University of North Carolina Press, 1986.

Rutland, Robert A. *The Newsmongers: Journalism in the Life of the Nation, 1690–1972.* New York: Dial Press, 1973.

Salmon, Lucy Maynard. *The Newspaper and the Historian,* New York: Oxford University Press, 1923.

Schellie, Don. *The Tucson Citizen: A Century of Arizona Journalism.* Tucson: Tucson Daily Citizen, 1970.

Schmitt, Jo Ann: *Fighting Editors: The Story of Editors Who Faced Six-Shooters with Pens and Won.* San Antonio: Naylor Co., 1958.

Sharpe, Ernest. *G. B. Dealey of the Dallas News.* New York: Henry Holt and Co., 1955.

Sibley, Marilyn McAdams. *Lone Star and State Gazettes: Texas Newspapers Before the Civil War.* College Station: Texas A&M University Press, 1983.

Sloan, William David, *American Journalism History: An Annotated Bibliography.* New York and Westport, Conn.: Greenwood Press, 1989.

Smalldon, James E. *Early American Newspapers: A Guide to Collecting.* Alhambra, Calif.: Paper Americana Press, 1964.

Smith, Page. *The Rise of Industrial America.* New York: McGraw-Hill Co., 1984.

Stratton, Porter A. *The Territorial Press of New Mexico, 1834–1912.* Albuquerque: University of New Mexico Press, 1969.

Taft, William H. *Missouri Newspapers.* Columbia: University of Missouri Press, 1964.

Turnbull, George S. *History of Oregon Newspapers.* Portland: Binfords & Mort, 1939.

Twain, Mark. *The Autobiography of Mark Twain Including Chapters Now Published for the First Time.* New York: Harper & Brothers, 1959.

Vanden Heuvel, Jon. *Untapped Sources: America's Newspaper Archives and Histories.* New York: Gannett Foundation Media Center, 1991. (This comprehensive report was prepared for the American Society of Newspaper Editors' Newspaper History Task Force.)

Wallace, Ernest. *Charles DeMorse: Pioneer Editor and Statesman.* Lubbock: Texas Tech Press, 1943.

Watkins, Albert, ed. *Publications of the Nebraska State Historical Society.* Vol. 20. Lincoln: Nebraska State Historical Society, 1922.

Watson, Elmo Scott. *A History of Newspaper Syndicates in the United States, 1865–1935.* Chicago: N.p., 1936.

Webb, Walter Prescott, ed. *The Handbook of Texas.* 2 vols. Austin: Texas State Historical Association, 1952.

Whetstone, Daniel W. *Frontier Editor.* New York: Hastings House, 1956.

White, William Allen. *The Autobiography of William Allen White.* New York: Macmillan Co., 1946.

Wilder, Daniel W. *The Annals of Kansas.* Topeka: T. Dwight Thacher, Kansas Publishing House, 1886.

Winkler, John K. *William Randolph Hearst: A New Appraisal.* New York: Hastings House. 1955.

Work Projects Administration. *Arizona: A State Guide.* New York: Hastings House, 1949.

———. *Colorado: A Guide to the Highest State.* New York: Hastings House, 1970.

———. *Copper Camp: Stories of the World's Greatest Mining Town Butte, Montana.* New York: Hastings House, 1943.

———. *Kansas: A Guide to the Sunflower State.* New York: Viking Press, 1939.

———. *Nevada: A Guide to the Silver State.* Portland, Oreg.: Binfords & Mort, 1940.

Young, John P. *Journalism in California.* San Francisco: Chronicle Publishing Company, 1915.

PAMPHLETS AND MONOGRAPHS

Billington, Ray Allen. *Words That Won the West.* San Francisco: Foundation for Public Relations Research and Education, 1964.

Carpenter, Edwin H. *Printers and Publishers in Southern California, 1850–1876.* Glendale, Calif.: La Siesta Press, 1964.

Dill, William. A. *The Newspaper's Family Tree.* Lawrence: Department of Journalism, University of Kansas, 1919.

———. *Growth of Newspapers in the United States.* Lawrence: Department of Journalism, University of Kansas, 1928.

Farrell, F. D. *Kansas Rural Institutions: IX. Country Weekly.* Manhattan: Kansas State College of Agriculture and Applied Science, 1953.

Graves, W. W. *History of Neosho County Newspapers.* St. Paul, Kans.: St. Paul Journal, 1938.

Hornberger, D. J. *Newspaper Organization.* Delaware, Ohio: Ohio Wesleyan University, 1930.

Mazzulla, Fred, and Jo Mazzulla. *Al Packer: A Colorado Cannibal.* Denver: Fred and Jo Mazzulla, 1968.

McMurtrie, Douglas C. *The Westward Migration of the Printing Press in the United States, 1786–1836.* Mainz, Germany, 1930. (Offprint From *Gutenberg Jahrbuch.*)

Official Report of the Semi-Annual Meeting of the Oklahoma Press Association. El Reno: Oklahoma Press Association, 1895.

Ray, Grace Ernestine. *Early Oklahoma Newspapers.* Norman: University of Oklahoma Bulletin, 1928.

Tennal, Ralph. "A Modern Type of Country Journalism . . ." *University of Kansas News-Bulletin* 14, no. 17 (1914).

Trahant, Mark N. *Pictures of Our Nobler Selves.* Nashville: Freedom Forum First Amendment Center, 1995. (A history of Native American contributions to news media.)

THESES

Hammond, Thomas Benedict. "The Development of Journalism in Missouri: The Newspaper." M.A. thesis, University of Missouri, 1922.

Mitchell, Marlene. "Washington Newspapers: Territorial and State." M.A. thesis, University of Washington, 1964.

MANUSCRIPTS

Original prospectus of *Missouri Gazette,* Pierre Chouteau Collection, Missouri Historical Society, Library and Collections Center, St. Louis.

Typescript of remarks by Mrs. Frank W. (Mamie Alexander) Boyd, delivered at the University of Kansas, February 10, 1967, on receipt of the William Allen White Foundation Award for Journalistic Merit. (Copy in the author's collection.)

DIARY

Hawler, H. G. 1860. Document Resources Department, State Historical Society of Colorado, Denver.

LETTER

Copy of letter from William Allen White, *Emporia* (Kansas) *Gazette,* to Rolla Clymer, Olathe (Kansas) *Register,* March 29, 1918. (In author's collection.)

MAGAZINES

American Newspaper Reporter, January 1, 1872.
Galaxy, December 1874.
North American Review, April 1866.

ARTICLES

Allen, Eric W. "Oregon Journalism in 1887," *Oregon Historical Quarterly* 38.
Chaplin, W. E. "Some of the Early Newspapers of Wyoming," *Wyoming Historical Society Miscellanies,* Laramie: Laramie Republican, 1919.
Colvin, Bill. "A Local Boy Made Good— Or Did He?" *Manhattan* (Kansas) *Mercury,* December 13, 1964.

Howes, Cecil. "Pistol-Packin' Pencil Pushers," *Kansas Historical Quarterly* 13.
Jones, Douglas C. "Teresa Dean: Lady Correspondent Among the Sioux Indians," *Journalism Quarterly* 49.
Kansas State Historical Society. "Lincoln in Kansas," *Transactions of the Kansas State Historical Society,* vol. 7.
Pfeiffer, Benjamin. "The Role of Joseph E. Johnson and His Pioneer Newspapers in the Development of Territorial Nebraska," *Nebraska History* 40.
Pound, Louise. "The John G. Maher Hoaxes," *Nebraska History* 33.
Rhodes, James Ford. "Newspapers as Historical Sources," *Atlantic Monthly,* May 1909.
Ripley, John W. "Another Look at the Rev. Mr. Charles M. Sheldon's Christian Daily Newspaper," *Kansas Historical Quarterly* 31.
Utley, Robert M. "The Custer Battle in the Contemporary Press," *North Dakota History* 22, nos. 1, 2 (January–April 1955).
Woolford, Sam. "Carry Nation in Texas," *Southwestern Historical Quarterly* 63.

INDEX

———◆———

David Dary is a native of Manhattan, Kansas, where his great-grandfather opened a general store in the 1860s after working on several western newspapers as a printer. He lived for several years in both Texas and Washington, D.C., working with CBS News and NBC News before returning to Kansas to teach journalism at the University of Kansas. Since 1989 he has been head of the School of Journalism at the University of Oklahoma.

Dary is the author of seven previous books on the West: *The Buffalo Book, True Tales of the Old-Time Plains, Cowboy Culture, True Tales of Old-Time Kansas, More True Tales of Old-Time Kansas, Entrepreneurs of the Old West,* and *Seeking Pleasure in the Old West,* which received a Spur Award as the best nonfiction book of 1995 from the Western Writers of America. *Cowboy Culture* was the recipient of the National Cowboy Hall of Fame Wrangler Award, a Spur Award, and the Westerners International best nonfiction book award.

A NOTE ON THE TYPE

This book was set in a typeface called Bulmer. This distinguished letter is a replica of a type long famous in the history of English printing which was designed and cut by William Martin about 1790 for William Bulmer of the Shakespeare Press. In design, it is all but a modern face, with vertical stress, sharp differentiation between the thick and thin strokes, and nearly flat serifs. The decorative italic shows the influence of Baskerville, as Martin was a pupil of John Baskerville's.

Composed by North Market Street Graphics, Lancaster, Pennsylvania

Printed and bound by Quebecor Printing, Martinsburg, West Virginia

DESIGNED BY ROBERT C. OLSSON